Anti-System Politics

JONATHAN
HOPKIN

Anti-System Politics
The Crisis of Market
Liberalism in Rich Democracies

OXFORD
UNIVERSITY PRESS

OXFORD
UNIVERSITY PRESS

Oxford University Press is a department of the University of Oxford. It furthers
the University's objective of excellence in research, scholarship, and education
by publishing worldwide. Oxford is a registered trade mark of Oxford University
Press in the UK and certain other countries.

Published in the United States of America by Oxford University Press
198 Madison Avenue, New York, NY 10016, United States of America.

Library of Congress Cataloging-in-Publication Data
Names: Hopkin, Jonathan, author.
Title: Anti-system politics : the crisis of market liberalism in rich
democracies / Jonathan Hopkin.
Description: New York : Oxford University Press, 2020. |
Includes bibliographical references and index.
Identifiers: LCCN 2019031627 (print) | LCCN 2019031628 (ebook) |
ISBN 9780190699765 (hardback) | ISBN 9780190699789 (epub) |
ISBN 9780190699772 | ISBN 9780190097707
Subjects: LCSH: Democracy—Economic aspects—Western countries. |
Capitalism—Political aspects—Western countries. |
Neoliberalism—Western countries. |
Western countries—Politics and government—21st century.
Classification: LCC JC423 .H7528 2020 (print) | LCC JC423 (ebook) |
DDC 320.51/3091821—dc23
LC record available at https://lccn.loc.gov/2019031627
LC ebook record available at https://lccn.loc.gov/2019031628

9 8 7 6 5 4 3 2 1

Printed by LSC Communications, United States of America

For Victoria

CONTENTS

ACKNOWLEDGMENTS

T HIS BOOK STARTED life, awkwardly, as a paper about the surprisingly timid reaction of Western electorates to the financial catastrophe of 2008 and the subsequent Great Recession. As I observed banks collapsing and politicians scurrying to rescue the "Masters of the Universe," my anxiety was tempered with the soothing thought that the neoliberal consensus had met its demise. As the dust settled and governments set about cutting social programs rather than reforming capitalism, I realized I had jumped the gun. But why did people vote for more punishment? Before I got very far in developing an answer to this question, people stopped voting for the punishment and any of the politicians associated with it. But what were they voting for instead? This book attempts to answer that question.

Mark Blyth, whose book *Austerity* is essential reading for anyone trying to understand anti-system politics, pushed me to develop my ideas into a book and commented on various drafts. David McBride at Oxford University Press has been a great source of encouragement and guidance, and has shown admirable patience as I have burned through deadlines. I am grateful for the opportunity to present my research at various seminars, at Oxford, Amsterdam, Leiden, the European University Institute, the Danish Institute for International Studies, the Bucharest University of Economic Studies, and the University of Westminster. I am very grateful for the feedback from all the participants, especially Ben Ansell, Renira Corinna Angeles, Elisabetta Brighi, Bjorn Bremer, Brian Burgoon, Pepper Culpepper, Clara Darabont, Hanspeter Kriesi, Petr Kopecky, Bo Rothstein, Christian Lammert, Claus Offe, Jakob Vestergaard, Guillem Vidal, and Boris Vormann. Alice Evans, Chase Foster, and Javier Ortega took the time to read draft chapters and provide helpful and detailed comments. Alexandre Afonso, Luis Cornago Bonal, Pedro Magalhaes, Scott Mainwaring, Nick Malkoutzis, and Carol Thanki provided help with data.

Many other colleagues have been a source of inspiration, support, and friendly criticism over the course of this project, notably Karen Anderson, Lucio Baccaro, Cornel Ban, Pepe Fernández, Scott Greer, Sara Hobolt, Wade Jacoby, Erik Jones, Dick Katz, Julie Lynch, Philip Manow, Matthias Matthijs, Kate McNamara, Andrés Rodríguez Pose, Waltraud Schelkle, David Soskice, Robin Varghese, and David Woodruff. Ken Shadlen not only provided great academic advice but also pretended to laugh at my jokes. Javier Ortega kept me sane by introducing a very British notion of 4 o'clock tea breaks at the historic Wright's Bar. The professional services staff of the Government Department at the London School of Economics (LSE) have been efficient and supportive, and Mark Bryceland in particular. Students at LSE are a joy to teach and have helped me shape my thinking.

Finally, I am grateful to my family for putting up with me during this project. Thanks to my parents, Gerald and Margaret Hopkin, my brother Alastair and my sister Victoria, and my brother-in-law Alec for their love and support over the years. We were devastated to lose Victoria in 2017, and this book is dedicated to her memory. *Grazie* to Silvia and Giulia, for being there. *Il secondo album e' sempre il piu' difficile.*

London, June 2019

Introduction: A Quick History of the Present

A BILLIONAIRE DECIDES to enter politics, after a successful business career first in real estate and then in the entertainment industry. A skilled communicator and salesman, he achieved celebrity status, his face appearing in glossy magazines, sometimes alongside leading politicians he counted as friends. Despite a history of legal troubles, heavy debts, and even alleged mob connections, as well as marital infidelity (and perhaps worse), for many his image is one of power and success. A political career is a natural step for such a talented self-publicist, especially when the existing political establishment is widely perceived as corrupt, self-serving, and incompetent. The billionaire stands for election and, to the astonishment of political observers across the world, wins the presidency, despite never having held any political office before. The pundit class and academic specialists are forced to rethink their worldview.

Or maybe not. The events I am describing took place a quarter of a century ago in Italy, and did not in fact lead to much fundamental rethinking of how democratic politics works. In 1993 Silvio Berlusconi, a Milanese real estate and media magnate, alarmed at the collapse of Italy's political establishment in the face of a sweeping anti-corruption drive, created a new political movement, Forza Italia ("Come On Italy"). Forza Italia became Italy's biggest political party in the 1994 elections, and Berlusconi formed a government in coalition with two other anti-system parties, the separatist Northern League and the "post-fascist" National Alliance. A system of government revolving around centrist parties that had ruled Italy for half a century had been overturned.

This political earthquake was too easily dismissed as a typically Italian exception to the rule of stable democratic politics in western Europe. And indeed, although Berlusconi and his allies introduced a crude, populist language to the previously arcane rituals of Italian politics, his victory was not a harbinger of fundamental change, and still less of the "new Italian miracle" he promised. But the fact that decades-old political parties could effectively disappear in the space of little over a year, and that someone as unsuited to office as Berlusconi could fill the gap, should have warned us of the vulnerability of our political institutions to a hostile takeover. Even in wealthy, consolidated democracies, the political system could be captured by anti-system forces.

Although Italy was by far the most extreme case, the political order of the postwar era was facing new challenges elsewhere, too. In the late 1980s and 1990s, new right-wing parties began to win sizable vote shares in Denmark, Norway, Switzerland, Austria, and France. These parties homed in on issues such as immigration and European integration, targeting the voters of mainstream center-right parties with xenophobic rhetoric. The chief beneficiaries of these developments were center-left parties, which by the late 1990s were in power in the United States and most of the European Union member states. But by the mid-2000s the Center-Left was in decline, too, their voters increasingly turning to fringe parties, or dropping out of formal political participation altogether.

Against this backdrop, the bursting of a housing bubble in the United States, combined with an over-leveraged and inadequately regulated financial system, set off the biggest economic crisis the world had seen since the 1930s. The same unpopular establishment politicians whose authority had been eroding for some time—among them, ironically, Silvio Berlusconi himself—were handed the task of rescuing the world economy. Inconceivable sums of money were mobilized to bail out banks and insolvent governments, while ordinary citizens were asked to pay higher taxes on their stagnant or falling wages, all while government spending was cut. It would have been surprising if there had not been a political backlash, but even so, most politicians, opinion leaders, and academics still contrived to be entirely taken aback by it.

The seismic events of 2016—first Britain's vote to leave the European Union, then Donald Trump's election to the presidency six months later—brought anti-system politics on to the front pages, but the pressure had been building for some time. The Greek Socialist Party (PASOK), after presiding over a catastrophic bailout and brutal austerity measures, was effectively wiped out in the 2012 election, its place taken by a radical left coalition, Syriza. In Spain, centrist Catalan nationalists pivoted to a radical policy of secession, while a powerful anti-austerity street movement directed millions of voters toward an entirely new political party, Podemos ("We Can"). In Italy, the Five Stars Movement, a party of ecologists and digital democracy campaigners led by a comedian, became the biggest party in the 2013 election. In Britain, Labour Party members elected veteran left-winger Jeremy Corbyn as their new leader in 2015, soon after the pro-independence Scottish Nationalist Party had won all but three parliamentary seats in Scotland.

Unlike Trump or the Brexit campaign, none of these movements had adopted an anti-immigration or culturally conservative message—quite the contrary. Instead, their campaigns focused on the failure of the political establishment to represent popular demands for protection from the brutal effects of the economic crisis. The banking bailouts and the austerity measures that followed them sparked popular outrage while sharpening preexisting political conflicts and discrediting incumbent political elites. Some of this outrage was channeled by right-wing anti-system politicians demanding tighter border controls and a reversal of globalization, but a good part of it went in a very different direction. Social movements demanding a more participatory form of democracy, an end to austerity, and a reining in of the power of the wealthy elite—the "one percent"—were just as much part of the story as the radical anti-migrant Right.

This book explains the rise of the xenophobic Right and the anti-capitalist Left as part of a common global trend: anti-system politics. It explains why anti-system politics is on the march, and why different forms of anti-system politics prosper in different places and among different types of voters. Its basic premise is that the political and economic "system" failed, and that anti-system movements are a predictable, and in many ways welcome, response to that failure. Dismissing angry opposition to the status quo as a result of racism, self-indulgence, or susceptibility to foreign propaganda is a serious mistake. What the anti-system Left and Right have in common is their shared rejection of the political and economic order governing the rich democracies at the beginning of the twenty-first century. This rejection is most powerful in the democracies where inequality is highest, and where the social and economic effects of the Global Financial Crisis have been most severe.

The reasons for the rise in anti-system politics are structural, and have been brewing a long time. The success of anti-system parties forces us to ask ourselves fundamental questions about the nature of our political and economic system, and the way in which the twenty-first-century market economy affects people's lives. Rather than dismissing anti-system politics as "populism," driven by racial hatred, nebulous foreign conspiracies, or an irrational belief in "fake news," we need to start by understanding what has gone wrong in the rich democracies to alienate so many citizens from those who govern them.

The Roots of "Anti-System" Politics

The term "anti-system" was coined by political scientist Giovanni Sartori in the 1960s to describe political parties that articulated opposition to the liberal democratic political order in Western democracies.[1] The economic and political successes of the postwar Western order ensured the dominance of political parties representing liberal democratic political ideas, such as liberalism, conservatism, Christian democracy, and social democracy. These competing ideologies were articulated by well-organized political parties with deep roots in society, which used the powers available to national governments to pursue and implement their distinctive visions of a better society.

For conservatives and Christian democrats, this meant protecting the capitalist economic order and resisting pressures from emerging social groups for cultural and political change. For socialists and social democrats, in contrast, it meant reshaping and reforming the capitalist system so that it could better accommodate their aspirations for an egalitarian society. Liberals were a minority force squeezed awkwardly between them, arguing for a society based around both individual rights and freedoms and less economic and social regulation. Across the Western democracies, these different party families formed the backbone of the political system, either sharing power in the coalition governments typical of continental Europe, or competing for it in the majoritarian democracies such as Britain or the United States.

Anti-system parties fundamentally opposed to liberal democracy enjoyed significant electoral support only in France and Italy. These parties represented the main available alternatives to democracy and the market system: communism, the ruling ideology of the Soviet bloc and China, and fascism, the ideology that had been defeated in World War II. With the memory of democratic breakdown in interwar Europe still fresh, and the Cold War a constant reminder that capitalism was not the only possible economic model, Sartori and others took threats to the postwar liberal order seriously. Communist parties averaged between 15 and 30 percent of the vote in France and Italy, the extreme Right far less. Anti-system ideologies also animated terrorist movements in Germany, Greece, Italy, Spain, and the United Kingdom.

The meaning of anti-system politics changed as the most economically advanced democracies evolved toward a quite different type of political and economic order, based on the primacy of markets over politics. The highly regulated form of capitalism that emerged in the aftermath of the war was gradually superseded by a more economically liberal model, as governments sought to dismantle nonmarket institutions and promoted an economy governed, wherever possible, by competition and the price mechanism. The main political parties progressively converged around this market liberal model, emptying electoral democracy of much of its meaning, as established political elites increasingly resembled a "cartel" offering a limited range of policy options.[2] The main political parties across the democratic world, from Left to Right, embraced a shared set of pro-market economic ideas. Politicians such as Bill Clinton, Tony Blair, Massimo d'Alema, and Gerhard Schroeder led their traditionally left-leaning parties over to what they called the "progressive center," from which they insisted that free markets and social justice were part of the same package.

Liberal democracy had become "neoliberal democracy," in which an open market model was no longer an object of political dispute and key decisions had been taken out of the electoral arena.[3] This new type of politics entrenched market liberal thinking in the policy regimes of the advanced democracies in a way that created the conditions for the backlash of the mid-2010s. It marginalized opposition to the decisive move toward trade openness, and in particular open capital markets, which were at the heart of the Global Financial Crisis and the Great Recession that followed. But it also meant that when the wheels came off the global economy in 2008, conventional democratic politics was unable to provide adequate solutions to the acute economic distress this caused. The main political parties across the Western democracies had invested heavily in the neoliberal ideas underpinning this failed system, and had farmed out the most important economic policy tools to nonelected bodies that had been completely wrong-footed by the crisis.

For this reason, contemporary anti-system politics should not be defined in terms of opposition to liberal democracy as such.[4] The xenophobic Far Right is undoubtedly a threat to liberal democracy, and the behavior of Trump, Salvini, Orban, and others in government is a cause for serious alarm. But there is no evidence that Western publics are becoming less supportive of democracy, or more xenophobic—quite the contrary.[5] The Five Stars Movement, nationalist movements in Catalonia and Scotland, and parties on the anti-system Left, such as Podemos, Syriza, and the Corbyn and Sanders campaigns, very clearly align themselves with progressive democratic values, advocating greater involvement of grassroots political organizations in political decision-making. Anti-system politics is born out of the failings of our political institutions to represent popular demands.

Thinking Theoretically about Anti-System Politics

This book mostly avoids the concept of "populism," which has become the accepted shorthand for anti-system politics in the political debate, in the media, and to some extent also in academia. Populism is usually defined as an anti-elitist discourse that purports to represent some morally charged idea of the "people" as a whole, while condemning existing institutions for betraying or failing to properly represent the people.[6] Most contemporary anti-system parties can be considered populist because, like the early populist movements of the late nineteenth century in North America and Europe, they express "a powerful sense of opposition to an establishment that remained entrenched and a belief that democratic politics needed to be conducted differently and closer to the people."[7] In other words, they advocate a different form of governance based more explicitly on the popular will. This certainly captures the essence of the anti-system movements discussed in this book, which all, in one way or another, demand that politics be more responsive to the people they seek to represent.

However, the term "populist" has also been used to label nativist and xenophobic political movements that reject pluralism;[8] politicians prone to dishonesty, corruption, and demagoguery; and even economic policymaking that prioritizes short-term over long-term objectives.[9] As a result, the term has inescapably acquired a heavily pejorative connotation, undermining serious and systematic analysis. Not only can describing opponents of the status quo as "populist" imply that they are somehow wrong-headed or even dangerous by definition, but it also leads to quite specific characteristics of some populist movements being implicitly ascribed to others that do not in fact share them. To describe Catalan nationalists, the Five Stars Movement, or Syriza as populist runs the risk of implying that these movements share the xenophobia and authoritarianism of Trump, Le Pen, or Salvini. To describe these movements as anti-system, however, precisely captures the uncontroversial fact that they all demand fundamental changes to the current political and economic "system."

The misuse of the concept of populism is unfortunate, because it obscures the very insightful distinction between "liberal" and "populist" ideas of democracy present in political theory.[10] In scholarly debates about democracy, "liberalism"—another term stretched beyond usefulness in contemporary political debate—is an idea of the political order that prioritizes the protection of individuals' rights in the face of the potential for government to tyrannically abuse its coercive power. Liberals prefer a system of divided government with little ability to pursue grand collective projects, which in practice implies a preference for free markets over government intervention in the economy and strict constitutional constraints on politicians' powers. Populism, on the other hand, sees democracy as a means for the implementation of the people's will, implying a greater scope for the state to shape the economy and society in line with the demands of the political majority, potentially to the detriment of the rights of minorities.

The anti-system parties studied in this book all, to a greater or lesser extent, adopt a populist view of democracy in this more specific sense of the word. They invoke the rights of the people to use the power of the state to protect the population as a collective, rather than to guarantee the rights of individuals. The anti-system Right identifies the people as being the national community (usually ethnically defined), whose interests must be protected against "outside" threats of migration, hostile foreign powers, international organizations, and terrorist groups. The state is the instrument for delivering this protection, even if it undermines the rights of minority groups and noncitizens. The anti-system Left instead identifies the enemy as the capitalist system, and often the wealthy groups who benefit most from it. The Left demands protection from the arbitrary decisions of unregulated markets that overturn peoples' lives by denying them work, dispossessing them of their homes, and starving the government of the resources to pay for welfare policies.

These ideas are far from new, nor have they always been regarded as hostile to liberal democracy. In fact, the nationalism and authoritarianism of the anti-system Right and the egalitarian interventionism of the anti-system Left were present in the political discourse and policy practice of governing parties through most of the postwar period. Conservative and Christian democratic parties have long been skeptical of the idea of a multicultural society where migrants enjoy full citizenship rights, and have also resisted demands for sexual and racial equality. Similarly, the social democratic and labor parties of today's Center-Left were once committed to providing substantial social and welfare benefits, expanding and enforcing workers' rights, and maximizing growth and employment. So why are these positions today mostly associated with anti-system forces?

The answer to this question is quite straightforward: the range of political positions represented by the established political parties has narrowed over time to the point where voters are left with little real choice at election time. The postwar period pitted political parties with very different visions of how society should be organized against each other, and voters were able to express their preferences for these different visions. Elected politicians had access to policy levers that could make a profound difference to the economic and social development of the countries they governed. Somewhere along the way, however, democratic governments ceased to reflect differences in political philosophies, and lost the ability to implement alternative policies. To understand anti-system politics, we need to understand the system it opposes: a set of institutions and practices that we can call "neoliberal democracy."

Priming the Backlash: Economic Fissures and Neoliberal Democracy

Anti-system parties and politicians tend to present themselves self-consciously as alternatives to a discredited establishment or elite. They accuse the mainstream politicians of behaving like Adam Smith's tradesmen, banding together in a "conspiracy against the public" to close the market to new entrants and cheat their customers by offering them a restricted choice.[11] Typically, the mainstream political parties are depicted as being indistinguishable from each other, their leaders a homogeneous collection of careerists devoid of principles, interested solely in winning political office, or maybe turning an illicit profit. There are plenty of examples of this kind of behavior to give these accusations credibility.

But the failures of establishment politicians cannot be reduced solely to venality or laziness. The narrowing of the political space owed much to the serious difficulties politicians began to face, especially from the 1970s on, in meeting citizens' demands. The slowing of economic growth meant that politicians had fewer resources to play with, while financial markets were becoming more difficult to control, limiting national governments' ability to tax profits or borrow to fund public spending. The political "cartel" of the late twentieth century emerged as politicians became increasingly pessimistic about the possibility of government intervention in the economy to deliver social improvements, and settled instead for a more laissez-faire approach, hoping that freer markets and lower taxes would keep their voters happy.[12]

The neoliberal program created losers as well as winners, but the return of economic growth in the mid-1980s and the huge gains made by some politically influential groups established small government and open markets as the consensus position in Western politics. Serious alternatives to the market system disappeared from the political debate. This neoliberal consensus suited elected politicians in a variety of ways. The emphasis on the market, rather than government, in determining the allocation of resources got politicians off the hook for citizens' economic fortunes. Politics became a battle not between competing visions of the good society, but competing teams of administrators of the market system, chosen on the basis of claims to competence and honesty rather than for their ideas.

The progressively broader role for markets in social life translated almost everywhere into higher inequality. Not only did markets tend to result in a more unequal allocation of resources, but the same neoliberal logic also undermined the kinds of nonmarket institutions that could mitigate these inequalities, such as progressive taxation and redistributive government spending. In the most extreme case, the United States, income inequality rose dramatically, with the top 1 percent of earners taking 20 percent of total income by 2010, double their share in 1980, while the bottom half traveled in the opposite direction, their slice of the pie dropping from 20 percent to a little over 12 percent in the same period.[13] Growing inequality led to rising social anxiety and health risks, especially among the most vulnerable groups, but also among higher-income groups, as even many of the "winners" from the market system were still exposed to economic threats.[14]

All of this may have been a price worth paying had the promise of improved economic growth and a "trickle down" effect of higher earnings across the rest of the economy come to fruition. Neoliberalism achieved some successes—notably defeating inflation and eliminating some wasteful and inefficient government regulation and expenditure—but it was unable to match the economic record of the postwar period. The typical household still enjoyed rising living standards in most countries, but poverty rates also increased. Viewed from the mid-2000s, the neoliberal experiment had yielded at best mixed results, and then in 2007 the intricate architecture of the emerging global financial system, a system built on the neoliberal philosophy of free markets and minimal government intervention, came crashing down, devastating lives across the world.

The extent of the damage—on any measure the Global Financial Crisis of 2007–2008 was the worst since the Wall Street Crash of 1929—was such that business as usual was no longer possible. The "sink or swim" creed of the neoliberals was hastily abandoned—for banks. The financial system was backstopped by governments through injections of capital, lines of soft credit, and even printing money to raise asset prices. These emergency measures were successful, at least in the sense that a catastrophic financial collapse and 1930s-style depression were averted.[15] But as soon as the panic in the financial markets subsided, policymakers attempted to revert to type with harsh austerity measures, leaving households struggling to rescue their own balance sheets.

The predictable, and indeed widely predicted,[16] consequence of this turn to austerity was a period of economic stagnation that has become known as the Great Recession. Not surprisingly, electorates in the rich democracies generally responded by voting out incumbents, not unreasonably blaming their economic pain on the politicians in charge at the time of the crisis. They were replaced by opposition politicians who were quick to claim that the crisis was the result of their predecessors' bad policies. Yet these elections changed little, and the new governments, locked into the same neoliberal model as their predecessors, quickly became as unpopular as those they replaced.

The crisis of the late 2000s contains all the basic ingredients for a political backlash: economic stagnation, high inequality, and a political system that blocked off any prospect of effective change. Across the democratic world, the share of the population benefiting from these economic and political arrangements has contracted to such an extent that the dominant political parties no longer have the votes to maintain themselves in office. The forty-year-long experiment in leaving people at the mercy of the market produced a top-heavy income distribution of a small number of big winners, a much larger group of losers, and a squeezed middle fighting to maintain its position in an increasingly insecure world. The political establishment had run out of ideas to make things better. The rise of anti-system politics reflects the exhaustion of neoliberal democracy: an economic model that ultimately only worked for a minority, and a political system that closed off alternatives to it.

But What about Culture?

A plausible challenge to this argument is that anti-system politics is about much more than economics. Donald Trump, after all, was a billionaire who proudly boasted of avoiding paying taxes and spent much of his campaign insulting liberals, Mexicans, and Muslims. Trump's campaign slogan, Make America Great Again, and his focus on capturing the votes of mainly white Americans, pointed to a backlash against the more ethnically diverse and culturally open society represented by the Obama presidency. A similar story has been told about Brexit and the rise of far-right politicians in Europe: the refugee crisis of the mid-2010s and a wave of terrorist attacks in France, Belgium, and Germany pushed voters weary of mass migration and rapid social change into the hands of "national-populists."[17] Norris and Inglehart describe this as a "cultural backlash."[18]

The evidence supporting this contention is that some survey data shows that immigration and security issues were at the top of public concerns across Western democracies over the decade following the financial crisis.[19] Some voting studies show that authoritarian attitudes, racial anxiety, and social trust are strongly correlated with the vote for the anti-system Right. Education levels perform better than income levels in predicting voting behavior, suggesting that the socialization effect of higher education is more important than economic circumstances in explaining Trump, Brexit, and the rise of the European Far Right. Most studies have failed to show conclusively that falling income predicts anti-system voting. So why insist that economic problems, and the neoliberal model more broadly, explain the political upheavals of the 2010s?

Cultural factors should not be dismissed, and cultural attitudes are of course part of the explanation for why some voters are likely to support anti-system options. However, immigration is a long way from being a novelty in Western societies, and the evolution of public attitudes on immigration does not provide a very compelling explanation for the rapid rise in anti-system politics in the post–financial crisis period. Instead, attitudes toward immigration in Western democracies have steadily become more liberal over the past decades.[20] The sharp rise in voting for the anti-system Right in some countries after the financial crisis does not coincide with any particular change in migration flows, or an increase in negative attitudes toward migrants. In any case, changes in attitudes toward migration are not a plausible explanation for the rise in support for parties of the anti-system Left or for secessionist parties that have mostly adopted progressive positions on migration.

Where culture can plausibly play a role is in conditioning the different kinds of anti-system appeals that attract different kinds of voters. It is true that right-wing anti-system forces have tended to perform better in the countries where strong labor markets have attracted greater inward migration flows, while left-wing anti-system parties have been stronger in countries with high unemployment and stronger outward flows.[21] But vote shares for the anti-system Right are negatively correlated with migrant presence at the local level, suggesting that openness to a xenophobic appeal, rather than any concrete negative experience of migration, is what drives voters toward these parties.

What explains openness to a xenophobic diagnosis of economic distress is the broader cultural and attitudinal characteristics of different social groups. Across the Western democracies, xenophobic and authoritarian attitudes are much stronger among older sectors of the population, and in particular among less educated citizens.[22] In contrast, younger and more educated voters are far more likely to have liberal or progressive social attitudes and to have positive views of migration. Not surprisingly, therefore, right-wing xenophobic parties are more successful among older, less educated, and particularly male voters, especially in economically declining regions.[23] In contrast, left-wing anti-system parties perform better among younger cohorts, often in the most economically dynamic urban areas.

Immigration and cultural rejection of it are not a good explanation for the broad phenomenon of anti-system voting, because opposition to the system can be expressed in very different ways. It is a simple matter of causal logic that the simultaneous rise of anti-system movements of such radically different kinds can only be convincingly explained by factors that they have in common, rather than those that differ between them. The failures of the neoliberal economy and its severe consequences for society generate the kind of anger that fuels anti-system voting, but that anger needs to be interpreted and mobilized in order for political change to happen. As Mark Blyth puts it, "structures don't come with an instruction sheet":[24] citizens may feel cheated and ignored, but the way they respond depends on the stories they are told about why things are happening and what should be done about them.

It is a great irony of the rise of anti-system politics that the voters most likely to vote for xenophobic anti-immigration parties are those least likely to be in contact with migrants, while the areas most exposed to migration have the least support for such parties. The success of the anti-system Right is not the direct result of the concrete impact of migration, but is instead a function of the ways in which economic change has affected the voters that are culturally most hostile to it. This book will show that anti-system voting is conditioned by the ways in which different institutions and policies distribute economic benefits and risks. The greater the impact of inequality and economic hardship, the higher the vote share for anti-system parties. Where older and less educated voters feel more threatened by economic change, right-wing xenophobic parties perform better than left-wing anti-system forces. Where younger citizens are the ones most exposed to the crisis, left-wing anti-system alternatives perform better than the anti-migrant Right.

Debt Matters: The Importance of Creditors and Debtors for Anti-System Politics

The impact of immigration is tied up with the decades-long process of economic globalization.[25] Immigration was just one aspect of this globalization, and in many ways less important than the growth in cross-border financial flows or trade liberalization. After the 1970s, governments in the West abandoned capital controls and encouraged developing countries to do the same, leading to a rapid acceleration of unregulated movements of money around the world, accompanied by growing financial instability culminating in the global meltdown of 2008. In the same period, successive rounds of international trade negotiations removed many barriers to trade, further restricting governments' ability to control their national economies. Globalization benefited large numbers of people in developing countries, and high-skilled workers everywhere, but many lesser-skilled workers in the West lost out.[26]

A constant theme in the discussion of the political and economic upheavals of the early twenty-first century is that globalization has created "winners" and "losers," and that anti-system politics is best understood as the product of the resulting social conflict. The distributional consequences of globalization are compounded by the ways in which the internationalization of the economy strips nation-states of their ability to respond to electoral pressures. Dani Rodrik describes this scenario as a "trilemma," in which open economies can only enjoy the economic benefits of globalization by either abandoning democratic responsiveness or pooling sovereignty at the supranational level. This framing is insightful and helpful, but it leaves much unexplained.

The countries that have faced the biggest political upheavals in the early twenty-first century are not impotent victims of the unstoppable process of internationalization of the economy, but rather some of its biggest champions. The United States was the main driver of the globalization push of the late twentieth century, with the United Kingdom an enthusiastic junior partner. The southern European countries have been among the most committed supporters of greater economic and political integration in Europe. On top of this, the countries most exposed to globalization—the small open economies of northern Europe—are the same ones that have coped best with the political consequences of the crisis. Whether or not nations participated willingly in the opening up of their economies to greater global competition, the ways in which they dealt with the consequences were very much a matter of political choice.

What this tells us is that globalization creates common pressures, but that rich democracies can respond to it in different ways, and that these responses depend on the political and economic institutions with which they have endowed themselves in the past. This book therefore focuses on the nature of party politics and the development of economic and social policies in the rich democracies, and finds that these variables explain why some countries have been far better equipped to survive globalization and its attendant economic shocks than others. Although the drift toward neoliberalism and the consequent challenges to democratic institutions are common across the whole of the rich world, some countries have protected their populations far more successfully than others. Where inequalities have been allowed to grow highest, and political institutions have been least able to address its consequences, anti-system politics has been most powerful. Anti-system parties are like antibodies: a reaction to the exposure of societies to an inadequately regulated market economy.

Globalization is important, but it should not blind us to the consequences of political choices made by politicians and regulators. When the financial crisis hit, capital markets had to be rescued by governments, in a sudden reversal of a power relationship that had previously subjected politics to the whims of the market. The way this rescue was performed, and the measures taken to deal with the subsequent economic downturn, was very much the product of political decisions made by states, which in large part passed the bill for capitalists' mistakes onto the people who had gained the least out of the neoliberal revolution. Banking bailouts and austerity were political choices, and citizens could not be expected to be indifferent to their consequences.

Capitalism against Democracy: It's Not a Love Story

This book draws on a very simple theory of political change in capitalist democracies to explain the rise of anti-system politics across the West. It sees this anti-system politics as part of what Karl Polanyi in his classic book *The Great Transformation* described as the "double movement" of capitalist development: as the logic of market exchange expands and threatens other valued forms of social interaction, "counter-movements" arise as people organize politically to demand protection against the market.[27] Polanyi's book was published in 1944, and focused on explaining the upheavals of the interwar period as political elites sought to reimpose the Gold Standard on a fragile social fabric. For Polanyi, the dramatic collapse of the global political order in the 1930s was the consequence of a bone-headed insistence on imposing the implacable logic of the "self-regulating market" on a fragile society, which led to a predictably violent reaction.

It has not escaped attention that the dynamics of the Global Financial Crisis and the Great Recession bear more than a passing resemblance to the interwar period.[28] The final years of the twentieth century presented sufficiently clear signs of a 1920s-style bubble to lead one economist to call them "the roaring nineties."[29] After the 2008 crash, the rescue of the financial system with a wave of liquidity did suggest some policy-learning from the disaster of the 1930s, but a premature turn to austerity suggested that other lessons had gone unheeded.[30] Keynes's *General Theory*, published at the height of the Great Depression, cautioned that under certain conditions, governments must address economic downturns through expansionary fiscal policy—a combination of tax cuts and/or higher public spending—or risk a self-fulfilling downward spiral of deflation and debt. Yet as the world economy emerged dazed from the financial emergency of 2007–2009, governments of every color across the rich democracies turned to austerity, with the predictable result that the recovery was stopped in its tracks.

If the parallels with economic policy failures in the 1930s were not stark enough, a collapse of political authority and the rise of anti-system movements soon followed. It is a matter of some surprise to this author that so many observers have either failed to notice the similarity or dismissed it as pure coincidence. There are, of course, many important differences between the 1930s and the world of the early twenty-first century, not least the dramatic improvements in living standards since then, and the development of sophisticated institutions of social protection that cushion all Western populations to some degree from the threats of financial and economic misfortune. Greece or the United States in the 2010s are certainly not Germany in the early 1930s. But it is hard to dispute that citizens' expectations that their democratically elected governments would help the whole of society participate in rising living standards have been disappointed.

Anti-system political movements on the left and right are all offering an answer to this disappointment. They all in their differing ways appeal to citizens who feel they have been ignored and that governments have preferred to protect the wealthy and powerful rather than ordinary people. They offer different remedies, some demanding the return of robust national borders, others the decentralization of powers to smaller subnational units, yet others the extension of supranational authority to allow for burden-sharing across national states. To reduce anti-system politics to cultural unease, the anxiety of the "left behind" or the "places that don't matter," or the revival of national sentiment misrepresents the phenomenon. At a very basic level, anti-system politics is about reasserting the power of politics over markets and money.[31]

Polanyi would not be surprised. The politics of the rich democracies since the 1970s have steadily eroded the power of politicians over markets, and his theory of the "double movement" predicts that a political reaction to reassert social interests over financial ones will follow. He also cautions that the existence of an anti-market revolt does not in itself solve the problem, and indeed the ways in which neoliberal institutions lock themselves in place, closing off avenues for the management of the market in the public interest, tend to create a dangerous impasse in which extremism can prosper. The anti-system wave pits the irresistible power of the market against the immovable object of society.[32] It took an unthinkable catastrophe to reconstruct capitalism in a more politically manageable form in the mid-twentieth century. This book is written in the hope that a better understanding of contemporary anti-system politics can contribute to moving toward a timely recalibration of the relationship between democracy and capitalism that puts markets in their proper place.

Where We Go from Here: The Structure of the Book

The rest of this book is divided into three parts. Part One places contemporary anti-system politics in the longer-term perspective of the conflictual relationship between capitalism and democracy over the past century. The first chapter outlines the evolution of the relationship between the market economy and political institutions of the Western countries over the last century, showing how capitalism and democracy have a fundamentally unstable relationship that produces regular political upheavals, of which the current turbulence is the most recent example. Attempts to reduce popular control over the market economy tend to provoke social reactions, which lead to government control over the economy being restored. The chapter shows how the shape of political institutions, and in particular the organization, interaction, and ideological identities of political parties, conditions the impact of markets on society, and how the dominance of liberal market ideas in the late twentieth and early twenty-first centuries weakened democratic participation and paved the way for a reemergence of political conflict through anti-system forces.

Chapter 2 analyzes the electoral successes of these anti-system forces, and shows how differences in the social, economic, and political institutions in the rich democracies determine the extent and nature of anti-system support. It shows that anti-system politics is stronger in countries that are structurally prone to run trade deficits, have weak or badly designed welfare states, and have electoral rules that artificially suppress the range of political options voters can choose from. It further shows that the ways in which welfare systems distribute exposure to economic risks predict whether anti-system politics takes a predominantly left-wing or right-wing direction. Right-wing anti-system politics is successful in creditor countries with very inclusive welfare states, as the most vulnerable economic groups express their fears that migratory pressures and transnational burden-sharing will undermine their generous social protections. Left-wing anti-system politics is stronger in debtor countries with "dualistic" welfare states, which particularly marginalize younger, more progressive-minded voters while protecting older, less educated citizens. The countries with the most limited welfare arrangements and most neoliberal institutions expose wide parts of the population to economic insecurity and therefore generate both left- and right-wing anti-system movements.

Parts Two and Three document the distinctive ways in which this anti-system politics has transformed some of the rich democracies. Part Two looks at the distinctive anti-system politics of the Anglo countries, driven by a populist, nationalist Right, but also an interventionist Left, and argues that these countries' enthusiastic adoption of market liberal policies has generated an intense demand for a political response to the resulting acute social stresses. Chapter 3 argues that the 2016 election in the United States is best understood in terms of the long-run consequences of the neoliberal turn in the 1970s, and the way in which the financial crisis of the late 2000s was addressed. Trump reflects one side of this anti-system response, while the rise of the Left in the Democratic Party reflects the other. Chapter 4 charts the very similar response to inequality and financial collapse in the United Kingdom, with the anti-system Right represented by the Brexit campaign, and the Left by Jeremy Corbyn's takeover of the Labour Party.

Part Three moves over to continental Europe and charts the anti-system politics arising out of the way the financial crisis shook the foundations of Europe's Monetary Union. Chapter 5 analyzes the Eurozone debt crisis as a conflict between creditor and debtor countries, pitting northern member states against the southern periphery, before looking at the distributional politics of austerity in the smaller southern Eurozone states of Greece and

Portugal. Chapters 6 and 7 chart the evolution of anti-system politics in Spain and Italy, respectively. These three chapters show that the southern European countries display a resurgent Left demanding greater burden-sharing at a European level and a strengthening of social protection at home. In contrast, the anti-system Right has been much stronger in the northern European creditor countries.

The final chapter assesses the implications of anti-system politics for the future of capitalism and democracy in the advanced countries. It argues that the current wave of anti-system support reflects the ultimate failure of the project of market liberalism, in that the limitations of the market logic have been laid bare by the financial crisis and the inability of the free market model to deliver prosperity and security. The answer to this crisis is likely to involve a reassertion of political authority over the market: either a revival of social democracy, the guiding ideology of the inclusive capitalism of the second half of the twentieth century, or a return to the nationalism and mercantilism of the interwar period.

PART ONE | CAPITALISM, DEMOCRACY, AND CRISIS

CHAPTER 1

Parties against Markets: The Rise
and Fall of Democratic Capitalism

Introduction

The political instability of the 2010s should have surprised no one. Capitalism
and democracy have always been in tension, and the easy relationship between
liberal democratic institutions and free markets proclaimed by some observers
at the end of the Cold War[1] was based on ahistorical delusions. The history of
capitalism is marked by the battle between economic forces pushing for the
primacy of profit and political forces demanding its regulation in the social
interest. Markets can create prosperity, but they also heighten inequality and
insecurity.[2] As a result, attempts to impose the logic of the market on democratic societies are fraught with difficulty, because citizens mobilize to respond
to threats to their economic and social well-being. However, popular mobilization is also fragile and difficult to sustain, leaving openings for pro-market
forces to push back against protective social institutions.

This chapter shows how democracy collided with the market economy
throughout the twentieth century, a collision at the root of the political and
economic instability of the early twenty-first century. Political parties are
the central protagonists in this story. Parties provide citizens with choices of
policy programs and candidates for political office at election time, and also
fill key government positions. But their role in democracies can go well beyond this minimalist contribution: historically, parties have articulated different social identities and visions of society, and sought to implement these
visions though government action. As Elmer E. Schattschneider put it in the
1940s, "democracy is unthinkable save in terms of parties."[3]

But political parties themselves evolved as patterns of democratic governance changed. In recent decades political parties became less and less able to perform the functions traditionally attributed to them, with the result that citizens felt less and less represented. The rise of anti-system parties is the direct consequence of the loosening of the bond between voters and the representatives they elect, and of the increasing perception that political parties serve a narrow elite of career politicians and insider interests. This crisis of political representation is the consequence of economic changes that have subjected Western societies to growing inequality and insecurity, while undermining the ability of political institutions to respond to popular pressures. The rest of this chapter shows how.

The Origins of Party Democracy

The first political parties were formed inside the parliaments of the protodemocratic regimes that emerged in western Europe and North America through the eighteenth and nineteenth centuries. These were described by Maurice Duverger as "cadre parties"[4]—loose associations of elites who agreed on common governing priorities. In the limited-suffrage regimes of that period, politicians had no need for highly developed local organizations to win over their small electorates of propertied men, and remained relatively detached from the rest of society. In the "rotten boroughs" of prereform England, many parliamentarians won election unopposed, or were able to win the votes of their tiny electorates through a mixture of local prestige, trading of favors, or simple bribery, such as plying voters with free alcohol. It was an unapologetically elitist form of government with limited representative ambitions.[5]

This early form of party democracy came under pressure in the second half of the nineteenth century, as mass movements representing the emerging industrial working class and landless peasants demanded political change. The socialist or labor parties established in the majority of Western countries demanded opportunities for political participation, and restrictions on the franchise were loosened, expanding the size of the electorate. These "mass parties," as Duverger called them, built networks of activists to support party candidates at election time, but also to build relationships with stable constituencies of voters. Mass parties sought to "encapsulate" their target electorate through party newspapers, social clubs, youth sections, summer camps, and so on. Voting for the party would become such an instinctive and natural act that, for many voters, it was unthinkable to support anyone else: partisan identification was born and provided democracy with a stable structure of political competition.

The economic system of the industrial age generated prosperity, but also extreme inequality: at the beginning of the twentieth century around half of pre-tax income typically accrued to the richest 10 percent of the population in Western countries.[6] Democracy, in contrast, was based on fundamentally egalitarian principles: it implied broad-based mass participation in political decision-making, giving the poor majority decisive influence over the conduct of government. This conflict between economic inequality and political equality was at the heart of elite resistance to democratic reforms in the nineteenth century: even apparently enlightened liberal thinkers as John Stuart Mill or the American Federalists feared that democracy would hand power over to an unruly mob that could threaten the rights of property-holders, the only social class considered worthy of political representation.[7] Mill, a supporter of extending voting rights, nevertheless argued that recipients of poor relief should not be enfranchised, on the grounds that "he who cannot by his labour suffice for his own support has no claim to the privilege of helping himself to the money of others."[8]

Ruling elites were particularly threatened by democracy because they were unaccustomed to having to win mass support for their plans. In some countries, such as Britain, elites were quick to build their own party structures. The Conservative Primrose League, which by 1910 had over two million members, organized meetings, speeches, and social events, and members swore allegiance to the Crown, the empire, and free enterprise. The Liberals, the other main party at that time, had built their own mass membership organization, centered around Joseph Chamberlain's Birmingham "caucus" of activists, which lobbied for trade protectionism. Although the labor movement initially worked with the Liberals to achieve worker representation, by 1900 the British trade unions founded their own Labour Party, which steadily supplanted the Liberals as the main alternative to Conservatism. For most of the period after World War II, UK electoral politics revolved around these two strong mass organizations, each reflecting distinctive political ideologies and social classes.

In other parts of Europe the path to democracy was far more conflictual. In Germany, Italy, and Spain the labor movement was torn between radical and pragmatic factions, a divide formalized after the Russian Revolution with the creation of communist parties. Reactionary ruling elites were reluctant to extend political rights to the working class, and the threat of the revolutionary Left led to the mobilization of more conservative sectors around fascism. It is easy to forget after seventy years of peaceful democratic rule in most high-income countries that the rise of mass politics between the wars also took the form of aggressive anti-liberal, anti-democratic, and some-times totalitarian movements. It is these parties, and their successor parties after World War II, that inspired Giovanni Sartori to coin the concept of "anti-system" parties.[9] These anti-system parties were directly responsible for overturning the democratic order between 1918 and 1945.

The interwar period witnessed the first attempt at reconciling mass pol-itics and market capitalism in Europe.[10] It was a period of intense political mobilization, as the working class pressed for political and social rights and demanded a greater share of economic output,[11] while governing elites sought to reimpose the macroeconomic discipline of the prewar Gold Standard. Their ultimate failure demonstrated, not for the first time in financial history, that unsustainable debt burdens and restrictive monetary conditions would lead to economic collapse and conflict.[12] The lack of protective social institutions to cushion labor from market adjustments drove industrial conflict and bol-stered anti-capitalist and anti-democratic political movements. The experi-ence of the 1930s revealed the limitations of the liberal order, showing that markets could break down under political pressure, potentially destroying democracy as well as capitalism.[13]

The human costs of the catastrophe were incalculable, but the economic costs can be measured: Thomas Piketty estimates that the financial damage caused by the two world wars and the intervening slump destroyed capital worth around four times GDP in Britain, France, and Germany.[14] This loss of wealth diminished the political influence of economic elites and facilitated a rebalancing of political power in favor of the laboring classes. The magnitude of the disaster convinced political elites that capitalism would need to learn to coexist with popular democracy, and with the political ideologies articu-lated by mass political parties: ideologies that were suspicious of unfettered markets.

The Democratization of Capitalism: Political Parties and the Welfare State in the Postwar Order

The defeat of fascism in World War II gave Western liberal elites the opportu-nity to rebuild the market system within a democratic framework, applying some of the lessons of the interwar period. Led by the United Kingdom's representative John Maynard Keynes, a long-standing critic of the post-1918 arrangements, and his US counterpart Harry Dexter White, the Bretton

Woods Conference in 1944 decided on a regime of stable, managed exchange rates, with capital controls and safeguards to deal with imbalances in international payments.[15] By averting the need for harsh domestic adjustments, these arrangements gave national governments the scope to adopt protective welfare policies and seek to maximize employment. The postwar order reestablished capitalist production while cushioning society from market instability.

This shift amounted to a "democratization" of capitalism in which the balance of power moved from international finance to the national state, which in western Europe and North America meant empowering democratically accountable governments.[16] Absent the threat of capital flight, popular pressure could be channeled into policies that cushioned society from the market while allowing capitalism to generate profitable investment. It was helpful that fascism and national socialism had been discredited—and in some cases, such as West Germany, formally outlawed—eliminating one potentially destructive avenue for market-curbing politics. A second nondemocratic threat to capitalism—Soviet-style socialism—was less easily defeated, and elites were concerned to prevent the labor movement in Western Europe being tempted by the communist option. The threat of communism and the strength of organized labor made a repeat of the interwar period's attempts to impose market orthodoxy unthinkable.[17]

This "democratic capitalism"[18]—the exercise of state power to tame the market and shape an economy in response to social needs—required organized political parties. Parties performed the key functions of recruitment and representation and the articulation of coherent political programs that could connect with the ambitions and interests of key social groups. The postwar period was a propitious time for government interventionism and social policy development, and in all the Western countries that had democratic elections at that time, governments pushed back against the laissez-faire orthodoxy that had failed between the wars. In the face of well-organized left-wing parties and unions, business and financial interests were incentivized, indeed perhaps coerced, into accepting class compromise, in the form of institutions that redistributed resources and risks more evenly between capital and labor. Political parties acted as the underwriters, mediators, and in some cases initiators of this new bargain between the employer and investor classes and the rest of society.[19]

Across the democracies, participation in government revolved around political parties representing the dominant ideological traditions of conservatism, liberalism, Christian democracy, and social democracy. All these parties favored, to varying degrees, the idea that governments ought to be involved in managing the economy by regulating finance, directing public invest-ment, running key industries and utilities, and using progressive taxation to fund social programs. This economic interventionism was embraced particu-larly strongly by socialist or social democratic parties, and their allied trade unions, and the growth of these organizations in the first half of the twentieth century hit its high point in the postwar period.[20] Protected by the fixed ex-change rates and capital controls of the Bretton Woods system, governments were now freer to use the levers of macroeconomic policy, such as interest rates and deficit spending, to pursue full employment.[21]

The strong economic growth Western countries enjoyed in the 1950s and 1960s provided governments with abundant resources to reward voters with concrete benefits in return for their support.[22] Government spending in the industrialized countries averaged around 10 percent of GDP at the end of the nineteenth century; by the end of the twentieth century it averaged 45–50 percent.[23] These opportunities incentivized party activism, and trade union membership, as well as high levels of citizen participation in elections. As mass parties took power and developed policy programs in accordance with their ideological outlook and electoral constituencies, they were able to use the state not only to achieve policy outcomes, but also to enhance and en-trench their own role in the political system.[24] Government spending created constituencies of beneficiaries that could identify the parties responsible as their protectors. The postwar "golden age" of inclusive economic growth was therefore also the golden age of the mass party.

The postwar period saw the consolidation of patterns of political repre-sentation whose essential stability underlined the grip mass political parties had over society. Early studies of electoral behavior showed that voters tended to identify with particular parties and vote in terms of partisan loyalty.[25] These loyalties reflected the stability of the key dividing lines—economic, religious, cultural—cutting through the electorate, which mass parties both reflected and reinforced.[26] Often partisan identities went well beyond the ballot box, influencing patterns of housing, schooling, leisure, and employ-ment. British workers socialized in working-men's clubs tightly connected to unions and the Labour Party, and Italian workers congregated in the *Case del Popolo* (People's Houses), social clubs close to the Communist Party. Party leaders stood at the head of organizations that were deeply embedded in both society and the state machinery, providing them with substantial clout in their exercise of government power.

Figure 1.1 illustrates the degree of party organization, and the extent of labor mobilization, at the height of the postwar golden age. Across sixteen consolidated democracies in 1970, 44 percent of workers on average were

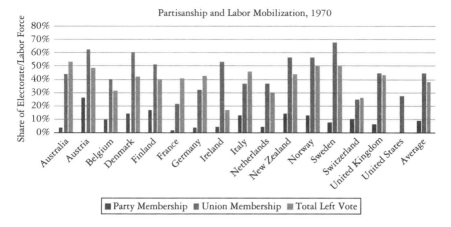

FIGURE 1.1 Mass Mobilization in the "Golden Age": Indicators of Strength of Organized Labor, 1970

union members, and left-wing parties won more than a third of the vote, while close to a tenth of the electorate on average were enrolled as members of a political party. In some countries, such as Austria, Denmark, Ireland, Sweden, and Norway, well over half of workers were in a union, while even in the United States approximately a quarter of the workforce was unionized. Party membership varied considerably, but in Austria more than a quarter of voters were members of a political party, while Denmark, Finland, Italy, and New Zealand were also above the average. Turnout in elections was very high in this period, averaging over 80 percent, with more than 90 per-cent of voters casting ballots in Australia, Austria, Belgium, Italy, and the Netherlands. High levels of popular participation in politics, added to high levels of worker organization, constituted a formidable counterweight to the power of wealthy capital owners.

The importance of mass participation can be seen in patterns of policy-making and ultimately in the income distribution. Figure 1.2 shows a strong cross-national correlation between trade union membership and levels of in-come inequality in the golden age period. The countries with high levels of trade union membership, and particularly those where unions were po-litically affiliated with the Left, delivered more left-leaning governments, with socialist/social democratic or labor parties gaining higher than average vote shares. Sweden is a paradigmatic case, with the Social Democratic Party (SAP) winning power already in the early 1930s and consolidating its grip on power, dominating governments until the 1970s. Trade union density reached 70 percent of the labor force in the 1960s, and continued to rise

FIGURE 1.2 Union Membership and Inequality, 1970s

before peaking at 90 percent in the 1990s.[27] Norway, Denmark, Austria, and Belgium all exhibited similarly high levels of left mobilization. These countries were in the forefront of welfare state development in the postwar period, developing extensive universalistic social protections, and achieving some of the lowest levels of inequality recorded in Western democracies.[28]

In other countries, the social democrats were less successful. This was not so much because the Left was not mobilized, but rather that it was divided among different left factions, principally because of a strong communist party to rival the social democrats. Finland, France, Germany, and Italy all had significant communist parties, and in Greece, Portugal, and Spain communism played a major role in the opposition to dictatorship. Conservative interests tended to coalesce around Christian democracy as an alternative to both socialism and liberalism. In Italy, the Christian Democrats (DC) dominated governments for nearly half a century, building an extensive welfare state offering generous protection for politically favored groups, such as public employees, small businesses, and retirees, in part as a strategic response to the communist-led labor movement.[29] In the continental and southern European countries a "Bismarckian"[30] occupation-based welfare predominated, in which work status defined access to social protection. Social and Christian Democrats had differing priorities and electoral clienteles, but both accepted the principle of generous social provision to compensate for the inequalities generated by the market.

In the English-speaking countries, both Christian democracy and communism were absent and political competition revolved around a straight battle between the organized Left pushing for welfare state expansion and a lay conservative Right mostly skeptical of the role of government in reducing economic inequality. Majoritarian electoral systems made coalition politics inviable and accentuated the zero-sum nature of distributional conflict, tending to undermine the labor movement's ability to win government power.[31] In Britain, Australia, and New Zealand, labor parties were relatively successful in winning government power on the back of a strong trade union movement, though in the 1980s neoliberal forces pushed back, reducing social protection considerably. In the United States, Ireland, and Canada, the labor movement was weaker historically and welfare more limited, especially in the United States where a combination of divided government, scale, and ethnic heterogeneity restricted the ability of the federal government to raise sufficient revenues to fund an extensive welfare state.[32]

The high degree of political mobilization characteristic of this period allowed the most economically vulnerable sectors of society to overcome their collective action dilemmas and challenge the structural power of wealth-holders. Under voter pressure, governments increasingly dedicated a large share of society's resources to the provision of old age pensions, disability benefits, family benefits, and unemployment compensation, all of which tended to redistribute resources from higher-income to lower-income groups.[33] Most voters were net beneficiaries of such policies, paying less tax than they received in social transfers, meaning that politicians could win elections by promising expansions of public spending.

The benign postwar environment of a stable international monetary order, entrenched popular representation, and egalitarian economic growth came to an end in the early 1970s. If the boom years of the postwar period had been a period of political constraints on capital, the 1970s and 1980s saw the gradual erosion of the system of capital controls that had facilitated popular governance of the economy. With the abrupt end to continuous growth and full employment, the dominant economic policy paradigm of the postwar era was suddenly open to challenge. Keynesian-style government intervention to secure full employment and the benign view of the state as an effective administrator of the economy were increasingly questioned, and neoliberal, pro-market theories made a comeback.[34]

The crisis of the 1970s sparked the reemergence of a clear conflict between capital and labor, fighting over the allocation of the pain of economic adjustment. Business was keen to push back against inflation and achieve wage restraint, as well as restore workplace discipline, which in countries as diverse as the United Kingdom, France, Italy, Spain, and Sweden had become severely compromised. The labor movement, in turn, was reluctant to give up on egalitarian income growth, and the 1970s were a period of intense labor mobilization in many Western countries. The destabilizing of the postwar arrangements provoked a high degree of industrial disruption as workers sought to maintain real wage levels in the face of inflation. Strike activity hit a postwar peak, and unions successfully mobilized a growing share of the labor force.[35]

In some countries, such as Germany, labor and capital reached cooperative bargains that sought to preserve investment and employment through wage restraint. But in many others, such as the United Kingdom, France, and Italy, governments responded to this climate of worker militancy by shifting their policy positions to accommodate labor demands. As a result, employers and investors were forced to take the strain in the form of reduced profits, either through inflationary pay demands, interruptions in production, or both. Concessions on employment law, inflationary pay increases, and increased public spending emboldened organized labor and undermined efforts to achieve price stability and bring government borrowing under control. Business interests were increasingly concerned that the capitalist system itself was under threat, and became more and more receptive to reversing the trend toward government interventionism.

Market Liberalism and Democracy: Shrinking the Space for Parties and Voters?

The market liberal (or neoliberal) turn was more than a set of alternative ideas of how to run the economy; it instead implied a very different kind of state and a different model of democracy. Democratic capitalism was, in William Riker's use of the term, "populist": it saw the role of government as responding to citizen demands, and actively intervening in society and the economy to meet the expectations expressed through competitive elections. Elected politicians, in this understanding of democracy, were entitled to manage the economy in accordance with the popular will, which in turn implied a more activist approach to markets, which were seen as technically improvable, and whose outcomes had little intrinsic normative value. Since it could be assumed that in a context of economic inequality the majority of the population would prefer a more equal sharing out of the national income, democratic capitalism implied political action to secure greater equality through the active management of the market economy.

The economists and philosophers whose ideas underpinned the liberal turn took a very different view. The capitalist system, built on free interactions of individuals and firms in competitive markets, was in itself a source of legitimacy, and its outcomes had the ethical status of resulting from individual acts of free will. In this view, clearly articulated, for example, in Milton Friedman's book *Capitalism and Freedom*,[36] market exchanges had the virtue of not resulting from coercion, while government regulation and taxation were underpinned by the coercive use of state power, and therefore undermined liberty. Aside from the broader philosophical questions this argument raises, it clearly advocated a particular form of state: a minimalist government, able to define and enforce property rights and oversee monetary arrangements, but do little else. Popular democracy based on the majority will was not only an insufficient basis for interfering with individual rights and choices, it was not in fact a desirable value at all.[37] Democratic institutions should instead be designed with a view to preserving individual freedom. Individual wants should be satisfied by free, unrestricted exchange in the marketplace rather than collective action.[38]

This radical liberal conception of the state had major implications for political representation. Neoliberals saw left-wing parties and unions as vehicles for exercising coercion against individual rights in the form of restrictive regulations on trade and investment, confiscatory taxes, and fiscal and monetary policies that eroded property rights through inflation.[39] Democratic capitalism was a "populist" arrangement that "overloaded" the state with insatiable demands for social rights and expenditures.[40] The influential Trilateral Commission report *The Crisis of Democracy* lamented that "the operations of the democratic process [. . .] appear to have generated a breakdown of traditional means of social control, a delegitimation of political and other forms of authority, and an overload of demands on government, exceeding its capacity to respond."[41] The "overload" thesis implied bringing monetary and fiscal policy back onto a more conservative footing, by insulating them as much as possible from popular pressure.

The primary means of adjusting monetary policy was to orient central bank policy toward price stability, overriding other objectives such as full employment. A key tool for achieving this was central bank independence—the removal of direct partisan influence over interest rates, which would be set by "independent" experts rather than elected politicians. Central bank independence spread rapidly across the Western democracies as politicians became persuaded that giving up direct operation of monetary policy was the most effective way of controlling inflation.[42] This turn toward stricter monetary policy also had implications for government budgets, which could no longer be cheaply financed through central bank purchases. By the 1990s most Western governments were subscribing to "fiscal rules," binding themselves to borrowing limits, either through participation in the European Monetary Union, or in the case of the United Kingdom, as a way of preempting threats to financial stability. This delegation of political decisions to "non-majoritarian" agencies[43] run by technocratic experts has been described as a "hollowing out of the state."[44]

The new policy orthodoxy severely circumscribed government policy discretionality, and was ultimately successful in easing the pressure on governments to meet popular demands for redistributive interventions. As mainstream political parties progressively adhered to these restraints, the outcomes of elections became less and less important for macroeconomic policy, particularly in the Eurozone, where monetary policy was removed entirely from national control and fiscal policy was subject to strict limits. Some areas of policy difference did remain, with social democratic parties more likely to prefer public investment in education and training to enhance productivity, while conservative parties tended to prefer more private-sector oriented solutions to labor market problems.[45] But even in these "supply-side" areas, policy increasingly converged around market deregulation and privatization.

As well as entrenched monetary rigor, the neoliberal project was also keen to curb the power of trade unions. Tight monetary policy could discipline labor by forcing up unemployment, but regulatory reforms also weakened the bargaining power of organized labor by raising the costs of strike action and discouraging union membership. The United States and the United Kingdom were trailblazers in this regard, with the Reagan and Thatcher administrations deploying a variety of legal, political, and economic resources to weaken the most powerful unions. But even in continental and northern Europe, where union membership remained high, a steady stream of regulatory reforms undermined collective bargaining, weakened workplace organization, and challenged employment protections.[46] Industrial unrest fell steadily after the 1970s as a result. By the 1990s, strike action had become a rarity (see Figure 1.3). The decline of unions was a serious problem for parties of the Left, and indeed the Thatcher reforms in the United Kingdom had the explicit aim of fatally weakening the Labour Party as a political force.[47]

As party politicians progressively lost their central role in governing the economy, political parties' grassroots presence and voter attachment began to decline. Figure 1.4 shows that party membership as a share of the electorate peaked around 1960 at an average of 13 percent, and fell continuously through the first decade of the twenty-first century. Another measure of party penetration into the social fabric—the numbers of voters expressing attachment or identification with the party—also declined. Dalton and Wattenberg found that, in nine European democracies for which time series

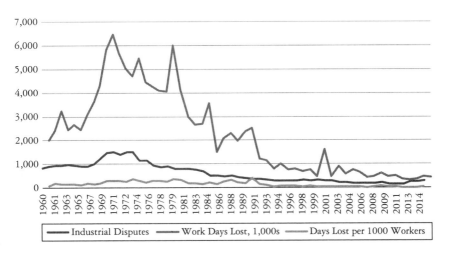

FIGURE 1.3 Industrial Disputes, 19 Democracies, 1960–2015
Source: Klaus Armingeon, Virginia Wenger, Fiona Wiedemeier, Christian Isler, Laura Knöpfel, David Weisstanner, and Sarah Engler, *Comparative Political Data Set 1960–2014* (Bern: Institute of Political Science, University of Berne, 2017).

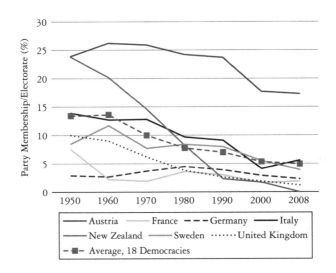

FIGURE 1.4 Party Membership in Selected Democracies, 1950–2008
Source: Susan Scarrow, *Beyond Party Members: Changing Approaches to Partisan Mobilization* (Oxford: Oxford University Press, 2014), p.96.

data was available, the number of voters who did not identify with any political party grew from around 30 percent in the mid-1970s to over 40 percent by the early 1990s, while the number of sympathizers with a party traveled in the opposite direction, from 40 to 30 percent.[48] Alongside the decline in membership, this reflected an increasing distance between party organizations and most of the electorate, threatening the future survival of the partisan structures that underpinned democratic politics.

The waning ability of mass parties to mobilize their loyal supporters and the interest of party elites in winning government power generated internal conflict as office-holders sought to appeal to broader electoral audiences, diluting parties' ideological identities and insulating themselves from grassroots pressures. This "catch-all" politics[49] set in motion a self-reinforcing shift away from the grassroots activists toward career politicians, and weakened parties' connections with their core voters. But delivering benefits to a broader-based and more fickle electorate was increasingly costly, pushing parties to use more and more government resources to secure their political and organizational survival. As economies ran into trouble from the early 1970s, governing parties were caught between the pressures of an increasingly demanding labor movement seeking continued wage rises and increases in public spending, on the one hand, and the financial pressures of rising deficits and nervous bond markets, on the other.

The decline of ideological appeals and the dampening of popular expectations about what government could achieve undermined the motivation of party volunteers and left parties short of the labor power that underpinned the mass party model. A new organizational form was therefore necessary, which relied less on the labor-intensive grassroots activism of the early phase of democracy, and could exploit more capital-intensive campaigning techniques revolving around television, mass advertising, and opinion polling.[50] But this new professionalized model both cost money and alienated parties' core electorates, accelerating the decline of traditional sources of funding such as party membership subscriptions and contributions from ancillary organizations such as trade unions.

The financial crisis of political parties could be addressed in two ways: public money or private donations. Public subsidies freed parties from some of the financial strains resulting from the increasing costs of electoral campaigning and the declining revenues accruing from membership fees. But they came at a reputational cost, as it did not escape public attention that it was the parties themselves that voted to divert taxpayer money to their own organizations, usually by making secretive agreements with their opponents.[51] Public funding was predictably unpopular among voters, but the alternative was just as bad: private donations pitted the broad, collective interest of millions of voters against the narrow, exclusive interests of corporations or wealthy individuals.[52] In the case of social democratic parties, private funding risked subordinating ideological and programmatic commitments to the needs of donors. The resulting scandals were hugely damaging to parties' reputations and their relationship with the traditional voter base.[53]

Public funding of political parties avoided the stark inequality of political influence associated with private donations, but it generated a new form of disconnect, by relieving parties of the need to maintain deep organizational roots among their social base. Instead of party conferences to represent the demands of the core constituency, party leaders could commission opinion polling to identify popular policies, and part of the activists' job of canvassing for support could be delegated to professionalized media-oriented campaign strategists. Elected politicians were increasingly able to operate at arm's-length from party supporters, and indeed very often built political careers inside metropolitan political elite circles, with little experience of grassroots activism. But this implied a far more superficial and volatile relationship between parties and voters, and a greater fragility of the party system as a whole.

After the Party: Cartel Politics and Democratic Disaffection

Electoral politics in the golden age period was characterized by high levels of stability, with parties enjoying reliable support from their core electorates. Lipset and Rokkan described Western party systems as "frozen," pointing out that "the party systems of the 1960s reflect, with few but significant exceptions, the cleavage structures of the 1920s. . . . [T]he party alternatives, and in remarkably many cases the party organizations, are older than the majorities of the national electorates."[54] Although the political turbulence of the 1970s brought an increased level of electoral instability, this remained largely true for the first decade of the twenty-first century, too. For example, in the year 2000, Britain, France, Germany, and Sweden were all governed by socialist or social democratic parties that had already held office in the immediate postwar period, and indeed had a century or more of history behind them.[55]

But the parties of the early twenty-first century, despite mostly keeping the same names, were very different from their predecessors of a few decades earlier. Parties that could once count on a reliable base of activists and a reservoir of loyal partisan voters were now extraordinarily fragile. As we have already seen, levels of party membership were in steep decline, with on average just one member for every twenty voters. Moreover their shares of the overall vote had also declined, not only because of the growing fragmentation of the vote, with growing shares going to new "challenger" parties, but also because voter turnout had been declining in the vast majority of democracies, very sharply in some, such as the United Kingdom and Italy, and more moderately in others. Another sign of parties' waning grip on their supporters was the growing share of the electorate willing to change their vote from one election to the next: electoral volatility (net vote share changes, calculated by summing the changes in party support between successive elections[56]) also reached its lowest point in the early 1960s, rising steadily until an even sharper rise in the 2010s (see Figure 1.5).

The growth in political disengagement should not be mistaken for a sign of passive contentment. There were strong indications that the

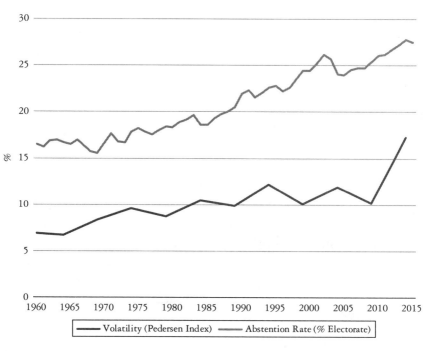

FIGURE 1.5 Indicators of Party Decline, 21 Democracies, 1960–2015
Source: Data for non-European countries from Scott Mainwaring, Carlos Gervasoni, and Annabella España-Najera (2017), "Extra- and Within-System Electoral Volatility," *Party Politics* 23(6): 623–635; Armingeon et al., *Comparative Political Data Set 1960–2014* (see Figure 1.3).

disenfranchisement implicit in the cartel party model was keenly felt by citizens, and that falling electoral turnout was a sign of frustration at the lack of options available, rather than of indifference to politics.[57] Party decline was matched by democratic disaffection, and growing numbers of voters expressed mistrust of politicians and the democratic institutions more broadly.[58] This frustration could be detected in declining turnout and, among those who voted, an active rejection of the traditional political parties and growing support for new parties, almost all of which in some way sought to present themselves as alternatives to the existing elites.

These developments reflected a fundamental weakening of political parties' ability to perform their traditional representative function as a link or "transmission belt" between identifiable social groups and the policy process. However, this did not pose an immediate threat to the survival of the established parties. With the safety net of public subsidies, parties could secure their survival as long as they were able to maintain adequate levels of electoral support, and the inertia of most voters' behavior and high barriers to entry for new parties provided a degree of protection against the loosening of their connection with the electorate. The main political parties became, in the words of Katz and Mair,[59] "cartel parties," colluding to preserve the existing party system and to limit the range of acceptable policy positions.[60]

Once social democratic parties had abandoned their commitments to public ownership of the economy and full employment, and conservative parties had accepted a substantial role for the state in protecting incomes and providing essential services, the stakes of political competition were lowered. Not by accident, sometime around the mid-1990s it became accepted terminology in public debate to refer to the rival establishment parties as being on the "center-left" or the "center-right"—the notion of a party not adjacent to the center proving seemingly inconceivable. The characteristic form of electoral competition of the cartel party era revolved around leadership competence, marginal variations in distributive politics, and (often largely symbolic) differences in cultural identities and values.[61] Political parties were no longer competing over different models of society, but instead over their ability to manage the only possible model: a market liberal society with an increasingly strained welfare state.

This sharp reduction in the range of policies on offer is depicted in Figure 1.6, which uses text analysis of party manifestos to estimate party positions. It presents the average trend on economic policy issues for the main political party families in western Europe since World War II: a centrist position would be represented by a zero on the vertical axis, a left-wing position by a negative score, and a right-wing position by a positive one.[62] At the start

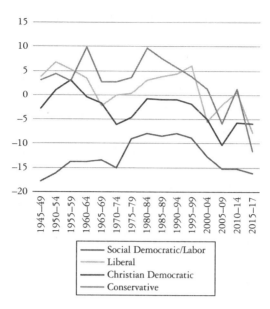

FIGURE 1.6 Average Economic Policy Positions for Each Party Family, 14–16 Democracies, 1945–2017 (Percentage of Right-Wing Statements Minus Percentage of Left-Wing Statements). The chart includes fourteen democracies for the whole period and adds Portugal and Spain after 1975.
Source: Andrea Volkens, Werner Krause, Pola Lehmann, Theres Matthieß, Nicolas Merz, Sven Regel, and Bernhard Weßels, *The Manifesto Data Collection: Manifesto Project (MRG / CMP / MARPOR)*, version 2018b (Berlin: Wissenschaftszentrum Berlin für Sozialforschung, 2018) (https://doi.org/10.25522/manifesto. mpds.2018b).

of the period, the gap between social democratic, socialist, and labor parties and the other three types was very large, reflecting the commitment of these parties to fundamental socialist transformation. However, over time the social democratic position moved in a centrist direction, while the liberal and Christian democratic parties, and later the conservatives, trended leftward, as they embraced the preservation of the most popular elements of the postwar welfare state. The turn back to the Left of the social democrats in the early twenty-first century, and in particular after the Global Financial Crisis, was matched by the other parties.

Voters may have been freer of partisan ties than ever before, but the range of choices on offer was far narrower. Key political cleavages or dividing lines that had structured politics during the postwar period, such as socioeconomic class or religion, ceased to be strong predictors of voting choice.[63] Voters had become detached from stable political loyalties, and rather than unthinkingly backing the same party every election, "began to choose" the politicians and policies that they preferred, voting in response to parties' programmatic offerings, leadership attractiveness, and performance in government.[64] But this emergence of a new, more mobile and fickle voter coincided with a curtailing of real political choice.

The decline of the mass party, once it began, was self-perpetuating and ultimately destructive of democracy. As Peter Mair documented in his prescient book *Ruling the Void*,[65] political parties, shorn of their ideological and social referents, became little more than state agencies charged with providing voters with a menu of options to exercise notional democratic choice within highly constrained parameters. Not only were elections less and less meaningful in terms of providing instructions and guidance for those governing, but political parties were less and less autonomous from the state in terms of their organization and funding, and as a result more insulated from popular pressure. But by distancing themselves from their core support and making superficial "catch-all" appeals to less committed voters, the established political parties were exposing themselves to much greater levels of electoral and political risk.

Neoliberal Democracy: Inequality, Plutonomy, and Governance by Markets

Cartel parties were an effective vehicle for governing the liberal order because they allowed democracy to serve capitalism, by securing mass consent for policies that insulated markets from the protectionist and redistributive instincts of voters, especially those in the lower- and middle-income brackets. Elections could come and go without significant disturbances to monetary and fiscal policies and regulatory institutions, which were determined to a large degree by international agreements and nonelected institutions either at the national or supranational level. Cartel politics rested on a shared belief between the main political parties that government could not, and should not, interfere too much with the workings of markets, so that voters had little opportunity to vote against market liberalism. Liberal democracy had become "neoliberal" democracy.[66]

But at the same time that cartel politics was making voters more politically powerless, the emerging liberal market economy was placing them under growing stress. Most obviously, the distribution of income was becoming more unequal. Figure 1.7 shows that in the large industrialized

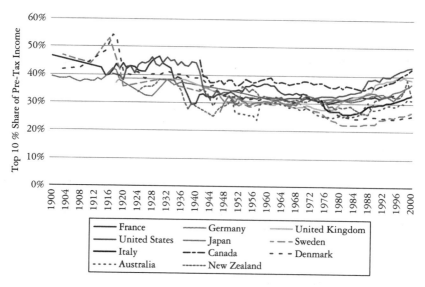

FIGURE 1.7 Top Income Shares in 11 Democracies, 20th Century
Source: World Inequality Database (https://wid.world).

countries the income share of the top decile declined dramatically through the interwar years and the postwar golden age, but from the 1980s on it began to rise again.[67] This reflected both secular changes in the economy and shorter-term political decisions. Thomas Piketty argues that this rise in inequality was driven by the recovery of capital after the turmoil of the two world wars, which led to the capital share of income following a clear linear upward trend across the Western democracies, reaching around 25–30 percent by 2010.[68] This implied a loss of 10–15 percent of GDP for wage-earners. And as the labor share of income was sacrificed, income inequality also inevitably increased, since labor was the main source of income for most households.

As the top income groups took a larger and larger share of the pie, their connection to the rest of society became correspondingly weaker. The emergence of the very wealthy as a distinct social group, with political interests dramatically at odds with the rest of society, was displayed with unusual candor in a notorious report produced by a Citigroup analyst, which described the United States and other similar countries as "plutonomies" where "economic growth is powered by and largely consumed by the wealthy few."[69] As billionaire investor Warren Buffett put it, "there is class warfare [. . .] But it's my class, the rich class, that is making war, and we're winning."[70] A clear indicator of the increasing power of the wealthy was that even as their share of economic output grew, their contribution to the public coffers through taxation, which had reached extraordinary heights in the immediate postwar period, was relentlessly cut.[71]

At the same time that this group enjoyed unprecedented wealth, life was becoming more precarious for most of the rest of the population. The danger of locking in market liberalism was that the policies it implied produced increasing inequality and insecurity, if not by design then as a predictable result of the deliberate weakening of egalitarian and protective institutions. Typically, these reforms—which became such an entrenched orthodoxy in policy circles that they began to be described using the neutered phrase "structural reforms"—sought to enhance market competition, reduce the frictions and restrictions on trade and exchange inherent in government regulation and redistribution, and give greater scope to the price mechanism, rather than political or social rights and institutions, to allocate resources.

We can see the destabilizing consequences of market liberalization very clearly in the world of work, the principal source of income for the vast majority of households. Market liberal reforms to the labor market sought to individualize as much as possible the contracts tying workers to employers. Collective bargaining, which offered workers greater protection from dismissal, better working conditions, and more equal wages, was subject to withering critiques from conservative economists and policymakers, who argued that it made labor compensation too inflexible, with damaging effects on company competitiveness and overall levels of employment.[72] Similarly, employment protection legislation—the laws regulating and restricting dismissals and guaranteed basic rights in the workplace—was considered to destroy jobs, hinder industrial adjustment, and raise labor costs. Finally, welfare policies designed to provide income guarantees for unemployed workers were criticized for discouraging workers from accepting jobs paying the market rate, and pushing up non-wage-labor costs because of the expensive social contributions required to finance them.

In markets for goods and services, a preference for light-touch regulation, both domestically and internationally, prevailed. In the national context, regulation of markets was seen as an impediment to economic efficiency, and economists were strongly influenced by ideas about regulatory capture[73] and the susceptibility of governments to legislate to protect special interests at the expense of consumers, which it is assumed would benefit from market forces. In the international arena, free trade was regarded as of unambiguous benefit for all, and the removal of formal and informal barriers to trade as making for greater economic efficiency and therefore prosperity.[74] Needless to say, state ownership of productive activities that could be delivered by the private sector was considered inefficient at best, and corrupt and wasteful at worst.

In financial markets, levers of government control over the investment function were also increasingly regarded as inefficient and politically undesirable.[75] Direct political interventions in the banking system, through state ownership of credit institutions, was discouraged, and in those countries where it existed programs of privatization were launched, often by governments of the center-left. But regulation of the banking system was also out of tune with the strong preference of the economic policy community for arm's-length supervision of credit, based on the belief that financial institutions had sufficient incentives to avoid practices that would imperil financial stability. Finally, government's own involvement in the credit system through its borrowing was increasingly circumscribed, with central bank monetization of government debt largely outlawed and the emergence of fiscal rules preventing government borrowing exceeding the narrow confines of automatic stabilizers in mild downturns.

The political success of market liberalism was all the more remarkable because many of the measures that mainstream politicians accepted as the orthodoxy were deeply unpopular. The former European Commission President Jean-Claude Juncker once candidly admitted, "we all know what to do, we just don't know how to get re-elected once we've done it."[76] For example, cuts to state pensions and other popular spending commitments provoked fierce public opposition, as did regulatory reforms to reduce labor protections and promote more "flexible" forms of employment. As a result, democratic accountability was fundamentally threatening to this new orthodoxy, and increasing efforts were made to circumvent democratic institutions in order to implement it, through the growing role of nonelected authorities described earlier. The market liberal economy required democratic politics be kept on a tight rein.

The emergence of this orthodoxy and its implementation to varying degrees across the rich democracies is all the more remarkable because the economic ideas that inspired it were far from uncontroversial even within the economics profession, and were very strongly contested outside it. Moreover, the evidence has mounted ever since that these ideas were fundamentally flawed, in some cases so obviously that one economist described them as "zombie ideas": no matter how often they are debunked, they keep coming back.[77] Even before the financial crisis of the 2000s, growth rates in the advanced democracies were slow to display signs of benefiting from the recommended reforms. Yet market liberal policies such as privatization and the deregulation of labor and financial markets were frequently presented as being essentially technical fixes designed to make economies work better, based on the kind of sound scientific advice that governments would seek before setting policy on, say, public health or climate change.

Presenting market liberal policies as scientifically grounded technical fixes meant that their distributional implications were rarely discussed. Policies designed to dismantle protective institutions such as restrictions on firing, collective wage negotiations, trade barriers, and limits to credit creation created both winners and losers. The underlying assumption of the structural reform agenda was that societies as a whole would be so much better off that the distributional effects of the policies were not worth much attention. But dismantling collective bargaining made low-skilled workers poorer,[78] the opening up of protected markets to new competition destroyed many jobs, and the expansion of credit inflated asset prices and generated income streams from poorer to wealthier citizens.

These policies inevitably increased inequality, poverty, and insecurity, placing a greater strain on welfare states. Even the OECD's own econometric analyses found that the reductions in employment protection legislation that it was advocating to member states were significantly predictive of increased inequality.[79] Market-friendly reforms also made for greater insecurity, as livelihoods were increasingly tied to market dynamics while, as a result of the same broad reform agenda, markets were becoming less and less predictable. The numbers of workers on temporary contracts, exposed to sudden losses of income as market conditions and employer needs change, dramatically increased.[80] Protections against dismissal for workers on permanent contracts were also relaxed.[81]

Yet governments in the high-income countries were busy attempting to contain social spending even as the demands on the welfare state accelerated.[82] Unemployment benefits were subject to increasingly strict conditionality, and many countries made moves away from state-backed pay-as-you-go pensions, introducing a greater private market involvement in retirement provision.[83] Provision of social housing was also pared back, exposing households to the vagaries of real estate and credit markets to a much greater extent than in the past.[84] Home ownership became increasingly important for living standards, but housing markets were made more subject to the fluctuations of the credit cycle, increasing households' vulnerability to financial shocks. Ordinary citizens were exposed to growing economic insecurity at work and through the life cycle.

By reducing the scope of collectively determined decisions and enhancing individual exchange, market liberalism accentuated inequalities of resources between economic actors and exposed weaker parties in economic exchange to greater uncertainty and insecurity. The structural shift in the political economy in favor of the wealthy was abetted by policy changes that limited the ability of governments to compensate the wage-earning classes for their declining share of income and the growing material uncertainty they faced. The arguments for reducing government's ability to regulate markets and redistribute income and risk rested on contested claims that rolling back the state would improve the performance of the economy overall, making everyone better off. But the 1990s and 2000s was also a period of weak wage growth, as well as rising wage inequality and, in most countries, welfare retrenchment.[85] The electorate could be forgiven for thinking that cartel politics worked largely in the interests of the wealthiest sectors of society, who saw their share of income grow almost everywhere, in some cases quite spectacularly.

The "Flaw in the Model": Market Liberalism and the Global Financial Crisis

The postwar period was unprecedented for the almost total absence of banking crises in the Western industrialized economies. The capital controls and strict financial regulation of the Bretton Woods era disincentivized or outright prohibited the kinds of risky behavior that could bring down financial institutions, and prevented problems becoming systemic. Credit was restricted and controlled in myriad ways, placing limits on the ability of corporations, households, and governments to build up high levels of debt. But as governments began to dismantle these restrictions in the 1970s, financial instability began to grow and banking crises and bubble dynamics subjected household finances to higher levels of volatility. Even the more prosperous groups were exposed to greater economic uncertainty under these circumstances, and the rise in inequality raised the stakes, with wrong decisions or simply bad luck in the labor or financial markets having potentially devastating consequences.

The financial collapse of the late 2000s is now so thoroughly studied and apparently well understood that it is difficult to believe that almost nobody predicted it.[86] The intellectual blinkers that contributed to this inability to anticipate the consequences of a long period of reckless lending and inadequate regulation gave it the appearance of an "exogenous shock," a "black swan" on the outer reaches of what was considered possible or even thinkable.[87] This element of surprise was not merited, as the 2008 collapse was quite easily slotted into the regular cycle of financial crises associated with volatile, mobile capital and arm's-length regulation of the banking sector, a cycle identified and reasonably well understood a long time ago by scholars such as Keynes, Minsky, and Kindelberger.[88] The crisis may not have been precisely predicted in its timing or it proximate triggers, but the signs of serious financial fragility had been identified by some astute observers.[89]

The failure to avert the crisis may have been to some extent a failure of policy design and individual judgment in the part of key actors, but at its heart it was an intellectual failure. Governments and regulators had been captured by market liberal thinking to such an extent that policy was based on the naive belief that market actors would avoid risky behaviors because it was in their self-interest to do so. The logical implication of this was that government regulation was either futile or counterproductive: investors had "skin in the game" and would not build positions that would endanger the financial system.[90] This fanciful idea was forcefully applied by luminaries such as Alan Greenspan, chair of the US Federal Reserve until just before the crisis, and Harvard economist Larry Summers, US treasury secretary under Bill Clinton, who actively resisted any drift toward greater regulation and oversight. After the fact, Greenspan contritely admitted to a congressional committee that he had detected a "flaw" in the free market model that had underpinned his lengthy tenure at the head of the global financial system.[91]

This flawed model was shared by many influential figures both in politics and academia, but it was also sustained by the very real gains that it delivered to Wall Street and financial elites across the Western democracies. Over the period preceding the 2008 crash, financial sector compensation soared, particularly in the United States and the United Kingdom. The beneficiaries of inadequate financial regulation used part of their gains to buy political influence, by funding political campaigns and extensive lobbying activities to protect their gains.[92] When the crisis hit, this infrastructure of political influence smoothed the path to the massive bailouts the governments resorted to in the face of a global economic meltdown. There was a compelling case that bailouts were necessary and that allowing systemic financial institutions to fail would have wreaked havoc across the world economy. But the bailouts were deeply unpopular, involving the sudden deployment of inconceivably large amounts of money to rescue financial assets mostly held by the wealthiest sectors of society.

The bailouts may have prevented a catastrophic collapse, but they were unable to avert the largest downturn across the industrialized world since the 1930s. Half of the twenty Western democracies for which we have data suffered negative median income growth between 2007 and 2014.[93]

Moreover, declining incomes were accompanied by significant reductions in the growth of government spending, creating further discontent as health-care, education, and other public services were pared back.[94]   But although the financial crisis and the "Great Recession" that followed it affected the whole global economy, it affected some countries far more than others. And the countries that were most affected by the crisis proved to be the countries most subject to anti-system political backlash in the 2010s.

Figure 1.8 shows that countries running high current account deficits—in other words, those that were importing more than they exported, and therefore were borrowing to finance spending—on the eve of the crisis had the worst performance in terms of median income growth in the years after-ward. Most of these countries had credit booms in the 2000s, which gave way to banking crises and in some cases sovereign debt crises after the 2008 meltdown. Current accounts on the eve of the financial crisis in the countries studied here varied from a deficit of over 15 percent of GDP in Greece to a surplus of 17 percent in the case of Norway. Figure 1.8 shows that the me-dian income losses during the financial crisis and the Great Recession were highest in the most indebted countries, especially Greece, but also Spain, Ireland, Italy, and Portugal.[95] Less indebted countries mostly had modest in-come gains in the same period.

The connection between high inequality and exposure to financial crises has been the subject of an interesting but inconclusive debate among economists. High inequality may have encouraged policymakers to loosen

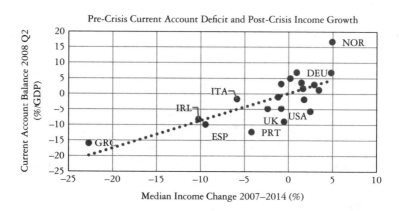

FIGURE 1.8 Pre-Crisis Current Account Deficit and Post-Crisis Income Growth
Source: OECD, "Current Account" (https://data.oecd.org/trade/current-account-balance.htm); OECD, "Income Distribution Database (IDD)" (http://www.oecd.org/social/income-distribution-database.htm).

financial regulation, leading to excessive credit expansion, asset price inflation, and unsustainable flows of capital to overheated economies that ultimately crashed.[96] But the correlation between inequality and crisis could equally be a spurious one: successful export economies—such as Germany and the smaller European social market economies—share a tradition of corporatist bargaining between labor unions and employers, in which wage moderation is traded for a more egalitarian wage structure and generous welfare arrangements.[97] Their low levels of inequality may therefore be only indirectly related to their current account surpluses, but either way, the populations of the surplus countries were far less exposed to the ravages of the crisis, and have had correspondingly lower levels of political instability, as the next chapter will show.

The historically large trade imbalances between surplus and deficit countries before the crisis meant that the former were building up financial claims on the latter: put crudely, surplus countries were also creditors, lending deficit countries the money to buy their exports.[98] This meant that the postcrisis adjustment was asymmetric: deeply painful for debtor countries such as those in southern Europe and the Anglosphere, more manageable for the export powerhouses of northern Europe. To balance their current accounts, the debtor countries needed to sharply reduce their consumption, cut real wages, and expand their exports to replace the lost demand. However, creditor countries, most of which also underwent significant banking crises, were retrenching at the same time, meaning that the debtor nations had little hope of achieving a balance without a large reduction in internal demand. The channel through which this reduction took place was a sharp tightening of credit conditions in the private sector and fiscal retrenchment (tax rises and spending cuts) in the public sector: in other words, austerity.

Creditor countries were also affected by the crisis, since the global downturn that followed the financial crisis undermined their export markets, and governments' reluctance to substitute external demand with internal demand by fiscal stimulus, in case it resulted in higher inflation affecting competitiveness, also implied a degree of austerity, though far less acute. Even in the relatively stable economies such as Germany, the Netherlands, or Austria, wage growth was anemic in the aftermath of the crisis and fiscal policy, after the initial stimulus in 2009–2010, was neutral or even contractionary, doing little or nothing to expand demand. Moreover, despite their overall creditor status, these countries were exposed to the debt crisis in two ways. First, banks that had invested heavily in risky assets, often in debtor countries, found themselves in deep trouble, some of them requiring direct government assistance. Second, the creditor countries of the European Union were first in line to finance rescue packages for the debtor countries on the Eurozone periphery. Although the costs of these bailouts in concrete terms had little incidence on government budgets, they were deeply unpopular among voters who themselves were also facing the consequences of the downturn, albeit less severely.

These troubles were real enough to have political consequences, but they paled in comparison to those suffered by debtor countries. Countries that were reliant on flows of capital from outside sustaining domestic consumption—such as Greece, Spain, Ireland, and the United Kingdom—had to drastically, and suddenly, rein in their spending. The loss of internal demand was especially hard to cope with because the same thing was happening to other countries, so there were no growing neighboring markets that could make up for it. Exporting one's way out of the slump was nearly impossible for these countries. Germany also suffered a short-term hit with the slump in demand from southern Europe, but its export-oriented economic model enabled it to grow in other markets, such as Asia, benefiting from the weakening of the euro currency. The United States was also hit by the crisis, but its status as the issuer of the global reserve currency gave it much greater flexibility to cope with the squeeze in demand. The weakness of these countries' welfare institutions ensured that large shares of the population suffered brutal economic and social consequences.

Conclusion

To recapitulate, the market liberal orthodoxy of the late twentieth century placed Western publics under a level of stress not seen since the 1930s. They had been subjected first to increasing inequality and insecurity, as labor market protections and welfare provisions were rolled back, while wealthy elites took most of the gains from economic growth. Then the market volatility generated by a separate plank of the neoliberal reform agenda provoked a global crisis, which cost millions of citizens their jobs and wrecked the household balance sheets of many more. Governments bailed out financial institutions to the disproportionate advantage of the wealthiest groups, while imposing harsh austerity on everyone else. Meanwhile, the promise that "tightening belts" would lead to a swift recovery proved to be entirely false, as the majority of citizens took years to return to their pre-crisis incomes, and in many cases were made permanently poorer.

One would expect this succession of events to provoke both a great deal of anger toward the politicians and financiers who had provoked the crisis and a clamor for a reversal of the policy measures that had caused the mess. The anger was real enough, as the heavy defeats of governing parties in post-crisis elections across the Western democracies attest. But policy change was far more muted than would have been predicted. Financial regulation was tightened, but without the radical measures, such as breaking up "too big to fail" institutions or tighter government controls on credit, that many demanded.[99] The bonus culture among top bankers persisted. Monetary policy remained loose, which relieved the pressure on households to some degree, but measures to expand the money supply focused on backstopping asset markets and easing pressures on bank balance sheets, rather than helping financially stressed households. The panic about government debt, led by controversial neoliberal economists such as Alberto Alesina,[100] Carmen Reinhart, and Kenneth Rogoff,[101] led to a doubling down on welfare cuts. Finally, the dominant response to post-crisis unemployment was further labor market deregulation, rather than government investment or other forms of fiscal stimulus.[102]

How could the spectacular unraveling of a set of contested political and economic ideas, which caused damage on a global scale, lead to so little policy change? The market liberal consensus that underpinned policy across the Western democracies after the 1970s proved surprisingly resilient.[103] There was no doubting that Western publics were anything but relaxed about the crisis and its consequences. But politics was slow to turn. There was no shortage of intellectual armory to bring to the problem, as the crisis sparked a lively debate in economics, with leading figures in the field challenging the neoliberal consensus and suggesting a range of possible reforms, from a return to expansionary fiscal policy, innovative ideas in monetary policy, and arguments for an increased role for public investment. But politicians in the main political parties were strangely reluctant to pick up on the opportunities to shift the policy agenda and respond to the demand for change. Their failure to react left the field open to enterprising anti-system politicians capable of cashing in on popular anger and resentment.

CHAPTER 2 | Explaining the Rise of
Anti-System Parties: Inequality,
Debt, and the Crisis

T HE HISTORY OF capitalism and democracy tells us we should have
expected years of rising inequality and a massive financial crisis to produce a political backlash. The tendency of financial crises to produce political upheaval, and often authoritarian reactions, is well documented. Yet
many observers have insisted that spectacular political shocks such as Trump,
Brexit, and the anti-system takeovers in the southern Eurozone had little to
with economics.[1] Instead, it is argued, immigration and social change are to
blame for pushing culturally conservative voters toward right-wing authoritarianism. The weakness of this explanation is immediately apparent: not
only have immigration and shifting cultural norms been a constant feature
of Western societies for decades, but in several countries political instability
has taken the form of left-wing movements that celebrate cultural change
and even demand solidarity with refugees. A theory that explains only some
anti-system movements is not a robust theory.

However, it is also true that the relationship between the economic shock
and its political consequences is often indirect and hard to pin down. Anti-
system parties are not necessarily supported by the most economically vulnerable citizens, and are present in economically successful countries as well
as those most affected by the crisis. What we need therefore is a theory of
anti-system politics that puts economic change at center stage, and that can

explain how the extent and nature of anti-system politics varies over time and across countries. This chapter presents such a framework, and then presents some evidence of how exposure to inequality and financial insecurity predicts anti-system politics better than cultural changes of patterns of migration. This framework then informs the case studies in the rest of the book.

What Is Anti-System Politics?

Anti-system political movements are defined by the system they oppose: they share a rejection of "the prevailing political or social order,"[2] and the values it represents. But anti-system parties do far more than agitate to overturn existing elites: they also express uncompromising opposition to the dominant form of political and economic organization, which for the current period means support for or acceptance of globalization and the institutional architecture of international cooperation that underpins it, a broadly pro-market position on economic and social policy, and support for the liberal order and currently existing national states. Anti-system politics also generally combines a blanket condemnation of the existing political class or establishment with demands for a greater degree of voter input into political decision-making.[3]

This oppositional attitude has led to the wide and sometimes indiscriminate use of the term "populism" to describe anti-system politicians. Certainly populism is a workable concept for describing the highly charged rhetoric, anti-elitism, and simplification of complex political problems characteristic of politicians like Trump, Beppe Grillo, or Nigel Farage. But there are also ways of opposing the existing political and economic order that do not reject basic liberal democratic values such as pluralism, the rule of law, and evidence-based policymaking. Aside from the definitional disputes surrounding the term and its highly charged normative implications, this book avoids relying on the concept of populism because it only very partially captures the nature of anti-system politics while at the same time attributing the same negative connotations to widely differing political movements.

In the public debate and even to some extent in academia, populism is often presented as antithetical to liberalism.[4] Unfortunately, liberalism is an equally misused concept, deployed variously to describe quite different and often incompatible political values. In the United States, a "liberal" is what in Europe would be described as a social democrat, favoring government intervention to secure economic fairness and equal rights for victims of discrimination. In continental Europe, "liberalism" means the exact opposite—a preference for limited government and free markets, giving primacy to individual rights, and especially property rights. It is therefore useful to distinguish between these two understandings of liberalism, which become important in defining the differences between anti-system political movements. Social liberalism emphasizes equality of rights and freedom from oppression on the grounds of gender, ethnicity, religion, or sexuality: positions that are often described, mostly pejoratively, as "identity politics." Economic liberalism emphasizes the protection of individual rights to interact in markets with as little government regulation and taxation as possible.

These two dimensions of liberalism are often conflated, with a generic populist wave pitted against the "liberal elite." But anti-system movements are not defined by their opposition to liberalism in the broadest sense, but by their rejection of "neoliberal democracy": the closed version of democracy that places the governance of the market outside the purview of representative politics. Their proposed alternatives, however, are quite varied. The anti-system Left rejects economic liberalism in favor of greater government intervention in the economy, but embraces social liberalism. The anti-system Right rejects some aspects of economic liberalism—in particular the global reach of markets and the permeability of national boundaries—but mostly favors a capitalist economy, while vehemently rejecting social liberalism. Both these forms of anti-system politics share a clear rejection of the existing order and the basic values underpinning it, and demand better representation for ideas that have not been adequately represented by the mainstream elites. But they have quite different diagnoses of the reasons for the failure of the existing order, and different prescriptions for overcoming it.

This approach to defining anti-system parties allows for a more precise definition than loose references to "populism." First, it does not require a party to be located necessarily in opposition. Some parties that we could consider to be anti-system, such as far-right parties in Denmark or Austria, or indeed radical left or green parties in some northern European countries, have participated in government coalitions, which is inconsistent with the anti-establishment logic of anti-system politics. Here I count parties as anti-system when their opposition to immigration, trade openness or the market economy in general, and current practices of democratic governance puts them outside the mainstream pro-market and pro-globalization positions associated with the mainstream parties over recent decades. This definition includes right-wing populists alongside left anti-capitalist movements and secessionist parties.

Second, this allows us to exclude from the analysis new parties that express opposition to the "establishment" and the entrenched governing elites, while remaining inside the mainstream consensus on economic policy. For example, Macron's "En Marche" movement and Ciudadanos in Spain are completely new political movements that have mobilized around the demand for change and in particular for turnover of governing elites, but whose discourse and policy proposals cannot be regarded as especially threatening to neoliberal democracy. These parties are best defined as challenger[5] or "outsider" parties rather than anti-system parties in that they challenge established elites, but not established democratic practices or the liberal market economy.

The positioning of anti-system parties on the economic dimension is central to our argument. Although these parties can adopt markedly different positions on the values dimension, on the economic dimension they almost universally favor positions to the left of the mainstream parties whose voters they are competing for. As left-wing anti-system parties push the boundaries of economic discourse to the left, right-wing anti-system parties push social and cultural values to the right of the existing consensus. This directly compromises the attempts by mainstream parties to control the terms of political debate. By advocating closing borders to migratory movements (which are mostly driven by economic motives) and demanding looser monetary and fiscal policies, these parties have extended the range of political options available to voters. In a period of deep economic crisis, alternative political forces have exploited voter discontent to break the neoliberal cartel. Although these positions appear beyond the pale to many supporters of existing arrangements, it should be noted that border restrictions and political control of monetary and fiscal policies were well within the range of acceptable policies during the "golden age" era. In many respects the current crisis of representation is little more than a return to a conflictual and competitive political environment.

Figure 2.1 illustrates these patterns of anti-system politics and their relation to the established party system, drawing on a two-dimensional mapping of political positions commonly used in political science.[6] The horizontal dimension charts positions on the standard socioeconomic left-right scale, which ranges from a more "statist" position on the economy, favoring more government regulation and redistribution, to a more "liberal" one emphasizing less regulated markets, lower taxes, and less government spending. The vertical dimension charts parties' positions on the social-cultural dimension, depending on whether they emphasize conservative and authoritarian social values or more liberal and progressive values.[7] On the right, mainstream conservative parties and Christian democrats mostly adopt more

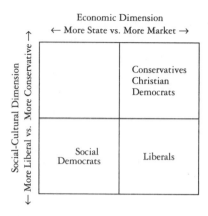

FIGURE 2.1 Dimensions of Competition in the Established Party System

pro-market positions on the economic dimension, and more socially conservative positions on the social-cultural dimension. Liberal parties are both economically and socially liberal. On the left, social democrats, at least in the recent period, have moved toward rather centrist positions on the economic dimension, combining support for, or at least acquiescence in, liberal markets, but with some compensatory redistribution. They are increasingly associated with very liberal positions on the social-cultural dimension.

These four party families have dominated the party systems of the Western democracies since World War II.[8] On the whole, the positions they have adopted reflect a prevailing centrist consensus, consisting of economic liberalism with some redistribution, combined with positions on the social-cultural scale that range from very liberal to moderately conservative. A large open space can be seen in the top left-hand corner combining social-cultural conservatism and statist economic positions. The increasingly centrist orientation of social democratic parties also left a growing space to their left on the economic dimension. In a context of economic difficulty, these two spaces presented the opportunity for anti-system parties to win support by offering a more economically interventionist approach.

This schematic representation of the emerging patterns of party competition around the turn of the century is supported by the available data on party positions. Political scientists have used two distinct ways of systematically comparing political positioning: expert surveys[9] and content analysis of political documents such as electoral programs.[10] Figure 2.2 uses the latter, since expert survey data only covers Europe. The parties are from twenty countries in western Europe, North America, Australasia, and East Asia that have been democracies since at least the 1970s, and the positions are taken

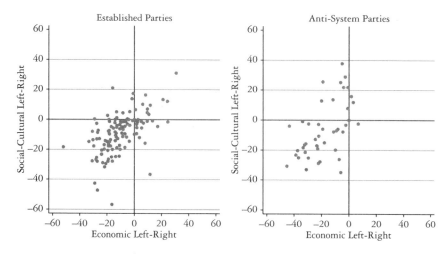

FIGURE 2.2 Party Positions on Sociocultural and Economic Dimensions, Established Parties, and Anti-System Parties

from the most recent party manifestos available, between 2010 and 2017. Central and eastern European democracies are excluded from the analysis, in part because their party systems have not been sufficiently stable to distinguish established parties from anti-system parties. The left-hand chart plots the positions of the established parties on both the economic and social-cultural scales, while the right-hand chart plots the positions of the anti-system parties.

Established parties here are those that are affiliated with the main party Internationals[11] or European Parliament Party Groups (for European Union member states) representing the liberal, conservative, Christian democrat, and socialist party families.[12] Some new political parties, such as Macron's En Marche in France and Ciudadanos in Spain, are therefore coded as established, since their centrist positions on most issues mean they cannot be realistically described as anti-system. Mainstream conservative parties in the Euroskeptic Alliance of Conservatives and Reformists in Europe group, like the UK Conservatives, are coded as established parties, the others, such as the Danish People's Party, are clearly located on the anti-system Right. New parties that have been excluded from government office are coded as anti-system, as are groups with clear anti-system discourses but that have participated in national government, such as The Finns and the Austrian Freedom Party (FPO). Most Green parties in Europe—those belonging to the European Green Party group—are also coded as part of the established party system, given their long experience of working with the other mainstream party families in national parliaments and in the European institutions. Ethnoregionalist parties in the European Free Alliance group that do not advocate secessionism are also coded as "established."[13]

The right-hand chart plots the positions of the parties coded as "anti-system" on the same two dimensions. These are parties outside the established Internationals and European party groups, which with few exceptions are internationally affiliated with organizations on the anti-system Right,[14] or on the anti-system Left.[15] Ethnoregionalist parties seeking secession are also coded as anti-system, as is the Italian Five Stars Movement (M5S), which is ideologically ambiguous, but unequivocally oriented toward fundamental political system change. Table 2.1 lists the anti-system parties in the dataset used for Figure 2.2. Note that anti-system forces that have taken over existing parties—as has occurred in the established parties of the United Kingdom and the United States—are not included in this list.

The established parties in the left-hand chart are mostly bunched around a position just to the left of center on both economic and social-cultural issues—outliers are mostly very small parties of little relevance to government formation. The main axis of competition runs diagonally from the moderate Left on both dimensions to a rather centrist position. A large area of this map of possible political positions remains essentially unoccupied, leaving voters with more radical attitudes unrepresented. There are two quadrants that are particularly neglected: the comprehensively liberal position of free markets and progressive values on the bottom right, and the combination of state interventionism in the economy with cultural authoritarianism on the top left.

The right-hand chart shows that anti-system parties have tended to be located almost exclusively on the center and left of the economy dimension, but represent a wide range of positions on the social-cultural dimension. With the addition of anti-system parties, the economic dimension is extended out leftward, while the social-cultural dimension is extended out rightward. These measures are inevitably imprecise and fail to capture the nuances of party positions, and also leave out cases of anti-system factions inside established party organizations, such as the Tea Party or Trump strand of the Republican party, the socialist Left wing of the Democratic Party led by Bernie Sanders, and the Labour Party under Jeremy Corbyn. But these data are suggestive of broad patterns of party competition. The established party system left gaps for enterprising anti-system politicians to exploit on the left of the economic policy debate and on the right of the social-cultural debate, since these were the areas that established parties were failing to represent adequately.

TABLE 2.1 Anti-System Parties in 20 Democracies

	Left and Ethnoregionalist	Right
Australia		One Nation
Austria		Freiheitliche Partei Österreichs Bündnis Zukunft Österreich
Belgium	Parti du Travail de Belgique/ Partij van de Arbeid van België	Front National; Vlaams Belang
Canada	Bloc Québecois	Reform Party
Denmark	Socialistisk Folkeparti Enhedslisten—De Rød-Grønne	Dansk Folkeparti
Finland	Vasemmistoliitto	Perussuomalaiset
France	France Insoumise Parti Communiste Français Front de Gauche	Front National
Germany	Die Linke	Alternative für Deutschland
Greece	Syriza Kommounistikó Kómma Elládas	Chrysí Avgí LAOS Anexartitoi Ellines
Ireland	Sinn Fein People Before Profit	
Italy	Sinistra e Liberta' Liberi e Uguali Movimento 5 Stelle	Lega Fratelli d'Italia
Japan	Japan Communist Party	
Netherlands	Socialistische Partij	Partij voor de Vrijheid
New Zealand	Alliance	New Zealand First
Norway	Rødt	Fremskrittspartiet
Portugal	Bloco de Esquerda Coligação Democrática Unitária	

(Continued)

TABLE 2.1 Continued

	Left and Ethnoregionalist	Right
Spain	Podemos Izquierda Unida Esquerra Republicana de Catalunya Bildu	
Switzerland		Schweizerische Volkspartei Lega di Ticino Mouvement Citoyens Genevois
Sweden	Vänsterpartiet	Sverigedemokraterna
UK	Sinn Fein Scottish National Party Plaid Cymru	United Kingdom Independence Party Democratic Unionist Party

Anti-System Parties and the Gap in the Electoral Market

Studies of voter attitudes confirm that anti-system parties have tapped into unmet demand in the electorate. Socially conservative attitudes—such as opposition to same-sex marriage or drug legalization and hostility to immigration—are strongly held by large sectors of society in most Western countries, particularly among older generations.[16] Yet established political parties, even those on the mainstream Right, have tended to acquiesce in the liberalizing reforms promoted by centrist or center-left parties, and in some cases conservative parties even proposed such reforms themselves (for example, the UK Conservatives under David Cameron brought in same-sex marriage in 2013 as part of their coalition agreement with the Liberal Democrats). The growing size of the more socially and culturally liberal shares of the electorate[17] have clearly pushed the balance of power in the party system in a more liberal direction, which opens up space for a "cultural backlash" on the right.[18] This creates the potential for politics to revolve around "culture wars," as the more liberal younger generations push for further reforms and older more conservative voters fight back.[19]

But there has been also been a serious decline in political competition on the economic dimension, reflected in the clustering of the established party system around centrist positions in Figure 2.2. The previous chapter described how the established parties moved toward an increasingly centrist position on economic issues, combining less regulated markets, a less active role for government in managing the macroeconomy, and the maintenance, rather than the expansion, of existing social rights. This was particularly the case for social democratic parties, whose historic commitment to Keynesian macroeconomic interventionism and extensive welfare provision were effectively abandoned between the 1980s and the early 1990s. This coincided with a shift in the support base of center-left parties away from the traditional blue-collar working class, and toward a more heterogeneous coalition in which the educated middle classes predominate.[20]

The relationship between this neoliberal economic policy consensus and voter preferences in Western countries is unclear. On the one hand, some studies have shown that the average voter position has shifted to the left during the neoliberal period,[21] while others show that voters have on average moved to the right,[22] or that voter preferences on the economic dimension have converged around a broadly centrist position.[23] But on specific policy questions there is strong evidence that voters prefer greater government action to combat economic problems such as unemployment and inequality. In the UK, survey data shows that two-thirds of voters believe inequality is too high and that governments should act to redistribute from rich to poor, a number that has barely shifted for thirty years.[24] In the United States, support for progressive taxation to reduce inequality is also surprisingly high,[25] while, more predictably, a majority of French respondents expected government to act to reduce inequality.[26] Yet policy over recent decades has generally moved in a very different direction: the established parties converged on a neoliberal model of lower welfare spending, limited labor rights, and less progressive taxation, which has brought higher inequality.

As a result, voter preferences had difficulty filtering through into policy measures, as the public were only allowed a limited range of options to choose from at election time, This was particularly acute in the countries where the neoliberal strategy was executed most thoroughly, the United Kingdom and the United States. In the United Kingdom, Labour's abandonment of government interventionism and overt redistribution coincided with a dramatic drop in voter turnout, which Evans and Tilley link to Labour's neglect of working-class interests from the mid-1990s on.[27] In the United States, a similar exclusion of the interests of lower-income voters from effective democratic representation has been documented by numerous researchers.[28] This foreshortening of democratic choice, especially marked in the two-party politics of Britain and the United States, provided an opening for politicians offering popular policies rejected by the established parties.

This is all consistent with an explanation of anti-system politics as a predictable response to the failure of the established party systems in the rich democracies to offer the kinds of policies that voters were actually demanding.[29] The steady erosion of support for the governing "cartel" of parties was visible well before the financial crisis, and there is also strong evidence that parties were failing to represent and implement mass preferences, particularly in regard to economic policies. This presented a gap in the electoral market, but to fill this gap successfully, anti-system forces had to offer what the established parties could not: an alternative to neoliberalism.

Anti-system parties have in common a rejection of the constraints imposed by the neoliberal model of democratic governance, but the anti-system Left and the anti-system Right draw on very different sources of ideological inspiration. The anti-system Left draws on what Ronald Inglehart describes as "postmaterialism" and others have described as liberal or left-libertarian social-cultural values. The anti-system Right draws on conservative or even authoritarian social-cultural values. The high degree of political polarization around these alternative visions of society that has emerged in some Western countries gives some plausibility to Norris and Inglehart's claim that anti-system politics is primarily a conflict over social-cultural values, and that the different sides of this conflict feed off each other. This "culture wars" thesis is reinforced by the high salience in public debate of some of the key issues that mark these dividing lines, most notably immigration and the status of ethnic and religious minorities in Western societies.

As the rest of this chapter will show, the patterns of support for anti-system parties in Western democracies suggest otherwise. In fact, divisions over economics are at the heart of the surge of anti-system parties. One of the reasons this is so difficult to observe clearly is that our instinctive resort to binary divisions forces the anti-system parties into a box labeled "populist," set against the mainstream or establishment forces. But anti-system parties are just as opposed to each other as they are to the establishment. The "system" is being attacked on both flanks, but anti-system parties differ fundamentally in what they propose replacing it with. Contemporary politics in Western democracies pits three broad ideologies against each other, in a way deeply reminiscent of the interwar period. The primacy of liberalism in the early twenty-first-century political economy, just like in the 1920s and 1930s, is contested by ideologies that purport to bring the market economy under control in order to safeguard key political and social values. Those ideologies are nationalism (or sometimes fascism), on the one hand, and socialism or social democracy, on the other.[30] The inspiration for the anti-system Right is the former and for the anti-system Left the latter.

Markets against the People: Anti-System Critiques of Neoliberalism

The social authoritarianism and xenophobia associated with far-right political movements is a familiar enough story. Donald Trump's appeal to white America, his demonization of illegal immigrants and Muslims, his misogyny, and his often violent rhetoric sits comfortably alongside his relaxed attitude toward white supremacists in America and his open support for far-right politicians elsewhere, such as Benjamin Netanyahu in Israel or Jair Bolsonaro in Brazil. Similar traits can be observed across the spectrum of the anti-system Right in Europe. Lurid warnings of immigrants, especially Muslims, "invading" and "taking over" the continent, and appeals to harsh repression of illegal immigration and the implementation of tight border controls are a staple of the Far Right. Demands for a restoration of conservative social values on sexuality and the family are also typical. These positions are so at odds with the dominant values of mainstream politics, and evoke such horrific memories of fascist experiences in the past, that relatively little attention is paid to what the Far Right says about economics.

The anti-system Right's hostility to liberalism goes well beyond social and cultural issues and extends to deep suspicion of the kind of market system that has resulted from the neoliberal project. This suspicion stems from discomfort with the ways in which a market system based on individual rights can trump collective identities and values, such as community and nationhood, loyalty, and hierarchy, that are dear to the anti-system Right. It is not so much the inequality produced by the market system that is seen as problematic, but the way in which it subverts the kind of inequality inherent in some preferred system of social stratification.[31] As a result, the anti-system Right frequently embraces mercantilist and protectionist policies, because the market cannot be allowed to undermine its vision of the collective national interest. Immigration controls are not only a way of providing cultural protection and safeguarding its particular view of national values but also a way of ensuring preference for citizens over foreigners in access to the labor market and the welfare state.

The anti-system Right often selectively subscribes to aspects of the neoliberal program, albeit constrained within the nation-state framework. The first wave of right-wing anti-system parties, which emerged in France, Italy, Austria, Switzerland, Denmark, and Norway in the late 1980s and early 1990s, adopted relatively liberal economic policy positions, protesting high taxes and government regulation.[32] These positions appealed to a social base that included large numbers of petty bourgeois voters, such as shopkeepers and the self-employed, a historic staple of the Far Right.[33] As the process of globalization evolved and neoliberalism became entrenched, large numbers of voters with right-wing social-cultural predispositions began to face high levels of economic insecurity. Small business owners faced growing threats from the dismantling of regulatory protections, which exposed them to competition either from low-cost production overseas or from large domestic corporations. Blue-collar workers in general were threatened by increasing trade openness, which exposed them to fierce competition.[34]

These developments provided an opening for an anti-system Right with an explicitly economically protectionist orientation.[35] The Northern League in Italy was an early mover on this, advocating tariff barriers to protect northern Italian manufacturing from Chinese competition, and moving toward a Euroskeptic position at a time when all other Italian parties were enthusiastic supporters of further European integration. The Austrian Freedom Party under Jorg Haider and the Swiss People's Party (SVP) also adopted strongly Euroskeptic positions, alongside their anti-immigrant stance. Although the anti-system Right varies in its position on economic policy across Europe, often obfuscating between neoliberal and protectionist positions, hostility to the process of European integration and to economic openness more broadly has been a common feature.[36] In the United States, Trump's campaign message was openly protectionist, promising a trade war with China and a renegotiation of the NAFTA trade deal with Canada and Mexico. Other movements on the anti-system Right, such as the Dutch Freedom Party (PVV) and the Swiss SVP, have been less opposed to free trade per se, while right-wing supporters of Brexit in the United Kingdom have combined hostility to immigration with a quixotic appeal to global free trade outside the European Union.

The increasing pressures on the welfare state, which have become particularly acute since the financial crisis, have opened up the space for an appeal to "welfare chauvinism": the restriction of welfare rights to "deserving" citizens and the exclusion of migrants from social protection.[37] The Brexit campaign made great play of the purported pressures on the National Health Service and other areas of social provision due to "uncontrolled immigration" from other European Union member states. The Sweden Democrats (SD), who made an electoral breakthrough in 2018, not only emphasized the supposed security and cultural threat posed by the Swedish government's decision to welcome large numbers of refugees, but also highlighted the purported costs for Sweden's generous welfare state. The SD went as far as demanding "multicultural financial statements" for local government services to distinguish between money spent on Swedes and that spent on migrants, in order to prioritize the former.[38] Trump's mantra of "America First" has been copied wholesale by European anti-system politicians, such as the leader of Italy's League, Matteo Salvini, who called for Italian citizens to have preferential access to education and welfare services over migrants.[39]

The anti-system Right also exploited popular disgust at the politics of the post-crash financial bailouts. Super-rich bankers drawing outsized bonuses after taxpayer-funded bailouts were an easy target for anti-system politicians, and the parties of the anti-system Right were not slow to join the chorus of condemnation of the financial system. The Tea Party movement in the United States, the precursor to Trump's 2016 campaign, mobilized directly around resentment over the bailouts and opposition to plans by the Obama administration to offer financial assistance to in-debted mortgage-holders and other needy groups.[40] Trump himself railed against Wall Street in his presidential campaign and promised to reform tax loopholes that allowed hedge funds to pay lower taxes than most Americans.[41] Salvini was similarly critical of financial bailouts in Italy, frequently pointing to connections between the center-left Democratic Party and a failing Tuscan bank.[42] And the anti-system Right in the cred-itor countries of continental Europe were visceral in their opposition to financial bailouts of weaker debtor states of the South, and indeed of their own banking systems.

The anti-system Right's critical attitude toward the world of finance was to be expected given the unpopularity of the banking sector after the crisis, but it also connects with a deeper tradition in the Far Right of hostility to the world of money, often tinged with anti-Semitism. This found its clearest expression in the far-right movements of central and eastern Europe, where parties such as Viktor Orban's Fidesz and Jaroslaw Kaczyński's Law and Justice party (PiS) established "illiberal" regimes openly critical of the global neoliberal order. Fidesz saw "globalization, ne-oliberalism, consumerism, privatization to foreign investors and cosmopol-itanism . . . aimed at establishing the world dominance of certain economic and political powers."[43] The success of this discourse can be traced back to the dire consequences of Hungary's experience of financial liberalization, which allowed an accumulation of unsustainable external debt before the 2008 crisis, leading to an IMF bailout. The Orban government's nation-alist response was to harshly tax foreign banks and companies, nationalize pensions, and force banks into renegotiating the terms of household debts.[44] In Poland, the financial crisis was less severe, but the PiS also tempered past liberalization measures with an expansion of welfare support for families and government interventionism in markets.[45]

This kind of market skepticism was more established in the central and eastern European Right than in western Europe,[46] but it illustrates the opportunities presented to the anti-system Right by increased economic insecurity and inequality. While accepting the basic principles of a market economy, especially private property and a certain work ethic, the anti-system Right can simultaneously advocate government interventions that protect the domestic market from foreign competition (usually described as unfair or "rigged" in some way), a greedy or corrupt financial system, and uncontrolled immigration. While neoliberalism establishes the principle that prices allocate resources and discrimination against goods, services, and indeed people on the basis of nationality should be suppressed, the anti-system Right instead insists that the nation comes first, and that markets should be organized around that national favoritism. They therefore attack institutions of economic integration that prevent national governments from limiting the freedom of workers to cross borders or companies to relocate, and advocate a return to national sovereignty that would allow governments to properly defend the interests of their people.

Alongside the right-wing nationalist appeal, present in almost all Western countries, substate nationalist and secessionist movements also prospered in multinational states such as Canada, the United Kingdom, Belgium, Italy, and Spain. These movements mostly shun the anti-immigration and anti-trade discourses of the right-wing nationalists, and appeal to a less socially and culturally authoritarian electorate. Usually located in small and relatively prosperous regions such as Flanders, Catalonia, the Basque Country, and Scotland, these parties have less reason to embrace protectionist discourses, and instead advocate secession from their host states while remaining inside the European Union. They share with the right-wing nationalists some resentment over burden-sharing in welfare arrangements, but they mostly adopt progressive discourses around social policy, and mobilize a younger and more educated electorate, so, with the exception of Italy's Northern League, they have much in common with the anti-system Left.

The anti-system Left opposes contemporary neoliberalism with a much more consistent critique of the idea of the market economy and a commitment to greater equality.[47] Markets are seen as a source of inequality and injustice, curbing individual freedom rather than enhancing it. While the anti-system Right mostly accepts the market economy, while rejecting its globalized version, the anti-system Left opposes globalization on the grounds that it entrenches the injustices of the market system, while adopting a tolerant line on immigration and refugees. Unlike the nationalist Right, these parties mostly embrace the cultural diversity brought by migration and generally refuse to blame stagnant living standards and pressures on the welfare state on migrants. Instead, the fault lies with capitalist exploitation and the post-crisis austerity policies, which have impoverished the weakest. The answer is to enhance the role of government in the economy, reversing welfare cuts and labor market deregulation. The wealthy elite—the so-called one percent—and corporations are often blamed for the crisis, austerity, and poverty, while the political elite—often lambasted as a "caste" of privileged elites, is blamed for minding its own interests rather than those of the people.

Several anti-system Left movements acknowledge a socialist or communist heritage. Syriza in Greece identifies with "twenty-first century socialism."[48] The German left party Die Linke has its origins in the PDS, the Party of Democratic Socialism, the successor to the East German Communist Party.[49] The main coalition of the French anti-system Left, France Insoumise, consists of a splinter group from the Socialist Party called Socialist Left, allied with the French Communist Party and other radical left-wing groups,[50] The Bloco Esquerda (Left Bloc) in Portugal has roots in parties that claim a socialist heritage, while the other main force on the Portuguese anti-system Left, the Unitary Democratic Coalition (CDU), is led by the Portuguese Communist Party. Bernie Sanders in the United States describes himself as an "independent socialist," while Jeremy Corbyn in the United Kingdom also identifies with the socialist tradition. These parties' long-standing identification with the Marxist or socialist Left places them in an unambiguously antagonistic position toward neoliberalism and toward the market system in general. The centrist drift of most established social democratic parties generated a large pool of dissatisfied voters on the left who could be attracted by this kind of message.

The other main strand of the anti-system Left hails from a "left libertarian" or "postmaterialist" tradition. Left libertarianism, like socialism, is hostile to the market system because of its excessive materialism and disregard for social ties and for the environment, but it parts company with socialism in its distrust of "the centralized bureaucratic welfare state and the hegemony of professional expertise in public policy and society,"[51] Left libertarians have often allied with other radical left groups, so they can be found in many of the anti-system Left coalitions mentioned in the previous paragraph. In some cases, they have formed parties that retain a distinctive left-libertarian identity, such as the parties of the Nordic Green Left in Scandinavia, and Green parties in countries such as Germany, Austria, and the Netherlands. Green parties have in many cases entered the mainstream, becoming reliable coalition partners for the established parties, such as in Germany, where they governed with the Social Democrats under a centrist leader, Schroeder. Elsewhere they have remained in an anti-system position, often with limited vote shares.

The anti-system Left also contains parties that are less easy to classify. Podemos in Spain is generally perceived as aligned with the Left, but shuns too clear a formal identification with the socialist tradition (partly because it competes with the Spanish Socialist Party) and seeks to appeal beyond ideological boundaries, while at the same time invoking classic socialist aims such as redistribution of income and wealth, the regulation of finance, and the broad reconfiguration of political power.[52] Another prominent case that is much harder to classify is the M5S in Italy. Some scholars have classified it alongside Podemos as a new kind of "technopopulist" party, which avoids any clear ideological identification in favor of supposedly "practical" and "technical" solutions to political problems.[53] Unlike Podemos, however, M5S avoids any reference to socialism in its discourse, and its only coherent ideological resemblance is with postmaterialist and environmentalist movements, although these do not constitute the movement's dominant identity. It is therefore only tentatively defined as an anti-system Left party.

Anti-system Left parties have varied attitudes toward globalization and European integration. Most have strongly opposed post-crisis austerity measures, and in Eurozone countries that faced externally imposed austerity as part of their financial bailouts, this was their central political message, and in the case of Podemos, the main reason for the party's creation. However, opposition to austerity did not necessarily follow a Euroskeptic logic: while Podemos and M5S at various times hinted at a referendum on euro membership, Syriza's position was to demand greater solidarity from creditor countries in the Eurozone rather than to seriously contemplate "Grexit." Some veteran politicians on the anti-system Left, such as Jean-Luc Mélenchon in France and Jeremy Corbyn in the United Kingdom, expressed Euroskeptic views on the grounds that the European Union institutionalizes a neoliberal idea of the market economy. Others, however, see the European Union as a potential arena for transnational cooperation to bring global capitalism under the people's control.[54] The anti-system Left has rarely expressed hostility to migration, and anti-racism is a core part of most of these parties' political identities.

In short, anti-system politics has taken a critical stance toward the neoliberal economy and the way in which globalization and European integration have affected economic and social well-being. Anti-system parties are similar in their demand for some form of political intervention to cushion the vagaries of global markets, with an emphasis on capital flows, foreign investment, and monetary hawkishness on the left, and a focus on immigration, and to

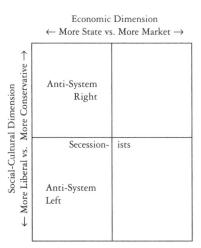

FIGURE 2.3 Dimensions of Anti-System Politics

some extent trade, on the right. The Left in the debtor countries advocates burden-sharing both within and across societies, while the Right in creditor countries is instinctively hostile to bailouts of other nations. These anti-system parties share a rejection of the incumbent political elites and the broad policy consensus they represented, a consensus around broadly market liberal policies in the economic sphere and an increasingly liberal position on social and cultural issues too. Where they part company is in their radically different attitudes to social and cultural change. If the anti-system Right is culturally conservative and the anti-system Left culturally liberal, then it makes little sense that they should both be protesting against the system because of fears about immigration. Instead, their common rejection of neoliberalism is a much more compelling explanation.

Exposing the Flaws: Anti-System Politics Meets the Global Financial Crisis

The success of anti-system politics is directly related to the extent of the economic and social failure of the neoliberal policies that have dominated in Western countries over the last decades, charted in chapter 1. The greater the economic distress caused by the failures of the market system, and the smaller the share of voters that unambiguously benefit from it, the bigger is the pool of potential anti-system voters. Anti-system voting is higher, all else being equal, where income growth has been lowest, where inequality and insecurity are highest, and where the financial crisis had the most damaging consequences for the social fabric: in short, where markets wreak the most damage. This should be visible both over time and across space: in periods of economic distress, anti-system politics can be expected to grow more than when the economy is performing well, and anti-system voting can be predicted to be higher in places—countries or regions—that have suffered the most from economic problems.

The vulnerability of the established political parties to an angry and disenfranchised electorate was exposed by the global financial collapse of the late 2000s and subsequent austerity. Standard models of voting behavior, which predict that voters vote down governments in economic hard times, suggested that incumbent parties would suffer defeats.[55] But historical scholarship also shows that deep financial crises also provoke nativist and nationalist backlashes as voters respond to economic anxiety by blaming outsiders and seeking the protection of the nation-state.[56] In contemporary democracies, financial crises threaten the wealth holdings of voters,[57] while resulting austerity measures saddle the costs of bailouts on economically vulnerable groups.[58]

The evidence that the crisis led to heightened political stability is clear. Figure 2.4 presents data on electoral volatility in twenty-one Western democracies over the post–World War II period, and shows that disruption to normal patterns of politics tends to coincide with periods of economic crisis, such as the early 1980s, the early 1990s, and especially the late 2000s. Volatility—the net change in party vote shares between two successive elections[59]—rose sharply after the Global Financial Crisis: out of fourteen postwar elections where net changes in party support exceeded 30 percent, seven of them came after 2008. This vote-switching disproportionately negatively affected governing parties, as Figure 2.5 shows, leading to unusually heavy losses of governing parties and very high levels of government turnover: in just four out of the sixteen western European countries did the governing parties or coalitions survive intact the first election after the crisis. Incumbent defeats in the midst of an economic crisis could be expected, but the numbers of votes lost by incumbents was far higher than the historical norm, in some cases up to 30 percent (Figure 2.5): more than half of the cases of incumbent losses of more than 10 percent of vote share in the whole postwar period occurred after 2008.

Few governments survived the first election after the crisis. In the United States, the Republicans lost the White House two months after the financial collapse and banking bailout of September 2008. In the United Kingdom the

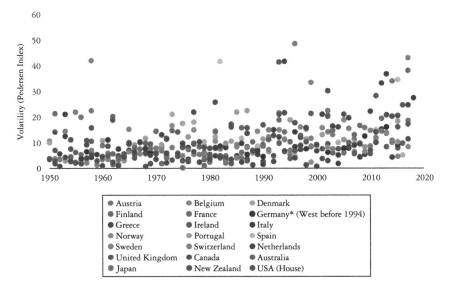

FIGURE 2.4 Electoral Volatility in 21 Democracies, 1950–2018
Sources: Ruth Dassonneville, *Net Volatility in Western Europe: 1950–2014*
(University of Leuven, 2015); Scott Mainwaring, Carlos Gervasoni, and Annabella
España-Najera (2017), "Extra- and Within-System Electoral Volatility," *Party
Politics* 23(6): 623–635.

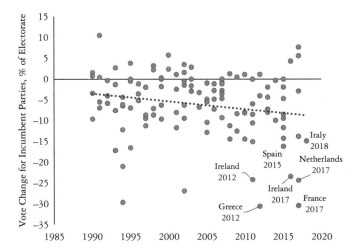

FIGURE 2.5 Incumbent Vote Change, 16 European Democracies, 1989–2018
Source: Klaus Armingeon, Virginia Wenger, Fiona Wiedemeier, Christian Isler,
Laura Knöpfel, David Weisstanner, and Sarah Engler, *Comparative Political Data Set
1960–2014* (Bern: Institute of Political Science, University of Bern, 2017).

Labour government of Gordon Brown limped on until 2010 before falling to defeat, shedding almost a third of its vote. Spain's Socialist government under Zapatero fell in 2011, and the conservative Popular Party (PP) under Mariano Rajoy won an absolute majority. Nicholas Sarkozy lost the French presidency to the Socialist Hollande in 2012 and Italy's center-right coalition government under Berlusconi fell in 2012 and was defeated in the polls in 2013. The prominent exceptions to this trend were German Chancellor Angela Merkel and Canadian Prime Minister Stephen Harper, both of whom presided over less severe financial crises.

Governing parties not only were defeated, but in many cases also polled historically low vote shares. The most spectacular case is that of the Panhellenic Socialist Party (PASOK) in Greece, which after regaining power in the immediate aftermath of the crisis had to preside over the Troika bailout and was almost annihilated in the 2012 election, dropping from 43.9 percent to just 13.2 percent of the vote in less than three years. But other governing parties also suffered historic defeats. The French Socialists and their allies lost 38.4 percent of the vote between 2012 and 2017, the Parti Socialiste falling to just 7.5 percent in the legislative elections, its poorest result ever. Fianna Fail, in charge during Ireland's banking crisis, lost the support of 24.4 percent of the Irish electorate in 2011, while Fine Gael and the Labour Party, which entered into coalition in 2011, lost 23.4 percent between them in the subsequent 2016 election. The Dutch Labour Party (PvdA) dropped from 24.8 percent in 2012 to just 5.7 percent in 2017, another historic low. Such heavy defeats of governing parties were rare during the postwar period, yet became common after the financial crisis.

Figure 2.6 shows the relationship between the depth of the crisis and the average electoral punishment meted out to governing parties in elections after 2008. Although governing parties everywhere suffered in the post-crisis period—in no country did incumbents increase their vote share in the first post-crisis election—,the losses tended to be higher in countries that suffered most in the crisis. Incumbent parties in countries with low or negative median income growth were more likely to suffer heavy losses.

Volatility can take the form of heavy defeats for governing parties to the benefit of opposition parties, resulting in simple alternation between established political forces, and in most of the elections immediately following the crisis this was the case. Labour's defeat in the United Kingdom benefited the oldest political party in Europe, the Conservative Party, the Gaullist Sarkozy in France gave way to the Socialist Party, and even in Greece it was the established conservative opposition, New Democracy, that won power after the implosion of PASOK. The first round of post-crisis elections was

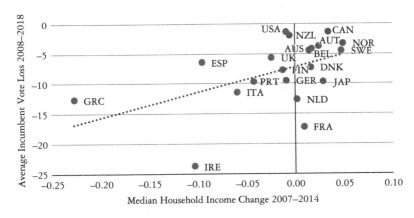

FIGURE 2.6 Median Income Change and Average Incumbent Vote Loss after the Crisis

Source: Armingeon et al., *Comparative Political Data Set 1960–2014* (Vote Change) (see Figure 2.5); OECD, "Income Distribution Database" (Income Change).

consistent with typical patterns of economic voting, with the punishment of incumbents matching the depth of the economic downturn. But the second round of elections under economic conditions that had improved little and in some cases had become even worse, gave voters the difficult choice of reinstating the parties that had presided over the beginning of the crisis, or sticking with incumbents who had failed to pull the economy out of it. This presented obvious opportunities to anti-system forces.

Figure 2.7 shows average support for anti-system parties since 1989 in twenty-one Democracies in western Europe, Australasia, North America and East Asia, and breaks that average down into averages for left and right anti-system parties. As we can see, anti-system parties have been present throughout the period since 1989, but there has been a consistent increase over time in anti-system vote share, as well as a jump in frequency of high anti-system shares since the late 2000s. The pattern mirrors the trend in electoral volatility, with elections increasingly likely not only to throw up heavy defeats of mainstream parties, especially those in government, but also spikes in support for anti-system parties. This suggests that many voters were sufficiently exasperated by the political and economic situation that they felt the need to send a much stronger signal than simply voting for the established alternatives. Anti-system party vote shares had rarely reached 15 percent before the crisis, afterward the total rises to almost unprecedented shares of over 25 percent, with left-wing anti-system forces gaining particularly strongly.

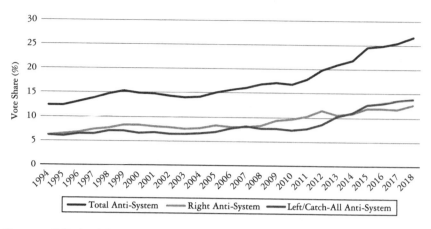

FIGURE 2.7 Anti-System Vote Share, Western Europe, 1994–2018
Source: Armingeon et al., *Comparative Political Data Set 1960–2014* (see Figure 2.5).

This combination of harsh electoral defeat for incumbents, and the high support for anti-system parties, implied that electorates were doing far more than simply prompting government alternation to "throw the bums out." Instead, major changes, and even wholesale realignments, of party systems were emerging. Subsequent elections saw not only heavy defeats for incumbent parties but also pluralities for previously marginal political forces. If the first elections after the crisis mostly resulted in incumbent defeats, the subsequent post-crisis votes presented voters with a different kind of choice. Business cycles in the postwar period involved short periods of recession followed by much longer periods of expansion, meaning that opposition parties benefiting from economic voting in one election had good prospects of taking credit for the economic recovery in the next. The economic pain of the post-2008 period was unprecedented in both depth and duration, so by the time of the second or third post-crisis election, two sets of incumbent parties or coalitions would be targets for voter ire. For many voters in Western democracies, this meant that the whole governing elite was discredited, opening up a space for anti-system politicians to move beyond traditional limits to their support.

This safety valve of retrospective voting and government alternation explains the delayed reaction of Western electorates to the economic cataclysm they were facing. In countries where electoral and legislative politics revolves around rival parties or coalitions alternating in power, the crisis offered opposition parties the opportunity to win election by pinning the blame on incumbents' policies, and promising that their approach would provide an answer. But the failure of economies to recover within the usual electoral cycle meant that the new incumbents' analysis of the crisis was quickly falsified and voter frustrations prompted a search for some other alternative. By the second or third post-crisis election, such alternatives could credibly claim that the existing political establishment had failed, and that only a clean break with the system could improve things.

Why It's "the Economy" and That's Far from Stupid

The broad pattern of conventional alternation followed by an anti-system backlash can be observed in most of the Western democracies, but the extent and form of this anti-system surge varied. For example, in the United Kingdom the Conservatives blamed the incumbent Labour government for the severity of the financial crisis, arguing that they had "overspent" and that Britain's high fiscal deficit required a dose of austerity to reduce wasteful government programs and overgenerous welfare. The Brexit vote of 2016 came after the failure of six years of this austerity to improve living standards. Much the same pattern can be seen in Spain, where the severe defeat of a Socialist government and the election of a conservative government in 2011 led to austerity and an aggressive labor reform, and the surge of anti-system forces in 2015. The same dynamic also played out in the opposite ideological direction: in France the Gaullist president Sarkozy lost the first post-crisis election to the Socialist Hollande, but the failure of the conventional political Left to bring about any significant policy shift or economic results led to the near annihilation of the Socialist Party five years later. In Greece, Portugal, and Ireland, both the center-left and the center-right parties alternated responsibility for managing their countries' Troika bailouts before elections brought a sharp turn to the anti-system Left. In the United States, the crisis brought Obama to the White House, but the 2016 election saw powerful anti-system pressures on both the Left and the Right.

But the differing fortunes of anti-system forces across Western democracies are anything but random. Instead, there are clear patterns, not only in the extent of anti-system voting, but also in the type of anti-system parties that are most likely to prosper at different times and in different places. Anti-system parties emerged first in the strong welfare states of continental and northern Europe, but have been unable to dislodge established parties from power, or shake the policy consensus of economic openness and generous social protection in those countries. Where anti-system parties have had the biggest impact is in the weaker or more divided welfare states of the English-speaking democracies and southern Europe. Anti-system parties took longer to break through in those countries, but did so with dramatic force after the financial crisis. These different patterns of anti-system success reflect fundamental differences in political and economic institutions: their electoral systems, the extent of economic redistribution achieved by their welfare states, and their exposure to international financial markets.

Electoral systems play an important role in the development of anti-system politics. In countries with proportional representation (PR) and low thresholds for entry into parliament, anti-system forces can gain representation more easily, because voters are less likely to vote tactically for one of the established parties in order to avoid "wasting" their vote. This kind of PR is common across continental Europe and Scandinavia, and allowed voter discontent to be defused more easily, with anti-system parties of the right and left libertarian parties winning substantial vote shares as early as the 1990s. In southern Europe, the democratic systems established in the 1970s adopted forms of PR with quite high electoral thresholds to discourage voters from supporting extremist parties, with the result that anti-system forces had greater difficulty winning representation. In the "pure" majoritarian systems such as the United Kingdom and the United States, the established parties have enjoyed even greater protection from outsider parties, who struggle to win any seats even with substantial numbers of votes. These more "closed" electoral systems tend to magnify shifts in popular support, and contributed to anti-system politics breaking through with greater force in the 2010s.

Electoral systems may mediate the emergence of anti-system politics, but cannot easily explain electoral change, since in most countries electoral systems remain constant over long periods. However, electoral systems do make different kinds of economic and social arrangements possible. Proportional representation countries tend to be "coordinated market economies," which are economically open and have strong exporting industries, alongside generous welfare states and strong labor representation. Under PR, inequality is generally lower, because these countries tend to include a wider variety of social interests in the policy process, and also commonly have other integrating institutions, such as strong trade unions and generous welfare systems, that ensure that inequality is kept under control.[60] Countries with more majoritarian or closed electoral systems generally lack these integrating institutions and have weaker welfare states and higher inequality, exposing their citizens to greater economic insecurity.

This combination of political integration and protective social institutions is strongly related to anti-system politics. The peaks in total anti-system support after the 2008 crisis correlate strongly with economic inequality (measured as the post-tax Gini coefficient), as Figure 2.8 shows. The highest anti-system scores are found in Italy, Greece, the United Kingdom (the Leave vote in the EU referendum) and the United States (the vote for Trump in 2016), all countries with high inequality. Similarly, the lowest anti-system vote shares after 2010 are to be found in countries such as Belgium, Ireland, Germany, and Finland, which have lower levels of inequality. This is entirely as one would expect if economic anxiety were driving anti-system voting, as inequality is a reasonable proxy for levels of objective economic insecurity at the country level, and the post-crisis environment escalated this insecurity dramatically. In the most developed welfare states, labor market institutions make it harder to shed labor in response to lower demand, and people who do lose their jobs or suffer drops in income are protected to a high degree by unemployment or other social benefits and public assistance to retrain and find new work. In the higher inequality countries these institutions are either absent or have insufficient resources to compensate for economic misfortune, leaving citizens more exposed to the force of market fluctuations.

Worse, these same high inequality countries suffered more severe crises than the more egalitarian countries, because they had mostly built up high levels of external debt, which forced them to sharply reduce their consumption when international financial flows dried up. The biggest political crises can all be found among these high-inequality, high-debt countries: out of six countries in Figure 2.8 with Gini coefficients of higher than 0.30, all six of them have seen major upheavals in their political systems involving

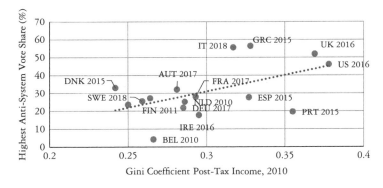

FIGURE 2.8 Inequality and Peak Anti-System Vote, Western Europe and United States, 2010s

anti-system movements or candidates taking over government, or forcing major constitutional changes. Although anti-system parties have joined government coalitions in three of the creditor countries (Austria, Finland, and Norway) and made gains in three others (Sweden, Netherlands, and Germany), they have remained peripheral actors in their party systems. In several debtor countries they have become central political actors. In Greece and Italy openly anti-system parties have taken over the national government, and in Portugal and Spain anti-system parties have underpinned the governing majority. Spain's second most populous region, Catalonia, came close to secession. In Britain, a majority voted in a referendum to leave the European Union, creating constitutional havoc and potentially throwing the country's economic model into chaos. And, of course, Trump became president of the United States.

Why Left and Right Reactions? How Welfare States and Labor Markets, Not Migration, Explain Anti-System Voting

The extent of the anti-system backlash after the Global Financial Crisis can be predicted by three broad variables: the electoral system, the welfare system, and a country's exposure to international financial conditions. These factors are tightly related to each other, so that countries with closed electoral systems also tend to have weaker welfare protections and are more exposed to financial shocks than those with open electoral systems, strong welfare states, and financial surpluses. But we can go further and show how these same factors also predict which types of anti-system parties—whether right-wing nationalist or left-libertarian and socialist—are likely to prosper in different institutional and economic environments.

One clear pattern that emerges is that left-wing anti-system parties have been more successful than the Right in southern Europe. Syriza's election victory in 2015, supplanting the socialist party PASOK, is the most striking example of a left backlash in a country subject to by far the worst post-crisis slump of any established Western democracy. But a similar pattern can be observed in Portugal and Spain. In Portugal the Socialists formed a governing alliance with the anti-system Left in 2015 to turf the conservatives out of power, while the Spanish Socialists also averted "Pasokification" by shifting to the left under Pedro Sánchez and forming a government with the support of the anti-system Left Podemos. Finally in Italy the main anti-system force is the M5S, which is not as clearly aligned with the Left, but makes a similar appeal.

As debtor countries suffering harsh austerity imposed from outside, southern Europeans have little scope for turning to economic nationalism and protectionism, which would have high costs. Syriza flirted with the idea of leaving the euro, but ultimately caved in to external pressures, and instead pressed European allies—largely unsuccessfully—to adopt a more forgiving approach to Greece's debt problems.[61] A similar appeal to wider European burden-sharing is present in the discourse of Podemos. The internationalism and emphasis on the value of solidarity, and the focus on the misdeeds of financial institutions, rather than the scapegoating of immigrants, is a logical response to the predicament of Europe's indebted periphery, since debt relief would benefit the majority of citizens with little wealth, at the expense of the financial elite.[62] Moreover, these countries have suffered very high unemployment in the Great Recession, leading many citizens to migrate, often to member states in the North of the European Union. An appeal to open borders and tolerance of migrants also addresses the interests of large shares of the population in the South, underpinning support for the Left.[63]

The flipside of this pattern is reflected in the relative advantage of the anti-system Right over the anti-system Left in the creditor countries of northern Europe. Whereas in Portugal, Greece, and Spain the Far Right has struggled to make much headway, it has enjoyed big successes in Switzerland, Austria, France, and Denmark, polling well over 20 percent at times in those countries, and significant shares also exist in the Netherlands and Norway. The sudden rise of the AfD in Germany and the Sweden Democrats in the 2010s, albeit with lower vote shares, also fits into this pattern. In the creditor countries of Europe, an appeal to national self-interest and a rejection of burden-sharing, consisting of opposition to immigration and financial bailouts of weaker Eurozone members, has an obvious appeal. This appeal can more coherently be made by the anti-system Right with its traditional opposition to globalization and international cooperation.

Figure 2.9 presents data on the electoral fortunes of anti-system parties of the Left and Right in Europe, charting the distinct trends in creditor and debtor nations (measured by pre-crisis current account balances: creditors run surpluses, and debtors run deficits). Although there is a good degree of noise and the distinction between creditor and debtor nations is less meaningful for borderline cases, the patterns of voting confirm that the anti-system response skews to the left in debtor countries and to the right in creditor countries. The chart resembles a crocodile: the upper jaw showing the

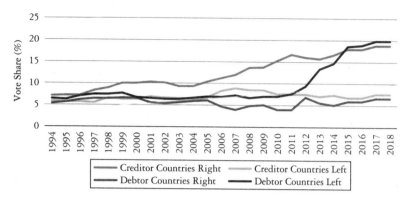

FIGURE 2.9 The "Crocodile Chart": Left and Right Anti-System Vote Shares, Creditor and Debtor Countries

rise of the anti-system Left in the debtor countries and the anti-system Right in the creditor countries, the lower jaw showing how the anti-system Right in the debtor countries and the anti-system Left in the creditor countries have flatlined. By 2018, support for the anti-system Right was around 19 percent in creditor countries, compared with around 7 percent in debtor countries. In contrast the anti-system Left won on average just short of 20 percent of the vote in debtor countries, but only around 8 percent in creditor countries.

The anti-system Right has also enjoyed success in the United Kingdom and the United States, the two English-speaking democracies at the epicenter of the financial crisis. This suggests that exposure to a "sudden stop" in capital inflows can also lead to a strong right-wing backlash. However, both of these countries have also had significant movements on the anti-system Left: Jeremy Corbyn's takeover of the Labour Party in 2015 and the party's strong electoral showing under his leadership in 2017, and the strong support for the Bernie Sanders campaign in 2016 and subsequently, show that debt crises can provoke anti-system responses on both sides of the ideological divide. Neither can this be explained in terms of the depth of their economic problems: although the financial meltdown hit the United Kingdom and the United States first, and brought about generalized crisis of their entire financial system, the recovery was far stronger than in southern Europe, and their median income growth, while weak, was not much below some of the northern European surplus countries (Figure 2.8).

What does mark out the two Anglo-Saxon cases from the rest is their very high levels of inequality and weak institutions of social protection. As subsequent chapters will show, the United Kingdom and the United States spent much of the period after the 1980s chipping away at their welfare states, weakening trade unions, and deregulating their labor market, while financial market reforms opened up spectacular gains for the wealthiest groups. As a result, economic insecurity affected larger shares of the population than in most other Western democracies, while high inequality meant that the economic recovery left many people behind as gains were concentrated at the top. If anti-system politics is a function of exposure to economic risk, the United Kingdom and the United States should be expected to experience a very high level of anti-system voting.

Extending our analysis to the structures of the labor market and the institutions of social protection and redistribution adds further insights into the patterns of anti-system voting across countries and over time. Extensive research has shown that right-wing nationalist and anti-immigrant parties do not generally attract support from a wide and differentiated selection of voters, but instead focus on particular regions, demographics, and occupational groups. The typical voter for right-wing anti-system parties is an older blue-collar worker, usually male, in a region in economic decline, and with socially conservative views—the so-called white working class.[64] Although the cultural dimension of political conflict appears to be most salient in the communication of the anti-system Right, its voters are very often economically dissatisfied, but frame this dissatisfaction around issues such as immigration and globalization, rather than the classic left-right dimension of markets and redistribution.[65] This raises the question of why these kinds of voters have supported anti-system parties in larger numbers in the creditor countries compared to the debtor countries?

The answer to this question does not seem to revolve around exposure to immigration. Historic immigration levels are higher in the creditor countries of northern Europe than in the South, but the South has had greater recent increases, and parts of the Mediterranean coast have been on the front line of the refugee crisis, particularly in southern Italy and Greece. Although there is tentative evidence that local-level exposure to large volumes of refugee arrivals makes voters more likely to vote for the Extreme Right,[66] the poor performance of right-wing anti-system parties in the broader regions where refugees arrive suggests little effect. Anti-system Right voting in northern Europe tends to be higher in economically declining regions—such as rural or postindustrial areas—which have the least immigration, and lower in dynamic areas, such as large cities, with more immigration.[67] Finally, migration is usually countercyclical, increasing in periods of economic expansion and declining during downturns, even though hostility to migration tends to increase during downturns,[68] suggesting that the objective facts about migration are not what is driving anti-migrant sentiment.

Conservative cultural attitudes are a better predictor at the individual level of support for right-wing anti-system parties than contact with migrants, but this effect does not explain differences at the societal level. On average, conservative social-cultural attitudes are more prevalent in southern and eastern Europe than in northern Europe,[69] yet votes for the anti-system Right are lowest in the South, highest in the East, and somewhere in between in the North. What we need is a better understanding of how cultural predispositions interact with economic circumstances to produce a political reaction: some of the time voters with culturally conservative or even socially authoritarian values will stick with mainstream, established parties, but under certain circumstances an anti-system party can "activate" these predispositions. Patterns of distributional conflict emerging out of a rapid process of market liberalization followed by a major financial crisis and harsh austerity are a likely "trigger" of this switch.

Anti-system right parties have been able to convince large numbers of culturally conservative voters that migrants and international burden-sharing constitute a threat to their well-being. This is more likely to be a compelling argument when these voters are indeed suffering economic distress. Although creditor countries maintained comparatively generous welfare states and suffered far less in the aftermath of the financial crisis than debtor countries, some groups still had objective reasons to feel aggrieved. Austerity measures may have been harsher in the debtor countries of southern Europe and the Anglosphere, but spending cuts and revisions to social entitlements were also present in the creditor countries. Losing entitlements, at the same time as important migratory flows and pleas for financial assistance from European partners, provides an obvious opening for the anti-system Right.

Germany is a case in point: after reunification, its economy suffered high unemployment and slow growth, only recovering after a series of labor reforms and restrictions of welfare entitlements, which forced down wages, allowing German exports to become competitive again.[70] This had dramatic consequences, particularly for lower-skilled workers, and wage inequality in Germany accelerated far more quickly than in comparable countries, leaving parts of the labor market exposed to rapidly deteriorating conditions.[71] Support for the far-right AfD, as in most of the rest of Europe, was higher among lower-skilled and lower-income groups, in rural areas with an aging population.[72] In contrast, the share of foreigners living in an area had a negative effect on voting for the AfD, a result that replicates similar research in Austria.[73] Research into support for the far-right Sweden Democrats produces similar results. Sweden, like Germany, accepted far more refugees than most other European states, and the anti-system Right appealed to anti-migrant and anti-refugee sentiment quite directly, with apparent success. But a careful analysis of voting patterns shows that voter exposure to welfare cuts, declining wages, and increased job insecurity are a stronger predictor of the right-wing anti-system vote than exposure to migrants.[74]

This offers a perhaps surprising explanation for patterns of left- and right-wing anti-system voting across creditor and debtor countries. In southern Europe, inequality is higher than in the North, but welfare states are very "dualistic" or selective in their provision, disproportionately protecting older, male workers at the expense of younger and especially female citizens, who are denied full labor rights and access to welfare.[75] The typically most socially authoritarian parts of the electorate—older male workers or pensioners with lower levels of education—are relatively well cared for in these countries, enjoying stable employment with predictable wages and generous pensions. They are therefore less inclined to vote against existing arrangements. Whereas older blue-collar workers in the North are relatively exposed compared to the past,[76] and compared with younger and more educated citizens, in southern Europe it is the other way around: youth unemployment, even among graduates, is very high, and welfare support for the young unemployed is patchy. Economic risk is highest among demographic groups—the young, women—likely to have more culturally liberal attitudes and be more receptive to a left-wing anti-system appeal. As a result, parties such as Podemos, Syriza, and the M5S are the primary beneficiaries of voter discontent in southern Europe.

Table 2.2 maps out the ways in which creditor and debtor status, combined with welfare state types, produces characteristic types of anti-system politics. Creditor countries with strong welfare states have more limited anti-system votes, skewed to the anti-immigrant and welfare chauvinist Right. Debtor countries, meanwhile, are divided into two broad types according to their welfare state structures. In the South of Europe, the anti-system response has been skewed to the left, and right-wing anti-system parties have been weaker. The far-right Golden Dawn in Greece polled only 7 percent at its peak, Portugal has not had a significant far-right party, and in Spain the right-wing party Vox only appeared in 2018. The exception is the Northern League in Italy, which experienced a dramatic rise in 2018 to 18 percent of the vote. The League, however, has much more in common with the anti-system Right in northern Europe, since northern Italy is an industrial powerhouse that has suffered a very similar deterioration in labor market conditions and welfare protection. In the South of Italy, which has a more typical southern European social structure, the left-leaning M5S is the

TABLE 2.2 Welfare States and Main Anti-System Forces

Creditors	Debtors	
Strong welfare state (low inequality, less severe crisis)	Dualistic welfare state (high inequality, more severe crisis)	Residual welfare state (high inequality, more severe crisis)
Right-wing anti-immigrant, anti-bailout movements	Northern Italy (League)	Right-wing anti-immigrant movements
Germany (AfD) Sweden (SD)		UK (Brexit) US (Trump)
	Left-wing anti-austerity movements	Left-wing anti-austerity movements
	Spain (Podemos) Greece (Syriza) Italy (Five Stars)	UK (Corbyn, Scottish Nationalists) US (Sanders)

main anti-system force. The third broad type of anti-system politics corresponds to the Anglo-American economic model, with weak welfare provision and high exposure to economic risks across the social spectrum. There we see strong anti-system responses on both sides, with right-wing anti-migrant forces pressurizing the established Center-Right, and anti-austerity left forces assailing the established Center-Left.

These patterns fit the evidence far better than an explanation revolving around immigration and cultural change. Anti-system voting is not highest in the places most exposed to immigration, if anything the opposite is the case. Support for the anti-immigrant Right is highest in "the places that don't matter": in areas of economic decline, with few migrants but more "left behind" voters, with poor economic prospects, lower levels of education, and more culturally authoritarian attitudes.[77] Examples of these areas are the US Rust Belt, the post-industrial North of England, eastern Germany, or the very North of France. Migration is concentrated in more dynamic regions where voters are less likely to feel economically anxious, and there are higher shares of younger and more educated citizens with more culturally liberal attitudes. Large metropolitan areas such as London, Paris, Berlin, or Milan are not a happy hunting ground for the anti-system Right. There, voters tend to support the established parties, or if they vote against the establishment, they support anti-system forces on the Left.

Conclusion

These cross-national patterns offer a useful starting point in analyzing anti-system politics, and suggest a basic theory to explain political instability after the financial crisis: the more societies are exposed to economic and financial distress, the more likely it is that anti-system forces will win greater shares of the vote. In extreme cases, where economic stresses have been the strongest, anti-system politics can even supplant and replace the established party system. In contrast, in countries where the economic and social institutions cushion the population from economic risks and secure a more equal distribution of economic benefits, anti-system politics has more limited success. This explains why Trump was able to take over the American presidency, or why the Greek Left was able to win power, while the anti-migrant Right in northern Europe has not made sufficient gains to take over the government.

Parts Two and Three of this book take this theory and apply it to a series of country studies that will show the mechanisms through which anti-system political movements of different kinds can win support in different political, social, and economic contexts. Part Two focuses on the two major cases of anti-system politics in the English-speaking world, looking at the consequences of decades of rising inequality and financial instability in the United States and the United Kingdom. These two cases illustrate the long-run effects of the market liberalization in the two countries that pioneered the neoliberal turn: a turn to economic nationalism, represented by Trump and Brexit, and a return of the radical Left, represented by Sanders and Corbyn. Part Three then turns to the crisis of the Eurozone, and the successes of the anti-system Left in the debtor countries of southern Europe. These cases show how the financial crisis morphed into a debt crisis that stripped national governments of much of their ability to cushion the population from economic threats, leading to a powerful anti-system response that was for the most part directed against the institutions imposing austerity measures rather than against migrants.

PART TWO | CURBING
TRANSATLANTIC
NEOLIBERALISM

| American Nightmare: How Neoliberalism Broke US Democracy

I N 2016, THE electorate of the United States delivered probably the biggest political shock in its modern history, electing the unlikely figure of Donald Trump to the presidency. Although not the first example of voters overturning the established order, this event brought anti-system politics to the heart of the world's most powerful democracy. Barely taken seriously when he launched his political career, Trump more or less single-handedly blew apart the American party system with a mix of old-fashioned xenophobia, economic protectionism, and a reality show persona. Perhaps the least of the world's worries, Trump also exposed the limitations of political science: barely any serious scholarship contemplated the rise to power of a man like Trump in an established, rich democracy. Trump's election is to political science what the financial crash of 2008 was to economics.

Trump's rise is deeply intertwined with the financial crisis and with the longer term political shifts resulting from the market liberal turn of the 1980s. If Trump is the most spectacular example of anti-system politics, the United States is the most extreme case of the subjection of society to the brute force of the market. These two stylized facts are not unconnected. The destabilization of US politics shows how an obsessive drive for marketization, high levels of income inequality, an unstable financial system, and constraints on political choice provoke political revolt. The United States took the lead in driving forward the neoliberal agenda in the 1980s under the leadership of Ronald Reagan, with the result that what was already a weak welfare state with high levels of economic inequality hit unprecedented levels for the rich democracies. The United States remains an outlier on most measures of income distribution, to such an extent that although average incomes are very high by global standards, many Americans face greater material hardship than their counterparts in much poorer countries.

It is therefore hardly surprising that anti-system politics should have exploded so powerfully. But although Trump has taken most of the headlines, the United States also saw a revival of the Left, in the form of Bernie Sanders's unexpectedly strong bid for the Democratic nomination in 2016. If "liberal" was a term of abuse used by conservatives disturbed by the progressive ambitions of Democrats such as Barack Obama, Sanders self-identified as a "democratic socialist," a taboo label for which he was the sole representative in the United States Senate. These developments are all the more striking because until very recently, mainstream politics seemed to be completely dominated by pro-market, pro-business forces in both parties, with the right wing of the Republican Party pushing hard for further reductions in government regulation and welfare provision, while the Democrats embraced globalization and the expansion of a liberalized financial industry. In the space of little more than two years, politics was turned on its head, with the return of socialist ideas on the left and the growth of economic nationalism and protectionism on the right.

The events of 2016 also reveal that there are very different ways of responding to the upheavals of economic inequality and financial instability, and these different ways appeal to different social constituencies. Trump responds to the anxieties of older, whiter, and generally less well-educated Americans about the rapid changes in society and the economy, emphasizing the dangers of globalization and advocating a combination of economic protectionism and social authoritarianism. Sanders and other leading personalities on the left, such as Alexandria Ocasio-Cortez, appeal to a younger and more progressive-minded electorate, offering an increased role of the government in protecting people from the destabilizing effects of market capitalism. Both reject the corporate-led "winner-take-all" politics centered on the horse-trading in Washington, DC.[1] The emergence of both kinds of anti-system politics at the same time indicates that they are best seen as rooted in a common rejection of economic injustice and the demand for politics to respond to popular needs, rather than a somehow unrelated rise in xenophobia and social authoritarianism.

More Inequality and More Insecurity: The Consequences of the Market Liberal Project

The first part of the puzzle is to understand how the United States found itself in the socially fragile situation that provoked the upheavals of 2016. The American economic model stands out among the rich democracies for its strong emphasis on private property, the virtues of the price mechanism, and skepticism about government interventionism to address inequalities.[2] The US welfare state, despite the expansions of the New Deal in the 1930s and the New Society in the 1960s has consistently lagged behind western Europe, trade unions are traditionally weak, and organized labor has never enjoyed the luxury of a strong political party that represented unambiguously left-wing values.

As a result, American living standards are more dependent on market forces than elsewhere in the rich world. Liberalizing reforms from the 1980s on implied what Jacob Hacker has called the "privatization of risk."[3] The decline of trade unions raised wage inequality, as workers with valued skills and exit options made gains and those with weaker bargaining power lost out. Jobs with comprehensive healthcare benefits became more and more scarce. Access to housing and income in retirement were increasingly left to the market, making households' basic economic security dependent on movements in financial markets, and the mortgage and housing markets in particular. This model means that voters in the United States have been on average far more exposed to the fluctuations of the market system over recent decades than in other advanced economies. Wrong financial choices, sometimes driven by date of birth, ill health, or random chance as much as smart decision-making, can bring disaster.

Uncertainty is compounded by inequality. Figure 3.1 charts the percentage growth in income of American households for each fifth of the income distribution since the 1970s. We can see that before tax, income growth was massively concentrated among the top 20 percent of households, whose income doubled between 1980 and 2015, while the other groups grew by around a third over the same period. This contrasted with the relatively equal distribution of income growth in the postwar period, where all groups made similar relative gains. Taxation and redistributive government transfers compensated for a good part of this differential growth, as we can see from the post-tax incomes reported in the right-hand graph in Figure 3.1. But given the very large differences in absolute levels of income between the top 20 percent and the rest, this still allowed the gap to grow much wider: in 2015 the average yearly post-tax income in the top quintile was $215,000, compared to just $33,000 among the bottom 20 percent (see Figure 3.2).

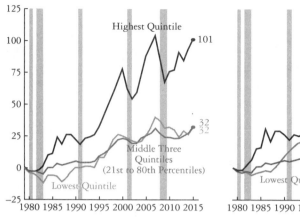
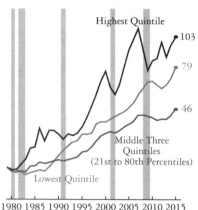

FIGURE 3.1 Cumulative Income Growth (%) for Households at Different Points in the Distribution, United States 1979–2015
Source: Congressional Budget Office, "The Distribution of Household Income, 2015," November 8, 2018, Summary Figure 2 (https://www.cbo.gov/publication/54646).

Clearly, higher income groups did better than most, but these numbers obscure the huge divide inside the top income group. Figure 3.1 averages out income gains across the whole of the top 20 percent of the income distribution, but Figure 3.2 reveals that most of these gains were taken by the highest-earning one percent. The Congressional Budget Office data shows that this group of 1.2 million households earned on average $1.9 million per year before tax, putting them on a quite different scale than other Americans. The very wealthiest earn a much larger share of pre-tax income than in other rich democracies, and this share rose spectacularly from around 10 percent for most of the postwar period to 23 percent in 2007, a return to the levels of the 1920s. That the wealthiest one percent of Americans should have taken almost a quarter of pre-tax income in the years before the two biggest financial meltdowns in history is no coincidence, since the booms that preceded them delivered spectacular gains to the capital-rich and those who service them in the financial and other sectors. Figure 3.2 demonstrates starkly how the top one percent stand out not only compared to low-income groups, but even compared to those just below them.

These trends reflect a "decoupling" of wage growth from productivity growth ever since the 1970s. The American economy has been producing more output per worker over time, but the typical worker's wages have risen

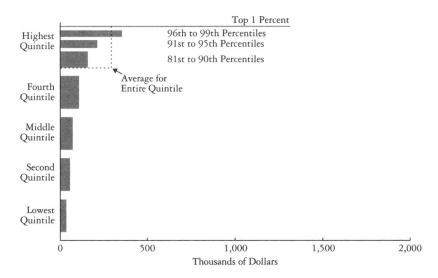

FIGURE 3.2 Average Post-Tax Yearly Income for Households at Different Points in the Distribution, United States 2015
Source: Congressional Budget Office, "The Distribution of Household Income, 2015," November 8, 2018, Figure 7 (https://www.cbo.gov/publication/54646).

much more slowly, if at all: between 1972 and 2010, US productivity grew by 84 percent, while median wages lagged way behind, increasing only 21 percent.[4] As a result, most Americans' incomes increased by less than the average for the whole economy.[5] The gains, instead, were concentrated among a relatively small slice of the population, which enjoyed spectacular increases in income. Headline rates of economic growth therefore give a very misleading picture of typical living standards in the United States.

The United States also stands out for the high level of instability of incomes. Fluctuations in the business cycle have had a greater impact on living standards over time because of the more limited cushioning of incomes by the welfare state and labor market institutions.[6] As well as very high inequality of incomes between individuals, the United States also has very high levels of income volatility (the variation in individual incomes across time),[7] for a variety of reasons. Limited employment protection rules make hiring and firing easier, hastening job losses during recessions. Most workers are not covered by collective agreements, facilitating downward wage adjustments during slumps, and increasing inequality as differences in workers' market value feed through more fully into the wage distribution. Limited income transfers for unemployed or low-paid citizens mean that incomes are smoothed less over the business cycle than in the other democracies with their more generous welfare policies. Overall, the US economic model exposes citizens to far greater degrees of economic and social risk than in other comparable countries.[8]

On top of labor market risk, Americans have also had to cope with the emergence of a financial system that has become increasingly unstable over time, and that exposes households very directly to fluctuations in financial markets. The process of "financialization" sparked by the deregulatory drive of the 1970s, 1980s, and 1990s led to a loosening of restrictions on consumer and mortgage lending, and a rapid expansion in household indebtedness. The weakening of social protection and policies to encourage individuals to make their own arrangements for managing economic risk, such as the promotion of individual retirement accounts and efforts to expand home ownership, led to most Americans having a direct stake in the vagaries of financial markets, and very often incurring debt to pursue financial gains. Moreover, university tuition rising eight times faster than wages has significantly increased the burden of student debt: 44 million Americans owed $1.4 trillion in student loans in 2015.[9]

The precarious existence facing many Americans has had a measurable impact on public health. The United States has higher levels of mental illness than other comparable countries,[10] and economic stresses have been directly linked to drug addiction and higher death rates for the sectors of the population most exposed to economic risk. African Americans and other non-white groups have long been at higher risk of poverty than whites, but recent studies show a striking increase in midlife mortality among white Americans, an inversion of a secular downward trend.[11] This rise, which did not affect other demographic groups, has been directly attributed to economic distress, and in particular the effects of deindustrialization and the loss of good manufacturing jobs in areas of the "Rust Belt."[12] At the start of the twenty-first century, large swathes of American society had experienced decades of stagnant or even declining living standards, making them ill equipped to cope with the dramatic economic shock that was about to hit them.

Captured: How the American Party System Locked in Neoliberalism

Why did Americans vote for elected representatives who took decisions that wrecked the economy and subjected them to acute economic distress? In a democracy, policies that delivered an ever greater share of the pie to a small wealthy minority would be expected to lead to some kind of electoral retribution. Yet these market liberal policies had the broad support of both major parties, and although elections were frequent and fiercely fought and party control of the key institutions fluctuated, the broad contours of economic policy changed little over time. Americans have consistently voted for candidates that celebrated the market system and showed little or no interest in regulatory protections for American workers or increases in welfare protection. Unlike in other rich democracies, the United States has never had an electorally significant party of the socialist Left.[13]

A common explanation for this historical weakness of the Left in the United States is that Americans appear to be less concerned about inequality than Europeans, and more ready to accept it as the price of a meritocratic society where hard work is rewarded.[14] This could lead to a lower degree of support for "big government," with Americans tending to prefer individual responsibility over social safety nets, especially voters who oppose redistribution on racial grounds.[15] But there is also evidence that Americans' views on equality and redistribution are less distinctive than is commonly believed. A sizable majority of Americans believe that inequality is too high and that income and wealth should be redistributed to reduce it.[16] Majorities consistently support more progressive taxation to pay for education, healthcare, and retirement pensions, and most Americans are also more than happy to contribute to food stamps and other forms of assistance for the poor.[17] Yet policy has for some time privileged tax cuts, especially for high earners, at the expense of spending on Americans' preferred social policies.

The US Constitution is part of the reason for this mismatch between voter preferences and policy outcomes. The restrictions on the powers of the federal level of government and the incentives for states to compete by offering lower taxes have contributed to a lack of financial resources to fund social policies.[18] The separation of powers between executive, legislature, and judiciary and frequent "gridlock" place obstacles in the path of major social reforms, and the overrepresentation of sparsely populated rural states biases policy in a conservative direction. Some historians argue that the US Constitution was designed with this conservative bias in mind.[19] But the constitutional framework has remained broadly constant over time, and cannot explain why inequality has grown so much in recent decades, when policy in the mid-twentieth century was so much more progressive and egalitarian.

Recent research by political scientists suggests that voter ignorance and cognitive inconsistency is to blame, leading voters to vote against their interests on issues such as fiscal policy and healthcare.[20] Others have argued that the Right has successfully mobilized working-class anxieties about issues such as race, gun control, and abortion to win support for regressive economic and fiscal policies.[21] Put more crudely, for many scholars the problem would be solved if only lower-income Americans voted in greater numbers for the Democratic Party. It is certainly true that there are important differences between the parties, and, in particular, that the Republican Party has moved heavily to the right on both economic and social/cultural issues in recent decades. McCarty, Poole, and Rosenthal have shown that congressional voting has become increasingly polarized and partisan since the 1970s, with most legislation dividing representatives along party lines, and the average position of Republican and Democratic legislators moving further apart.[22]

But it is also true that on key economic issues, the Democrats and Republicans have tended to adopt similar positions, pushing voter preferences out of the equation. Figure 3.3 presents a measure of the two parties' positions on economic policy issues since World War II, calculated from programmatic documents: a centrist position would be represented by a zero on the vertical axis, a left-wing position by a negative score, and a right-wing position by a positive one. We can see that as the Republicans move to the right from the early 1970s, the Democrats follow them, and apart from the 1996 election, where the two parties are quite far apart, they are mostly quite close together. The polarization is only clearly visible if we look at the parties' positions on

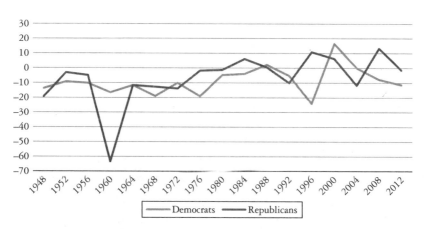

FIGURE 3.3 US Party Positions, Economy, 1948–2012, Percentage of Right-Wing Statements Minus Percentage of Left-Wing Statements

Source: Andrea Volkens, Werner Krause, Pola Lehmann, Theres Matthieß, Nicolas Merz, Sven Regel, and Bernhard Weßels, *The Manifesto Data Collection: Manifesto Project (MRG / CMP / MARPOR)*, version 2018b (Berlin: Wissenschaftszentrum Berlin für Sozialforschung, 2018) (https://doi.org/10.25522/manifesto. mpds.2018b).

sociocultural issues, where after 2008 in particular the Republicans moved sharply to the right while the Democrats moved to the left, opening out a significant gap, which can be seen in Figure 3.4.

The recent period of apparent polarization in American politics has masked a clear convergence between the parties on some of the key policy controversies relating to the economy and the distribution of income and wealth. After the conflictual politics of the 1960s and 1970s, the 1980s saw both parties adopt a broadly liberal, pro-market and pro-trade approach to the economy. The key ideas of the postwar period, such as a government-led demand that management to maintain full employment, careful regulation of financial markets, and redistribution through progressive taxation and public spending became deeply unfashionable on both sides of the partisan divide. The policies that have driven an ever wider gap between rich and poor, and indeed between the richest and the rest, enjoyed the active support of both Republicans and Democrats. The Reagan administration may have been the most aggressive promotor of neoliberal transformation, but the Democrats, after three successive defeats in presidential elections, accepted this broadly market liberal stance.

The Clinton presidency not only failed to reverse any substantial features of the Reagan marketization agenda, but in many respects moved it still further. Welfare reforms toughened eligibility and enforced labor market flexibility, while budgetary policy was more orthodox than under Reagan,

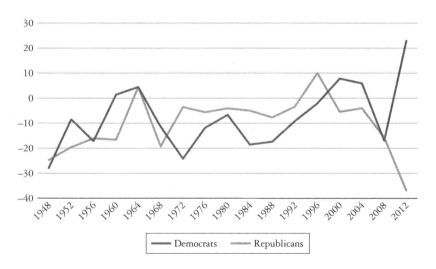

FIGURE 3.4 US Party Positions, Society/Culture, 1948–2012, Percentage of Right-Wing Statements Minus Percentage of Left-Wing Statements
Source: Volkens et al., *The Manifesto Data Collection* (see Figure 3.3).

with significant budget surpluses being used to pay down government debt. In the financial sector, the Clinton administration embraced deregulation, with Treasury Secretary Robert Rubin—formerly a leading Wall Street executive—aggressively pushing a deregulation agenda and protecting fiscal privileges enjoyed by hedge funds.[23] Finally, trade agreements, notably the North American Free Trade Agreement (NAFTA) concluded by the Clinton administration, and the entry of China into the World Trade Organization exposed American manufacturing to much greater international competition, hastening the decline in the industrial workforce.[24]

The pro-market, pro-openness shift spawned a growth model centered on the expansion of the financial sector at the expense of other parts of the economy. The industrial sector shrank, shedding the unionized and relatively well-paid and protected jobs typical of postwar manufacturing, while the service sector grew, creating large numbers of poorly paid jobs with limited security. The parties differed in their response to declining job quality, with Democrats favoring tax credits to supplement meager wages, while Republicans preferred tax cuts, which magnify the divergence of market incomes. But neither party was willing to embrace more active government intervention to raise low-skilled wages, build or rebuild institutions of collective bargaining, or restrict employer and investor freedoms to maximize profit unhindered by regulation. As conventional measures of unemployment fell, a growing share of the low-paid jobs created by the service economy was taken by migrant workers, although low-skilled immigration declined after the mid-2000s.[25]

The steady drift of the established parties toward pro-market positions was not driven by a similar shift in public opinion. Even though support for collectivism and welfare has historically been weaker than in most European democracies, survey data showed a growing concern about inequality and increasing support for policies that could deliver a more balanced distribution of income and wealth.[26] The neoliberal project may have had only lukewarm support among voters, but it was greeted enthusiastically by the wealthy business interests that funded politicians of both parties.[27] The increasingly loose regulation of political donations (notably the *Citizens United* decision, which freed up corporate funding of politics) meant that monied interests carried increasing weight in the American political process, leading to a growing gap between the views of the median voter and the positions adopted by congressional representatives.[28] Although this outsized influence of business is nothing new in American politics,[29] the rising share of income controlled by the top one percent since the 1970s meant that the wealthy enjoyed significantly enhanced bargaining power over politicians.

Seen from this perspective, American voters' apparent acquiescence in pro-wealthy policies makes more sense. Lower-income Americans are more likely to vote Democratic,[30] but policies introduced by Democratic administrations have in large part failed to compensate for the overall shift, supported by both parties, toward a much more pro-business consensus on financial regulation and fiscal and social policy. From the late 1980s, US politics exhibited a strong elite consensus around financialization, globalization, and a more market-driven distribution of income and wealth. The traditional party system was not able to protect Americans from the market, because the political parties, tied as they were to the demands of wealthy donors, failed to reflect the full range of policy preferences of American voters. Worse, close to half the electorate regularly failed to cast a vote at all, meaning their preferred policies were entirely without representation.

The high barriers to entry for new political leaders protected the mainstream parties and candidates from the consequences of growing voter dissatisfaction. From 1988 to 2008 the presidency was occupied by members of two families, the Bushes and the Clintons. Obama defeated Hillary Clinton in the Democratic primaries, and Jeb Bush failed to win the nomination in 2012, giving way to Mitt Romney, whose father had run for president in 1968. The 2016 primary season once again involved a Bush and a Clinton. This kind of dynastic inertia was suggestive of a closed political elite, in which insider candidates enjoyed considerable advantages in terms of fundraising, access to favorable media coverage, and support from the party machinery. To call these arrangements oligarchical[31] may be controversial, but this kind of endogamic recruitment of political leaders, alongside the incumbency advantages enjoyed by congressional leaders, ran the obvious risk of entrenching a self-referential elite hostile to political alternatives.

By the beginning of the 2010s there were clear signs of the electorate tiring of the choices available to them. Voter participation in the United States was historically lower than in Europe, and both presidential and congressional election turnout was on a downward trajectory since the early 1970s, although it recovered slightly in the 2000s. Survey data revealed increased disaffection with political elites and indeed with the democratic process more generally.[32] In one 2010 poll only 11 percent of respondents claimed to have high or very high confidence in Congress,[33] an extraordinary number considering that many of those polled must have given their vote to at least one congressional representative. This was down from 30 percent in 2004, suggesting a marked deterioration as the economy declined. The last thing American democracy needed was the worst economic crisis in almost eighty years.

Too Big to Fail or Too Connected to Fail? The Politics of the Financial Bailout

Not only did the neoliberal reforms described earlier expose US society to greater degrees of economic risk but the same faith in lightly regulated markets was also directly responsible for unleashing the financial turmoil of the late 2000s. The removal of regulatory restraints on credit growth and the relaxed regulatory approach to financial innovation brought the expansion of finance and a dramatic increase in leverage across the economy. Although the governing elites in the Federal Reserve and the US Treasury insisted that market mechanisms could adequately price risk and secure financial stability, the panicked deleveraging after the collapse of the US subprime mortgage market suggested otherwise. US regulators failed to understand the consequences of the loosening of credit standards inherent in the widespread securitization of mortgage debt, or the risks implied by large numbers of borrowers taking on unsustainable loans to speculate on a rising housing market. The government turned a blind eye as financial institutions built large and opaque exposures to credit derivatives that led to a complete breakdown of the financial system in late 2008.

Some economists have argued that inequality and financial instability are in fact closely connected.[34] As wages stagnate for the average worker, savings rates become increasingly skewed as surpluses accumulate at the top of the distribution. These savings are recycled through the financial system as cheap credit for lower-income groups, who need to borrow to sustain consumption and seek social mobility through leveraged bets on property markets. The resulting growth in credit destabilizes the economy as a whole, resulting in frequent financial crashes. First, by increasing leverage more generally in the economy, financialization made the US economy exceptionally vulnerable to financial shocks by encouraging speculative bubbles in housing and financial assets. Second, the growth of the financial sector had dramatic effects at the top of the income distribution, where successful leveraged bets could generate massive payouts to a select group of hedge fund managers and other financial operators, spiking the income share of the top one percent. Finally, by pushing down savings rates and facilitating high ratios of household debt to household income, living standards for many began to be reliant on easy credit conditions.[35]

Although most accounts of the crisis identify the US subprime mortgage markets as the key short-term trigger, its devastating effects were the consequence of a significant growth in debt, both in terms of the global imbalances that developed as some countries (including the United States) became heavily dependent on capital flows from others, and in the domestic economy as households and financial institutions became increasingly leveraged. The debt explosion was the direct consequence of deregulatory policies promoted aggressively by the United States both globally and locally. The collapse of the American, and then the global, financial system blew apart the intellectual rationale and the political legitimacy of the pro-market program, not only because such catastrophic events were not supposed to be possible in a free market system, but also because the seizing up of the credit system required the government to subvert the logic of free markets by staging a massive government intervention to bail out financial institutions and their creditors.

The bailout (the so-called Troubled Asset Relief Program [TARP], later formalized in the Emergency Economic Stabilization Act) allocated $700 billion of public resources to buy toxic assets and prop up the market, directly or indirectly rescuing the major US financial institutions from insolvency. This amounted to a bailout of the financial industry worth around 5 percent of US GDP, at a time when many Americans were facing serious hardship. The bailout may well have been the only way to stabilize the financial system and protect the wider economy, but the very close connections between the key political actors and financial sector leaders—Treasury Secretary Henry Paulson was a former CEO of Goldman Sachs, and many other leading figures in the administration and in the Democratic elite had financial sector experience—created an indelible impression that the bailout was more about protecting the interests of a close-knit political and business elite. Subsequent research in fact showed that the personal financial interests of congressional representatives were a statistically significant predictor of their legislative support for the Emergency Economic Stabilization Act.[36]

The unprecedented bailout of the US financial system highlighted the distance separating American voters from their political and financial elites. The passage of the act was hugely controversial. Most polls showed public opposition, and congressional representatives facing re-election came under heavy pressure from constituents to oppose the bill.[37] Protests underlined that the bailout involved channeling huge quantities of government money directly into the pockets of some of the wealthiest people in America, rewarding them for making spectacularly wrong decisions. Interestingly, opposition to the bailout spanned the political spectrum. Protests were organized by labor unions and anti-corporate activists on the left, but there was also outrage on the conservative right at the use of public money to protect bankers from the consequences of their recklessness. In the aftermath of the bailout, protest movements emerged on both left and right, constituting the founding moment for the anti-system politics that exploded in 2016.

The 2008 crisis came just weeks before the presidential election won by Barack Obama, who successfully presented himself as a break with the past, offering up slogans of "hope" and "change." This turnover in the executive did not, however, lead to dramatic changes in the policy approach to the financial crisis and resulting recession. Instead, his nominations to key economic policy positions suggested a high degree of continuity, with key financial sector insiders Timothy Geithner (New York Federal Reserve Chair) as Treasury Secretary and Larry Summers (Treasury Secretary under Clinton) as chair of the National Economic Council. These nominations suggested little appetite for a radical reform of the financial sector, and the fiscal stimulus adopted by the Obama administration came down on the conservative side of the scale, reportedly after pressure from Summers to reduce its size and prioritize tax cuts.[38] Obama's commitment to bipartisan, centrist policymaking and close ties to financial interests ensured that policy would continue to protect the banks and remain within the parameters of a broad market liberal approach for the rest of the economy.

Normal electoral turnover between the Democratic and Republican parties fell way short of any systemic transformation, and the Obama administration's policy response was oriented toward cushioning the effect of the crash on the broader economy and attempting to shore up the faltering financial system, rather than any root and branch reform. Alongside TARP spending, the Federal Reserve loosened monetary policy to the zero lower bound, and intervened heavily in markets by purchasing private sector assets such as mortgage-backed securities, building up holdings worth $2 trillion, around 15 percent of US GDP. Help was also extended to the auto industry, with the government-backed rescues of General Motors and Chrysler. Some provisions in the stimulus package (the American Recovery and Reinvestment Act [ARRA]) extended unemployment benefits and offered boosts to various forms of social assistance, while measures taken in the Making Home Affordable program offered help for underwater homeowners. But the assistance for the corporate and banking sectors dwarfed the help for indebted households, or those who face job losses as the recession deepened.

This policy response, although ambitious in comparison with previous downturns, was not sufficient to prevent a recession unprecedented for the postwar era in both its depth and reach, hitting the labor market, housing market, and stock market simultaneously. Survey data showed that by April 2010 about 39 percent of households had experienced either unemployment, negative equity, or mortgage arrears, which showed the extraordinary reach of the recession beyond the most vulnerable groups into the middle class.[39] Although unemployment did not reach record levels, peaking at around 10 percent, the rate of job loss in 2008–2009 was 6.1 percent of all employment, twice the level of the 1981 recession.[40] Employment recovery was slow, and underemployment high, with the labor force participation rate dropping to and remaining at under 60 percent of the active population.[41] Wages fell back to the levels of the late 1990s, remaining below 2007 levels for several years for the bottom 95 percent of the labor force.[42] Real median income for working-age households fell 10 percent between 2000 and 2009, a fall that began before the financial crisis but was dramatically accelerated by it.[43] Beyond the labor market, the recession had a major impact on the asset holdings of American families, lowering net wealth by 23 percent in 2007–2009, with 60 percent of all households losing net wealth.[44]

Since government was preoccupied with restoring order to the financial system by supporting the value of compromised assets, policy had a natural bias in favor of owners of capital and those in the financial industry who managed their investments. After the TARP had doled out government money to a handful of insolvent financial institutions, bailing out not only the recipients but also their creditors, yet more money was thrown at the industry through quantitative easing, which had the direct effect of pushing up asset prices, but was rather less effective at stimulating the broader economy, as financial institutions hoarded the cash. Given the very unequal distribution of these assets, quantitative easing effectively subsidized the recovery of the balance sheets of the wealthiest Americans. There is also evidence that very expansionary monetary policy is good for employment and wages,[45] but the majority of Americans who enjoyed little or even negative income growth over the past decade could be forgiven for not appreciating this point.

The Obama stimulus may have been deemed insufficient by many,[46] but as panic over the financial system began to subside, so did the support for, or tolerance of, expansionary policy among financial and policy elites. Early signs of the wind changing were the creation of a bipartisan panel on fiscal policy, the National Commission on Fiscal Responsibility and Reform (or Simpson Bowles Commission) in early 2010, less than eighteen months after the collapse of Lehman Brothers. Fiscal policy quickly turned contractionary as Republicans in Congress pushed through the Budget Control Act, which imposed $1.2 trillion of automatic cuts on spending—the so-called sequester—and most of the provisions in the ARRA expired. As a result government programs with important redistributive effects—such as programs for the unemployed, aid for underwater homeowners, healthcare, education, and other discretionary spending—were pared back.

As fiscal stimulus was reversed while quantitative easing was expanded to take the strain, the nature of the new post-crisis settlement became clear. The bailout of the financial sector would be protected and continued, but the household sector would have to cope with less, for fear of an implausible collapse in the credibility of the US Treasury. In short, the banks were too big to fail, but the American public was too big to bail. Nor was there any regulatory reckoning for the bankers to fear: the Dodd-Frank Act tinkered with some of the egregious flaws of the financial system without addressing the ways in which it generated instability.[47] The bonus culture was alive and well, and Wall Street's highest earners were able to quickly return to making outsized gains, thanks to the support of the US taxpayer and the Federal Reserve. As the American economy returned to growth, the lion's share of income gains were still accruing to the highest earners: astonishingly, by 2013, 95 percent of income gains since the start of the recovery had gone to the top one percent.[48]

It may be an oversimplification to claim that policy focused primarily on restoring normal service for wealthy investors and financiers, while the vast majority suffered stagnating incomes and declining economic security. But as the richest one percent quickly got back to where they were on the eve of the crisis, while the most Americans were left trailing behind, it was easy to draw that conclusion. As the chaotic events of 2008 faded into the past and attention shifted to the debt ceiling and the sequester, the crisis of an overleveraged and greedy financial sector was skillfully spun as a crisis of an overleveraged and greedy government; what Mark Blyth called "the greatest bait and switch in human history."[49] This kind of distribution of economic gains and losses is politically unsustainable in a democracy, especially in hard times, and in 2016 it unraveled.

Too Big to Bail: American Voters and the Financial Crisis

We have seen that the American system of government managed to rescue its financial system and its wealthiest citizens but proved incapable of generating a policy mix that would offer the "99 percent" the same degree of protection from the consequences of the downturn. Policy toward the financial sector reflected the outsized influence of financial interests in US politics, and as a result exacerbated the disconnect between voters and the political leadership. The American public was on the front line of the fallout from the financial crisis, and faced a severe economic shock that the rudimentary US welfare state was ill-equipped to weather.

The route to the political shocks of the 2016 electoral cycle was laid down by the political choices made during the crisis and its immediate aftermath. But the backlash was not a simple revolt of the groups most damaged by the crisis. Instead, the first wave of protest came from relatively economically secure and politically conservative voters, in the form of the Tea Party. This movement was inspired by a televised rant by financial commentator Rick Santelli in February 2009 complaining about the Obama administration's plans to help underwater homeowners (or as he called them, "losers").[50] Tea Partiers, drawn primarily from the older white middle-class suburban and rural population, mobilized opposition to the Obama administration and the more moderate elements of the Republican leadership, pressuring the GOP to adopt a harder line against the Democrats' liberal plans. Tea Party rhetoric emphasized the threat to "traditional" American values of small government that they saw as present in the thinking of the Founding Fathers and embedded in the Constitution. The rise of the Tea Party is also frequently attributed to a fearful reaction of American whites to the election of the first black president.[51]

Tea Party supporters were mostly economically comfortable, albeit usually not from the very high end of the wealth scale, and had retirement income and asset values to protect. But the wealth of the middle class fell sharply between 2007 and 2010, while that of the top decile increased,[52] in part because the middle class had a greater share of capital tied up in the collapsing housing market. This group feared being on the hook for any expansion of social protection, because it was not wealthy enough to avail itself of the tax "planning" resources used by one percenters.[53] The perceived threat to their healthcare rights from the Obama administration's plans to extend help to the uninsured was also a source of acute anxiety, given the likelihood of this group of older Americans having much greater healthcare needs than the younger population.[54] Tea Partiers saw their rights threatened by bad government policies and redistribution to the poor and ethnic minorities. The much lampooned slogan "Get Your Government Hands off My Medicare" reflected a belief that these programs consisted of rights built on contributions through a long working life, and should therefore be distinguished from the "handouts" to the unemployed or other younger or working-age groups.

There was also a powerful response on the left to the financial crisis and the bailout, although it took longer to emerge. The Occupy movement, which gained prominence with the occupation of Zuccotti Park in New York in September 2011, fully three years after the peak of the financial crisis, was very unambiguously a protest against the inequality and economic pain inflicted by neoliberalism and the banking collapse.[55] The Occupy movement drew inspiration from the Arab Spring, and in turn sparked similar mobilizations in other Western countries, notably in London in the United Kingdom and in southern Europe. Initial sparks for the protest were education budget cuts in California, leading to protests in various University of California campuses in 2010–2011. Unlike the Tea Party, which used traditional media and territorially based grassroots organizing, the Occupy movement used social media much more extensively.[56]

Where the Tea Party movement took its intellectual lead from shock-jock radio commentators and the right-wing media, the Occupy movement drew on the ideas of an older generation of left-wing scholars such as Judith Butler and Naomi Klein, as well as younger organizers. Key slogans clarified that inequality was a central concept for the Occupy movement: "We are the 99 percent" popularized the academic work of Piketty and others documenting the concentration of income around the top one percent. The location of the protests, at the heart of the New York financial district, the use of the label "Occupy Wall Street," and a concern with abuses of power by corporations and the excessive debt burdens of students and others identified the workings of the market system as a target. The Occupy movement appealed particularly to young people, many of them highly educated and carrying student debt but not in well paid jobs, and therefore hit hard by the weak economy and policy choices that protected creditors over debtors. Unlike the Tea Party, Occupy sought to represent less economically protected groups and express a vigorous critique of the market system.

But much of the Occupy rhetoric was directed at the failings of politicians and the flaws and limitations of American democracy, and here it shared common ground with the Tea Party. One Occupy slogan was "banks got bailed out, we got sold out," highlighting how the crisis had led to a bailout of wealthy financial institutions, at the expense of the general public. But Wall Street was not the only target: Occupy also took aim at the politicians responsible for the decision to side with the banks, condemning "a political system rigged to serve only the very wealthy."[57] In fact, as well as a critique of capitalism, the Occupy movement was also articulating a critique of American democracy and attempting to develop an alternative form of participatory politics. This emphasis on "bottom-up" action and a hostility to elitist and oligarchical forms of decision-making were part of the reason the more active phase of the movement largely petered out within a year. Alongside a long-standing suspicion of hierarchy in leftist social movements, the Occupy movement was one of the first attempts in a democracy to use the Internet to bypass traditional forms of political organization. This "horizontalist" approach proved incapable of sustaining large-scale political action for long, and the Occupy movement lacked the kind of economic and logistic assistance that the Republican donor community offered the Tea Party.

The Tea Party and the Occupy movement both represented fundamental challenges to the established party elites. Many Tea Partiers saw the Republican leadership as too close to corporate interests and unconcerned with the interests of grassroots conservatives. The Occupy movement was equally frustrated with the slow pace of change under the Obama administration and its finance-friendly appointments to key positions. Yet the 2012 presidential election pitted the incumbent Obama against a wealthy financier, Mitt Romney, as a mainstream Republican candidate, suggesting a return to "normal" politics after the upheavals of the financial crisis. The Tea Party did make a significant impact on the politics of the Republican Party, but it was also relatively easily co-opted by wealthy elite groups who themselves had been pushing to roll back government regulation and reduce taxes, especially on the very wealthy. The Occupy movement suffered the fate of many such movements, failing to transform the spontaneity and energy of a leaderless wave of agitation into a coherent organization that could pressure government into changing policy. The Democratic Party had no primary season, and no credible independent candidate emerged to represent the groups mobilized by Occupy.

The 2012 election entrenched the new policy equilibrium that had emerged after the financial crisis. The Democratic administration and the Federal Reserve were taking responsibility for holding the financial system together, while Republicans were fighting to push back against the kinds of fiscal policies that would protect the wider public and counteract the skewed market income distribution. Below the surface of the apparently highly polarized partisan politics in Washington, DC, politics continued to prioritize the interests of the financial sector, while most Americans continued to struggle. Real pre-tax income for the top one percent grew by 37 percent between 2009 and 2015, fully 52 percent of total US income growth for the period. Logically, the remaining 48 percent of income gains had to be shared out over the remaining 99 percent of the population, whose income had still not recovered from the losses incurred during the crisis.[58] Neither the Obama administration nor the Republican leadership had a compelling story about how this could be rectified. Any change would have to come from outside the system.

"The System Is Rigged": Trump against the GOP

Donald Trump's election to the presidency, like the financial crisis of 2008, was a big surprise to the pundit class and to the academic community, leading to frenetic attempts to make sense of it. The bewilderment generated by Trump's victory is compounded by the fact that his personality and much of his rhetoric is anathema to the high-income, highly educated classes of Washington, DC-based political analysts and Ivy League university professors that shape elite opinion. This plausibly explains the widespread failure to anticipate Trumpism, and the grave difficulties many have faced in understanding it after the fact. Trump represented a revolt not only against the political elite but also against much of the media and the "experts" of the academic and policy world. Leading figures in the Republican Party—the "never Trumpers"—openly criticized Trump as unsuitable for office, and refused to back his campaign. Their rejection of him, far from undermining his chances, became one of his biggest selling points.

Trump's rise is best explained as a broad-based rejection of the existing political establishment and its failure to protect the living standards of the majority. Trump offered a clear break with the conventional language and practices of professional politicians. Unlike all the other primary candidates he was facing, Trump had no experience of elected office or public administration, nor even any stable partisan affiliation, having variously supported Democratic, Republican, and Reform Party candidates. He could therefore credibly offer something new to an electorate that had good reason to feel poorly represented by the political establishment, presenting a fantasy of the tough businessman coming into politics and cutting through the ambiguities, compromises, and broken promises of professional politicians.

Trump's crude rhetoric and use of threats and insults to his opponents also broke with convention, and identified him as being different from the mainstream elites that had brought so many disappointments. An eloquent illustration of his outsider credentials was the heckling he faced at the Alfred E. Smith Memorial Foundation Dinner, a charity event that presidential candidates typically attend just a couple of weeks before polling day.[59] What appeared at the time to be a publicly humiliating experience, as assorted billionaires and other Manhattan luminaries expressed their revulsion at Trump's off-color rhetoric, proved to be a harbinger of many Americans' readiness to vote against the establishment. This aggressive language tapped into the resentment and anger that many voters felt at the failures of politicians to address the threats to their well-being. By taking a hard line on the purported culprits, Trump signaled a possibility of dramatic change in how the country was governed. In a context where Americans' trust in political institutions was at a historic low, this had considerable appeal, and the outrage it evoked only served to confirm his apparent outsider status.

In a crowded primary field, Trump's strategy was to belittle—sometimes literally (he referred to fellow primary contender Marco Rubio as "little Marco")—his opponents as weak insiders. As well as confirming his appeal to voters keen to see someone take on what many perceived as a self-serving political elite, his high-intensity rhetoric also made great news copy, providing Trump with abundant media coverage and circumventing the usual media channels. His Twitter use was also key to this strategy, with the continuous flow of simplistic critiques of President Obama and proposals of easy solutions to various political problems winning him a huge audience of millions of followers who accessed Trump's views without intermediaries. This media strategy, building on Trump's carefully constructed notoriety as a celebrity over the years, allowed him to bypass the usual channels of campaign funding, which could have exercised some control over his message, and aided his claims to represent a new departure able to shake up the entrenched Washington elite.[60]

Trump's rhetoric has been the subject of much anguished commentary, focusing not only on its racist and authoritarian overtones, but also its crude, often incoherent and grammatically defective use of language, and a breezy approach to factual accuracy. But leaving aside his frequent use of claims that are either demonstrably false or at the very least dubious, it is misleading to infer that he has no clear political message. The slogan of his presidential bid, "Make America Great Again," was a clear appeal to voters who felt that government had been insufficiently patriotic and had failed to protect American citizens from global threats, both economically and in terms of security at the border. His 2015 book *Crippled America*[61] addressed "the bedrock of this country—the middle class—and those 45 million Americans stuck in poverty (who) have seen their incomes decline over the past 20 years." Trump claimed to share their "disenchantment and frustration" at a "deadlocked" Congress and an executive branch guilty of "incompetence beyond belief."[62]

A key element of Trump's discourse was to propose a retreat from the elite consensus of economic openness and the embrace of globalization through free trade agreements. He made frequent reference to Chinese competition and its effects on American jobs, and criticized agreements such as NAFTA and the proposed Trans-Pacific Partnership (TPP) and practices of offshoring that shifted production from the United States to cheaper countries. Avoiding technocratic language, Trump made simple promises to bring back industrial jobs from overseas by renegotiating trade deals in America's favor.[63] This set him apart not only from the Democrats, who had been cheerleaders for free trade ever since the early 1990s, but also from most Republicans. Trump counterposed to this "globalist" consensus a form of economic nationalism summarized in another slogan he revived, "America First."

Trump's economic nationalism dovetailed neatly with his other key message, which was opposition to immigration.[64] His anti-immigration rhetoric focused on illegal immigration (mostly from Mexico), but also the threat of Islamist terrorism. By zooming in on two aspects of immigration that evoked threats to physical security, Trump was leveraging increasing concern at illegal immigration in some southern states, with the broad fears many Americans had about global jihadism. The anti-immigration message merged easily into dog-whistle politics relating to America's history of race politics, with Trump supporters proving to be predominantly white. However, Trump avoided overtly racist remarks about African Americans, directing his most offensive invective mainly to Mexicans and Muslims. The dubious legality and impracticality of his two main policy ideas in this regard—a border wall along the Mexico border and a ban on Muslims entering the United States—provoked predictable outcry, which almost certainly assisted Trump in mobilizing support and entrenching him as the outsider candidate, the only candidate serious enough about dealing with the alleged problem to propose tough solutions.

The provocative nature of Trump's rhetoric focused a great deal of media attention on his various violations of Washington protocol and his ambitions to run the presidency with an authoritarian and possibly racist governing style. As well as firming up Trump's support base, the nature of political commentary and the mobilization of a variety of left-wing groups against his ideas distracted attention from the reasons why his message could prove attractive to many Americans in the middle and bottom of the economic hierarchy. Trump's aggressive style and promises of economic interventionism were particularly powerful among middle- and working-class whites living in areas that had suffered from deindustrialization. These groups were at the front line of disruptive economic changes, as documented not only by the income and employment statistics, but also by the dramatic data on public health risks, most notably the recent apparent decline in life expectancy among white non-Hispanic Americans.[65] Trump's promises to intervene to stop American corporations moving jobs overseas, and claims that he could reopen coalfields (by loosening environmental regulations) resonated in areas that had been shedding industrial jobs for years.

Trump was the only Republican candidate offering a serious program of economic interventionism to address the consequences of the financial crisis and the secular decline in living standards among middle-class white Americans. The combination of trade and labor (through immigration control) protectionism with promises of public infrastructure investment and restrictions on outsourcing contrasted with the broadly neoliberal approach adopted by other leading Republicans. In a context of economic insecurity not only for poorer Americans but also for large sections of the middle class, the success of a brash candidate promising to restrict and control market mechanisms in the interests of middle America had an obvious appeal. His apparent distance from the monied interests that typically financed Republican candidates gave his promises credibility. Trump mobilized large numbers of blue-collar voters in the primary campaign,[66] reflecting his ability to offer something different for some of the social groups that had suffered the most from economic change and the shock of the financial crisis.

"Feel the Bern": The Return of the American Left

While Trump was tearing up the rulebook in the Republican primaries, the Democratic primary campaign also came under pressure from anti-system forces, although this time with a different outcome. Hillary Clinton was a consummate insider, having spent eight years in the White House already and as a former Senator for New York, and was associated with the Democratic establishment both in terms of personal history and political positioning. Her husband, Bill, brought not only his experience of running a campaign machine and an extensive network of supporters, but also a track record of centrist, and mostly enthusiastically pro-market and pro-trade, policy positions. The Clinton campaign enjoyed abundant financial backing, in part from the same core group that had funded previous Clinton campaigns to the tune of billions of dollars.[67] After defeat by Obama in 2008, a frequent observation made by political commentators was that 2016 was "her turn," appearing to confirm the worst features of insider politics in the United States.

Unlike in the fragmented Republican primary, the only opponent Clinton faced was independent Senator Bernie Sanders, whose "socialist," identity was considered way beyond the pale of mainstream American politics. Sanders's campaign focused on economic issues, emphasizing inequality, the excessive political influence of the wealthy and, particularly, the Wall Street banks, and the damaging effects of trade agreements on working Americans.[68] Sanders campaigned for more progressive taxation, a financial transactions tax to pay for social programs, reductions in student debt, universal healthcare through a single-payer system, raising the minimum wage, and extending workers' rights to organize in the workplace. Way to the left of most American politicians, Sanders emphasized how such policies were standard in European countries, citing the case of social democratic Denmark as a model to emulate. Sanders represented progressive positions on issues of sexual and race equality, cannabis use, and foreign policy (he was a vocal opponent of the Iraq War). These relatively radical positions contrasted with Clinton's pragmatic and strategic approach to politics, which was centrist in orientation and technocratic in presentation.

As well as having a clear left-wing identity, Sanders was able to claim similar "outsider" status as Trump. Although he had extensive political experience on launching his bid, having been mayor of Burlington, Vermont, then winning election to the House and ultimately the Senate, Sanders had maintained formal independence from the Democratic Party, the only Senator to do so. Alongside this formerly nonpartisan positioning, Sanders also expressed an open rejection of established practices of political finance in the United States and advocated campaign finance reform. Sanders opted not to seek large donations or draw on Super PACs and other standard fundraising practices used by other candidates, and instead raised money through small contributions.[69] By identifying as an independent socialist and shunning wealthy donors, Sanders was successfully able to present himself as free of the ties and shady arrangements many Americans associated with their political representatives in Washington, DC, again in sharp contrast to Clinton, whose lucrative speeches to Wall Street audiences gave the exact opposite impression.[70]

Unlike Trump, Sanders did not win, facing as he did a single well-organized and experienced candidate with extensive backing from the Democratic Party machine, wealthy donors, and progressive media outlets. But he did win unexpectedly high levels of support, both financially and in terms of primary votes. The Sanders campaign raised well over $200 million,[71] and won 43.1 percent of the primary electorate, or well over 13 million voters, taking several states, although the final result was never seriously in doubt. Moreover, the Sanders campaign mobilized considerable attention on the left, particularly among many younger voters, and drew larger crowds to his events than his rival, and indeed than Republican candidates.[72] This apparent enthusiasm gap between the two Democratic candidates was compounded by the strong impression, nourished in particular by the publication of leaked e-mails from the Democratic National Committee, that Sanders represented change and an insurgency against the entrenched power of machine politicians personified by the Clintons. The leaks revealed hostility to Sanders among the Democratic leadership and attempts to bias the primary process in favor of Clinton. The emergence of a vocal faction of Sanders supporters refusing to back Clinton, the so-called Bernie or Bust movement, further damaged the Democratic nominee by entrenching her image as a ruthless insider.

Alongside Trump's success in the Republican contest, the primary season revealed that a very large proportion of the most politically engaged Americans were prepared to contemplate nontraditional candidates and policy positions, and were keen to reject the policy consensus and personnel of the political establishment. Alongside Sanders's 13 million votes and 43 percent share, Trump received the support of 14 million Republican primary voters, or 44 percent, the highest ever for a GOP candidate.[73] These two purportedly outsider candidates, both of whom had shunned their party for long periods, amassed not far away from half the votes of the most engaged party supporters, a clear rejection of the political establishment on both sides.

Although there were very obvious differences between Trump and Sanders, their policy positions had in common a rejection of the neoliberal consensus. Both opposed aspects of trade liberalization, and, albeit in very different ways, both proposed measures to protect American workers from the harsh consequences of market forces, through social democratic measures for Sanders, and through potential trade barriers and immigration controls for Trump. Again in different ways, both showed an ability to connect with victims of economic change: Sanders appealing more to younger voters struggling to build their careers in a period of crisis, Trump to the "white working class" stricken by the decline of traditional industrial employment as well as the older, more prosperous "Tea Party" electorate. Both presented a contrast with the broadly pro-market, pro-trade consensus of both Hillary Clinton on the Democratic center-right and the myriad insider neoliberals in the Republican primary field. And finally, Trump won his primary, turning the 2016 election into a battle between a Democratic insider and a Republican outsider.

Trumped Up Voters? How Anti-System Politics Took Over the White House

Trump's victory in the 2016 presidential election was met with astonishment and anguish among political scientists and pollsters,[74] in part because most thought it was inconceivable and predicted his defeat, in part because his style and views were so far removed from the conventions of the American presidency. Trump's intemperate rhetoric, his lack of political experience, and the accusations of corrupt and even sexually abusive behavior should have made him an unappealing candidate for the median voter. The improving economy should have benefited the incumbent Democrats, according to theories of economic voting, although electoral history also suggests increasing likelihood of the incumbent party losing the White House after two or more mandates. Hillary Clinton's carefully planned campaign used modern data science to calculate which demographics had to be targeted to get her over the line.[75]

Political scientists have proposed two broad explanations for the result, which have frequently been pitched as mutually exclusive alternatives. On the one hand, Trump's inflammatory rhetoric on immigration, race, and gender issues, combined with the strong correlation between authoritarian, misogynist, and racist attitudes and support for Trump, has underpinned an explanation of the result in terms of race politics and a "white male" backlash against the liberal cosmopolitan elitism purportedly represented by Hillary Clinton. On the other, Trump's success among lower-income white voters in Rust Belt states such as Pennsylvania, Michigan, and Ohio drew attention to the role of economic grievance and opposition to trade liberalization among some of the losers from globalization. The debate has become confused as the normative implications of these two narratives become entangled with the empirical evidence. For example, accounts of the troubles of the "white working class" have been critiqued for appearing to justify illiberal and authoritarian values,[76] while analyses of the importance of race in voting patterns among low-income whites have appeared to dismiss the importance of the "legitimate concerns" of these voters.[77]

What emerges from the data is that both race and economic status matter in American elections, and 2016 was no exception. Trump unsurprisingly performed far better among whites than African Americans or Hispanics, but he was not very different from previous Republican candidates in this regard. The racist overtones of Trump's campaign were reason to expect that the 2016 vote would be more defined by racial divides than previous elections, and survey data has strongly suggested this was the case. Trump supporters in the Republican primaries scored higher on measures of racial resentment than supporters of other candidates.[78] But even before Trump's campaign began, race had begun to divide American voters into distinct camps, as whites became increasingly likely to identify as Republicans, and nonwhites as Democrats, in the course of the Obama presidency.[79] As a result, analysis of the 2016 vote has tended to focus on race to the exclusion of other factors such as economic grievances. According to this view, Americans had simply become racially polarized, because of demographic change and the trauma for many white Americans of an African American president.[80]

However, a number of the areas that swung heavily to Trump had delivered comfortable victories for Obama in 2008 and 2012. The underlying premise of the racial divide thesis is that white Americans voted for Trump because of their anxieties about cultural change, triggered by the eight years of the Obama presidency. But this fails to explain why the cultural anxiety was not present when Americans elected Obama—twice. Moreover, the factors that allegedly motivated disgruntled white voters to support Trump on the basis of his nativist appeal were not new: immigration had not increased particularly sharply under Obama compared to previous presidents, nor had Obama followed policies that favored African Americans over others in any noticeable way. After a brief blip during the financial crisis, American voters' attitudes toward immigration became more, not less, favorable over the decade prior to Trump's election to the presidency.[81] Race had long been a strong predictor of the vote in American politics, but it is counterintuitive to suggest that race mattered more in the 2016 election than it had in two previous elections in which an African American candidate was actually on the ballot.

One of the reasons that disentangling the effects of the Obama presidency in polarizing racial attitudes from the effects of economic grievance is that Obama was elected in the midst of the financial crisis. His presidency therefore coincides very closely with the period of the most acute economic distress in recent American history, although, as we have seen, economic grievance had far deeper roots than the financial crisis. Another reason the role of economic factors fails to emerge clearly in the data is that, as a Republican candidate, Trump was always likely to win disproportionate support higher up the income scale: Republican voters on average had higher incomes than Democrats in previous elections,[82] so the positive correlation between income and support for Trump is not surprising. The most sophisticated attempts to demonstrate the relative weight of race over economics have used survey data to analyze the characteristics of voters who shifted from the Democrats to Trump between 2012 and 2016, and have found that these voters scored particularly highly on a measure of racial resentment.[83] But these same voters were peculiarly unconcerned with race when they voted for Obama in the first place, often twice, before supporting Trump in 2016.

Trump won the election, despite losing the popular vote to Clinton, because he carried, with very slim margins, three key Electoral College states that had previously been solidly Democratic, and that had been hit hard by the crisis and the decline of manufacturing industry: Michigan, Pennsylvania, and Wisconsin. There is compelling evidence that Trump's ability to reach beyond the electorate that supported defeated Republican candidates

McCain and Romney, and in particular to mobilize support in Clinton's "blue wall" states, did involve middle- and lower-income voters in economically troubled areas. For example, exit poll data suggests a substantial swing to Trump among lower-income voters (income <$50,000) and a swing to Clinton among higher-income voters, and particularly those with incomes higher than $100,000, while the swing to the Republicans was higher in lower-income areas[84]. In other words, differences in economic performance across different regions of the United States translated into changes in support for Democrats and Republicans, with Clinton winning by big margins in the more dynamic states on the two coasts, and Trump outperforming previous Republican candidates in the areas of the Rust Belt that had suffered most from industrial decline and were receptive to his promises to revive the manufacturing heartlands.

Of course, this appeal was far more effective among white voters than other groups, given Trump's barely concealed nativism (expressed in particular through his championing of "birtherism"—the claim that Obama had been born overseas) and attacks on illegal immigration. Combined with economic protectionism and hostility to environmentalism, Trump's rhetoric offered a solution to the problems faced by lower-income whites, promising jobs and a return to their status privileges over nonwhite Americans. Clinton, in contrast, offered very few concrete promises of major change, lacking a strong message beyond her own competence and experience, alongside the chance of breaking through the glass ceiling of male presidencies.[85] Her economic stance was pro-globalization, and accommodating of the interests of big corporations and financial institutions, and indeed her campaign was the biggest beneficiary of Wall Street donations.[86] If Obama was the change candidate in 2008, and Romney's tax-cutting agenda offered little promise of economic improvement for struggling Americans in 2012, Trump's promises to "drain the swamp" and "make America great again" may have been vague and lacking policy detail, but alongside his long-standing opposition to trade liberalization, they represented the possibility of a break with the existing policies that had left many Americans still waiting for an upturn in their fortunes.

Trump managed to combine economically comfortable, yet fearful, voters and resentful economic losers together in one nihilistic package. The illiberalism of the Trump campaign was not just visible in its racism, but also in its anti-globalism. Steve Bannon, a key intellectual inspiration of the Trump campaign, made this very clear in a revealing interview in 2018, in which he railed against the theory of shareholder maximization, the offshoring of American capital, and the impact of deindustrialization on working-class communities.[87] As he crudely put it, "The elites save themselves. [. . .] If you're an asset holder, if you owned real estate, stocks, or intellectual property, if you're an owner, you had the best run in human history, okay? If you're a deplorable, you got ****ed. You know why the deplorables are angry? Look, you have socialism in this country for the very wealthy and for the very poor. And you have a brutal form of Darwinian capitalism for everybody else. You're one paycheck away from oblivion. [. . .] Dude, this is ****ed up." The appeal of this kind of message for a society under severe economic and financial strain that political leaders had done little to address is obvious.

Conclusion

In sum, Trump's election on an openly protectionist program against a liberal free trader like Clinton is as much a backlash against neoliberal policies as about America's long history of race politics. Americans had been subjected since the 1970s to extensive retrenchment of the protective and redistributive institutions of the welfare state, progressive deindustrialization in once prosperous regions accentuated by trade policy, and finally to a spectacular financial crisis, all of which increased poverty, income and wealth inequality, and economic insecurity. Trump's aggressive economic nationalism and refusal to pay lip service to the screeds of the neoliberal consensus may have been singularly unconvincing to economists and elite opinion leaders, but that acted as a qualification for many of the lower-educated voters he was appealing to. By offering trade barriers and an end to illegal immigration, Trump had a story to tell about how America could be made "great again." Offering an alternative to the market liberal orthodoxy for the first time in decades proved a winning move for key sectors of society exhausted by short-term economic pressures and long-term relative decline.

On the center-left, Clinton's failure to win the presidency can be adduced to many specific, short-term factors, such as her own lack of clarity of message, the underlying misogyny of many American voters, and her vulnerability to scandals real or manufactured. But her defeat was also the consequence of the resentment felt in some traditionally Democratic blue collar areas at the economically and socially liberal culture she represented, which offered them neither economic opportunity nor the comfort of a privileged cultural status. The unexpected success of Bernie Sanders in firing up more radical and younger elements of the Democratic base with a more aggressive critique of Wall Street and deregulated markets confirms that the desire for change was not limited to the Republican electorate. In 2016, a neoliberal, pro-trade orthodoxy that had informed government policy for the best part of forty years was attacked from both sides, and ultimately wound up defeated. And as the next chapter shows, a similar story can be told about Britain's vote to leave the European Union just six months earlier.

CHAPTER 4 | Taking Back Control: Britain
Turns against the Market

R ARELY CAN A political message have so swiftly turned against its author than British Prime Minister David Cameron's pitch to voters on
the eve of the 2015 election: "Britain faces a simple choice—either stability
and strong government with me, or chaos with Ed Miliband." Opinion polls
predicted Miliband's Labour Party would win the election but fall short of
a majority in Parliament, meaning that it would need the help of the secessionist Scottish National Party (SNP) to govern. In the event, Cameron's
Conservative Party surprised everyone, including perhaps the prime minister
himself, by winning a narrow majority that kept him in office and allowed
him to dispense with his coalition partners, the pro-European Liberal
Democrats. The celebrations in Downing Street must have been tempered by
the realization that Cameron's promised referendum on Britain's membership in the European Union would have to go ahead. Little over a year later,
having lost the "Brexit" vote, Cameron resigned, ushering in perhaps the
most unstable period in British politics since the 1930s.

Like Trump's election in the United States, which it preceded by less
than six months, the Brexit vote was an anti-system vote, a vote of rejection of the existing political establishment and the economic policies it had
implemented since the 1980s. The EU referendum created a binary choice for
British voters, a choice between the political establishment and those outside
it. Remain was the status quo position, supported by the Bank of England,
business associations, the trade unions, and every major political party

represented in Parliament, although a significant faction of the Conservative Party campaigned for a Leave vote. In other words, anyone seeking to cast a protest vote had little reason to vote Remain, unless they were convinced by the dire warnings delivered by the Treasury and the Bank of England that leaving would make a bad economy even worse.

Just as Trump's victory mobilized entrenched racial divides in the United States, Brexit reflected a long-standing skepticism about European integration in British society. But at the same time, enthusiasm for Brexit was a minority interest, confined largely to the right wing of the Conservative Party: Europe only became a salient issue for British voters *after* the referendum had been called, and even more so in its aftermath. How did what was a marginal concern for most voters come to dominate the political agenda, making and destroying political careers, and destabilizing the British economy? This chapter will argue that Brexit formed part of a wider anti-system revolt in Britain, which replaced the centrist politics of the 1990s and 2000s with a deeply polarized politics pitting half the country against the other. The Conservative Party lurched to the right to become the party of Brexit, Labour elected the most left-wing leader in its history, and Scotland embraced a party committed to independence from the United Kingdom.

Just as in the United States, the story I tell cuts through the politics of identity and personality to home in on the underlying economic and social fractures driving the anti-system vote. Brexit is the consequence not of Britain's participation in an unpopular European project, but of the political choices made by British governments in recent decades, and the inability of the governing elites to respond to the consequences of these choices. Like the United States, the United Kingdom adopted a markedly neoliberal economic strategy after the 1970s, and again like in the United States, this led to rapid increases in inequality, economic insecurity, and severe industrial decline in many regions. As a pioneer in the liberalization of financial markets, Britain found itself at the epicenter of the Global Financial Crisis of 2008. The incumbent Labour government responded to the crisis by backing full bailouts of the financial sector, before giving way to a Conservative-led administration that imposed harsh austerity measures on a fragile economy. The crisis and subsequent slump left large parts of society exposed to economic threats. The anti-system backlash took diverse forms, inspired by inclusive and egalitarian principles as well as nationalistic and xenophobic impulses, but had in common a rejection of the political establishment and its long-standing economic policy consensus.

The Neoliberal Project in the United Kingdom: Freer Markets, Less Government, and More Inequality

The upheavals in the British political system in recent years, as in the case of the United States, can be traced back to the ways in which the financial collapse of the late 2000s exposed large sections of society to economic distress and uncertainty. It is no surprise that among the rich democracies these two most market-oriented economies have suffered the greatest post-crisis political turbulence. Britain was a pioneer of social policy development in the postwar years, establishing relatively generous state pensions and unemployment benefits as well as publicly funded health and education systems,[1] while strong trade unions secured relatively equal shares of income across the distribution. But poor economic performance in the 1970s provided neoliberals in the Conservative Party with an opportunity to launch a successful assault on the postwar economic model, inspired by the same ideas that fueled the Reagan reforms across the Atlantic.

The Thatcher revolution in the 1980s "rolled back" the British welfare state, marginalized trade unions, and deregulated labor and financial markets, making household living standards more dependent on market forces than in the rest of Europe. As a direct consequence of these reforms, inequality exploded: in the 1970s the Gini coefficient of inequality for the United Kingdom was comparable to Germany, and much lower than in France, but by 1990 it had come close to converging with the United States (see Figure 4.1). The main drivers of this change were increased divergence in wages between higher- and lower-paid workers,[2] cuts to welfare benefits,[3] and less progressive taxation. What is most striking about the UK case is both the extent and the suddenness of the change, most of which occurred in the space of little more than a decade in the 1980s and the early 1990s. Most other European countries showed only moderate changes in the income distribution in the same period.

The dramatic rise of inequality was halted in the 1990s and 2000s, as Thatcher's successors softened the hard edges of the neoliberal project, but the longer-term impact of the Thatcher era was to transform Britain into a market liberal economy along US lines, with lower levels of social protection than other western European countries and a growing tendency for income to be channeled to the highest earners. Even during the period of Labour government after 1997, the top of the distribution performed far better than everyone else: the top 10 percent grew its share of pre-tax income

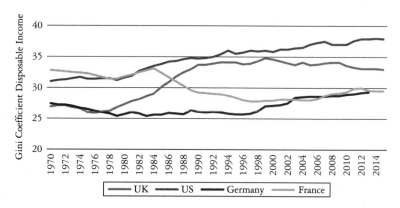

FIGURE 4.1 Post-Tax Inequality, UK, US, Germany, and France, 1970–2015
Source: Frederik Solt, *Standardized World Income Inequality Database* (https://fsolt.org/swiid/).

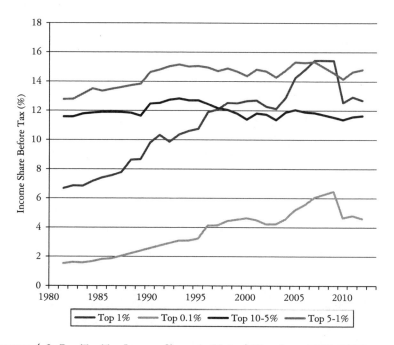

FIGURE 4.2 Pre-Tax Top Income Shares in United Kingdom, 1980–2012
Source: World Wealth and Income Database, http://wid.world/country/united-kingdom/

from 28.4 percent to 42.6 percent in 2007, before dropping back in the wake of the financial crisis. But what is even more striking is that the top one percent, whose share almost trebled to over 15 percent between 1979 and 2007, accounted for most of this change; those just outside the top 5 percent of earners actually saw a decline in their share.[4] Figure 4.2 also shows that the top 0.1 percent—the top thousandth of the distribution—trebled in the same period, reaching over 6 percent.

Market forces increased inequality not only between households but also between regions. Just as income growth was mostly concentrated among the top tenth of earners, economic growth became geographically concentrated in the areas where high value-added industries were located, particularly London, the home of most financial services activity, and larger cities in general. As manufacturing industry declined and financial and business services expanded, a wide gap opened up between London and the South-East and the declining industrial heartlands of Northern England, South Wales, and the West of Scotland. These latter regions were kept afloat through the redistributive effects of public spending, which was highly vulnerable to the brutal fiscal shortfall caused by the financial crisis.

As well as higher inequality, the shift toward a more market-oriented economy also exposed households to greater uncertainty and insecurity. The liberalization of the financial sector fueled a rapid expansion of credit to finance consumption and home loans, leading to a boom and bust cycle as house prices fluctuated sharply. Personal debt skyrocketed, while the state withdrew from supplementary pensions provision, encouraging workers to invest in private pension plans subject to market volatility and predatory management fees. Much of the country's social housing was sold off, encouraging social tenants into private homeownership, where some made big capital gains, while low-income groups without capital were increasingly pushed into the private rental sector with more uncertain tenures. Increased leverage made households more vulnerable to financial instability by encouraging participation in speculative bubbles, especially in housing assets. As the savings rate declined, high ratios of household debt to household income left households increasingly reliant on easy credit conditions.[5]

In short, the pro-market reforms of the 1980s led to greater economic inequality and unpredictability. The economic fortunes of the average Briton became more dependent on market forces, market forces that were less and less easily controlled by government, while the skewed income distribution concentrated a larger share of income growth at the top. Median income did grow consistently during the 1979–2007 period, but after the financial crisis all groups suffered significant income losses, including the top decile: average wages actually fell in real terms between 2007 and 2015.[6] The putative trade-off between inequality and insecurity and higher-income growth may have made some sense before the financial crisis, but in its aftermath inequality and insecurity were all that was left.

Beyond Left and Right: How British Parties Stopped Fighting over Economics

The kind of inequality and insecurity seen in Britain since the 1980s is difficult to sustain in a democracy, since the winners at the top are far outnumbered by those who are left behind by economic growth. Yet while poverty rapidly increased, British governments reduced the tax burden on upper-income groups and restricted spending on popular social policies. What is even more remarkable is that this policy mix remained substantially unaltered even after the Conservatives were defeated in 1997, and the Labour government that replaced them presided over the spectacular rise in top income shares charted in Figure 4.2. This is all the more paradoxical because survey evidence shows that British voters remained extremely attached to redistribution and the welfare state, even as their governments pushed the market liberal agenda. Figure 4.3 reveals that for all the talk of "rolling back the state," support for reducing government spending among British voters

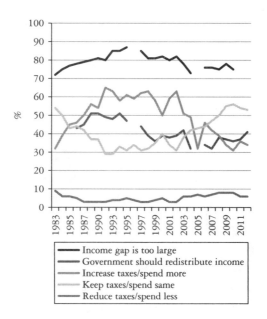

FIGURE 4.3 Attitudes on Income Redistribution, Taxation, and Spending in the UK, 1983–2012 (% Supporting)

Source: Alison Park, Caroline Bryson, Elizabeth Clery, John Curtice, and Miranda Phillips (eds.), *British Social Attitudes: The 30th Report* (London: NatCen Social Research, 2013) (www.bsa-30.natcen.ac.uk).

was vanishingly small throughout this period, while the vast majority felt that income inequality was too high.

The fundamental reason for this entrenching of a market liberal orthodoxy in Britain is that by the 1990s the Labour Party had proved incapable of winning power on a left-wing platform, and concluded that the centrist voters it needed to attract would not tolerate any deviation from a pro-market, low-tax agenda. Labour's problems were tied up with the decline of the traditional class-based battle lines of the British party system, in which Labour won support predominantly from manual workers, especially in industrial regions, while Conservatives enjoyed solid support from middle-class households, especially in rural areas and in southern England.[7] The deindustrialization of the 1980s and 1990s decimated the Labour Party's traditional base, forcing it to seek votes among middle-income voters in the more prosperous parts of the United Kingdom.[8]

Labour's failure to win back power led to an internal shift as pragmatic and centrist forces sought to recover ground by accepting much of the Thatcherite settlement, and working within a broadly pro-market framework. This process reached its height with the election of Tony Blair as party leader in 1994. Blair immediately set about detaching Labour from its traditional roots, rewriting the party constitution to eliminate references to state ownership of the economy, and distancing himself from the party's traditional support base in the trade union movement.[9] As Labour camped out in the center of the political spectrum, the Conservatives under John Major also adopted a more accommodating tone, stepping back from Thatcher's unpopular plans to outsource healthcare and education to private companies. The resulting convergence around a central position of free markets combined with modest welfare provision was described by one author as "Blaijorism."[10]

To secure the votes of "middle England," Blair's Labour promised fiscal restraint and a focus on preventing inflation. In an economy where households had taken on high debt burdens and many voters had variable interest mortgages on their homes, fears of financial instability under a Labour government were central to the Conservatives' electoral message. The Labour response was to commit to strict fiscal rules, and delegate monetary policy to the Bank of England, while loudly applauding the City of London's contribution to the UK economy.[11] Labour's decision to accept and work within the constraints of a highly financialized economy closed off most avenues for fundamental change. Instead, Labour's ambition was to draw on finance-related tax revenues to pay for a limited expansion of the welfare state.

As a result, Labour's victory in the 1997 election brought no dramatic shift in fiscal policy; indeed, if anything, fiscal policy was initially tighter than a Conservative government would have followed. The significance of these policy choices was to effectively end the debate on macroeconomic policy between the major political parties, since the Conservatives found little to object to in either move. Not only was Labour's policy stance perfectly in line with the market liberal orthodoxy of the "Washington Consensus," but it was instrumental in seeking to align other parties of the "center-left" with these positions, notably in the "Third Way" summit held in Florence in 1999, with Bill Clinton and various European leaders in attendance.[12] Moreover, under Blair the United Kingdom continued to champion liberal market reforms in the European Union, and fatefully the Labour government opened the UK labor market to workers from the new 2004 member states with immediate effect. This led to a rapid influx of low-wage labor from Poland and other eastern European countries that would prove a key driver of support for Brexit in 2016.

This does not mean that no differences remained between the parties: the Blair government made considerable efforts to address problems of poverty, increasing public spending on healthcare and education, improving support for working households on low incomes, and raising state pensions. Incomes for households in the bottom half of the income distribution grew more quickly than for those in the top half, excepting the top decile, which outstripped all other groups.[13] This odd pattern of redistribution from the middle to the bottom and the top reflected the awkward coalition between lower-income groups and the financial elite that Labour had constructed. The strategy was a Faustian pact in which the Blair government offered the City of London a "light touch approach [to] financial regulation."[14] In the celebrated words of Labour minister Peter Mandelson, the party became "intensely relaxed about people getting filthy rich, as long as they pay their taxes."[15]

Labour's newfound enthusiasm for open markets and light touch regulation removed one of the main areas of political disagreement in British politics, such that by the 1990s the positions of the major parties on the most important issues of economic and social policy appeared increasingly similar. Figure 4.4 shows that the policy positions of the major parties, after diverging dramatically in the 1970s and 1980s, began to converge in the 1990s. Figure 4.5 shows that this convergence was particularly clear on economic issues, with Labour moving toward a more pro-market position through the 1980s, 1990s, and 2000s, and the Conservatives becoming less hostile to public spending after the departure of Margaret Thatcher. The main challenger to the two big parties, the Liberal Democrats, occupied the increasingly tight space between them. British voters could have any government

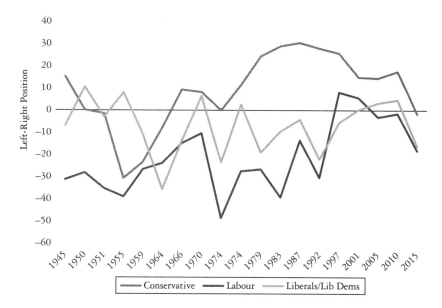

FIGURE 4.4 Party Positions, UK, 1945–2015, Percentage of Right-Wing Statements Minus Percentage of Left-Wing Statements
Source: Andrea Volkens, Werner Krause, Pola Lehmann, Theres Matthieß, Nicolas Merz, Sven Regel, and Bernhard Weßels, *The Manifesto Data Collection: Manifesto Project (MRG / CMP / MARPOR)*, version 2018b (Berlin: Wissenschaftszentrum Berlin für Sozialforschung, 2018) (https://doi.org/10.25522/manifesto. mpds.2018b).

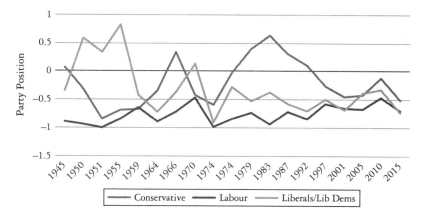

FIGURE 4.5 Party Positions on State/Economy UK, 1945–2015, Percentage of Right-Wing Statements Minus Percentage of Left-Wing Statements
Source: Volkens et al., *The Manifesto Data Collection* (see Figure 4.4).

they liked, as long as it subscribed to the attenuated market liberal positions the major parties were committed to.

This pattern of convergence was aided by Britain's "majoritarian" electoral system, based on single-member districts, which places a premium on parties' ability to win "marginal constituencies" where seats can be won from rival parties. For Labour, this meant that a vote in these districts was far more valuable than in their traditional heartlands, where Conservative support was limited, so the party's strategy was focused disproportionately on the needs of "floating" voters in around 100 constituencies that could be won from the Conservatives. These tended to be small towns and suburbs, particularly in the Midlands and the South of England, which had often done relatively well out of the economic changes of the 1980s. The 1992 election, Labour strategists concluded, had been lost among precisely those voters, and for those reasons;[16] the party therefore needed to eliminate voters' fear of tax rises and excessive spending on welfare, competing with the Conservatives by adopting many of their policies.

As Labour entrenched its grip on power in the 2000s, the Conservatives opted for a similar strategy to attempt to claw back power. David Cameron, elected party leader in 2005, attempted to ditch the party's socially conservative image and committed to matching Labour spending plans, in a fascinating flip-side of the pattern in the 1990s. The Conservatives aligned with the Labour government's macroeconomic positioning and had little reason to object to its enthusiasm for financial market deregulation. The main rival to the two-party cartel, the Liberal Democrats, barely diverged from this consensus themselves, focusing on opposition to Blair's support for American military intervention in Iraq. This lack of ideological diversity among elected politicians was matched by an increasingly narrow social and professional intake. The Labour parliamentary party in particular had fewer members with a working-class or trade union background, and a growing share of London-based, university-educated political professionals, who had served as political advisors before standing for election.[17] In the run-up to the financial crisis, British party politics was easily characterized as a complacent clique.[18]

Not only did voters appear to have little choice at election time, but the parties themselves became increasingly distant from their grassroots. The Labour Party was founded as the political arm of the trade union movement in 1900, and historically relied on the unions for funding and mobilizing the working-class vote. But in the Blair years, the unions were seen as a liability for Labour's image, and the party sought alternative means of funding, often in the form of individual donations from wealthy individuals, which by 2001 constituted 45 percent of its income.[19] Not only did this anchor Labour to a pro-business position but it was also a source of embarrassment, as private donations were sometimes linked to sleazy favors, such as the exemption of the Formula One competition from a ban on tobacco advertising after a million pound donation to Labour from Bernie Ecclestone, CEO of the racing group.[20]

Partisan convergence may have been useful for attracting flows of capital into the United Kingdom, financing consumption and raising asset prices, but it was bad news for democratic legitimacy. The Blairite commitment to neoliberal economics, albeit with a modicum of anti-poverty measures, dramatically reduced the degree of choice on offer in UK general elections. The broad similarity between the parties' economic policy positions meant that elections were no longer very decisive in shaping policy. Voters dissatisfied with economic conditions would be hard pressed to find a way of expressing a preference for change without moving outside the established party system.

Breaking the Cartel: The Threats to the British Two-Party System

The costs of cross-party consensus for the legitimacy of the British system of government were reflected in a dramatic fall in voter participation during the 1990s, with turnout dropping to less than 60 percent in 2001, the lowest on record in the United Kingdom, and one of the lowest in western Europe.[21] Low turnout alone would not necessarily imply any particular democratic malaise, though the drop in voter participation did occur after Labour's shift to centrist positions under Tony Blair. Turnout was lowest among younger voters: less than 40 percent of 18–24-year-olds, and less than half of 25–34-year-olds, voted in the 2001 and 2005 elections.[22] As the party system and conversation between political leaders became less representative of society, voters either dropped out of political participation or looked for different ways of expressing their demands.

Although turnout fell across the United Kingdom, there were significant variations across regions: it was highest in the prosperous South, and lower in the areas furthest from London. The twenty constituencies with lowest turnouts in the 2017 election were all low-income areas, in Scotland or Northern England, which had been Labour strongholds for decades. This was a clear sign that working-class voters were losing enthusiasm for a party that was increasingly rooted in London and less and less representative of their social and cultural traditions.[23] The constituencies with the highest turnout, in contrast, were high-income areas, all of them marginal constituencies, mostly in the South of England, contested between Labour, Conservatives, and the Liberal Democrats.[24] Economic decline combined with political neglect to alienate large swathes of voters in nonmetropolitan Britain. It is hard not to conclude that this rising abstention rate reflected dissatisfaction with the lack of available alternatives, and a feeling of low voter efficacy. Many voters appeared to wonder, "What is the point?"

Figure 4.6 gives a longer-term picture of the structural shifts in voting and nonvoting since World War II (the chart presents shares of the total registered electorate to capture turnout as well as party support). The decline of the two main governing parties, Labour and Conservative, is clearly visible: at their peak in the 1950s, they commanded the votes of 80 percent of the electorate, and well over 90 percent of votes cast. By the early 1990s, the number of voters actively supporting the party of government, or indeed either of the two parties that have provided every prime minister since the war, fell to embarrassingly low levels. In 2005, Tony Blair's Labour Party won a comfortable parliamentary majority with only 35 percent of the vote, on a turnout of little over 60 percent: Labour was able to govern with the active support of less than a fifth of the electorate. Average turnout in local council elections in the United Kingdom was only around 33 percent in 2016, and below 50 percent in local and metropolitan mayoral elections.[25] In European

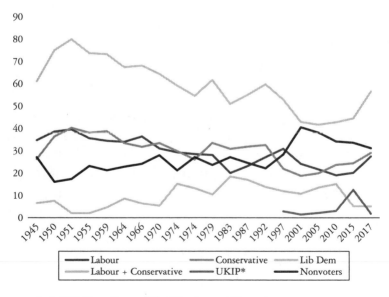

FIGURE 4.6 UK-Vote Shares (% of Registered Voters)

Parliament elections, turnout was also low at 35.4 percent (for 2014), the second lowest in the EU15, after Portugal.[26]

Those voters who did cast a vote were more and more likely to desert Labour and the Conservatives for anti-system parties, as Figure 4.7 shows. In 1997 the Referendum Party, a campaign for a referendum on EU membership bankrolled by James Goldsmith, won 2.6 percent of the vote as the Conservative vote collapsed. The UK Independence Party (UKIP), which advocated withdrawal from the European Union, also contested Westminster elections for the first time in the same year, and saw its vote share climb steadily through the 2000s, before leaping to a spectacular 12 percent in 2015, electing just one MP (a defector from the Conservatives). In European Parliament elections, where proportional representation increased the opportunities for small parties after 1999, it performed even better, growing its vote steadily to finish second in 2009 and first in 2014, with 26 percent of the vote, pushing the governing Conservatives into third place.

The Green Party also made steady gains, winning representation in the European Parliament and in the devolved assemblies in Wales, Scotland, and London, and finally a parliamentary seat (Brighton, a south coast city with two universities within easy reach of London). Respect, a party founded by renegade Labour MP George Galloway and drawing on support from leftist fringe group the Socialist Workers' Party, mobilized in mainly Muslim areas around opposition to the Iraq War, twice winning election to Parliament, in 2005 and 2012. The far-right British National Party (BNP) picked up almost 2 percent of the vote in 2010, focusing on low-income white voters in declining industrial towns, especially those with some presence of migrants

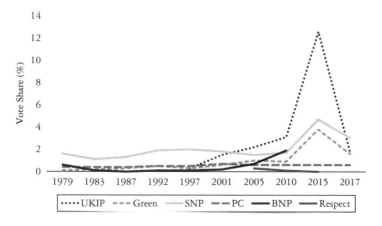

FIGURE 4.7 Anti-System Party Support, 1979–2017

from Muslim countries. Even more unusually, a family doctor managed to be elected MP for the constituency of Wyre Forest in 2001 on a single-issue campaign to save a local hospital from closure (he was re-elected in 2005).

These successes for minor parties marked a departure in British politics, which had no tradition of independent candidates in the postwar period. These parties articulated political identities and ideas that were effectively locked out of the system by the ruling duopoly. The Conservatives and Labour were both committed to continued membership in the European Union, supported the contentious Iraq War, and shared a basic belief in the virtues of the market system mitigated by an adequate welfare state. They supported trade openness and free-flowing global capital, enthusiastically lobbied for the City of London, and encouraged foreign investors to buy up British assets, including in key strategic sectors, and even to run public services. There were important differences of emphasis and over preferred beneficiaries of social policy, but neither contested the basic features of the post-1979 growth model of the United Kingdom.

The challenger parties, in contrast, all contested aspects of this consensus. This was most evident on the Far Right. The BNP was an exemplar of far-right racist nationalism, with strong authoritarian tendencies and a heavy focus on immigration and other purported threats to British identity.[27] UKIP shared some of these characteristics, but lacked the BNP's appeal to violent youth, representing instead authoritarian social values and opposition to immigration, and of course exiting from the European Union.[28] The market liberal consensus, in particular its focus on frictionless trade and free movement of labor, was unambiguously rejected by these parties, which attacked the governing parties as a closed elite of established politicians, contemptuous of popular opinion.[29] Right-wing anti-system forces grew from around 2–3 percent of the vote in the late 1990s to 13 percent in 2015.

The anti-system Left in Britain rejected market liberalism and advocated greater state involvement in the economy and the protection or expansion of the welfare state. Initially this achieved only limited support. The Respect Party represented left-wing positions on economic issues, but its main focus was campaigning against Western foreign policy, notably in the Middle East.[30] By the 2000s the Greens had moved beyond their environmentalist origins and also adopted a strong anti-war and anti-capitalist message,[31] typical of left-libertarian parties. As on the anti-system Right, pejorative references to the "Westminster parties"[32] and similar anti-establishment rhetoric[33] were a central part of the discourse on the anti-system Left.

Even though the foundations of the two-party system were steadily eroding, Labour and Conservative parties continued to form governments with parliamentary majorities, leaning on the distortions of the electoral system. But as economic conditions turned toxic after 2007, their lack of popular backing placed the system under unsustainable pressure. With impeccable timing, Tony Blair resigned in spring 2007, handing the baton to his deputy, Gordon Brown, after a prolonged dispute over the leadership. Brown therefore had the misfortune of taking over just as Britain's bloated financial sector, which had sustained economic growth during Blair's period in office, began to collapse. Gordon Brown had barely moved the furniture into Number 10 Downing Street when reports came in of anxious savers queuing outside branches of Northern Rock, a bank based in the North-East of England: the first bank run in the United Kingdom since the nineteenth century.

Gordon Brown Saves the World . . . Well, Just the Banks: The United Kingdom and the Global Financial Crisis

The financial crisis in the United Kingdom followed similar dynamics as those in the United States—unsurprisingly, given the tight connections between financial markets in the two countries. Although most accounts identify the US subprime mortgage markets as the key trigger of the global crisis, Northern Rock was an early victim when debt markets ran into trouble in 2007. The bank had expanded rapidly into the mortgage market by offering loans to customers without down payments, operating on thin capital buffers, and dependent on short-term financing. The government quickly acted to stem contagion by first extending liquidity support, then guaranteeing all deposits, and finally nationalizing the bank in early 2008. This established a pattern repeated throughout the financial crisis of attempts to find a market-based solution, with the help of emergency central bank liquidity, then adopting government guarantees to shield institutions from the consequences of their exposure, and finally surrendering to the need for overt government rescues of struggling banks.

For several months it appeared that Northern Rock could be dealt with as an isolated problem, and Labour attempted to maintain its broad lax approach to financial regulation, resisting a full government takeover until it became unavoidable.[34] But as the American financial markets began to collapse in late summer 2007, other institutions were dragged into the front line. After the Lehman Brothers' bankruptcy, fears about the solvency of financial institutions spread worldwide, seizing up London's interbank markets and drying up liquidity for its institutions. The most troubled banks, the Royal Bank of Scotland (RBS) and Halifax-Bank of Scotland (HBOS), along with the smaller Bradford and Bingley, all of which were heavily reliant on wholesale funding, failed and had to be bailed out and mostly nationalized, with the government guaranteeing their liabilities and taking majority stakes, while the Bank of England provided easy access to liquidity.[35]

The UK Parliament was in midterm when the crisis hit, so the incumbent Labour government, which still had a majority in Parliament, had the opportunity to develop its own policy response to kick-start the economy and cushion households from the effects of the recession that would inevitably follow. In line with the incoming Obama administration and most governments in Europe, the United Kingdom adopted a stimulus package worth around 1.5 percent of GDP to buoy domestic demand as consumers retreated to contemplate their tattered balance sheets.[36] But the sheer magnitude of the crisis quickly translated into a collapse in tax revenues and a spike in government borrowing, with the deficit reaching 10.3 percent of GDP by 2010.[37] Even this level of deficit spending could not cushion the economy from a significant GDP contraction of 6.3 percent, declining real wages (as the pound depreciated), and falls in house prices.[38]

The amounts of money involved in bailing out the banks were mind-boggling to an electorate accustomed to politicians arguing over the cost of small changes to health or education spending: saving Northern Rock alone involved government loans and guarantees of upward of £55 billion,[39] a figure equivalent to around half the government's annual spending on healthcare. The total cost of Britain's intervention in the financial system was eye-watering: the United Kingdom spent 26.8 percent of GDP on assistance to banks between 2007 and 2011.[40] The Bank of England itself described the bailouts as "the largest UK government intervention in financial markets since the outbreak of the First World War."[41] Meanwhile, even with government stimulus measures, households were facing real hardship, with frozen or falling wages, collapsing asset values (especially house prices), and in some cases job losses. In this context, Prime Minister Gordon Brown's skilled management of the crisis won little praise outside elite circles: he was widely derided for a slip of the tongue during a parliamentary debate, where he boasted "not only did we save the world" before correcting himself to the embarrassing "we saved the banks."[42]

The opposition Conservatives were quick to exploit popular outrage, dropping their previous commitments to match Labour's spending plans and abandoning their initial bipartisan approach to dealing with the banking crisis. Seeing an opportunity to skewer Labour for the downturn and exploit the explosion of national debt to roll back welfare spending, David Cameron began to blame the crash on Labour's "profligate" behavior in government. Familiar tropes of austerity made their appearance, with the Conservatives accusing Labour of "failing to fix the roof while the sun was shining," " 'maxing out' the national credit card," and insisting on a period of "belt-tightening" to "balance the books."[43] This was successful in defeating Labour in the 2010 election, but the Conservatives fell short of a majority and had to form a coalition government with the Liberal Democrats.

Labour's defeat marked a significant shift in policy, with the Cameron government committing to a stringent program of austerity in an optimistic attempt to eliminate the United Kingdom's structural budget deficit in five years. This plan fell in line with the abrupt end to Keynesian responses to the crisis in Europe and the United States around the same time, dismissing concerns by most economists that contractionary fiscal policy would depress demand at a time when heavily indebted British households were busily deleveraging their stretched balance sheets.[44] Not only did this mean an end to any attempt to use fiscal stimulus to promote growth, it also shifted the burden of adjustment very heavily onto recipients of government spending. Unlike other European countries that balanced deficit reduction between tax increases and spending cuts, the British austerity plan prioritized cuts to welfare and discretionary government spending.[45]

Predictably, this change of government failed to offer much relief to hard-pressed British voters. Although employment recovered to a degree that surprised most economists, growth and wages stagnated, leading to a relaxation of the pace of fiscal tightening in 2012 and an abandonment of the initial five-year deficit reduction plan. Productivity growth after the crisis dropped to zero, and domestic demand was constrained by the attempts of both households and the government sector to deleverage at the same time. Wages were frozen, by deliberate government policy, in the public sector, but also barely grew in the private sector. Uniquely among the advanced democracies, in the United Kingdom experienced declining wages even though the economy expanded between 2007 and 2015:[46] wages fell by more than in any OECD country except Greece (see Figure 4.8). This was facilitated by the United Kingdom's flexible labor market rules and the depreciation of the pound, which meant that nominal wage stagnation meant real wage cuts. Ominously, this wage stagnation coincided with a sharp rise in migration from the troubled countries of southern and eastern Europe.

Not only was the United Kingdom's overall economic performance comparatively poor in the post-crisis period, but the pain was also far from evenly

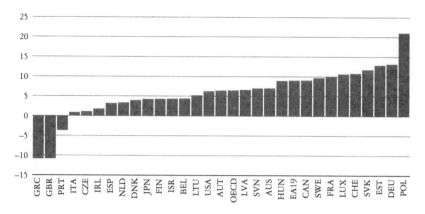

FIGURE 4.8 Cumulative Real Wage Growth, 2007–2015 (%)
Source: OECD, "Employment Outlook 2016" (https://www.oecd-ilibrary.org/employment/oecd-employment-outlook-2016_empl_outlook-2016-en).

distributed. Britain's growth model already generated high levels of inequality before the crisis, with economic growth concentrated in a handful of sectors located predominantly in the South-East of England, where house price and income growth outstripped the rest of the country. As the economy began to recover from the crash, the same imbalances were reproduced. The South-East quickly recovered, and by 2016 London was producing almost double the UK average Gross Value Added (GVA) per capita, while all UK regions apart from London, the South-East, and the West had lower GVA than their pre-crisis peak.[47] Although the United Kingdom's aggregate economic performance was poor, the lived experience of most parts of the country was even worse.

It is therefore unsurprising that the United Kingdom entered a period of political turbulence in the mid-2010s. The government that presided over the financial crisis had been dismissed, but its successor proved unable to generate a strong recovery, instead subjecting the households to harsh austerity in a failed attempt to eliminate the government deficit within one legislature. However the form the turbulence took was less predictable, and indeed more or less completely unexpected. After a long period of relative quiescence, in which dissatisfaction with the party system had been expressed largely through passive abstentionism rather than activism, political elites were taken aback by the scale of the rejection of the status quo. It is an indication of the degree of disconnect between voters and establishment politicians that this outcome should have come as a surprise.

I'm a Voter, Get Me Out of Here: How Britain Turned against Its Political System, Even before Brexit

Labour's predictable electoral defeat in 2010 was a spectacular one: the party lost around a million votes and ninety-one seats, polling just 29 percent of the vote, its second lowest share since World War II. But the unpopularity of the major parties was reflected in the Conservatives' failure to win outright, even after thirteen years in opposition. In contrast, the centrist Liberal Democrats won their highest-ever vote share, dominating the election campaign to such an extent that both Cameron and Brown fell over themselves to "agree with Nick" (Nick Clegg, the Liberal Democrat leader) during a televised debate.[48] The decline of the two main parties was reflected in a joint vote share of only 65 percent, the lowest since 1910. Turnout was just 65.1 percent, the third lowest in the history of universal suffrage in the United Kingdom. This collapse of the two-party system meant that Britain faced a coalition government for the first time since World War II.

The success of the Liberal Democrats did not, however, usher in a new centrist politics in the United Kingdom. In the 2015 election the Liberal Democrats paid a price for their involvement in the coalition, losing two-thirds of their vote share. The big winners from this shift were not the established parties, but antisystem forces such as UKIP and the Greens, which quadrupled their vote to 12.6 and 3.9 percent, respectively, and the SNP, which almost tripled its share (taking 50 percent in Scotland, and winning all but three MPs there). The losses suffered by the Liberal Democrats were the deepest of any party in postwar Britain, while the UKIP's rise was the second largest in the same period. The year 2015 saw the largest net change in the vote of any election since 1931, while the election held just two years later in 2017 produced the second-highest volatility score for the same period. Not only were elections increasingly unpredictable, they were also producing fundamental changes in political alignments and shifting power toward anti-system forces.

As the established political parties lost their grip on power, British politics took a plebiscitary turn. Before 2010 there had been only one UK-wide referendum—the vote to confirm Britain's membership in the then European Economic Community in 1975—and a handful of referendums over devolution reforms in Scotland, Wales, and Northern Ireland. In 2011 a UK-wide referendum was held over electoral reform, and in 2014 a referendum over independence, negotiated between the Scottish Executive and the Cameron government, was held in Scotland. The Scottish referendum may not have brought the breakup of the United Kingdom, but it indirectly set off a chain of events that led to the rapid polarization of British politics and the vote to leave the European Union. Scotland had been a bastion of the Labour Party for decades, but Labour had steadily lost ground in devolved elections to the Scottish Parliament,[49] and in 2011 the SNP won control of the Scottish government. The SNP's appeal combined a "civic" form of nationalism with promises of generous public spending and progressive values on social issues, outbidding Labour on its left.

The Scottish referendum may have produced a clear win for the Unionist position of remaining within the United Kingdom, but the pro-independence campaign mobilized large numbers of especially younger voters, leading to a rapid narrowing of the expected pro-Union advantage.[50] The coalescing of anti-system sentiment around the pro-independence position fed on itself, as it forced the Westminster establishment parties to set aside partisan advantage and form a united front in favor of the Union. Some 1,617,989 Scottish voters supported independence (44.7 percent of a historically high turnout of 84.6 percent), especially younger voters, and voters in low-income areas in particular, including a high proportion of Labour voters who defied the party's pro-Union position.[51] Labour was placed in the awkward position of campaigning on the message that Scotland and the United Kingdom were "better together," alongside a Conservative government that was deeply unpopular north of the border.

The political cost of keeping Scotland within the United Kingdom fell heavily on Labour. The SNP quadrupled its membership in the year following the referendum and was able to run an energetic campaign in the general election of 2015, winning half of the vote in Scotland.[52] Due to the workings of Britain's First-Past-the-Post electoral system, this vote share converted into the SNP winning fifty-six out of the fifty-nine Scottish electoral districts, effectively wiping out not just Labour, which lost all but one of its Scottish MPs, but also the Liberal Democrats, who lost ten of their eleven seats. The SNP produced the unusual result that, for the first time, a different party had won in each of the United Kingdom's constituent nations: the Conservatives in England, Labour in Wales, the SNP in Scotland, and the Democratic Unionists in Northern Ireland. This political fragmentation was compounded by the success of UKIP, which won almost four million votes (mainly in England) but just one parliamentary seat; the Greens, who won more than a million votes, held onto their one MP.

The quirks of the electoral system delivered a very slim parliamentary majority for the Conservatives, despite their winning little more than a third of the vote across the United Kingdom. Labour's collapse in Scotland destroyed any hope of its winning power, and brought the resignation of its leader, Ed Miliband, leading to a sharp shift in the party's leadership and direction toward an anti-austerity stance. Under the new rules established in 2014, the new leader would be elected by a free vote among all party members, with candidates requiring the support of at least 15 percent of Labour MPs.[53] This reform, aimed at enhancing membership influence over the leadership and reducing the weight of party office-holders, led to the election of long-standing left-wing dissident Jeremy Corbyn. This outcome had previously appeared so unlikely that some Labour MPs lent Corbyn their nominations simply to allow him into the contest, despite not supporting his campaign.[54] There could be no clearer indication of the stark disconnect between the party leadership and the party members that Corbyn's victory appeared so unthinkable. In the event, Corbyn not only won, but won comfortably, with a large majority of almost 60 percent of the vote, in a four-way contest.

In case there were any doubts that this represented a clear rejection of Labour's incumbent leadership, Corbyn's rhetoric during the campaign was witheringly critical of the largely pro-market, centrist strategy that Labour had followed during the Blair-Brown years, and of the inability of the party membership to influence policy. Corbyn stood on a "clear anti-austerity platform," promising "to give Labour Party members a voice in this debate."[55] The main themes of Corbyn's discourse were unambiguous opposition to the Conservative government's program of cuts to welfare benefits and public services, rejection of recent British foreign policy, especially in the Middle East, and a change in economic policy to promote state-led investment through monetary expansion, described as "people's quantitative easing," and more progressive taxation.[56] He also advocated renationalization of privatized utilities such as the railways, the abolition of university student tuition fees, and a substantial rise in the minimum wage. Although Ed Miliband had pushed for a more left-oriented stance in his five years as leader, he was reluctant to push Labour all the way to a fiscally expansionary position, instead adopting a cautious commitment to reducing the deficit through "sensible reductions in public spending."[57] Corbyn cut through all that and promised "an end to austerity."

By late 2015, Britain was in the sixth year of a program of fiscal retrenchment that was originally scheduled to clear its budget deficit one year before. Yet at the end of the 2014–2015 financial year, the government was still borrowing 5 percent of GDP, or £92 billion, while total public debt had hit 87.5 percent of GDP, more than double the level prior to the financial crisis.[58]

Painful spending cuts, especially for local governments, and drastic measures to curb welfare spending had caused severe hardship for wide sectors of British society. Among the measures introduced were cuts to housing benefits for tenants living in properties with spare rooms (the so-called "bedroom tax"), a household-level cap on benefits that affected families with large numbers of dependents, cuts to council tax allowances for low-income families, more restrictive tests to qualify for disability allowances, cuts to tax credit entitlements, and the freezing of child benefits, as well as the exclusion of higher-rate taxpayers from child benefits. All told, it was estimated that these measures amounted to cuts of £19 billion per year, or around £470 for each working age adult in the United Kingdom.[59]

This squeeze was accompanied by increases in taxation, which reduced disposable income, especially for the top 10 percent of households. The impact of austerity was quite selective, and targeted in such a way as to protect key support bases of the Conservative Party, notably the retired, who were exempted from most of the welfare cuts, and whose state pensions were not only protected from inflation but also indexed in line with wage increases or 2.5 percent, whichever was highest (the so-called triple lock). The working-age population bore the brunt of austerity, and the cuts to welfare were compounded by the collapse in wage growth: in 2016, UK workers were still on average paid less in real terms than before the financial crisis, leaving them around 20 percent worse off than if wages had maintained their pre-crisis growth pattern.[60] It was this austerity-fatigued society that was to be asked, in June 2016, whether it wished to remain in the European Union.

It's Not Europe, Stupid: How the European Union Took the Blame for British Austerity

By 2016, the British public was heartily sick of its political class and the grim economic situation that had existed since the financial crisis. Even so, most observers expected that voters would follow the recommendation of the prime minister, most of the Cabinet and the ruling Conservative Party, all the other political parties represented in Parliament except UKIP (one seat) and the Democratic Unionists in Northern Ireland (eight seats), the trade unions, business groups, the Bank of England, and the major international economic institutions such as the IMF and the OECD. But the "establishment" was not only weaker, but also more divided than it might have appeared. Over one hundred Conservative MPs joined the Leave campaign,[61] and the bulk of the right-wing media, including Rupert Murdoch's *Sun*, the best-selling tabloid newspaper, were vociferous advocates of Brexit. Moreover, the various Leave campaigns were not short of money or marketing expertise, enjoying substantial financial backing (in part of dubious provenance) and skillfully deploying targeted social media messaging.[62]

The result of the Brexit referendum took British politics by surprise in part because it appeared to make little logical sense. Economic forecasts, with barely any exception, pointed to serious economic costs if the United Kingdom voted to leave. Moreover, Brexit was predicted to be most damaging to the regions that voted for it—the agricultural East and postindustrial North and Midlands of England—because they were the most exposed to the costs of reduced access to the European single market,[63] and they were the most dependent on EU structural funds.[64] Much of the campaign focused on the alleged costs of EU migration to local communities and public services, yet the areas that voted most strongly to leave were those with the lowest levels of migration,[65] while studies showed clearly that migrants are net contributors to government finances, and provided essential staff for public sector organizations such as the National Health Service rather than burdening it.[66] In sum, one could be forgiven for concluding that British society had simply lost its mind and voted for its own demise.

This would be to take the Leave vote too literally. The evidence points toward the EU referendum acting as a lightning rod for a range of social tensions in post-crisis Britain, many of which had little to do with the European Union itself, whose workings have long been poorly understood by the British public. The United Kingdom was certainly one of the member states where support for the European Union had been historically lowest, and British voters were mostly unsympathetic to the European project. But EU membership was a low salience issue, and only a minority of voters held firm opinions on European integration.[67] While nationalist sentiment was clearly present in the Leave vote, with Leave voters identifying most strongly with British, and especially English, nationalism,[68] this sentiment had to be mobilized and connected to the question of EU membership to produce the Leave vote. The ways in which this was achieved drew heavily on the drivers of anti-system politics that we have observed across the rich democracies.

Although there was a small faction of left-wing advocates of Brexit—so-called "Lexit"—and one major Labour donor (John Mills) was involved in funding the campaign, the Leave message was pitched at the electorate most receptive to right-wing anti-system parties in other countries: older, less-educated voters in declining regions. The slogan of the official Leave campaign headed by former mayor of London Boris Johnson was "Take Back

Control," which appealed to voters disoriented by the apparent inability of governments to manage social and economic changes. To this extent Brexit can be seen as part of the broad family of anti-system right-wing politics, combining Euroskepticism, anti-globalism, and hostility to immigration and the cultural change it implies. Immigration was a key theme of the unofficial Leave campaign, Leave.EU, headed by UKIP leader Nigel Farage. Most notoriously, Farage launched a poster campaign depicting a "caravan" of thousands of refugees with the slogan "Breaking Point," and also suggested that Turkey's application to join the European Union could lead to millions of Muslim migrants to the United Kingdom.[69]

So did anxiety about immigration cause Brexit? Certainly numerous surveys showed that immigration was high on the list of voter concerns in the years preceding the referendum, and immigration control and the impact of immigration on public provision of healthcare and welfare benefits were key reasons for voter concern about EU membership.[70] Survey data showed that Leave voters were far more likely than Remain voters (47 percent compared with 16 percent) to consider immigration the top priority for government action, and immigration was the top issue in the referendum decision for 20 percent of voters.[71] Goodwin and Milazzo found that changes in migration were correlated with the Brexit vote at the local level, with rapid increases in the migration population a better predictor of Leave voting than overall levels of migration.[72] Alongside the growing support for the anti-migrant Far Right in Europe, the Brexit vote appeared to fit in with a broad pattern of mass migration and rapid cultural change fueling anti-system voting.[73]

Any political project attracting the support of over half the electorate will contain voters with diverse characteristics, and undoubtedly some proportion of Leave voters were motivated by a broad cultural anxiety that mixed hostility or fear of immigration with a feeling that European Union membership undermined British identity and sovereignty. For example, it has been pointed out that the lion's share of support for Leave came from socially conservative voters in prosperous rural and suburban parts of England who were—or at least felt—relatively unaffected by economic problems.[74] Much like Republican identifiers in the United States who supported Trump out of partisan commitment, these voters could have been expected to support Brexit even if the vote had been held in a context of economic optimism. Rather than economic distress, many of these voters were animated by their rejection of high levels of inward migration, which reached a net figure of over 200,000 at the height of the Euro crisis as unemployed workers from the Eurozone periphery sought work in the United Kingdom's open and flexible labor market.

But the actual patterns of migration, and the available evidence on their impact, suggests that migration was not a sufficient, and maybe not even a necessary, condition for the victory of the Leave campaign. First of all, migrants gravitate to the areas where a growing economy generates the best employment opportunities, which were also the places where voters were least likely to support Brexit. In the central boroughs of London, the most ethnically diverse area in the whole of the United Kingdom and a magnet for migrant workers, support for remaining in the European Union approached 80 percent. In strongly Brexit-voting areas such as the North-East of England and the West Midlands, the former mining communities in South Wales and Yorkshire, or the agricultural heartlands of East Anglia, the migrant share of the population was a fraction of that in the large cities or university towns where the Remain vote won. Leave voters may have cited immigration preferences more than economic preferences in survey research,[75] but the Leave vote was higher in areas with lower immigration.

The referendum result makes a lot more sense if we observe the objective economic characteristics associated with the Leave vote. The Leave vote prospered most among low-income and less-educated voters. Of voters with no more than secondary education, 78 percent voted Leave, as opposed to just 26 percent of university graduates; and 66 percent of those with monthly earnings below £1200 voted Leave, compared with 38 percent of those earning over £3800.[76] Age, which is strongly correlated with education and partly with income, was also a strong predictor of Leave voting, with 61 percent of over-65s supporting Brexit, compared with just 40 percent among the under-30s.[77] Older, less-educated, and lower-income voters had the highest propensity to support Brexit, and were also the groups most likely to hold socially authoritarian and nationalistic attitudes: an anti-migrant appeal was always likely to appeal to these voters, not because they were particularly exposed to migration, but rather because they were hostile to migration in principle, a pattern we observe across the rich democracies.

The Brexit vote was able to leverage anti-immigrant sentiment into an anti-establishment vote with the help of the very real economic distress that these voters had faced ever since the financial crisis. Leave voters perceived significantly more threats to their future standard of living than Remain voters, and were far more likely to take the view that life in Britain was worse than in the past.[78] The most Brexit-supporting demographic types were concentrated in economically declining "left behind" areas, which were those most exposed to economic threat. One indicator of this was the price of real estate: Ben Ansell of Oxford University has shown that the level of house prices was a powerful predictor of the level of support for remaining in the

European Union, not only at the regional level, but also down to the level of local council wards (the smallest administrative unit, usually containing just a few thousand voters).[79] House prices reflect the attractiveness of an area and the number of people seeking to live there, and is therefore an appropriate proxy not only for economic opportunity, but also for the kind of demographic pressure associated with immigration. The richer and more popular an area, the more likely it was that its residents voted to stay in the European Union.

Voters in Leave areas may have expressed grievances about immigration, but they were not in fact particularly affected by it. In any case, the available evidence suggests very strongly that migration has been broadly of benefit to the United Kingdom: not only were migrants, and especially migrants from the European Union, net fiscal contributors, actually alleviating pressure on UK public services, but there was no strong evidence of downward pressure on wages or increased native unemployment resulting from EU immigration.[80] The United Kingdom did not have a higher share of foreign-born than other comparable countries, nor did immigration increase more than in similar countries, and in any case most of the United Kingdom's increase was down to non-EU, rather than EU, immigration.[81] Further, the United Kingdom had the highest share of highly skilled migrants of any comparable country. Yet there was a consistently higher level of concern in the United Kingdom about migration than elsewhere in Europe. The UK government responded to public concern by commissioning a committee of experts (the Migration Advisory Committee [MAC], chaired by the London School of Economics Professor Alan Manning) to assess the impact of immigration, but the only clearly negative effect it found was an increase in house prices.[82] And as we have seen, this affected Remain-voting areas more than Leave-voting areas.

The Leave vote is therefore best understood as a protest vote, not against unbearable pressure from immigration, but from the precise opposite: economic, and demographic, decline. The neoliberal reform agenda followed by British governments since the 1980s had the effect of increasing inequality not only between different occupational groups, but also between different areas and regions. The destruction of manufacturing industry in the United Kingdom, which began under Thatcher in the early 1980s and accelerated under Tony Blair's government in the 1990s and 2000s, left vast swathes of the United Kingdom with little productive infrastructure, reliant on government transfers for support. These "left behind" areas declined further as younger, more educated citizens left to build careers elsewhere, leaving a population of older, less–educated, and generally poorer voters who were disproportionately inclined to vote to leave the European Union. Figure 4.9 presents some basic patterns of voter types in the EU referendum, and provides a clear picture of a Leave vote driven by economic neglect.

Figure 4.9 shows that age was a strong predictor of voting Leave in the referendum, probably because many older voters fondly remember Britain

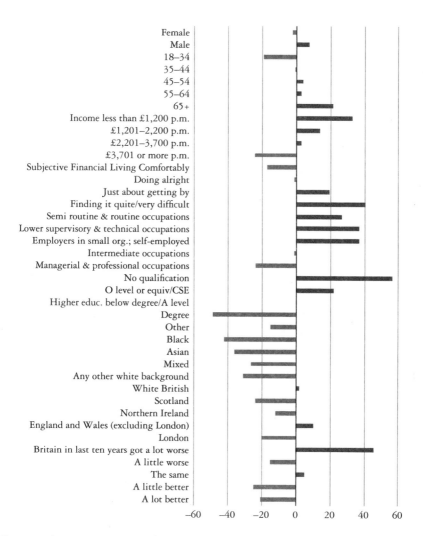

FIGURE 4.9 Determinants of Leave/Remain Vote
Note: A positive value denotes more Leave voters than Remain voters displaying the relevant characteristic/attitude.
Source: Data from Kirby Swales, *Understanding the Leave Vote* (London: NatCen Social Research, 2016), data annex (http://natcen.ac.uk/media/1319221/understanding-the-leave-vote-formatted-table-annex-final.xlsx).

as it was before it joined the European Economic Community, and because discomfort with immigration tends to be higher among older voters, but also because there were more of these voters in economically declining areas. Similarly, voters of white British ethnicity (who themselves are more likely to be older) were also more likely to vote Leave, as were those living in England and Wales, but outside London, rather than in Scotland and Northern Ireland. But Figure 4.9 also presents a clear pattern of economic disadvantage and pessimism present in the Leave vote. The lower the income, the lower the subjective financial well-being, and the more pessimistic the view of the way Britain had changed in the preceding decade, the higher the support for Leave. Moreover, this mapped onto the kinds of individual-level characteristics that we know are good predictors of economic disadvantage: the higher the level of qualifications, the more likely a voter was to have voted to remain in the European Union, with Remain winning 74–26 among university graduates, and Leave enjoying an even bigger advantage (78–22) among voters with only secondary education. This is reflected in the strong support for Remain in London, where average incomes and levels of education are highest, and the victory of Leave in every other region of England and Wales.

If Brexit was all about immigration, then we are left with the puzzle of explaining why voters most affected by immigration were least moved to leave the European Union. Subjective concern about immigration may predict the Leave vote, but objective factors point instead to Brexit responding to the ways in which the United Kingdom's deep economic crisis affected different groups, and different areas, to differing degrees. Statistical analyses of the vote have shown that support for Leave is regionally strongly associated with the impact of foreign trade on manufacturing industries,[83] and with the impact of government austerity measures.[84] Economic change was mostly likely to be detrimental to lower-skilled workers in these regions, and welfare cuts were most likely to hit voters with lower incomes. The data shows that these regions, and these types of voters, produced the strongest support for Leave.[85]

Although Britain's economy did recover more quickly from the financial crisis than some European countries, this recovery was not felt in all parts of the country: the South Yorkshire region suffered an economic contraction similar to Greece.[86] Stern warnings from the Bank of England that Brexit could damage the economy had little credibility among voters reeling from years of recession. The political scientist Anand Menon discovered this at a public debate in Newcastle, in the North-East of England, during the referendum campaign, when his suggestion that the United Kingdom could face a decline in GDP after Brexit met the response, "That's your bloody GDP, not ours!"[87] Many voters had lost trust in economists and civil servants after their failure to anticipate the financial crisis or indeed the depth of the subsequent recession, a distrust skillfully exploited by the Leave campaigner Michael Gove, who famously claimed that "people have had enough of experts."[88]

The Leave campaign successfully connected austerity fatigue with immigration and the United Kingdom's financial contributions to the European Union to mobilize these lower-income voters in hard-up regions. Although the strain on Britain's public services was the direct consequence of the financial crisis and the Conservative Party's insistence on closing the deficit through cuts to government spending, the Leave campaign deflected the blame onto migrants and the European Union, claiming that the health service was a victim of "health tourism" and that Brexit would free up £350 million per week to spend on the NHS. The real impact of health tourism was trivial,[89] and the £350 million figure swiftly debunked, but both claims were politically effective. In the post-crisis context of stagnation or decline in living standards and severe constraints on public spending, this illusory "Brexit dividend" was a powerful appeal. The counterargument from the Remain side, notably from the Treasury and the Bank of England, failed to hit home. The policy "establishment," and the party elites that had provided it with political cover, were no longer able to hold together a failing economic model.

The Aftermath: Brexiting Is Hard to Do

Brexit is unusual in the panorama of anti-system politics in that the referendum vote mandated a clear course of action on a visibly binary matter: membership in the European Union. While Trump could finesse his building of the border wall, the ban on Muslims, or his vague commitments to bring jobs back to America, the vote to leave the European Union presented an inescapable instruction to formally exit from a set of institutions, rules, and contractual commitments that were deeply embedded in the everyday life of the United Kingdom's government, economy, and society. The complexity and risk involved in such an operation may well have been the cause of the shocked expression on the faces of key Leave campaigners such as Boris Johnson on the morning after the vote, when it dawned on them that their victory brought with it a responsibility to unravel over forty years of political, economic, and legal development.[90]

The immediate consequence of the referendum result was the resignation of David Cameron, followed by a leadership election in the Conservative Party to choose a new prime minister. The leadership campaign pitted Brexiters against Remainers, and although all the candidates publicly committed to respecting the mandate to leave the European Union, the pathway for leaving and the extent to which Britain would maintain strong ties with the continent were up for grabs. Theresa May's victory in the contest came despite her having campaigned for Remain in the referendum; however, her credentials as a hardliner on migration stood her in good stead to stand as a compromise candidate to maintain party unity, particularly in the absence of a high-profile Brexiter candidate.

May's political strategy was slow to take shape: her repetition of the meaningless slogan "Brexit means Brexit, and we are going to make a success of it" was a gift to satirists. However, her first conference speech as party leader hinted at a recognition of the limits to Britain's neoliberal growth model and the need to build a more cohesive society, insulated from the pressures of globalization. She described the Brexit vote as a "quiet revolution," resulting from the "division and unfairness . . . between a more prosperous older generation and a struggling younger generation. Between the wealth of London and the rest of the country. But perhaps most of all, between the rich, the successful and the powerful and their fellow citizens."[91] Her promised response to these injustices involved not only Brexit, but also government action to promote strategic British industries, invest in regional development, regulate markets to protect the most vulnerable, and even secure worker representation on company boards.

Media attention around the speech focused on May's provocative claim that the cosmopolitan idea of being a "citizen of the world" actually meant being a "citizen of nowhere," which chimed with her reputation as a closed-border nationalist. But what was extraordinary about May's speech was its recanting of decades of free-market thinking in the Conservative Party, dating back to the mid-1970s. This shift owed much to her close advisor Nick Timothy, a steelworker's son from the Midlands with a suspicion of globalization and a determination to win over the working class to Conservatism.[92] Shortly afterward, May laid out her approach to Brexit, which clearly ruled out full membership in the Single Market and EU Customs Union by drawing two "red lines": that Britain should be free of the jurisdiction of the European Court of Justice, and should no longer be subject to the principle of "freedom of movement," which outlawed restrictions on migration from EU countries.[93] This strategy appeared designed to placate the hard Brexiters within the Conservative Party, at the expense of alienating centrists and much of the business community.

Having laid down her markers, May sent the European Union a formal letter notifying it of Britain's intention to leave, and set off a process that, according to Article 50 of the European Union Treaties, would conclude with "Brexit" two years later. She then called an early election in the hope of extending the Conservatives' thin majority, and winning valuable room for parliamentary maneuver. Opinion polls put the Conservatives way ahead of the Labour Party, which was still recovering from post-referendum internal strife, and whose leader, Jeremy Corbyn, was considered an electoral liability. The 2017 election, far from delivering May a comfortable majority, instead left the Conservatives with thirteen fewer seats than before, and reliant on the Democratic Unionist Party from Northern Ireland in the House of Commons. The 2017 election confirmed British voters' capacity to surprise their political leaders. Although the election result was a disaster for Theresa May, she did actually increase the Conservatives' vote share by over two million votes, the party's best performance since 1992. Unfortunately for her, Jeremy Corbyn's Labour Party won nearly 13 million votes, just over 40 percent of those cast—the party's best performance since Tony Blair's inaugural election victory in 1997.

Considering the background to the election, this was all the more extraordinary: after the EU referendum, twenty-three of the thirty-one members of Labour's Shadow Cabinet resigned, and a motion of no confidence in Corbyn's leadership was placed by Labour MPs in July 2016, which he lost by 172 votes to 40. But instead of resigning, Corbyn held on, and forced a leadership challenge, which, with the help of a dramatic expansion of Labour's membership, he won comfortably. A clear gap had opened up between Labour's grassroots, strongly supportive of Corbyn, and the party elite and most of the news media, deeply opposed to him and his left-wing identity. Most observers—and many Labour MPs—predicted that Corbyn could only be dislodged by a crushing electoral defeat, and fully expected this to be the outcome of May's snap election. Instead, Corbyn outperformed not only his critics but also apparently his own team's expectations: the party ran a defensive campaign, focused on retaining supposedly vulnerable Labour seats, rather than seeking gains at the Conservatives' expense.

With Corbyn's Labour winning 40 percent of the vote, and 42 percent of the vote won by the now pro-Brexit Conservatives under May, the overwhelming majority of British voters had backed parties that in differing ways rejected the open-economy market-liberal consensus of the pre-Brexit era. The sole remaining representative of this consensus, the centrist, pro-European Liberal Democrats, won a paltry eight seats. The message of the 2017 election was clearly that Britain needed to change, but the nature of the desired change was harder to fathom. The Conservatives were becoming more clearly identified with Brexit, and their increased vote share was in large part the consequence of hoovering up much of the electorate of the now redundant UKIP. But Labour, whose official position was also that the referendum result should be respected, had mostly mobilized younger voters, attracted by Labour's promises of cheaper housing, an end to austerity, and the abolition of university tuition fees, voters mostly hostile to Brexit. This so-called youthquake created a Brexit dilemma for Labour, whose heartlands had mostly voted Leave in the 2016 referendum.[94]

Labour's difficulties paled into insignificance compared to Theresa May's political strategy, which was left in tatters by the loss of her parliamentary majority. Worse, she now needed the votes of the Democratic Unionist Party (DUP), whose core demand that Northern Ireland should leave the European Union on exactly the same terms as the rest of the United Kingdom not only was a minority view in the province, but also was inconsistent with the Irish government and the European Union's insistence that Brexit should not lead to border controls in Ireland. May's own "red line" of leaving the EU Customs Union, in order to placate Brexiters who imagined the United Kingdom free to run its own independent trade policy, was also inconsistent with maintaining an open border in Ireland. The solution she negotiated with the European Union—the so-called backstop tying the United Kingdom to an open border—ultimately broke the government's majority apart, with the DUP and many right-wing Brexiters in the Conservative Party (organized around the European Research Group faction) rejecting the proposed Withdrawal Agreement in late 2018.

The failure of May's strategy culminated in her resignation in May 2019, after four unsuccessful attempts to win parliamentary approval for her plan, and a humiliating postponement of Britain's exit date to October 2019. Her failure could certainly be adduced to personal limitations, the poor election result, and the machinations within her own party, but the Brexit saga also reflected more fundamental divisions within British society and politics. Brexit split both the Conservative and Labour parties, with around 42 percent of Tory identifiers voting Remain in the referendum, while 36 percent of Labour identifiers voted Leave. As the Conservative government took responsibility for delivering Brexit, it not only alienated some of its traditional voter base, but also much of the business community; in one symbolic moment, Boris Johnson was reported to have dismissed concerns about the economic impact of Brexit with the words "**** business!"[95] Meanwhile, Labour faced a different problem—the young, left-leaning voters underpinning Corbyn's Labour project were in their vast majority opposed to Brexit.[96] In these circumstances the normal working of party and parliamentary politics broke down.

Brexit was always going to be difficult to deliver, requiring as it did a fundamental rewiring of the British legal and economic order, which would likely cause significant economic disruption. It was made all the more complex by the way it laid bare the weaknesses of the major political parties. Labour and the Conservatives both formally committed themselves to the Leave position, but their party elites were in their majority skeptical about Brexit, particularly in the Labour Party. The attempt by Theresa May to conduct negotiations with the European Union secretively and with little input from the rest of the Conservative Party, let alone the opposition parties represented in Parliament, brought an unprecedented divide between the House of Commons and the government. In Spring 2019, Parliament effectively took control of the Brexit process by rejecting May's proposed Brexit deal, while simultaneously rejecting a series of alternative plans in successive parliamentary votes. The result was paralysis and a postponement of the Brexit date that May's government had previously set in law.

The European elections of 2019 delivered the electorate's response to these failures: the Brexit Party, a new party founded by former UKIP leader Nigel Farage, polled a spectacular 30 percent of the vote, mostly at the expense of the Conservatives, who finished fifth with just 8.8 percent, their lowest ever vote share in any election in modern history. Labour was also punished for its ambivalence over Brexit, finishing third behind the Brexit Party and the pro-European Liberal Democrats, and also losing significant numbers of votes to the Greens, another a pro-Remain party. The European elections reflected a country that was increasingly fragmented but also polarized between a "hard Brexit" position, on the one hand, and a complete rejection of Brexit, on the other, with the compromise positions of the Labour and Conservative leaders supported by barely a quarter of voters. The 2016 referendum had created two new political identities—Leave and Remain—which were more strongly felt than the traditional partisan identities of Conservative and Labour. The anti-system revolt seemed to have created a new and perhaps lasting realignment of British politics.

Conclusion

Britain's anti-system turn shows the limitations of the neoliberal project: the exposure of society to the volatility and inequality generated by markets creates its own backlash, as different social groups turn against the market system in their different ways. Not only was Britain as exposed as any country to the wreckage of the financial crisis, it also responded to the downturn by imposing harsh austerity, exacerbating its social costs. It was perhaps not to be anticipated that the outcome would be a vote to leave the European Union, but Brexit falls into the typical pattern of right-wing anti-system voting elsewhere, focusing on immigration and targeting older, socially authoritarian voters in declining regions. Labour's leftward turn under Corbyn reflected an anti-system turn fueled in particular by the economic grievances of a progressive generation of younger voters, and a broader public rejection of austerity.

Britain's anti-system politics is similar to that in the United States, with extreme inequality and high levels of financial market openness spreading economic anxiety across large sectors of society, and pitting younger, progressive voters against older, more socially authoritarian ones. In the Eurozone, in contrast, anti-system politics followed a different pattern, as Europe's debt crisis pitted not only social sectors but also member states against each other, producing distinct patterns of anti-system politics: more left-wing in debtor countries, more right-wing in creditor countries. The next section explains why.

PART THREE | THE BREAKING
OF EUROPE

CHAPTER 5 | The New North-South Divide:
Bailout Politics and the Return of
the Left in Southern Europe

THE EURO AREA might seem an unlikely case of neoliberal overreach
sparking an anti-system backlash. Western Europe is the home of the
social market economy, that hybrid of capitalism and social protection which
has delivered not only some of the highest living standards in the world but
also relatively equal distributions of income and wealth. What is more, the
European banking system had appeared to be quite cautious in its approach
toward the kinds of financial innovation that sparked the meltdown of Wall
Street and the City of London. When the crisis hit, most European countries
could count on generous social shock absorbers to cushion society from the
worst effects of the downturn. Confident in the robustness of the European
social model, European leaders responded to the crisis with Schadenfreude: in
September 2008, German Finance Minister Peer Steinbruck claimed that
"the financial crisis is above all an American problem,"[1] while French
President Nicolas Sarkozy declared the demise of "the unconstrained Anglo-
Saxon market model."[2]

Within weeks of Steinbruck's dismissive comment, governments across
continental Europe were bailing out their own banks, shelling out sums
just as unprecedented as those mobilized in Washington, DC, and London.[3]
Europe was also caught up in the inevitable slump following the crisis, with
an even worse hit to GDP than in the Anglo-Saxon world: Germany suffered

a drop in output of almost 7 percent, compared to just under 4 percent in the United States. But far worse was to come as jittery financial markets began to lose confidence in the stability of the euro currency itself, pulling money out of the weaker economies of the Eurozone and necessitating a massive bailout of sovereigns costing, on one estimate, 1.6 trillion euros. This sovereign debt crisis stopped Europe's post-crisis recovery in its tracks, and the fiscal austerity imposed as a condition of the bailouts pushed the weaker countries into a double-dip recession whose effects lasted most of the decade of the 2010s.

This economic disaster predictably wreaked havoc on the political systems of the countries most exposed to the debt crisis, but it also destabilized the economically stronger countries who felt compelled to bail them out. Anti-system politicians made hay in this environment. The countries that suffered the most from the crisis—Greece, Italy, Spain, and Portugal—also experienced the deepest political crises, with anti-system movements challenging the political establishment, and in the case of Greece and Italy, winning control of the government. These countries were all exposed to a collapse in financial market perceptions of their creditworthiness, and had to request financial assistance from their neighbors, which was conceded only on condition that they cut back on their social programs and raised taxes. This not only piled the pain onto more vulnerable parts of the population, but also likely aggravated the economic crisis by depressing demand.[4]

It may not be surprising that anti-system politics prospered in the southern Eurozone in the midst of the worst slump since the 1930s. However, despite the financial bailouts very visibly and painfully subjecting the southern countries to harsh austerity decided by supranational institutions at the urging of foreign governments, right-wing nationalism was not the prime beneficiary (with the partial exception of Italy). Instead, movements of the anti-system Left, mobilizing the discontent of the younger, mostly highly educated, and politically progressive parts of the population, made the biggest gains, taking over the government in Greece, and sustaining coalition governments in Portugal, Spain, and Italy. The anti-system Right, in contrast, was the big winner in the northern Eurozone, where outrage at the costs of bailouts mobilized a nationalist, socially authoritarian vote.

The conflict between creditor and debtor countries drove a wedge into the Eurozone, but anti-system politics mainly played itself out within the individual member states, as different social interests fought over the distribution of the burdens of economic adjustment. A key feature of these internal battles was the way in which the crisis and its effects were filtered and cushioned by systems of social protection at the national level. Creditor countries had strong welfare states and less acute economic problems, but they were still affected by rising inequality, slow wage growth, and cuts to welfare entitlements that particularly affected the kinds of older, less-educated voters sympathetic to the anti-system Right. Debtor countries suffered worse crises, but their systems of social protection had a major bearing on the ways the costs of the crisis were distributed: southern European welfare states tended to protect pensioners and older male workers more than younger citizens, who were more inclined to protest by supporting the anti-system Left.

The depth of the crisis and the effects of welfare state design offer a compelling explanation of the rise of anti-system politics in the Eurozone. This focus on post-crisis economics fits the facts rather better than the conventional wisdom that immigration and the refugee crisis of the mid-2010s fueled anti-system politics. The European citizens on the front line of the humanitarian crisis in the Mediterranean—especially Greece, Spain, and southern Italy—did not support the xenophobic politics of the anti-system Right. Instead, the anti-system vote in the southern countries has mostly tended to the left, reflecting the economic concerns of younger disenfranchised voters, rather than the cultural panic of the older generation. Part Three will show how the euro crisis fueled anti-system politics in Greece, Portugal, Spain, and Italy.

Catching Up with Europe: The Euro and the Short-Lived Southern Success Story

Southern Europeans were historically among the most enthusiastic supporters of European integration, equating Europe with a process of economic, social, cultural, and political improvement that had few serious political opponents until the euro crisis.[5] The acceleration of integration in the 1990s was embraced by political elites with the apparent acquiescence of most of the population in southern Europe, and full participation in the euro became a shared objective of all mainstream political parties, with only the communist Left—a group with a long tradition across the South—opposing European Monetary Union (EMU).[6] This convergence around the European single market project defused the deep ideological divides that had run through southern European politics for most of the twentieth century, pitting Left against Right in often violent conflict. The Right accepted democratic rule and the welfare state, while the Left abandoned previous commitments to overturn capitalism and embraced the Western democratic order, in the form of NATO and the European Union.[7]

The European project initially appeared as a free lunch to the new southern member states. Inward investment rose, and sales to European markets expanded.[8] As the economy grew, governments had a great deal of scope to improve their limited social programs and expand public employment, an opportunity that the political parties seized to distribute jobs, social benefits, and infrastructure investment to their supporters. Extending pensions rights, rolling out new benefits for disabled and unemployed workers, and increasing public spending of services such as healthcare not only addressed a genuine social deficit but also established lasting relationships between voters and parties. Governing parties also exploited the opportunity to fill the growing public payroll with supporters, many of them party members.[9] While the Left was most enthusiastic about public spending, the Right also curried favor with voters by exempting certain groups or economic sectors from some of the resulting fiscal burden, at times openly facilitating tax evasion.

This rapid growth of the welfare state, as southern Europe sought to catch up with the highly developed social policies of northern Europe, collided with the increasingly market liberal ethos driving European integration, reflected in the completion of the single market and the move toward monetary union. The market liberal agenda was being driven not only by the European institutions but also by central bankers and business elites in southern Europe looking to liberalize domestic markets, rein in public deficits, and discipline labor. These groups saw the Euro project as a useful lever: unsustainable spending promises would be curtailed by the fiscal restraints implied by monetary union, while the abandonment of national currencies would rule out resort to devaluation and curb wage-driven inflation.[10]

The fiscal, monetary, and regulatory reforms required by EMU enjoyed wide support among the major southern European political leaders and was largely accepted by voters, too. However, EMU set in chain a process of detachment of political parties from their electorates, and especially on the left. EMU meant giving up any prospect of independent macroeconomic policy, sounding the death knell for leftist parties' traditional ideological ambitions. The need for fiscal restraint also put a brake on the kinds of partisan government spending that could compensate for these ideological compromises. The structural funds agreed to as part of the discussions around monetary union at Maastricht softened the blow to some degree,[11] but the inability of parties to offer either grand transformational visions or even more prosaic forms of electorally profitable welfare spending fundamentally changed their relationship with voters.

In this more austere environment, exacerbated by the recession of the early 1990s, political parties in southern Europe found themselves in a legitimacy crisis[12]. In Italy, the entire party system collapsed, as I will explain in chapter 7. In Spain, Felipe González's Socialist party, and in Portugal the center-right Social Democrats, were both mired in corruption after years in government.[13] In Greece, both the major parties—the conservative New Democracy (ND) and the socialist PASOK—were hit by a regular flow of scandals. At the same time, parties were converging around the need for fiscal prudence, welcoming the Maastricht Treaty as an opportunity to tie their hands in the face of domestic pressures for deficit spending and inflationary wage rises.[14] Paradoxically, the weakness of southern Europe's national political elites facilitated the push toward EMU, because public trust in national political institutions was significantly lower than trust in the European Union.[15] The euro was seen by many voters as a means to entrench northern European living standards and resolve long-standing governance problems.

As a result, the sacrifices necessary for euro entry were broadly accepted, and the Maastricht criteria proved a valuable external constraint, empowering national governments to take unpopular decisions by invoking outside pressures. But the flipside of this external constraint was a disempowering of the electorate to influence government choices, and an increasing role in policymaking for unelected officials, at both the domestic and supranational levels.[16] In the short term, the convergence criteria were met and euro entry was achieved, with Greece and Spain in particular enjoying spectacular economic growth, which smoothed over any political misgivings over the process. But this insulation of policy from popular influence would prove to be unpalatable in harsher economic conditions.

Spain, Italy, and Portugal entered the first wave of monetary union in 1999, while Greece entered just two years later. The principal effect of euro membership was to dramatically reduce borrowing costs for the southern countries, as markets perceived lower risks of default, pushing down interest rates. But even these much lower rates were still higher than in the strong economies of northern Europe, leading financial institutions and, to some extent, households in the North to invest heavily in higher-yielding southern assets.[17] The resulting boom conditions brought easy financing of government debt, presenting politicians with new opportunities to reward their supporters. Greece was the most enthusiastic in exploiting these new tailwinds, running growing deficits after euro entry to finance spending such as an increase in public sector employment (which grew as a share of employment from 19.3 to 20.7 percent between 2000 and 2008)[18] and lavish infrastructure spending such as the Athens Olympics, while falsifying government accounting to hide the true extent of government borrowing.

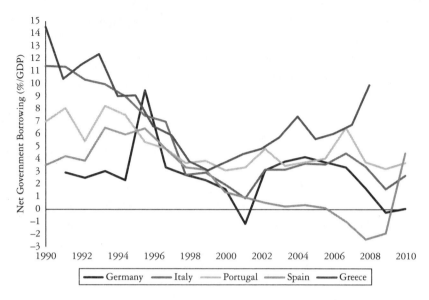

FIGURE 5.1 Government Borrowing in Germany and Southern Europe, 1990–2008 (%GDP)

Source: International Monetary Fund, "World Economic Outlook Database," October 2013 (https://www.imf.org/external/pubs/ft/weo/2013/02/weodata/index. aspx).

Figure 5.1 shows that although Greece clearly ran excessive fiscal deficits, the rest of southern Europe was not obviously out of line with the virtuous Germany, and markets and policymakers were relaxed about the buildup of debt in a context of strong economic growth. What became apparent after the crisis was that policymakers had been targeting the wrong things. Fiscal deficits were not a good measure of the South's increasing financial vulnerability, because vast flows of capital from northern Europe were encouraging private households and businesses to build up debt. These capital inflows, attracted by the higher yields and apparent safety of euro-dominated assets, led to booming real estate markets, which provided many opportunities for politicians to extract bribes and political donations through their control of regulations and the planning process. This resulted in a dramatic increase in household debt, which far outweighed the more frequently discussed fiscal vulnerabilities of the southern Eurozone. Spain was particularly exposed to any downturn in the housing market, as households leveraged up to fund real estate speculation.

As became clear after the Global Financial Crisis in 2007–2008, the South's credit-fueled growth model was vulnerable to a sudden stop in very similar ways to the highly financialized economies of the Anglosphere. This dynamic of indebtedness can be seen clearly in the evolution of the current account balance of Eurozone member states after Greece joined the single currency in 2002 (Figure 5.2). The current account is a measure of whether countries are net savers or net borrowers: a current account deficit means that a country imports more than it exports, and invests more than it saves, with the difference necessarily being made up by capital inflows. The current accounts of Greece, Spain, and Portugal reached extraordinarily high negative levels in the period prior to the financial crisis, meaning that they were financing their consumption by borrowing from foreigners who were buying assets from them. Greece's current account reached 16 percent of GDP, meaning that if anything happened to undermine foreign investors' appetite for Greek assets, Greek households would suddenly find themselves having to cut their spending by an equivalent amount.

Figure 5.2 also shows that Germany, in contrast, was consistently running large current account surpluses, corresponding to capital flowing out of Germany, as German households and companies spent less than they earned. To simplify, Germans and other northern Europeans were saving large amounts, and investing their savings in, for example, Spanish real estate or Greek government bonds. Northern Europeans were creditors, southern Europeans were debtors. When the financial crisis hit, creditors sought to pull their money out, while debtors came to the realization that they could not meet their liabilities out of their falling incomes. The resulting sudden stop to investment, and the rapid reining in of spending, dragged the whole Eurozone economy into recession and exposed the fragility of European banks

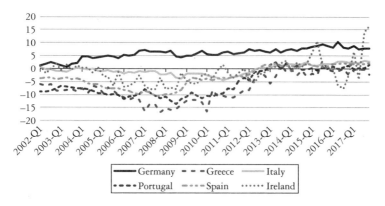

FIGURE 5.2 Current Account Balance, 2002–2017 (%GDP)
Source: OECD Data (https://data.oecd.org/trade/current-account-balance.htm) (retrieved June 29, 2018).

in both North and South. But the banking crisis and recession were experienced less as a shared problem, and more as a conflict between northern countries anxious to protect their assets, with southern countries fearful of falling into debt bondage. Anti-system politics played out very differently in these different contexts.

Debt, Austerity, and the Great Recession in Southern Europe

The sudden stop materialized once the credit boom in the United States and Europe ended in 2007. As in the United States and the United Kingdom, the very high current account deficits the southern countries had been running meant a very painful adjustment in consumption was necessary once capital inflows slowed. But unlike in the United States and the United Kingdom, southern Europe faced a further constraint: as Eurozone members they had no monetary autonomy, and limited fiscal autonomy. While the United States and the United Kingdom could both float their currencies and intervene through central bank quantitative easing to facilitate adjustment and rescue financial institutions, the debtor countries of the Eurozone could do neither while they remained in the euro. Moreover, their ability to use fiscal policy to counteract the debt deflationary dynamics unleashed by the financial crisis was constrained, first by European Union rules, but more importantly by the unwillingness of investors to lend money to governments whose fiscal position was deteriorating rapidly.

Figures 5.2 and 5.3 shows the extent and speed of the adjustment the debtor countries were subject to. Greece's current account deficit peaked in early 2007 at an extraordinary 16.5 percent of GDP (a GDP that was about to shrink dramatically). But Portugal and Spain were not far behind, with peaks of 13.5 and 10.5 percent, respectively, in late 2007 and early 2008. As the crisis began to bite, domestic consumption collapsed, reducing spending on imports as the capital flows sustaining these deficits came to a "sudden stop." The current account adjustment was huge in absolute terms: Greece's deficit amounted to $53 billion in 2008, but had been closed to just a tenth of that figure by 2013; in other words, Greece reduced its external borrowing by around $40 billion in just 5 years, a reduction achieved almost entirely by cutting consumption, as Greek GDP fell by 30 percent. The other southern countries also made dramatic adjustments, with Portugal reducing its $31 billion deficit tenfold by 2013. These adjustments dwarfed in relative terms

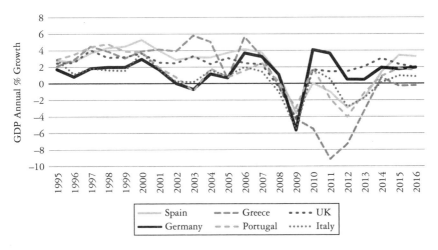

FIGURE 5.3 Europe's Double Dip Recession (%GDP)
Source: OECD, "Gross Domestic Product (GDP)" (https://data.oecd.org/gdp/gross-domestic-product-gdp.htm) (retrieved June 7, 2019).

those of the other big debtor countries, the United States and the United Kingdom, who benefited from borrowing in their own money, and who were able to deploy quantitative easing in order to ease the debt burden.

Although a financial crisis of such size and scope would inevitably affect all the advanced economies, the nature of EMU, and the policy choices made by its governing institutions, not only magnified its effects but also distributed them in a way that was catastrophic for southern Europe. First, a currency union meant that there was no possibility of the exchange rate bearing any of the strain of adjustment, meaning that domestic prices and wages would have to do all of the work, a process otherwise known as "internal devaluation." Second, the European Central Bank's particularly hawkish view of inflation meant that there was little possibility of allowing any of the adjustment to be accommodated by inflation. As well as having an asymmetric inflation target that biased toward tighter policy, the European Central Bank was much more institutionally and politically constrained than the other major central banks, so that it took far longer than the Federal Reserve or the Bank of England to adopt unconventional measures to loosen monetary conditions. As a result, Eurozone inflation remained very low, which meant that nominal wages and prices were the only route to adjustment. To make this even more difficult, the creditor countries of northern Europe, the southern countries' main trading partners, were also retrenching, albeit on a smaller scale, at the exact same time, making it almost impossible for the southerners' devaluation to deliver the kind of export-led growth that might have preserved living standards. Third, the high levels of debt, both public and private, that the South had built up during the boom years were all the harder to reduce given the low inflation rate and stagnant or falling real incomes.

As if this was not enough, the low interest rates that resulted from the policy response to the crisis did not benefit the South for very long, as doubts about sovereign solvency brought a financial panic and a fire sale of southern debt. European Central Bank President Jean-Claude Trichet's anxiety to quickly restore policy rates to more normal levels brought a premature rate hike in spring 2011, which had the predictable effect of exacerbating the panic. As spreads returned to pre-euro levels and beyond, southern governments had no defense against rising borrowing costs, and Greece and Portugal, along with Ireland, had to be bailed out by the Troika of the European Central Bank, European Commission, and International Monetary Fund (IMF). In ex-change for financial assistance, the governments of the troubled states agreed to implement detailed reforms of taxation, public spending, public admin-istration, and market regulation, and they accepted close monitoring from the Troika to ensure reform commitments were upheld. Although Spain was spared a formal Economic Assistance Program (EAP), by mid-2012 it was forced to request up to €100 billion of financial assistance from the European Union's European Stability Mechanism (ESM) to allow the Spanish govern-ment to recapitalize its banking sector.

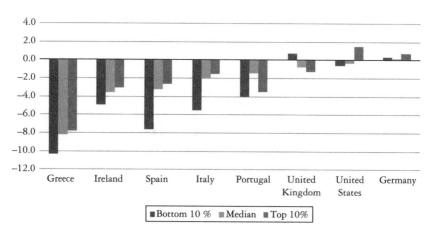

FIGURE 5.4 Annual Percentage Change in Household Disposable Income between 2007 and 2013, by Income Group
Source: OECD, "Income Distribution Database" (http://www.oecd.org/social/income-distribution-database.htm) (retrieved June 7, 2019).

The Eurozone's sovereign debt crisis brought to an abrupt end the South's fleeting recovery from the 2008 crash, as Figure 5.4 illustrates. While the United Kingdom and the United States returned at least to anemic growth after the end of fiscal stimulus, the Eurozone fell into a double-dip recession. Even in the main creditor country, Germany, economic growth fell back close to zero, but in southern Europe GDP shrank once again, returning to growth only in 2014. This was the consequence of the restrictive fiscal policies imposed as a condition of financial aid, which forced southern European governments to target primary budget surpluses even at a time when the private sector economy was shrinking rapidly. As well as coping with falling income and deleveraging, households also faced higher taxes and cuts in government transfer payments. Not surprisingly, investment and consumer spending fell sharply, and in the absence of any offsetting increase in demand in export markets, the economy as a whole shrank, making households poorer than before the crisis.

Although at the time of the bailouts Troika officials claimed that these policies could be consistent with economic growth, the IMF subsequently admitted that the recessionary consequences of the measures were massively underestimated.[19] In the case of Greece, the degree of austerity demanded could only result in a deep recession, and given Greece's untenable level of external debt, a deep economic slump was perhaps inevitable. However, the extent of the squeeze Greece was exposed to was ultimately counterproductive, since by shrinking the size of GDP it increased the relative size of Greece's debt and made investors even more wary of the risk of default. US Treasury Secretary Tim Geithner afterward claimed that the devastating effects on Greece's economy were intended as a strategy to force it out of the Eurozone,[20] while Yanis Varoufakis, briefly Greece's finance minister in 2015, wrote that European leaders were well aware that austerity would make it impossible for Greece to pay off its debts.[21]

Greece was an extreme case, but even in the other debtor countries there is legitimate suspicion that the painful consequences of the conditions of financial assistance were a feature rather than a bug. If the Eurozone periphery were to return to competitiveness, they would have to reduce their unit labor costs, and with a fixed exchange rate and low inflation, the only way to do that was through a deep recession, which would force down wages. Protective institutions such as collective bargaining rights, unemployment benefits, and restrictive regulations on firing workers stood in the way of this "internal devaluation," and would have to be dismantled. Europe bailed out troubled Eurozone sovereigns, but at the price of a deep recession and the loss of workplace and social rights that had been hard fought. In other words, the recession in southern Europe was the consequence of a deliberate strategy designed to enforce a neoliberal policy agenda of fiscal restraint, welfare retrenchment, and flexible labor markets.[22]

This painful economic adjustment was the result of political choices made by institutions that did not respond to any direct electoral mandate: the European Central Bank, the European Commission, and the European Council. These choices had important distributional consequences, pitting European Union member states against each other, while also dividing the populations of member states. Northern European politicians placed the blame for the crisis squarely with the southern Europeans; a notorious example had a former Eurogroup head, the Dutch social democrat Jeroen Dijsselbloem, justifying the tough austerity in moral terms, claiming, "You can not spend all the money on drinks and women and then ask for help."[23] Whether or not he believed this was a valid metaphor, the reality was that northern European electorates were sending a very clear signal to their own politicians to "keep their boots on Greece's neck," and ensure the profligate South did not escape punishment for its irresponsibility.[24] The result was a destructive austerity program that at best was badly designed and based on completely wrong estimates of its economic effects,[25] and at worst could be seen as a punitive attempt to defeat moral hazard and show that bailouts were not a free lunch.

On top of contraction and austerity, southern Europe also had to come to terms with a dramatic loss of political autonomy. The EAPs agreed with Greece, Portugal, and Ireland, and the Financial Assistance Facility Agreement with Spain consisted of hundreds of detailed and specific measures of fiscal, regulatory, and administrative policy required of the recipients, alongside detailed provision for surveillance and monitoring of progress.[26] These measures had harsh distributional consequences and were bound to provoke political opposition. Yet, faced with the choice of government insolvency or a financial bailout with strings attached, elected politicians opted for the bailout, thereby giving up their policymaking autonomy and their ability to respond to voter preferences. Instead of taking their cue from the electorate, policymakers had no choice but to respond to the price signals coming from the bond markets and to the political demands of the foreign governments and international organizations that could protect them from these markets.

The extreme nature of Greece's funding problems led to a unique degree of intervention from the EU-IMF "Troika," which stripped the government of key aspects of national sovereignty. Strict and detailed budgetary targets not only eliminated much of the discretionary power of the Greek government to decide how to raise revenue and how to spend it, but also set very detailed requirements for the structure of the public administration. Moreover, the budgetary demands made of the Greeks by Troika officials were so draconian as to drive the Greek economy into a deep depression, with dramatic economic and social consequences. Once the Greek authorities had made the decision to accept financial assistance, the process of determining how and when the money should be paid back was effectively decided unilaterally, and in a way that shifted the pain mostly onto the Greek population. The bailouts may have been presented as financial assistance to the stressed southern Europeans, but they were just as much about helping European banks, whose balance sheets were not ready to cope with further losses, and northern European governments, anxious to shift the blame for their domestic financial ailments onto the "irresponsible" debtors.[27]

The socialist PASOK government in Greece, which had initially triggered the crisis by revealing the full extent of the fiscal tricks played by its predecessor conservative (ND) administration, quickly found itself deeply unpopular as it attempted to fend off market pressure by forcing through austerity measures. As the economy entered into steep decline, the impossibility of securing market funding at sustainable rates became apparent, and the prime minister, George Papandreou, sought outside help, thus becoming the executor of the Troika's demands for even more harsh austerity. The lack of any formal channel of accountability for the Troika institutions meant that Greek voters had no obvious route for expressing their feelings directly to those responsible, although a wave of street protests and strikes made them clear. As the situation deteriorated and further financial assistance became necessary, Papandreou attempted a last-ditch appeal to the Greek electorate by promising a referendum on a second round of financial assistance, which involved a private sector "haircut" on Greek debt. Papandreou's move was condemned as "irresponsible" by key EU political leaders, outraged that the delicate negotiations to keep Greece afloat should be conditioned by appeals to democratic consent.

In the event, Papandreou was forced out and a caretaker administration led by a former central banker, Lucas Papademos, saw the negotiation of the second bailout through to its conclusion. The new program involved further stringent fiscal demands, and the Eurogroup of Eurozone finance ministers also insisted that the leaders of the major Greek parties commit to the program, so as to avoid further political upheavals. Immediately after the agreement was reached, elections were held, in which PASOK not only lost but was electorally obliterated. Yet the alternation of power and the arrival of a new conservative government could not change the essential facts: Greece remained unable to stick to its fiscal targets, the economy was in freefall, and within three years a further bailout was required. The economic collapse and the evident inability of Greece's elected politicians to do anything but implement harsh austerity decided by outsiders had a devastating effect on public confidence in the main governing parties.

Portugal faced a similar dilemma shortly afterward, though its fiscal situation was less desperate than Greece's and the political stakes were lower, given the low political salience of the small Iberian state. Again, stringent detailed budgetary targets were imposed. The Portuguese program already incorporated some of the lessons of the failed Greek bailouts, but still set unrealistic targets for deficit reduction and underestimated the contractionary effect of austerity on GDP, which dropped by 6.1 percent in the first two years of the program.[28] By 2012 GDP had contracted by almost 10 percent from its 2008 peak, and despite growth returning, it remained almost 6 percent lower in autumn 2015. The third country to need a formal bailout, Ireland, also suffered a dramatic contraction of output after the government rescue of its banking sector in turn provoked a run on government debt. Ireland had the deepest recession in the industrialized world between 2007 and 2010, with a GDP decline of 21 percent and fiscal deficits of up to 12 percent.[29] Eurozone bailouts were anything but a free lunch.

Who Got Bailed Out? Inequality and Precarity in the Mediterranean Social Model

The impact of this economic shock to households and businesses in the Eurozone periphery was unprecedented in the history of postwar Europe, and far exceeded that faced by debtor countries outside the Eurozone. Figure 5.4 shows that for all four southern European countries and Ireland, household disposable income fell all the way across the income distribution in the half-decade following the crisis. Median income fell by over 8 percent in Greece, 3 percent in Ireland and Spain, 2 percent in Italy, and 1.5 percent in Portugal; the bottom decile took a 10 percent hit in Greece, almost 8 percent in Spain, nearly 6 percent in Italy, and 4 percent in Portugal. There are simply no comparable income losses anywhere in the advanced democratic countries since World War II.

One of the most powerful indicators of the extent of the crisis is the rise in unemployment. Figure 5.5 shows the extent of the damage in southern Europe. By 2013, 27 percent of the Greek workforce were unemployed, and

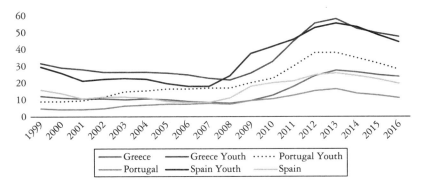

FIGURE 5.5 Unemployment and Youth Unemployment in Southern Europe, 1999–2016 (%)
Source: OECD, "Jobs" (https://data.oecd.org/jobs.htm#profile-Unemployment) (retrieved 7 June 2019).

joblessness reached 26 percent in Spain, and 16 percent in Portugal; among those under twenty-five years old, the unemployment rate reached 58 percent and 55 percent in Greece and Spain, respectively, and 38 percent in Portugal. These levels were far higher than the European average, and much higher than in the Anglo countries that also faced harsh adjustment. Wages for those able to stay in work, on the other hand, held up well in comparison, at least in Portugal and Spain.

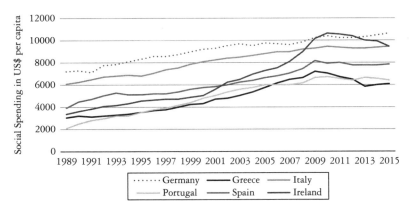

FIGURE 5.6 Social Spending in Germany and the Eurozone Periphery, 1989–2015
Source: OECD, "Social Spending" (https://data.oecd.org/socialexp/social-spending. htm) (retrieved June 7, 2019).

Unlike the British and American cases, where welfare states had been pared back as early as the 1980s, southern Europe had experienced an expansion of social protection through the 1990s and 2000s as their economies integrated more deeply into European markets (see Figure 5.6). Ireland stood out, briefly converging with levels of spending on social protection in Germany, while Greece, Spain, and Portugal steadily narrowed the gap. The result of these developments was a very distinctive social and economic model in which overall inequality was relatively high, but with a differently structured income distribution than the Anglo countries, where economic insecurity affected large sectors of society. In southern Europe inequality reflects a "dualization" of the economy: highly polarized exposure to market forces, in which some groups, usually older citizens, enjoy generous protections, while others, especially the young, are highly vulnerable.[30] This has important implications for the way in which anti-market sentiment is expressed politically, and it explains why the dominant form of anti-system politics in the South has been the anti-capitalist Left rather than the nationalist Right.

The type of capitalism that emerged as the southern countries democratized reflected the imprint of the authoritarian conservatism[31] that informed policy over much of the postwar period, and even the fascist legacy that was strongest in Italy, but also had some influence on its southern neighbors. Markets were carefully controlled, and the state was actively involved in either regulating production or directly managing it through government ownership, a legacy of the corporatism popular in the prewar period. Economic governance sought to entrench existing hierarchies in order to protect the privileges of dominant social groups: namely the church, the machinery of the state (particularly the armed forces), and the financial and business classes. State interventionism and welfare state development reflected the interests of this dominant social bloc, but also aimed at pacifying social conflict and containing worker militancy, one of the main threats to social stability. This legacy dovetailed counterintuitively with a strong communist tradition on the left, leaving little space for liberal or social democratic ideas. When transitions to democracy began in Greece, Spain, and Portugal, pressures from the communist Left pushed for the same tools of state interventionism to be used in favor of the interests of the occupational group most supportive of the Left: industrial manual workers.[32]

Social protection in southern Europe developed along Bismarckian[33] lines, providing unemployment coverage and pensions mainly to state employees and workers in large firms able to bear the high social insurance contributions that financed the system. These were therefore occupational welfare systems: the families of these largely male welfare beneficiaries were covered indirectly, as nonwaged women and young people not yet integrated into formal employment had few social rights of their own. Moreover, welfare provision tended to vary considerably with occupational status, creating significant inequalities of provision that often reinforced rather than mitigated existing market inequalities. These inequalities mirrored similar discrimination in the regulation of labor markets, where some core workers enjoyed very strong protection against dismissal compared to others. Finally, social spending was low in relative terms compared to other Western democracies, especially in the southern European dictatorships.

The patterns of party competition that became established as democracy was consolidated left their mark on the emerging system of social protection. From the 1970s, welfare provision expanded rapidly as democracy brought new political pressures for public spending and regulation—pressures that were exacerbated by the consequences of the recession of the late 1970s and early 1980s, and of the structural adjustments of the 1980s that led to rises in unemployment. The decline of authoritarianism and the growing influence of trained economists socialized into liberal market thinking[34] influenced policy in a liberalizing direction, but at the same time the presence of significant communist and socialist parties and trade unions pushed for a continued role for government in redistributing income and protecting employment. Parties used government budgets to design welfare and other spending policies to direct resources to favored groups and localities, on clientelistic lines. As a result, social protection became tied to political allegiances, and responded to electoral pressures as well as to social and economic needs. The arrangements that emerged out of this process of institutional development have been described as a "southern" or "Mediterranean" model.[35]

These social, economic, and institutional conditions determined how the crisis of the late 2000s affected different social groups and therefore conditioned the type of political reaction that resulted from it. Greece and Spain in particular had a serious long-standing structural unemployment problem, which was particularly acutely felt among the young. Labor market regulation in southern Europe has been highly dualized, in that labor rights vary across different occupational groups to a much greater degree than in most other Western democracies.[36] This dualism favored "insiders"—workers who enjoyed stable employment contracts in large firms or the public sector, and who were very expensive and sometime legally impossible to fire. The high regulatory barriers and high nonwage costs of employment in southern Europe have combined to endow a large cohort of older, usually male workers with high job security, welfare, and pension rights, rights whose defense are a priority for trade unions. In contrast, the "outsiders"—younger workers and, in particular, women and migrants—face much higher risk of unemployment, less job security, and less (sometimes no) welfare protection than their peers in other European countries.[37]

This dualism distributes economic security in starkly different ways at the individual level, although the social consequences are mitigated somewhat by the survival of a very familistic culture in which a high degree of economic protection and redistribution takes places within households and extended kinship, and sometimes friendship, networks.[38] For example, women's lower labor participation, and usually lower employment status, is in part also a reflection of a traditionally patriarchal culture in which women were expected to rely on the men within their families (fathers, then husbands) for not only income but also welfare rights. The sustainability of these arrangements depended not only on women's willingness to accept the economically subordinate position they implied, but also the availability of a sufficient number of stable, well-paid jobs for male workers. The persistence of high levels of unemployment since the 1980s, and the resort on the part of governments to a series of labor reforms that facilitated the creation of flexible, short-term contracts with lower social contributions and therefore welfare rights,[39] has meant that family reproduction has ground to a halt, with a collapsing birth rate and high numbers of young people remaining in the parental home well into adulthood.[40]

These institutional peculiarities mean that despite a high level of income inequality at the household level, large parts of the population of southern Europe enjoy quite high levels of social protection, in contrast to the Anglo-Saxon democracies with similarly high headline figures for inequality.[41] On top of this, most southern European households are insulated from economic shocks by relatively high levels of financial and housing wealth—wealth that is also distributed more equally than in most other advanced democracies.[42] In Greece, Italy, and Spain, the bottom 60 percent owns 17–18 percent of net wealth, and 12 percent in Portugal, compared with just 2.4 percent in the United States and 6.5 percent in Germany.[43] The very high levels of home ownership, and a historically rather high household savings rate, mean that the average family unit in southern Europe is an owner-occupier and often has some other forms of capital (often real estate). This acts as a buffer against the failings of a labor market that has struggled to provide sufficient numbers of well-paid jobs to sustain the population. Unemployed youth are saved from indigence by the availability of free accommodation in the parental home, and by financial support from family members who belong to the more protected groups. The dualization of social risks is therefore absorbed to a large extent within the family.

The southern European countries enjoyed a rapid expansion of the public sector after democratization, but this proved difficult to sustain over the longer term. In the immediate aftermath of dictatorship, the social protection gap relative to the rest of Europe provided governments with room to increase public spending, and they exploited the opportunity to provide key support groups with public sector jobs and generous pensions. But by the 1990s, government spending had come close to converging with European standards, and opportunities to increase public resources by addressing the most glaring failings of their tax revenue systems were exhausted. Public sector employment growth therefore slowed, and as demographic changes fed through, the growth in pension spending baked into unfavorable demographic trends began to erode the space for other forms of social policy.[44] Figure 5.7 shows that in southern Europe, pensions accounted for a larger proportion of social spending than in the rest of Europe.

When the crisis hit, this pattern of welfare spending, skewed heavily toward the old, determined a distribution of economic pain that fell primarily on the young. Younger workers were disproportionately likely to be employed on temporary contracts, and were therefore the first to be fired when companies had to shed staff. Moreover, welfare systems that rewarded seniority and years of service in stable employment provided little in the way of income support for the young unemployed, many of whom were not entitled to unemployment benefits. Although the austerity measures and structural reforms imposed by the Troika were not necessarily regressive themselves, the overall pattern of cutting social spending, which actually fell in real

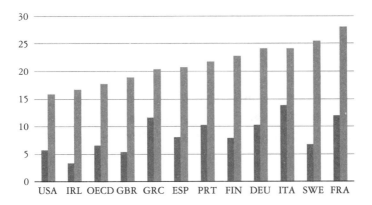

FIGURE 5.7 Total Social Spending and Pensions Spending, 2007 (%GDP)
Source: OECD, "Social Spending" (see Figure 5.6). The dark columns represent pensions spending, the lighter columns represent overall social spending.

terms in the bailout countries (see Figure 5.6), affected the young far more than the old. This proved to have important political consequences, since these younger citizens were at the forefront of the opposition to the management of the crisis.

Backlash: The Turn to the Anti-System Left

If the size of the economic shock that hit southern Europe made some kind of political backlash almost inevitable, the form that backlash took was less predictable. Among the different kinds of economic protectionism available in the anti-system menu, nationalist Euroskepticism would have seemed a logical response. The European Monetary Union exposed the periphery countries to financial volatility, while at the same time depriving their governments of the kinds of monetary, fiscal, and regulatory powers that might have offered some protection against them. When the financial crisis blew a hole in governments' budgets, the European authorities were slow to develop a coordinated response, and ultimately provided financial assistance too late and on harsh terms that increased the economic costs and distributed them in rather regressive ways.[45] That Europe had thrown the South overboard was an easy argument to make. As Adam Tooze put it, "if one wanted to write a script to bolster the claims of anti-system politics in Europe, it would look like the policy position of the [European] commission."[46]

Yet while nationalism and authoritarianism were on the rise in the Anglosphere and in eastern and northern Europe, southern Europe took a turn to the left. The political beneficiaries of the crisis in Greece, Portugal, and Spain, and to some extent in Italy, were more pro-European, culturally liberal, and economically progressive than the anti-system movements elsewhere. Northern European voters proved very receptive to the narrative presented by right-wing populists complaining about the costs of bailing out badly behaved southerners, but southern Europeans for the most part shunned nationalist resentment (the main exception to this, Italy, is discussed later). Instead, the Euro crisis proved an opportunity for the Left to break up the existing party cartels in the South and challenge their unquestioning adherence to the pro-market logic of European integration.

Unlike in the United States or most of the rest of Europe, immigration was marginal to the political debate in Greece, Portugal, and Spain, even though all had experienced quite dramatic increases in immigration in the period preceding the crisis. Neither was the refugee crisis resulting from the conflict in Syria central to the surge of anti-system voting, even though all were on the front line of the refugee crisis, because of Spain's proximity to North Africa and Greece's location close to the Middle East. Instead, political upheavals in the 2010s were clearly connected to the financial crisis and the frustrations resulting from national governments' inability or refusal to intervene to ease economic distress. This is clear from the timing of the electoral shocks, the kinds of political discourses of the anti-system parties that gained at the expense of incumbents, and the characteristics of the voters who opted to vote against the system. The peculiar characteristics of the southern European welfare systems are key to understanding why the post-crisis backlash benefited the anti-system Left far more than the anti-system Right.

Greece: From Troika to Pasokification

The political transformation unleashed in Greece in the early 2010s could be the most overdetermined event in the history of European electoral politics. The depth of Greece's crisis, the evident complicity of a corrupt national political establishment in allowing it to happen, and the brutal and punitive conditions of the successive European bailouts made some kind of backlash unavoidable. Not surprisingly, the deepest economic crisis in Europe produced a period of unprecedented instability, with five general elections and six prime ministers in the decade after the financial crisis began. Out of the fourteen most volatile elections in post-crisis Europe, three were in Greece: in the May 2012 election the net change in party vote share reached 33 percent, the fifth most volatile election in any western European country since World War II.

This panorama of instability was in fact highly unusual in contemporary Greek history. Since the restoration of Greek democracy after the rule of the military junta in 1967–1974, Greece had settled into a relatively stable two-party system underpinned by two rival political dynasties: the Papandreou and Karamanlis families. After 1981 the combined vote share of the socialist PASOK founded by Andreas Papandreou, and the conservative ND party, founded by Konstantinos Karamanlis, barely fell below 80 percent, and aided by an electoral system that reinforced this bipartism, they dominated government formation. Members of the Karamanlis and Papandreou families held the prime minister's office for a total twenty-five years in the post-1974 period, and even Costas Samaras, ND prime minister in 2012–2015, had roomed at Harvard with George Papandreou, Andreas's successor.[47] The tight-knit nature of the governing elite perhaps contributed to attenuating political conflict, but had the consequence of highlighting the cartel-like dynamics of Greek politics.

This apparently sclerotic pattern of political control was blown apart by the economic collapse and the series of humiliating bailouts successive Greek prime ministers could do little to avoid. Despite power having been shared between PASOK and ND during the boom years when Greek public finances went out of control, PASOK, in office from 2009, bore most of the political cost. Prime Minister George Papandreou not only came clean on the trickery behind Greece's official budget figures, but was also in charge during the key period of the first two bailouts, a moment of national humiliation as well as economic collapse. The 2012 election, coming on the heels of the second bailout and a brief period of technocratic government under former central banker Papademos, saw the third-biggest electoral collapse of any major political party in postwar western Europe—the PASOK, which had governed Greece for a total of twenty-one years since 1974, dropped from nearly 44 percent of the vote in 2009 to just under 14 percent three years later. By 2018 it had just eighteen members in the Greek parliament, and merged into an alliance with half a dozen other small parties on the center and left.

The main beneficiary of PASOK's demise was a political group on the radical left, Syriza. Figure 5.8 shows the transformation of the Greek party system over the successive post-crisis elections, and leaves little doubt that the most important material shift in Greek politics was the effective replacement

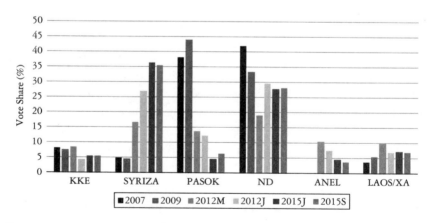

FIGURE 5.8 Patterns of Party Support, Greece, 2007–2015
Source: Klaus Armingeon, Virginia Wenger, Fiona Wiedemeier, Christian Isler, Laura Knöpfel, David Weisstanner, and Sarah Engler, *Comparative Political Data Set 1960–2014* (Bern: Institute of Political Science, University of Berne, 2017).

of PASOK by Syriza. This shift was spectacular enough to merit its own neologism, "Pasokification," meaning the cannibalization of a mainstream center-left party by the radical Left. The main party of the Right, ND, also suffered important losses after the crisis, losing almost half its vote share, but it recovered ground in the second election of 2012 and was able to maintain its status as the main potential governing party, despite some defections such as the creation of a small hard-line nationalist party, Independent Greeks (Anexartitoi Ellines – ANEL), and the emergence of a violent extreme-right party in Golden Dawn (Chrysí Avgí – XA).

The post-crisis period saw a rapid fragmentation of the political space in Greece, with not only the decline of both components of the post-Junta two-party system, but also a growth in the vote share of small parties, many of them new, and an increased turnover as a succession of new alliances emerged to seek parliamentary representation. In the May 2012 election the joint vote share of the two largest parties, at that point ND and Syriza, amounted to just 35 percent, less than half the post-junta norm. This meant an increasingly coalitional dynamic to government formation, as it became much harder for any single party to achieve a parliamentary majority. A further indicator of political crisis is the dramatic collapse in electoral participation: from an average of above 80 percent until 2009, voter turnout dropped to 65 percent in May 2012, and to just 56 percent in the September 2015 vote. Throughout the period, strikes and street protests, often violent, clearly expressed the anger Greek citizens felt about the economic losses they were suffering.[48] The signs of popular disillusionment and alienation from the political system after the crisis were unmistakable.

There is a consistent logic to this pattern of political change. As in other cases, the immediate impact of the crisis was to bring a change of government, but in the form of an orderly turnover within the established parameters of the political system. Prime Minister Kostas Karamanlis (nephew of the founder of his party, ND) was forced into an early election in autumn 2009, suffered a heavy defeat, and George Papandreou (son of the founder of his party, PASOK), took over. In the space of three years, Greece suffered a 25 percent drop in GDP, while financial assistance implying harsh austerity was negotiated by the existing political elite. Papandreou's appeal to popular consent by suggesting a referendum on the Troika bailout arrangements was slapped down by European leaders. In the run-up to the 2012 election, Greece was governed by a grand coalition of PASOK and ND under the stewardship of Papademos, a former European Central Bank vice president. The position of the established political class was that Greece's euro membership was to be preserved at all costs, and that they had little option but to accept the conditions being offered. Any voter wishing to oppose the bailout would have no choice but to support political forces from outside the established party system.

Part of the fragmentation of the Greek party system took the form of splinter groups—usually based on defections of parliamentary representatives elected with PASOK or ND—who still occupied positions within the broad mainstream of European politics, such as DIMAR (Dimocratiki Aristera – Democratic Left), a social democrat group, or Potami (The River) and EK (Enosi Kentroon – Centrist Union), both centrist liberal parties. But the big winners were anti-system parties that not only adopted more radical positions on the economy and society, but also expressed vehement opposition to the European bailouts and their implications. The total anti-system vote share in May 2012—summing the votes of Syriza, the Greek Communist Party (KKE), Golden Dawn, the far-right LAOS (Popular Orthodox Rally), and the nationalist Independent Greeks, amounted to 45.6 percent, far surpassing other elections in Europe. The anti-system parties all occupied relatively radical positions on the social-cultural dimension but were center or center-left on the economy: Golden Dawn and ANEL were less right-wing than ND on economics but further to the right on social-cultural issues, while Syriza was way to the left on both compared to PASOK, and the KKE is the most radical party on the left of the economic dimension.[49]

The effect of the post-crisis electoral shake-up was to move the average position of the Greek parliament substantially to the left on economic issues, while it became increasingly polarized on the social-cultural dimension. This is entirely in keeping with the predicted response of a society facing a dramatic loss of economic security: parties that promised to address these economic challenges were able to win votes from the established parties, whose corruption and incompetence were ultimately responsible for Greece's problems, and who were also the material executors of the austerity measures that had created such discontent. The anti-system parties all rejected the existing approach to the debt crisis with varying degrees of realism and coherence.

The emergence of the far-right Golden Dawn, from almost zero to nearly 7 percent of the vote, was the most disturbing development of the Greek crisis. Emerging out of a violent neo-Nazi street movement, Golden Dawn used aggressive xenophobic language to condemn the European Union, the Troika, and the euro, and to demand the full exercise of Greek sovereignty by leaving the Eurozone.[50] Its use of extremist language to condemn its opponents and what it viewed as Greece's enemies, and its violent street activism, often directed at migrants, put it outside even the normal range of right-wing anti-system parties. Golden Dawn won support particularly in districts of Athens with a high immigrant population, and its typical voter was young and unemployed with an intermediate level of education,[51] while it also recruited better than the average among farmers and business owners.[52] Its vote share, however, at just under 7 percent, was low and failed to rise in subsequent elections.

The other main anti-system response on the nationalist right, the Independent Greeks party, was a more typical European-style populist party, drawn mainly from the mainstream conservative right but rejecting the European bailouts, presenting itself as a "patriotic trench" to protect Greeks from the financial threats they faced.[53] Independent Greeks was born out of the conservative wing of the protest movement against the Troika, railing against the way the bailout had stripped Greece of its national sovereignty.[54] Voters for the Independent Greeks were often former supporters of ND, but were hostile to ND's support for European financial assistance and particularly likely to blame the European Union for Greece's economic problems.[55] Like Golden Dawn, Independent Greeks drew on long-standing far-right rhetoric about Greek national identity and articulated opposition to the bailout as an affront to the Greek nation, using often demagogical language such as equating Troika interventions to the German occupation in World War II.[56] The party also emphasized its own connection to the grassroots and associated itself visibly with the anti-austerity street protests, while dissociating itself from the left values of the rest of the anti-austerity movement.

While Golden Dawn and Independent Greeks together polled between 10 and 15 percent of the vote after 2012, the anti-system Left, comprising chiefly Syriza and the communist KKE, was much more significant electorally. The KKE peaked at just over 8 percent in January 2012, before reverting to its typical vote share of around 5 percent subsequently. The KKE has long been the most consistently Euroskeptic party in Greece, opposing euro entry and depicting the European Union as representative of the Western pro-capitalist values that the Greek Communists had long fiercely opposed.[57] It was therefore predictably opposed to the European bailouts.

The big winner in the anti-system wave in Greece was the leftist coalition Syriza. Syriza emerged out of SYN (Coalition of the Left, Ecology, and Social Movements), a loose coalition of former KKE modernizers, feminist and ecologist groups, and other groups on the new (non-Communist) left. Typical of such groups, it won support mainly from the highly educated, often public sector workers[58] attracted by its emphasis on "postmaterialism": issues such as the environment, multiculturalism, and enhancing citizen participation in democracy.[59] In 2001 SYN incorporated a varied range of small leftist groups into a new formation, Syriza, which was more open to social movements.[60] After the financial crisis began, Syriza unequivocally opposed austerity measures and backed popular protests, strikes, and civil disobedience, and with the formation of a grand coalition between ND and PASOK after 2012 to push through the bailout it found itself perfectly placed to exploit popular fury at the economic pain implied by the measures.

The failure of the ND-PASOK government to prevent yet a third bailout with onerous conditions brought its collapse and early elections in the worst possible conditions, sealing the fate of the post-junta party system. Syriza, led by Alexis Tsipras, went into the election campaign on a firmly anti-austerity ticket, promising to renegotiate the terms of the impending bailout and to secure a writedown of most of Greece's public debt, as well as a stimulus program led by the European Investment Bank—demands that the Troika and key EU governments were unwilling to contemplate.[61] At the same time Syriza maintained a tolerant stance on immigration and a broadly pro-European outlook, insisting that Greece's problems could be resolved within the EU framework by a shift in EU-wide policy toward greater solidarity with the debtor nations. Finally, it emphasized the need to "transform the political system to deepen democracy" by decentralizing power and enhancing popular participation in the decision-making institutions. This proved a winning message: Syriza's vote grew from under 5 percent in the immediate aftermath of the crisis to over 26 percent in January 2015, with the big breakthrough coming in the two 2012 elections. Syriza dominated particularly among civil servants (winning an estimated 43 percent of their vote), and among younger voters, housewives, and students.

Syriza's electoral victory in 2015 did not deliver a comfortable parliamentary majority, so it went into a coalition with the nationalist Independent Greeks, the other main anti-bailout party, rather than the pro-bailout center-left parties such as PASOK and DIMAR. The appointment of Yanis Varoufakis, a well-known critic of the bailouts, as finance minister suggested the intent to confront the European Union over Greece's financial needs and reject the existing terms for the third Greek bailout.[62] The Independent Greeks had an even more aggressive attitude toward the bailouts: their leader, Panos Kammenos, claimed that "Europe is being governed by German neo-Nazis."[63] The government's hope was that European leaders could be persuaded to ease the fiscal pressure on Greece, with a positive message on solidarity, backed up by the implicit threat of a chaotic "Grexit," which could destabilize Europe's fragile financial markets.

The Tsipras government, having predictably failed to move opinion in the key capitals of the European Union, was presented with the stark option of accepting the conditions on offer, or foregoing the proposed financial assistance, which would have left Greece close to financial meltdown. Consistent with Syriza's closeness to the popular mobilization against austerity and its rejection of the cartel politics of the pro-bailout parties, Tsipras attempted to overcome the impasse by inviting the Greeks to vote in a referendum on the bailout measures, which the government recommended rejecting. A decisive victory for the "No" vote in the referendum failed to sway the European Union, and Syriza opted to accept the bailout on terms that were if anything worse than before, calling yet another parliamentary election to obtain retrospective citizen consent for the retreat. Syriza's position on the euro was a pragmatic compromise between the need to do something to alleviate Greece's economic suffering and the surprisingly robust level of support in Greece for continued euro membership, as well as a realistic assessment of the dangers of any financial confrontation with Greece's creditors. Whether or not this political strategy made sense as a way of addressing Greece's economic crisis, it proved a very effective political strategy, as Syriza won re-election and was able to entrench itself in office.

Although Greece was also hit by the refugee crisis of 2014 on, with many Greek islands being located geographically on the front line of the refugee route from Syria, the timeline of economic collapse and electoral reaction points unequivocally toward its politics being driven by the nature and extent of the financial crisis, bailouts, and subsequent austerity. Greece's economic crisis was such that few groups were insulated from serious hardship, opening up opportunities for anti-system parties to make spectacular gains. Although the anti-system Right profited from the crisis, the Left made the biggest gains, appealing to the vast army of unemployed or underemployed youth and the public sector workers most affected by budget cuts. The main victim of this shift was PASOK, reduced to a rump of especially older voters and farmers. Adherence to the harsh austerity and liberalizing reforms imposed by the Troika appealed to a smaller and smaller share of the electorate: mainly ND's core vote of older voters, especially pensioners, farmers, small business owners, and the self-employed.[64] A political offering of economic protectionism, either of a nationalist or of a social democratic kind, was the most likely to prosper in the midst of a deep depression. The fact that the costs of adjustment were falling particularly on younger "outsider" voters, explains the greater success of the left narrative.

Spectacular though Greece's economic and political collapse may be, it is best seen as an extreme example of the patterns seen in other Western democracies since the late 2000s, rather than as a unique event. "Pasokification" may have been avoided elsewhere, but social democrats across Europe were hemorrhaging votes. Mainstream parties were colluding to protect the existing economic arrangements, and losing vote share, in most other democracies. Citizens have expressed increasing signs of resentment and mistrust of their political elites almost everywhere. The Greek case is simply off the scale in terms of the economic and social catastrophe wrought by the financial crisis, and, not surprisingly, its political consequences were far more powerful.

Portugal: A Quiet Revolution

Shortly after Greece's sovereign debt crisis began, Portugal also hit trouble and signed up to an Economic Adjustment Program (EAP) with the Troika in 2011. The slide toward the bailout coincided with the collapse of the Socialist-led government of José Socrates and the dissolution of parliament for new elections. The election campaign was dominated by the financial crisis and the ongoing bailout negotiations, yet the bailout was negotiated by a lame-duck Socialist government supported by the mainstream parties on the center and right: the Social Democrats (PSD), despite the name a mainstream party of the Center-Right, and the conservative Right (known as Centro Democrático e Social-Partido Popular, or CDS-PP). Finnish EU Commissioner Olli Rehn, with an eye on the concurrent election campaign in his home country, publicly stated that Socrates's original austerity plans had not been harsh enough, and that the bailout could not go ahead without Finnish support.[65] This interaction between elections in creditor and debtor countries reflected the weak position of the latter, with Portugal facing default if a rescue was not negotiated within weeks.

The bailout agreement was negotiated under the Socrates administration but came into effect under the new center-right government of Pedro Passos Coelho. However, only the parties of the anti-system Left—the Communist-Green alliance Unitary Democratic Coalitions (CDU), and the radical Left Bloc (Bloco Esquerda – BE)—opposed the agreement, and their parliamentary representation was not large enough for this to affect the prospects of the program coming into force. As in Greece, the electoral response to the financial crisis initially took the form of government turnover from within the established party system that had signed up to harsh austerity dictated by the Troika. The Socialists (PS) suffered a historic electoral defeat, losing over 8 percent of the vote compared to the previous election, and hemorrhaging twice that amount since winning power in 2005. The PSD gained most from the PS's losses, and the anti-system Left saw no immediate benefit from its opposition to austerity, but a warning sign was that the 2011 election saw the lowest turnout since the first democratic elections after the Portuguese revolution, at 58 percent.

Not only did the measures mandated by the Troika cause significant pain, but the Passos Coelho government also exploited the bailout to push its neoliberal agenda even further.[66] As the effects of the austerity measures fed through, the center-right government quickly began to suffer the political consequences, too, dropping precipitously in the polls to below 30 percent within a year of taking office as the economy declined.[67] After exiting the bailout program in 2014, Passos Coelho sought to hang on to power by forming an electoral coalition with the CDS-PP—called Portugal à Frente, or PàF—which would maximize the joint seat share of the two parties. This strategy failed dismally, with the PàF polling just 38 percent—12 percent less than its combined vote share in 2011, falling 13 seats short of a parliamentary majority (see Figure 5.9). The PS recovered to 32 percent, but the big winners were the anti-system Left, with the Bloco Esquerda doubling its vote to 10 percent, while the communist CDU also marginally increased its vote. The combined anti-system Left amounted to 18.5 percent and thirty-six parliamentary seats. This opened up the opportunity of a forming a center-left coalition with the PS, and after a doomed attempt by Passos Coelho to remain in office, a Socialist minority government, led by António Costa and supported in parliament by the radical left parties, was formed in November 2015.

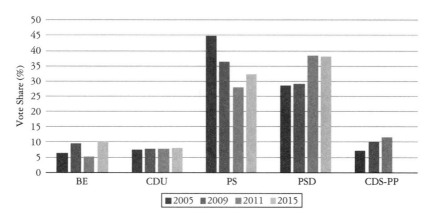

FIGURE 5.9 Patterns of Party Support, Portugal 2005–2015
Source: Ministério da Administracão Interna do Portugal (https://www.eleicoes. mai.gov.pt/legislativas2015).

This marked a sharp shift to the left in Portuguese politics, and the new government was the most clearly anchored on the left since the revolution. The main message represented by the anti-system Left, and more cautiously by the Socialists, was that austerity needed to be stopped and the state could and should help economic recovery through redistributive spending. Both anti-system left-wing parties demanded a restructuring of Portugal's public debt and a renegotiation of the EAP. The losses of the center-right were consistent with an anti-austerity wave in the election: the voters most likely to desert the PSD were those on low incomes or who had lost their jobs in the crisis, whereas higher-income groups were more likely to remain loyal.[68] It is difficult to interpret these results other than as a backlash against the harsh policies implemented by the Passos Coelho government under the tutelage of the Troika. At the time of the 2015 election, the Socialists and the Social Democrats (the main party of the center-right) had between them presided over the worst period for the Portuguese economy in decades.

Within the anti-system Left there were marked differences between the two main parties. The CDU alliance between the Portuguese Communist Party (PCP) and the Ecology Greens Party (PEV) drew on the historic tradition of the communist Left, a key player in the Portuguese revolution of the 1970s, and combined it with a Green agenda. The party symbol—a hammer and sickle and a sunflower—neatly illustrates the awkward juxtaposition of these two parties, one formally still a Marxist-Leninist movement, the other emerging out of the postmaterialist turn of the late twentieth century. The PCP articulated a long-standing anti-system position, opposed to European integration and to the capitalist system in general, bitterly criticizing the Troika, and at times adopting a nationalistic, Euroskeptic discourse, as seen in its slogan: "for a patriotic and left politics."[69] It played a role in the anti-austerity protest movement through its tight connection with the largest Portuguese trade union, the CGTP (Confederacão Geral dos Trabalhadores Portugueses), which was heavily involved in organizing resistance to the Troika measures through strike action and demonstrations.

The BE, formed as an alliance of various socialist and other radical left parties in 1999, located itself politically in the space between the CDU and the Socialists, combining anti-austerity discourse with a more left-libertarian politics, reflecting its younger activist base. While the PCP is a traditional mass-based left party, the Left Bloc has a looser and more decentralized organization, and has proved more open to social movements,[70] which is key to its growth in the period of Troika austerity. It has been close to youth-oriented street protest movements such as Geração à Rasca ("Desperate Generation") and Que se Lixe a Troika ("**** the Troika").[71] It has focused on opposing government cuts and privatizations and defending worker rights, especially "precarious" workers on short-term contracts, and protecting families from eviction. Compared to the Communists, the BE has particularly targeted the youth vote, playing up the perceived nonresponsiveness of the mainstream parties.[72] While the Communists have been open to the idea of leaving the European Union, the Left Bloc's position is analogous to Syriza in Greece, advocating reform of, rather than exit from, the Union, although euro exit has been discussed by some BE exponents.

As in the other southern European countries, the pattern of electoral support for the anti-system Left reflected the harsh consequences of austerity measures, particularly for vulnerable groups such as the young, disproportionately likely to suffer unemployment, and for public servants subjected to nominal wage cuts. Portugal stood out in southern Europe for the extent to which public opinion turned against the European Union as a result of the bailout and its accompanying austerity measures.[73] Clear majorities of voters rejected austerity: even a majority of center-right voters disagreed that "austerity was necessary to balance the government books," while among radical left voters, 93–94 percent disagreed with the statement.[74] The anti-austerity position of the radical left parties was clearly communicated over the period preceding the 2015 election, and clearly marked them out against the mainstream PS, PSD, and CDS-PP, which in varying degrees identified with the need for the Troika program.[75] However, there were also marked differences in social support: while the communist CDU had the highest share of pensioners among its electorate, BE had the lowest, reflecting the latter's closer connection to the new social movements that mobilized against the Troika.[76]

The extreme Right made no electoral inroads after the crisis in Portugal.[77] A small group, the Party of National Renovation (PRN) attempted to mobilize around the themes of immigration and national sovereignty, but performed dismally, winning 0.3 percent of the vote in 2011 and 0.5 percent in 2015. Despite a severe economic downturn and the humiliating experience of a financial bailout with harsh austerity measures attached, Portuguese voters remained unmoved by right-wing nationalist appeals. Immigration was not as prominent an issue in Portugal as in other southern European countries, since the refugee routes generally avoided Portugal, and net immigration was lower in Portugal than in most of the rest of western Europe.[78] The kinds of older voters typically supportive of right-wing populists in northern Europe tended to stay loyal to the mainstream, cartel parties: the PS and PSD in particular.

Opposition to austerity and the Troika instead came almost entirely from the left, since the population most affected tended to be younger, labor market, and welfare "outsiders." As a result, Portugal joined Greece in responding to the crisis by electing a left-anchored government that aspired to reverse austerity, within the European Union. Favored by an incipient recovery of exports and strong capital inflows,[79] the Costa government was able to halt some privatization plans, pensions cuts, and other austerity measures, and raise the minimum wage; to counterbalance this increased spending, public investment was cut back.[80] Although budgetary policy actually remained in line with European targets, Costa was able to claim that austerity had been abandoned, with the result of a booming economy.[81] Unlike in Greece, these favorable winds vindicated the critical discourse of the anti-austerity parties, and Portugal's leftist government found itself the poster child of the anti-austerity movement in Europe.[82]

Whatever It Takes: The Political Costs of Eurozone Austerity

The Eurozone crisis placed the European Union under extraordinary strain, as markets panicked, leaving the weaker, more indebted member states struggling to avoid financial collapse. The European institutions reacted to save the euro currency, offering "monetary solidarity,"[83] but failing to protect the weaker members from severe economic distress. The bailouts of Greece, Ireland, and Portugal may have saved them from crashing out of the single currency, but the price was harsh austerity for their citizens, and an accumulation of debt comparable to wartime. The effects of austerity were made worse by the refusal of European policymakers to act when it became clear that the debt crisis had derailed the recovery. While the US Federal Reserve and the Bank of England eased the pressure on their economies by slashing interest rates and printing trillions of dollars of new money to buy up financial assets, the European Central Bank continued to be more preoccupied with the threat of inflation, raising interest rates briefly in 2011 before cutting them again, and delaying quantitative easing until 2015.

The political costs of the Euro crisis can be seen in the destabilization of European party systems. Not only did Greece embrace anti-system politics, electing a government opposed to the bailout regime, but the northern European countries who had put up much of the money for the rescues also saw their own political backlash. Hard-pressed voters in the North may have been spared the fate of Greece, but still faced far from buoyant economic conditions: Germany's relative success in the post-crisis period was won on the back of a stoic degree of wage restraint, and an increase in wage inequality, which by the late 2010s was higher than in Britain.[84] Economic growth in the creditor countries, such as Netherlands, Austria, and Belgium, was weak, and Finland suffered lower growth than even Spain and Portugal in the decade after the crisis. The strong economies of northern Europe may have been accumulating trade surpluses, but the living standards of their citizens barely saw the benefit. Policy mistakes subjected the whole Eurozone to lower growth than it could have enjoyed.

At times of scarcity, distributional conflict becomes more difficult to manage, and political polarization is a predictable result. As Greece protested against the onerous conditions of European financial assistance, hard-up Germans and Finns could be forgiven for wondering why *they* should be paying to bail them out. Northern European politicians were understandably reluctant to come clean about the importance of bailing out the South for their own banks, which had lent recklessly during the boom years and risked collapse in the event of a Greek government default.[85] But by shifting the blame for the financial crisis entirely onto the debtors, they presented an opening to the nationalist Right, long opposed to Europe-wide burden-sharing. Parties such as The Finns or Alternative for Germany (AfD) exploited the southern European crisis to challenge European solidarity, demanding priority for their own citizens. This discourse was all the more effective when mainstream politicians such as Angela Merkel were themselves implying that southerners were guilty of ignoring the wisdom of "living within one's means."

What is more surprising is the relative weakness of the anti-system Right in the countries subject to bailouts with their attendant austerity measures and loss of sovereignty. Notwithstanding occasional tantrums, such as the Greek president greeting Merkel on a visit to Athens with a demand for war reparations,[86] nationalist revanchism was surprisingly muted in the South. Not only did the anti-system Right prosper far less than the Left in Greece, but in Portugal (as well as Ireland) no right-wing anti-system party appeared at all. This was all the more surprising, since the whole of Mediterranean Europe had to bear the lion's share of the burden of dealing with the Syrian refugee crisis of the mid-1990s, which outside Italy failed to ignite far-right sentiment. Instead, the backlash mainly benefited the Left, as in Ireland, where the mainstream political parties Fine Gael and Fianna Fail held on to power, despite some electoral turbulence and gains for the left-wing Irish Republican party Sinn Fein.

Here I have argued that the failure of the southern European anti-system Right to exploit the financial bailouts is the product of the way in which welfare states distributed the costs of the economic crisis. Young people are far more likely to espouse socially liberal views and tolerate immigration and diversity, and they were also the main victims of the crisis. Youth was the driving force behind mass movements protesting against austerity in Greece and Portugal, which grew into political parties capable of winning substantial vote shares and ultimately winning political power. The mainstream parties of the third bailout country, Ireland, held off the anti-system threat more successfully, in part because of the more generous welfare arrangements that the country's rapid growth had financed, and in part because of the high mobility of the Irish labor force, which responded to the crisis through mass migration. The other main victims of the Euro crisis, Spain and Italy, did not get off so lightly, as the next two chapters explain.

CHAPTER 6 | Spain: Boom, Bust, and Breakup

Introduction

By spring 2011, Greece, Portugal, and Ireland had all resorted to financial bailouts, and the "bond vigilantes"—investors betting against the bonds of heavily indebted countries[1]—turned their fire on Spain and Italy. Spain's beleaguered Socialist government under José Luis Zapatero responded with austerity measures that did little to stave off the market pressures but did hurt a population already reeling from a collapsing property market and an unemployment rate of 20 percent. On May 15, 2011, protestors filled Madrid's central square, the Puerta del Sol, and refused to leave for weeks, despite attempts by the police to clear the area. In Barcelona, a similar protest occupied the Plaça de Catalunya for a whole month, punctuated by violent clashes with the Mossos d'Esquadra, the Catalan region's police force.

As well as opposition to austerity measures, what became known as the *indignados* movement (or "15-M," after the date it began) protested the use of bankruptcy rules to evict underwater mortgage-holders from their houses. Spain had experienced a spectacular real estate boom in the late 1990s and 2000s, which turned into a bust after 2007. Unlike in the United States, where insolvent homeowners could simply "walk away" from their loans, Spanish borrowers could be evicted for missed payments and still be left on the hook for the remaining debt, with interest and charges. One of the leaders of a group protesting this plight, Ada Colau, rode the wave of protests to become mayor of Barcelona, Spain's second biggest city, at the head of a left-wing anti-austerity coalition. A similar coalition won control of the

City Council of Madrid, and the leaders of the *indignados* movement also founded a left-wing anti-system party, Podemos, that won dozens of seats in the Spanish parliament on an anti-austerity platform.

So far this is a familiar story: a debt-crippled southern European country forced into austerity, whose victims of unemployment, eviction, and spending cuts mobilized a left-wing protest movement that challenged the system, and where the anti-migrant Right made little impact. But here Spain diverges from the pattern in ways that shed light on the complexities of anti-system reactions. Little more than a year after the 15-M protest, a second front of anti-system politics was opened as a million protestors marched through Barcelona, demanding independence for Catalonia. Ada Colau's administration found itself pulled this way and that as the anti-austerity front divided along national identity lines, part of her coalition sympathizing with the ideologically hybrid Catalan nationalist movement, the rest aligning with the Spain-wide left project of Podemos.

Ada Colau's dilemma illustrates how group identities shape anti-system politics, and offers insights into the different ways in which the tensions arising from economic crises can be mobilized. The cultural and political roots of Catalan nationalism, relating to linguistic rights and the demand for self-determination, were long-standing, but the crisis turbo-charged these grievances. The Catalan independence campaign articulated the austerity fatigue of one of Spain's richer regions, resentful of what many Catalans regarded as an excessive fiscal burden imposed by an illegitimate state. In most of the rest of Spain, Catalonia's demands were given short shrift, and a polarizing dynamic was unleashed between competing nationalisms. In Spain, austerity politics pitted older, economically comfortable voters against younger, more precarious voters who suffered most of the economic cost of the crisis, but it also pitted one of the richer regions against the central state in a fight over the territorial distribution of the fiscal burden, and ultimately over the existence of the state itself. An economic conflict intersected with a conflict over identities, but, as this chapter will show, the issue of immigration barely registered.

Spain in the Euro: A Mediterranean Bubble Economy

This crisis hardly came out of nowhere, yet the prevailing view of Spain prior to the upheavals of the 2010s was one of political, economic, and social progress. Spain's relatively peaceful transition to democracy had been hailed as a model for others,[2] and its economy grew strongly through the 1980s and the 1990s, achieving a smooth entry into the euro. As late as November 2008 commentators were still describing Spain as a "success story."[3] Although the slow pace of structural reforms came under criticism from the European authorities, the key indicators policymakers focused on were flashing green. The debt-to-GDP ratio had dropped from 73 percent before euro entry to just 41 percent by 2007, and Spain was running budget surpluses. Unemployment, always Spain's Achilles heel, had fallen from 22 percent in 1995 to just 8.2 percent in 2007. From euro entry in 1999 until the eve of the crisis in 2007, economic growth averaged a healthy 3.4 percent.[4]

Unfortunately these healthy numbers masked the fact that Spain had been experiencing its own variant of the housing bubble that wrecked the economy of the United States. The convergence of interest rates after the completion of European Monetary Union (EMU) meant that borrowing costs in Spain plummeted: from a peak of over 13 percent at the height of the currency crisis of 1992 down to just 2.5 percent by 2005.[5] Spanish banks began to lend at historically low rates, generating an unprecedented credit boom. As late as the early 1990s, buying a home in Spain meant finding a down payment of around half the property value, then taking out a mortgage at double-digit interest rates and repayment over very short terms (ten years was typical). A decade later, banks were falling over themselves to offer home loans of over 100 percent of the purchase price with repayment terms of up to 50 years. The result was the biggest housing boom in western Europe, surpassing even Ireland, Greece, and the United Kingdom. Compound annual house price growth in Spain was over 8 percent between 2000 and 2008.[6]

Economic fundamentals could explain some of this increase, as income growth had been healthy and high levels of migration added around 3 million people to the Spanish population between the mid-1990s and the mid-2000s, one of the highest rates in the European Union.[7] However, there was also a heavy speculative component: in 2008 Spain had the highest price-to-income and price-to-rent ratios in western Europe,[8] meaning that house prices reflected neither citizens' capacity to service mortgages nor to pay rent. Instead, the financial system was directing speculative capital into a rising market in the expectation of continued asset growth, which brought a dangerous degree of dependence on overseas borrowing. Classic bubble behavior resulted, with households leveraging up to cash in on rising prices by buying multiple properties, and high loan-to-value mortgages being offered to people with low incomes and uncertain employment prospects reminiscent of the American-style "Ninja" loans. Household debt almost doubled between 1999 and 2007, from 80 percent to 154 percent of GDP.[9]

Although buoyant tax revenues resulting from the housing bubble brought public debt down as private indebtedness was rising, this only encouraged politicians to fuel the boom, embarking on "white elephant" projects, such as economically unviable airports in small remote cities such as Ciudad Real,[10] or the construction of the spectacular City of Sciences in Valencia, designed by fashionable architect Santiago Calatrava, at a cost of well over one billion euros, four times its planned budget.[11] By leveraging low interest rates to raise cash for such adventures, politicians could both impress voters and create jobs, and also rake in money through bribes and political donations from real estate and construction interests.[12] Reforms liberalizing local savings banks in the 1980s and 1990s allowed politicians to control the allocation of credit to specific firms and development projects.[13] This meant that political parties' financial and electoral viability was tied up with the housing boom.

This had a baleful impact on the behavior of politicians. One extraordinary example of this was the so-called Tamayazo scandal in Madrid, where two politicians elected to the Madrid regional assembly on the Socialist[14] list failed to show up to the investiture vote, sinking an attempt to form a center-left administration and paving the way for the center-right Popular Party (PP) to take power. The bizarre no-show was rumored to be connected to a corrupt deal with property developers. Even more remarkably, the two main parties colluded to bury the case: the Socialists, after initially accusing the two of taking bribes from developers, eventually let the issue drop and the two defectors disappeared from politics, although one of them, Tamayo, subsequently reappeared as a director of a construction company. This extreme example of the entangling of business interests and political representation revealed not only a pattern of deeply corrupt behavior, but also collusion between the major political parties keeping their exploitation of the housing bubble off the political agenda.[15]

Although the political parties had every reason to throw caution to the wind in the pursuit of money and votes, there was less of an excuse for the failure of banking authorities to foresee the likely consequences of the biggest housing boom in Europe. While by 2007 total private debt in Spain had doubled from 91 percent of GDP on euro entry to 191 percent, and total capital inflows were worth 10 percent of GDP, the Bank of Spain reported reassuringly that "the central scenario will continue to be a mild and progressive change of business model from the real estate segment to others, . . . to the benefit of investment in capital goods and exports."[16] Yet just a few weeks later, real estate investment in Spain ground to a halt, with high-profile Valencian developer Llanera going bankrupt in October 2007 as construction sites across the country began laying off workers. As global financial conditions changed, the tap of credit for Spanish banks was abruptly turned off. As bankruptcies and layoffs followed, house prices went into free fall, undermining the balance sheets of banks, companies, and households.

From Bubble to Austerity: Spain's Sovereign Debt Crisis

The collapse of the real estate bubble in Spain led to a dramatic increase in unemployment as the construction industry, which accounted for a quarter of Spanish jobs at the height of the boom, ran out of cash, leaving many buildings half-finished. GDP contracted by almost 5 percent in 2008–2009, recovered slightly in 2010, and then declined still further as the Eurozone double dip recession took hold. The budget surplus quickly turned into a deficit of 11 percent of GDP as tax revenues dropped and laid-off workers claimed unemployment benefits. As government borrowing shot up, investors shunned Spanish government bonds and an initial round of austerity measures was introduced by the Zapatero government, with tax rises, pay cuts in the public sector, and cuts in transfers to the regional governments that were responsible for much of Spain's social service provision. This contractionary policy predictably depressed economic activity still further, reducing the denominator of the deficit-to-GDP ratio and canceling out the effect of austerity.[17] Public austerity was all the more devastating because the private sector was attempting to deleverage at the exact same time: Spain reduced its external borrowing from $151 billion in 2008 to a $20 billion surplus in 2013, an adjustment worth around 12 percent of GDP in just five years.[18]

This herculean effort was not enough to convince the bond vigilantes that Spain could repay its debts, and spreads continued to widen even after Greece, Portugal, and Ireland had been bailed out by the Troika. It was becoming clear that Spain would not be able to exit the crisis without help, and in the summer of 2011 Zapatero (alongside his Italian counterpart Berlusconi), received a letter from the European Central Bank (ECB) governor Trichet urging the immediate implementation of structural reforms and budget cuts, which was widely seen as a quid pro quo for ECB support in the bond markets.[19] The letter was relatively detailed, identifying specific measures, particularly in the labor market, that were required, such as dismantling Spain's long-established collective bargaining arrangements, loosening rules on temporary employment, and easing restrictions on firing workers.[20] Moreover, the letter implied action was urgent, with the need to supply "credible evidence" of intent to address fiscal sustainability and structural reforms within the month.

The purchase of billions of euros worth of Spanish bonds by the ECB in subsequent months—ECB holdings by December 2012 stood at €44 billion, almost 5 percent of Spanish GDP[21]—relieved the pressure, but by the following summer Spain was again in trouble as it missed its deficit target and the economy was back in recession, implying even more austerity if future targets were to be met.[22] The final straw that pushed Spain to seek European financial assistance was the weakness of much of the banking sector, which by spring 2012 was on life support in the form of ECB funding. By this time Zapatero's Socialist Party had been thrashed in the November 2011 elections, to be replaced by Mariano Rajoy's PP, which had fewer political qualms about following through with labor market reform and cuts to welfare spending. Yet although Spain was spared a formal Economic Assistance Program (EAP), by mid-2012 the Rajoy government was forced to request up to €100 billion of financial assistance from the European Union's European Stability Mechanism (ESM) to recapitalize the Spanish banking sector.

The eagerness of the new administration to carry out what its finance minister Luis de Guindos proudly announced to European Commissioner Olli Rehn as a "very aggressive" labor reform[23] may have influenced the decision to allow Spain to avoid a full sovereign bailout, with all the associated stigma. Spain introduced several liberalizing reforms in the labor market after the crisis. The most important of these, introduced by the Rajoy government in 2012 was in part designed to assuage European policymakers, but also responded to partisan preferences and pleased the Spanish business community.[24] Its main objectives were to weaken union workplace power, undermine collective bargaining, and loosen legal restrictions on dismissal.[25] European policymakers had insisted that Spain's collective bargaining arrangements, by legally imposing extensions of agreements in cases where bargaining broke down, hindered the real wage cuts required for Spain to restore competitiveness. The reforms achieved their goal, as wage growth was slower in Spain than in any other European country except Greece and Portugal, and some groups, particularly younger workers and women, saw their real wages fall.[26]

Even though the Spanish government embraced this "internal devaluation" route out of the crisis, the banking bailout still involved a degree of intrusive monitoring comparable to the Greek and Portuguese programs, but through different institutional mechanisms.[27] However, the fiscal measures demanded of Spain were not tied to disbursements for the banking sector, and so the government was able to miss deficit targets without sanction, easing the return to growth. Even so, the social and economic consequences of the crisis were severe. By the time Spain finally returned to growth, in the fourth quarter of 2013, the economy had shrunk almost 10 percent from its pre-crisis peak. Unemployment had soared to almost 27 percent by 2013, with youth unemployment at 55 percent.[28] Median income fell by 3.3 percent in real terms in 2007–2013, and the lowest 10 percent of earners lost 7.6 percent, the worst figures in the Eurozone after Greece.[29]

As in the American real estate crash, Spaniards also suffered acute financial stress, with many losing their homes as properties with underwater mortgages were repossessed by banks. Spain's restrictive bankruptcy laws allowed banks to sell off repossessed properties at firesale prices, landing some homeowners on the street but still owing the banks tens of thousands of euros. In early 2018 it was estimated that there had been 745,000 mortgage defaults since the crisis began, of which just over half a million resulted in foreclosure, and almost half of these involved families losing their primary residence (236,000 families).[30] Like unemployment and negative wage growth, these losses disproportionately affected the younger working-age population, who were most likely to have high levels of housing debt.

Work and Welfare in Spain: Youth Takes the Strain

In the midst of a devastating financial crisis, many families could not survive without help from the government. Spain's welfare model was in some ways more egalitarian, demographically balanced, and sustainable than its southern neighbors. While maintaining many of the typical features of the Mediterranean model, with its heavy reliance on social insurance funding and generous provision for pensioners, long periods of Socialist government had layered redistributive social policies onto the edifice inherited from the Franco dictatorship. As well as a comprehensive unemployment benefit, the state social security system provided contributory and noncontributory retirement and invalidity pensions, and by the 2000s public spending on social programs amounted to 20 percent of Spanish GDP, just a few percentage points lower than the most advanced welfare states of western Europe. Unlike Italy or Greece, Spain lacked very stark differences in the social security rights of different occupational groups, and pension spending was relatively redistributive.[31]

Where Spain's social model clearly failed was in the organization of the labor market. The Franco dictatorship had sought to curb labor militancy by establishing very strong employment protections, so that public servants and workers in manufacturing industries were almost impossible to dismiss without paying extensive compensation. These restrictions hindered job creation, contributing to soaring unemployment of over 20 percent, the worst in Europe, which the Socialist government of Felipe González addressed by introducing temporary contracts with lower dismissal costs. By the late 1980s, Spain had more temporary employees than any other country in Europe, and these mainly younger workers were the first to be fired in downturns.[32] Yet unemployment remained the highest in Europe after Greece, peaking at above 25 percent in the recession of the early 1990s. Youth unemployment (under-25s) peaked at 45 percent in the mid-1980s and mid-1990s.[33]

These dramatic figures obscure the numerous ways in which the strong family structure in Spain cushioned young people from the full consequences of their economic disenfranchisement. As in other Mediterranean countries, patterns of interfamily solidarity often fill in the gaps left by the welfare state, with older, usually male breadwinners able to financially support younger family members, and sometimes intergenerational transfers from retirees in the extended family. The whole structure rested on a typically Mediterranean pattern of widespread home ownership, which in Spain was even higher than in neighboring countries, with close to 80 percent of the population in owner-occupancy.[34] In the mid-2010s, 73.6 percent of Spanish youth (15–29) lived in the parental home.[35]

The pension system, although more sustainable than in Greece and Italy, accounted for around 9 percent of GDP at the time of the financial crisis, and grew to over 11 percent afterward. Pension spending expanded markedly during the 1980s with the introduction of noncontributory means-tested minimum pensions, while defined-benefit contributory pensions based on payments into the Social Security fund became increasingly generous, resulting in relatively higher contribution rates for the working-age population. A wave of early retirements to facilitate industrial restructuring in the 1980s also contributed to higher social spending on the elderly. As a result, in 2014 over-65s in Spain had average incomes of almost 99 percent of the population average, the fourth highest in the OECD,[36] while the poverty rate for the elderly was considerably lower than for the general population. The roughly nine million pensioners in Spain constituted a formidable voting bloc, which acted as a severe deterrent to attempts to rebalance welfare spending in favor of the young.

Policy developments in the 1990s and 2000s addressed this lopsided pattern of welfare provision in a piecemeal fashion without changing its basic logic. The devolution of many welfare policy areas to subnational authorities (the Autonomous Communities) allowed some regions to expand provision.[37] However, the bulk of social spending revolved around Social Security, which was an exclusive competence of the central state and enabled a degree of income redistribution between poorer and richer regions. This constraint was particularly salient in Catalonia, which became a heavy net contributor to the Spanish welfare state, an issue on which Catalan nationalist parties were able to mobilize electoral support. Interterritorial redistribution also took place through public investment and transfers to the regional governments in poorer regions, notably the Socialists' power base in the South.[38]

Spain's pre-crisis welfare system primed the anti-system politics of the 2010s. Social spending and labor market regulation favored the old over the young, exposing the latter to job insecurity, low pay, and unemployment. Regional imbalances placed the onus on the more economically dynamic regions to fiscally sustain the low activity rates and bad demographics of poorer regions. Finally, politicians manipulated spending decisions for political gain, and often appeared to connive in obscuring corruption from the public gaze. In good times, voters seemed to relax their scrutiny of politicians' behavior, but in hard times, economic grievance and political mistrust would prove a potent mix.[39]

The Political Backlash: From the Streets to the Vote

The immediate response to the crisis in Spain was a wave of demonstrations by the so-called *indignados* as austerity measures began to hit home. The movement combined political and economic grievances: the main targets of its ire were banks and the mainstream political establishment, and an early slogan was *No somos mercancías en manos de políticos y banqueros* ("We are not commodities in the hands of politicians and bankers").[40] The movement shunned ideological identities and focused on what united protesters: rejection of the existing system and a shared feeling of outrage, reflected in the label *indignados* to describe its participants. The protests were coordinated by established activist networks of environmentalists, anti-globalization groups, anti-war protesters, gay rights groups, students opposed to higher education reforms, and groups involved in protests against foreclosures and evictions.[41]

The protestors occupying the squares were mostly young, especially students and the unemployed or insecure workers: one of the core groups was named *Juventud sin futuro* ("Youth with No Future"). The protests made frequent allusions to the lack of choice between the major parties, perceived as equally culpable for the crisis, and demands for an overhaul of the party system.[42]

Alongside these mass protests, direct action groups sprang up around the foreclosure crisis.[43] The PAH (Plataforma Afectados por las Hipotecas), founded in Barcelona in 2009, emerged as a protest group lobbying for better treatment of underwater mortgage holders and helping victims with legal advice. Housing became the front line of the impact of financial instability on Spanish households, and unlike broad issues of unemployment and job insecurity, foreclosures pitted debtors against their creditors in a very direct and tangible way. The PAH movement challenged the mainstream political parties—both the PP and the Socialists, especially the former—for their failure to intervene in defense of those losing their homes, and organized a popular petition to demand legislative changes to wipe out foreclosure debts.

As in Greece and Portugal, it was the groups most affected by the economic consequences of the crisis that mobilized to challenge existing policies, principally younger citizens lacking job prospects and those caught up in Spain's housing crash. But party politics was pushing in the opposite direction. The first post-crisis election brought the defeat of the Socialist Party, which shed over four million votes, dropping to just over 28 percent of the vote—its worst performance since the restoration of democracy in 1977. Although the far-left Izquierda Unida (United Left) doubled its vote to almost 7 percent, the real winner was the conservative PP, which won its highest ever vote share, 44.6 percent, winning an absolute majority in the Congress, albeit on a historically low turnout of under 70 percent. There was a sharp increase in the fragmentation of the vote, as the joint vote share of the two main parties dropped from 84 to 73 percent.[44]

The blanket rejection of the political establishment expressed by the *indignados* likely discouraged disillusioned voters on the left from casting a vote or pushed them toward anti-system candidates, most of them nationalist parties in the Basque Country and Catalonia. The pattern emerging from the 2011 election was of increasing polarization around the territorial divide, with big gains for Catalan and Basque nationalist parties at the expense of the Socialists, who defended Spain's existing territorial settlement. On the other side of the divide, a new party, Union, Progress and Democracy (Unión, Progreso y Democracia, or UPyD), with centrist economic and social policies but fiercely critical of Catalan and Basque nationalism, grew to nearly 5 percent of the vote. This incipient polarization around the national-territorial dimension was almost guaranteed to be fueled by a PP government with an absolute majority. The PP's position on the territorial issue was of quite aggressive opposition to Basque and Catalan claims, reflecting both its long-standing identification with conservative Spanish nationalism and a strategic calculation: the PP was historically weak in those two regions and had few votes to lose, while a hard-line approach played well in other parts of Spain.

The PP's victory ushered in a program of austerity measures and structural reforms consistent with the policy priorities of the European Commission and the ECB. In particular, the Rajoy government's labor reform—imposed in the face of the outright opposition of the trade unions—created a tense industrial relations climate, leading to two general strikes in 2012. A round of spending cuts, with a cut to public sector pay and a freeze on recruitment, higher retirement ages, and increased income tax and VAT, satisfied Spain's European creditors but were predictably deeply unpopular with Spanish voters. In less than a year, the Rajoy government's approval rating fell to the levels of the previous Zapatero administration shortly before its crushing electoral defeat. In a measure of the discredit of the entire political establishment, 85 percent of those polled had no confidence in Rajoy as a leader, yet the Socialist opposition leader (now Alfredo Pérez Rubalcaba) had equally low ratings.[45]

The financial crisis was not only economically painful, but it also threw the complicity of the main political parties in the mismanagement of the banks into sharp relief. The highest profile example of this was Bankia, created out of a merger of Caja Madrid with several other smaller savings banks in 2010 to become the third-largest bank in the country. As Spain's housing market collapsed, Bankia found itself with large numbers of bad loans on its books and needed recapitalizing, but international investors refused to bite, and instead around €3 billion in shares were offloaded to small local investors, mostly Bankia depositors. As the financial slide continued, an injection of government money of around €22 billion was needed to save Bankia from collapse, and trading in Bankia equity was suspended, leaving thousands of small shareholders facing massive losses. The director of Bankia in this period was Rodrigo Rato, a former finance minister and a leading figure in the PP; it subsequently transpired that he and others had maintained a slush fund for private expenses, for which he received a prison sentence in 2017.[46]

The PP's weak moral authority to impose austerity was exacerbated by a series of corruption scandals that reached uncomfortably close to the party leadership. The "Gurtel" case, which had been the object of a judicial investigation since 2009, involved a long-running and systematic arrangement whereby PP officials took bribes from businesses in exchange for favors in assigning public contracts or planning permissions, which in turn were used by the party as a slush fund for political and campaigning expenses.[47] In early 2013, at the height of the Rajoy government's austerity drive, secret party documents were published showing regular payments from the slush fund to various party leaders, including (again) Rodrigo Rato, as well as several other former ministers. The findings of these investigations and their political ramifications formed the mood music of the Rajoy administration, exacerbating the salience of corruption as a major political issue for Spanish voters.[48]

By the time of the 2015 election, the Rajoy government was deeply unpopular, yet the main opposition party, the Socialists, were discredited by their own scandals and in no position to capitalize. While the PP lost more than three and a half million votes and their parliamentary majority, the Socialists not only failed to recover, but lost a further 7 percent of the vote (see Figure 7.1). The joint vote share of the two major parties, which had averaged over 70 percent since the early 1990s, dropped to only 51 percent, and their joint share of parliamentary seats, at 60 percent,[49] was the lowest since the first democratic elections in 1977. The main beneficiaries of this collapse of the established parties were two new parties contesting an election to the Congress of Deputies for the first time: Podemos on the left, which won just under 21 percent of the vote, and Ciudadanos (Citizens—C's), on the center-right, which won 13 percent.

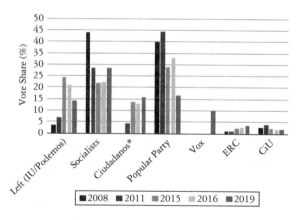

FIGURE 6.1 Patterns of Party Support, Spain, 2008–2019
Source: Klaus Armingeon, Virginia Wenger, Fiona Wiedemeier, Christian Isler, Laura Knöpfel, David Weisstanner, and Sarah Engler, *Comparative Political Data Set 1960–2014* (Bern: Institute of Political Science, University of Bern, 2017).
* For 2008, Unión de Progreso y Democracia.

Figure 6.1 shows that elections after the crisis represented a shift to the left in the Spanish political panorama. The PP lost out to Ciudadanos, which represented more socially liberal positions combined with a liberal economic stance, while the Socialists lost out to Podemos, which was clearly located further to the left on both dimensions. The other significant shift took place in Catalonia, where the left-wing nationalist party, the Catalan Republican Left (Esquerra Republicana de Catalunya, or ERC) defeated the center-right Catalan nationalist parties (Convergència i Unió, or CiU) for the first time, pointing to a radicalization of Catalan nationalism at the expense of the moderate centrists. Party competition in Spain was permeated by. the intense territorial conflict between the demands for self-government of nationalist parties in Catalonia and the Basque Country, and parties advocating a more centralized state.

These electoral trends follow a clear pattern of decline for the established parties and growth for new, mostly anti-system, parties. The source of these changes was the disenchantment of the younger voters most affected by the crisis and least attached to the established parties. Supporters of Podemos and Ciudadanos had a more negative view of the economic situation, and this was especially the case for the young.[50] In contrast, age was positively correlated with voting for the established parties, the PP and the Socialists, as the data in Figure 6.2. demonstrate starkly. On the left, the PSOE became a party of older, and usually less-educated, voters, and was especially strong in

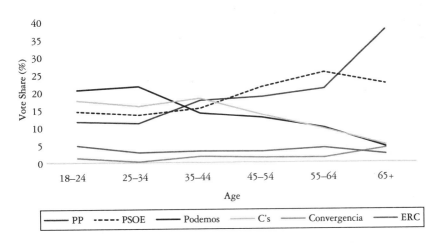

FIGURE 6.2 Party Support by Age in Spain, 2015
Source: Centro de Investigaciones Sociológicas (CIS), Post Electoral Survey, 2015 Election (Postelectoral Elecciones Generales 2015. Panel [2ª Fase], Estudio 3126. Madrid: CIS) (http://www.analisis.cis.es/cisdb.jsp).

the South, where the party used distributional politics to build an electoral stronghold. The PP had an even greater age skew: in the 2015 election, the PP's support among the over-65s was twice the average for all age groups. In contrast, support for Podemos and Ciudadanos declined with age. Figure 6.2 shows that this pattern also prevailed in Catalonia, where the center-right Catalan nationalist Convergència i Unió (CiU), like the PP, won twice as much support among the retired as among the electorate as a whole, whereas the Republican Left(ERC) was more evenly represented across age groups.

Anti-system voting was stronger among the young because they were the group most exposed to the effects of the financial crisis and the longer-term patterns of inequality and job insecurity in Spain. Data for 2014 showed that among 30- to 39-year-olds, around half were either unemployed or in temporary work, a figure that reached around a third even for university graduates. This group constituted a rich reservoir of support for anti-system parties such as Podemos and the left Catalan nationalists. In contrast, the Spanish welfare state was more successful in protecting the incomes of the old: retirees in the 66–75 age bracket had higher incomes than the average Spaniard, thanks to a relatively generous state-provided pension system.[51] These groups tended to stick with the established parties.

This age gap shaped the divide between established parties and anti-system parties, but other divides complicated the picture. Anti-austerity politics dragged the party system to the left, while the intensification of the center-periphery conflict pushed Catalan nationalism toward a more radical, secessionist position, provoking a hardening of attitudes among parties on the center and right opposed to any breakup of Spain. Unlike in most western European countries, the anti-system Right was slow to emerge. The rest of the chapter shows how this complex pattern of political competition shaped different forms of anti-system politics in the post-crisis period.

Podemos: The Political Wing of the Indignados

Podemos was formed in early 2014 after the publication of a manifesto signed by left-wing intellectuals arguing for the creation of a list for the European Parliament elections representing the ideas of the *indignados*. A Madrid university professor, Pablo Iglesias, emerged as leader of the new party, which after just a few months of existence won almost 8 percent of the vote, electing five members of the European Parliament. The party name, Podemos (We Can), evoked the Obama campaign of 2008, but its message was more radical: it demanded the reversal of austerity and the ousting of the political and financial elites responsible for economic hardship. By forming a party, Iglesias formalized and cemented the political structure that coordinated the various 15-M movements.[52]

Podemos's political message reflected its roots in the protest movements and its clear anti-system identity. It revolved around two familiar themes: opposition to the existing political order, and rejection of the current economic arrangements. Podemos initially dismissed the Spanish political system as fundamentally broken and in need of a new constitution that would dismantle the existing two-party system and its systematic corruption. This anti-elite discourse described the established party leaderships as *la casta* (the caste, after a popular book of the same name detailing political corruption[53]) and conflated the acronyms of the two main established parties (the PP and the PSOE) as "PPSOE," implying that they were indistinguishable, united in their neglect of the people. The concept of *la casta* extended beyond politicians to include bankers and corrupt business interests,[54] dovetailing with the party's critique of the economic order.

The economic discourse of Podemos placed it firmly on the anti-capitalist left, emphasizing the importance of protecting welfare rights, public education, and social services,[55] and advocating a greater role for the state in investment and the organization of the economy. Specific measures in the party's first electoral program in 2014 included the reduction of the working week to thirty-five hours, the reduction of the retirement age to sixty, and the revoking of all of the labor reforms implemented in Spain since the crisis.[56] Most of the party's main leadership figures had backgrounds in leftist politics, and Spanish voters certainly perceived to party to be located on the left.[57]

At the same time, party rhetoric sought to deny the relevance of the traditional left-right divide in politics, instead blaming political and business elites for society's problems.[58] Podemos did not shy away from its "anti-system" status, aspiring to be a "lever for political change in this country [. . .] so that citizens can take back democratic control of our institutions and destiny."[59] At the same time, Iglesias, when pointedly asked if he was "antisistema," replied, "We defend the health system, the education system, a system that defends social rights, the system that we live in, the product of many hard-working people."[60] Similarly, the party's position on the territorial divide in Spain reflected a neat triangulation: Podemos's official position was that they preferred Spain to remain intact, but that Catalonia should be entitled to hold a referendum on independence if a majority there wished.

The issue of the euro was also an awkward one for Podemos. On the one hand, its very existence was owed to the impressive wave of protests against the austerity measures whose ostensible purpose was to keep Spain in the euro. Yet reversing austerity while remaining in the Eurozone was impossible without a commitment from the European authorities, and in particular the ECB, to sustain Spain in the bond markets and commit to bailing out its banks or public institutions should they run out of funds. In a very similar approach to Syriza in Greece, Podemos proposed changes at the European level to relax the fiscal restrictions of the Stability and Growth Pact; develop greater coordination of fiscal policy at the European level, implicitly to facilitate redistribution from richer to poorer EU member states; and move toward the "democratization" of the European Central Bank, which should be required to hit targets for employment as well as inflation, and to permit the direct purchase of government debt to alleviate funding pressures on struggling states.[61]

Although Podemos resisted identifying itself as an ideological party and had ambitions to govern on behalf of the "people" as a whole, it was strongest among the same groups that typically supported the anti-system Left elsewhere: younger, more educated voters in urban areas, just like the activists that had launched the 15-M movement.[62] These voters had often previously voted for the Socialists, who lost disproportionately more younger voters in the 2011 election than those over 60.[63] Podemos voters, while they belonged to the generation most affected by the crisis, were not individually more likely to have suffered economic losses than other citizens. Instead, the party attracted the voters that were most politically engaged, rather than the most economically vulnerable groups, who tended not to vote at all.[64] But Podemos voters were more likely to have a negative view of their own personal economic situation and of the economy as a whole than those who remained loyal to the established parties, and they were also more likely to see political corruption as a cause of these problems.[65]

After its shocking burst onto the scene in 2014, Podemos continued to expand its support in subsequent elections. The local and regional elections of May 2015 presented major organizational and strategic challenges to the party, since it still lacked an entrenched territorial presence and was unable to monopolize the political space to the left of the Socialists, which consisted of fragmented and uncoordinated social movements in a number of Spanish cities. As a result, a decision was taken to present formal candidates for the regional but not the local elections, where instead Podemos offered support to like-minded candidates, mostly under the banner *Ganemos* (Let's Win).[66] This delivered some striking results, with radical left candidates winning the mayor's office in both Madrid and Barcelona (Ada Colau). After the regional elections held in most of Spain's Autonomous Communities in 2015 (with the exception of the Basque Country, Catalonia, Andalusia, and Galicia), Podemos contributed to the election of center-left administrations in five regions previously governed by the PP.

The November 2015 general election confirmed Podemos's momentum, as it won 5.2 million votes (a 20.7 percent vote share), only 300,000 less than the PSOE. This growth was facilitated by deliberate efforts by Iglesias to soften the party's image and adopt a catch-all approach, diluting some of its more radical messages, especially on economic policy and the euro.[67] The logic of this strategy was not only to maximize vote share, but also to make Podemos a possible coalition partner of the fading Socialists, paving the way to a governing role. This catch-all approach was easier to sustain on economic and social policy, where Spanish voters had a well-established preference for improved social protection, than on the other key cleavage in Spanish politics: the national/regional question. Here the polarization around the Catalan nationalists' increasingly radical stance threatened Podemos's electoral strategy and complicated the formation of a broad coalition of the left to combat austerity.

Against the System, Against the State: Territorial Politics and the Crisis in Catalonia

The battle over austerity interacted with Spain's territorial conflict, which has shaped post-Franco party politics, with regionalist and nationalist parties taking substantial vote shares in several of Spain's regions, known as "Autonomous Communities."[68] The political and identity dimensions of the center-periphery cleavage cross-cut the economic dimensions. Political centralization and Spanish nationalism have been associated with the political Right, while decentralization and support for nationalist claims in the periphery have been supported more by the Left. But in economic terms, Spain's fiscal arrangements imply substantial redistribution from the richer regions, such as Catalonia, but also Madrid, toward poorer parts of Spain. Claims to greater self-government for the wealthy regions have been opposed by the large southern regions that formed the bedrock of the Socialist electorate: Andalusia, Estremadura, and Castile-La Mancha.

A further layer of political complexity is that large numbers of citizens from these poorer regions of southern Spain migrated to the North, and particularly Catalonia, in the postwar period of economic expansion. This group and its descendants, mostly Castilian speakers, were less sympathetic to Basque and Catalan nationalism and tended to prefer state-wide political parties, especially the Socialists,[69] over the nationalist parties, creating an identitarian dimension of political competition and conflict. The PSOE has therefore historically adopted a pragmatic acceptance of a decentralized state, due to its large vote shares in the periphery regions and historic ties to Basque and Catalan nationalists in the opposition to the Franco regime. But this has placed the Socialists in an uncomfortable position, caught between the PP's hardline centralism and Spanish nationalism, on the one hand, and the national claims of Basques and Catalans, on the other.

In contrast to this, Spain's main conservative party, the PP, has benefited from adopting intransigent positions on territorial issues, with the main nationalist parties of Basque Country and Catalonia and the PP feeding off each others' hostility. Despite the polarized rhetoric, Spain's experience of frequent minority governments defused tensions, as Catalan and Basque nationalist parties often offered legislative support to Socialist or PP governments in exchange for a greater devolution of powers, and, conversely, the state-wide parties on occasion cooperated with nationalist parties in their respective autonomous regions.[70] But the election of a PP government with an absolute majority in 2011, at the height of post-crisis austerity, upset this equilibrium.

The PP's previous period in office with an absolute majority, in 2000–2004, had been marked by an escalation of tensions in the Basque Country, with the Aznar government passing a law banning political parties close to terrorist organizations, which directly excluded the Basque left nationalists from elections. But in the period following the financial crisis, it was Catalonia that took a radical turn. The traditional celebration of the national day of Catalonia (*diada*) on September 11, 2012, saw the biggest march in recent Catalan history, with banners demanding independence.[71] This impressive show of strength brought a seismic shift to the Catalan party system, as the main Catalan nationalist party, Convergència, dropped its traditional position of greater autonomy for Catalonia within Spain, and instead adopted secession as its formal policy. With this move, a pragmatic center-right party rooted in the Catalan business community, which had been the lynchpin of the region's governance, became an anti-system party.

This dramatic shift reflected the progressive loss of faith among Catalans in the institutions of Spain's semifederal arrangements, which devolved a wide range of powers to the regional governments but retained sovereignty, and the key fiscal and constitutional powers, in the hands of the central government.[72] The Catalan autonomous government (*Generalitat*) had voted through a revision to the region's statutory powers in 2006, only to find after a painstaking negotiation with the Zapatero government that the Constitutional Court quashed several articles and restated the doctrine of the unity of the Spanish state. The Court's decision, published in 2010, unleashed an angry reaction in Catalonia, including a major protest in Barcelona, where around a million people marched under the slogan, "We are a nation. We decide."

Survey data shows that popular support for independence, though growing, remained very much in the minority up until 2012. As Figure 6.3 reveals, the share of Catalans favoring independence rose in spectacular fashion, from 29 to 44 percent, in the year prior to the 2012 *diada* protest. The success of the pro-independence mobilization occurred at exactly the same time that Catalonia was also experiencing its own version of the Spain-wide anti-austerity protests of the *indignados*. These protests, often met with a brutal response by the police, reached their height in June 2011 with a mass protest blockading the Parliament building in Barcelona, leading to members of the Catalan government being helicoptered in to cast their votes for the spending cuts.[73]

The economic crisis created a particularly fraught situation in Catalonia, whose government was running a budget deficit of around €9 billion in 2010 and had the highest stock of debt of any Spanish region, putting it squarely in the sights of the Spanish government, the European Commission, and the financial markets.[74] Convergència appointed former Harvard economist

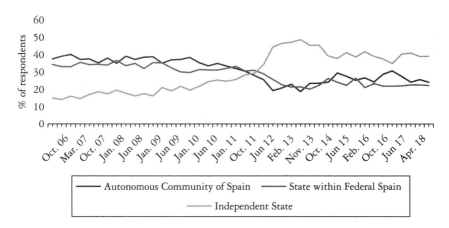

FIGURE 6.3 Preferred Relationship of Catalonia to Spain, 2006–2018 (Catalonia only)
Source: Centre d'Estudis Opinió, 2018, *EvoluCEO*: Valors Polítics, Question 30 "Relació entre Catalunya i Espanya"(http://evoluceo.ceo.gencat.cat/ceo/inici/evoluceo.html#/main/evolucio) (author's translation to English).

Andreu Mas-Colell to stabilize the finances of the Generalitat through a front-loaded adjustment that lopped almost 10 percent off the budget in 2011. This involved politically toxic measures such as a 5 percent salary cut for functionaries, cuts of more a billion euros to health spending and education, and fare increases on public transport. The Catalan administration came close to default in July 2012, requiring an emergency cash transfer from the central government to pay debts to Italian and German financial institutions.[75] As part of the austerity drive, the Generalitat also delayed payments to suppliers, including third-sector organizations delivering social services, as well as private companies.

The political consequences of these difficult economic conditions are clearly reflected in survey data on Catalans' political priorities, as we can see in Figure 6.4: from 2009 until 2015, unemployment and job insecurity was consistently the top issue cited as the most important problem facing Catalonia (with around 40–60 percent), with economic performance the second most important. In contrast, the problem of "Catalonia's relations with Spain" was way down the list of concerns at the height of the economic crisis; even in October 2012, when the massive march for independence took place on the *diada*, less than 8 percent of Catalans thought the national question was a priority. However, party politicians set about driving the issue to the top of the agenda. In response to the *diada*, the head of the Catalan government, Artur Mas, called a snap election only two years into his term, and promised to hold a referendum on independence if re-elected.

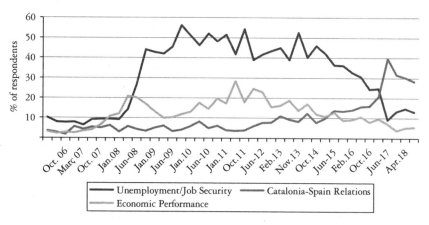

FIGURE 6.4 Issue Salience,* Catalonia, 2007–2018
* Response to question "Which do you think is the most important problem in Catalonia?"
Source: Centre d'Estudis Opinió, 2018 (see Figure 6.3).

This shift in strategy was a gamble on the Convergència's newfound support for independence restoring the dominant position of the conservative Catalan nationalism, close to business interests and pragmatic in orientation, which had controlled the Generalitat from 1980 until 2003, but had declined after the departure of its historic leader Jordi Pujol and a wave of corruption scandals.[76] Convergència had found itself increasingly challenged by the ERC, which had always been committed to independence, and by the even more radical pro-independence CUP (Candidatura de Unitat Popular, Popular Unity Candidacy). Catalan nationalism was hurtling toward the left: away from an essentially conservative movement based on business interests and rural voters, and toward a younger, more urban, and progressive nationalism.

Mas's gambit of promising a referendum on self-determination, was aimed at deflecting demands for radical social and economic change onto the more manageable terrain of identity politics. In this way the popular indignation over austerity, which had been as strong in Catalonia as in the rest of Spain, could be redirected onto the central government in Madrid. The 2012 election campaign focused heavily on the independence issue, evoking the Scottish success in winning agreement for a referendum to attract pro-independence voters to Convergència, and blaming the Spanish central government for the cuts.[77] This message fell on fertile ground, since Catalonia's status as a major net contributor to Spain's central government budget had provoked resentment for some time.[78] The Spanish government, rather than the Generalitat or the broader global and European financial crisis, could be blamed for unpopular austerity.

The election unleashed a polarizing dynamic that dominated Catalan politics and pushed nationalist politicians toward open disobedience of the law of the Spanish state. The election produced a hung parliament, leading Mas to form a parliamentary majority with the ERC, which left little room to row back on his promises of self-determination. This commitment clashed with the Spanish constitution of 1978, which not only sanctified the unity of Spain, but also retained the power to revise the constitution or hold referendums in the hands of the Congress of Deputies in Madrid. The new Catalan parliament, with a bare majority of seats for the nationalist parties first passed a motion in early 2013, declaring Catalonia to be a sovereign people and initiating a so-called sovereignty process (*procés*), then called a referendum on independence for 2014. Both these decisions were overturned by the Spanish Constitutional Court. Finally, a nonbinding vote on independence was held in November 2014, which remained, albeit ambiguously, within the law, and was largely boycotted by nonnationalist voters.

Having set in train the independence *procés*, the Catalan government lost control of it, with intense popular mobilization pushing the politicians toward ever more confrontational positions. Organizations such as the Catalan National Assembly (Assemblea Nacional de Catalunya, ANC) and Omnium Cultural organized frequent, almost daily demonstrations and other initiatives to intensify the push for independence, getting close to a million people onto the streets on several occasions. The failure to achieve any institutional progress and the refusal of the Rajoy government in Madrid to negotiate produced another snap election, in September 2015, which Mas pitched as a "plebiscite" on independence, promising secession within eighteen months if he were delivered a parliamentary majority. This time a broad pro-independence electoral alliance—Junts pel Sí (Together for Yes)—was negotiated between Convergència and the ERC, but again it fell short of an absolute majority, and was forced to rely on the radical anti-capitalist CUP for votes in the Parliament.

This pushed the nationalist coalition into an increasingly radical stance. Mas was forced out as the price of winning the support of the CUP for a new nationalist government, and was replaced by Carles Puigdemont, a long-standing supporter of the independence cause. The Puigdemont government pressed ahead with the independence agenda, this time pushing through a "self-determination referendum," with a bare majority of the Catalan Parliament, as the nonnationalist parties abandoned the chamber in protest. The referendum was declared unconstitutional by the Spanish Constitutional Court, but it went ahead anyway, though largely boycotted by nonnationalist voters, and affected by police repression.[79] In a final act of defiance, Puigdemont announced a unilateral declaration of independence, albeit suspended in effect, leading to the Spanish central government temporarily dissolving Catalonia's autonomous institutions and calling new elections, while Puigdemont and many other independence leaders were indicted on charges of "rebellion" and "sedition" by the Spanish judiciary.

These extraordinary developments represent in some ways the most extreme example of anti-system politics in this book. But the broad and heterogeneous nature of the pro-independence coalition, which ranged from the conservative, business-friendly center-right to the radical Trotskyite left, meant that anti-system politics in Catalonia was hard to fit into familiar categories of right or left. Pro-independence voters broadly came from two socially rather different, origins: on the one hand, younger, higher income, and more educated voters in the economically dynamic urban coastal areas of Catalonia, and on the other, conservative voters in the largely rural provinces inland.[80] What bound these voters together was a strong sense of

Catalan, rather than Spanish, identity, usually accompanied by habitual use of the Catalan language and disproportionately Catalan heritage (Catalan surnames are distinctive compared to those common in Castilian-speaking Spain). Survey data shows a strong linear relationship between family ties to Catalonia and support for independence: 75 percent of Catalans whose parents and grandparents were all born in Catalonia supported independence, while those born in Spain but outside Catalonia were the least supportive (12 percent).[81]

Many Catalans of non-Catalan origin descended from those that migrated from the poorest regions of Spain—especially Andalusia in the South—and Catalan heritage was therefore correlated with income and other social characteristics. Because of this, support for independence was positively correlated with economic status, with the unemployed and those with lower family incomes least supportive of independence. Higher-income Catalans were likely to feel most affected by Catalonia's status as a large net contributor to the Spanish state budget, a situation described as *espoli* (plunder) in radical nationalist discourse, captured more crudely by the slogan *Espanya ens roba* ("Spain steals from us"). A group of US-based nationalist academics, including Columbia University economist Xavier Sala-i-Martín, claimed that independence would bring a "fiscal dividend" from the prospect that "money that now goes to Spain, after independence would stay in Catalonia."[82] These claims were enthusiastically picked up by nationalist politicians.

The left wing of the independence coalition had much more in common with the anti-austerity movement of the *indignados*, and appealed in particular to younger voters, especially students and the precariously employed. The ERC, Catalonia's historic nationalist party, founded in 1931, occupied the space to the left of Convergència, attracting a younger, more urban, and more highly educated sector of the Catalan-speaking electorate.[83] Long before secession became the stated goal of the broader Catalan nationalist community, the ERC adopted an anti-system position, arguing for independence and the principle of Catalan popular sovereignty, even at the cost of breaking with the Spanish constitutional order.[84] The CUP also adopted a left pro-independence position, alongside a more radical participatory vision of political action, based on principles of direct democracy, representing a more fundamental challenge to the capitalist order and advocating a "socialist and ecologist" economic model.[85]

The opening of the *procés* served a useful purpose for all these parties by obscuring the deep divisions between the left and right wings of Catalan nationalism on social and economic issues and protecting Convergència from the political fallout of the austerity measures it had imposed after the crisis. This was reflected to a surprisingly transparent extent in the speeches of key Convergència leaders. Francesc Homs claimed "the left-right debate subordinates us to Spain," while Mas argued that "independence is not a right or left issue."[86] As Figure 7.3 shows, the *procés* shifted public concern away from the economic situation and toward the issue of Catalonia's constitutional status.

In terms of street protest, during the *procés,* part of the anti-austerity movement was subsumed into the independence movement. Once the intensity of the *procés* subsided after the 2018 elections, voters' focus on the independence question declined, and a new wave of anti-austerity mobilization directed at the Generalitat, once more under the control of the Catalan nationalist center-right, kicked off.[87] This highlighted the conflictual relationship between the nationalist Left and the nonnationalist Left, represented in Catalonia by a loose federation of groups aligned with Podemos, whose most prominent leader was Mayor Colau of Barcelona. Colau's position, like the Podemos line nationally, was that Catalans should be allowed to vote on independence but that she would campaign against it. Faced with the institutional conflict between Madrid and the Generalitat, Podemos was forced into an uncomfortable position, appealing for dialogue and condemning the repressive response of the Spanish central government, while simultaneously accusing the nationalists of irresponsibility.

The politics of Catalonia demonstrate the ways in which political contestation can be mobilized across different dimensions, and the interaction of political competition at different institutional levels. The established parties, particularly the PP and the Socialists, suffered the electoral costs of being associated with the failures of Spanish government policy in the euro era. But opposition to austerity could be framed in different ways. For the anti-system Left, represented by the movements aligned with the *indignados,* the problem was austerity and a corrupt political system that privileged financial interests. But in Catalonia anti-austerity politics cross-cut with the question of Catalan relations with the rest of Spain, allowing mainstream Catalan nationalists to shift the blame onto the central government[88] and the unfair fiscal burden placed on Catalonia to subsidize poorer regions of Spain. By turning austerity into a question of identity, the Catalan nationalist Right avoided the fate of the Spain-wide political establishment, but at the cost of adopting an unsustainable project of unilateral secession.

Whether the secession crisis would have arisen in the absence of the Constitutional Court's dilution of Catalan autonomy, or under a less hostile governing party than the PP, is hard to settle, but at the very least austerity and crisis had an escalating effect and economic grievances were central to the discourse of the pro-independence movement. Catalonia's debt problems and status as a net contributor to Spanish public spending greatly exacerbated the tensions over its constitutional status within Spain. The Basque Country, in contrast, did not see any significant rise in support for secession in the same period, even though the Basque nationalist movement has historically been far less comfortable within Spain. Basque nationalists attempted their own push for independence in the 2000s, which met with a similarly obstructive response from the central government. But one significant difference between the two cases is that the Basque Country and neighboring Navarre enjoy special fiscal arrangements, which are extremely favorable[89] and allow their respective governments to provide social services more generously than in Catalonia. Unlike Catalonia, which has seen Madrid and other regions overtake it in economic growth in recent years, the Basque Country is an economic success story, and its strategy for promoting innovation is seen as a model across Europe.[90] The crisis did not trigger any radicalization in the Basque Country, nor were Basque nationalists especially supportive of the Catalan *procés*.[91]

Franco's Revenge? Identity Politics and the Return of the Spanish Far Right

Given the high degree of salience of migration in most advanced democracies in recent years, Spain, alongside the other bailed-out states of the Eurozone (Portugal, Ireland, and Greece), stands out for the limited success of political parties mobilizing around nativist, anti-migrant positions. This is puzzling, since there are many features that would have predicted some kind of xenophobic backlash in these cases. The crisis hit these countries harder than any other in the Eurozone in terms of GDP and real income losses. Moreover, by resorting to financial assistance under onerous conditions, the four countries also very visibly gave up much of their national autonomy in terms of economic and social policy, as well as undergoing intrusive and humiliating monitoring of government business from external actors. Finally, all four countries had experienced substantial inward migration during the boom years, and in the case of the three Mediterranean countries, were on the front line of the refugee crisis of the mid-2010s.

Spain was a net exporter of labor for most of its recent history, but from the 1990s, the country experienced quite a dramatic demographic shift with substantial migratory inflows, chiefly from North Africa, parts of Latin America, and eastern Europe. At the onset of the financial crisis, around a tenth of the Spanish population were foreign nationals, a tenfold increase since the beginning of the century.[92] On top of this, Spain is just a few kilometers from Africa across the narrowest Mediterranean crossing, and has two enclaves—Ceuta and Melilla—embedded inside North Africa. Finally, Spain suffered in 2004 what remains the single deadliest jihadist terror attack in Europe. The potential for immigration to become a source of resentment in a country where over a quarter of the active population were unemployed at the height of the recession was obvious.

Instead, the major post-crisis development on the right was the growth of a political party, Ciudadanos, which barely mentioned migration in its messaging, focusing instead on overturning corrupt politicians and pushing back against secessionism. Ciudadanos was founded in 2006 in Catalonia in response to the growing radicalization of the Catalan nationalist movement, pitching its message at largely Spanish-speaking voters tired of the nationalist hegemony of the Catalan political system. The party mobilized opposition to policies promoting the use of Catalan language in the public services and autonomous institutions, and particularly in education, where Catalan was required to be the primary language in all public schools.[93]

Ciudadanos initially stood for election only in Catalonia, polling vote shares under 4 percent, but the radicalization of the Catalan nationalists in 2012 created an opportunity for growth. The party doubled its vote in the 2012 Catalan elections, exploiting the increasing salience of its signature issue—the rise of Catalan secessionism—and the inability of the weakened Socialist Party to hold on to its base of nonnationalist voters. As the economic crisis continued and austerity measures were imposed by both the Spanish central government and the Generalitat, Ciudadanos joined Podemos in riding the wave of resentment toward the established parties. The Ciudadanos leader, Albert Rivera, like Pablo Iglesias significantly younger than the other party leaders, quickly won a high media profile across Spain, offering a mix of commitment to the unity of Spain, strong rhetoric against the corruption of the established politicians, and liberal economic reforms.[94] This political positioning earned the party the label "the Podemos of the right."[95]

Ciudadanos aimed at different kinds of voters in different arenas. In Catalonia, its main target was the electorate of the Spain-wide parties, especially the Catalan Socialists, who had long straddled a difficult tension between the strong Spanish identity of a part of the party's voters, and the more Catalan nationalist sympathies of its party leadership. By offering a more uncompromising rejection of Catalan nationalism coupled with a more centrist position on other issues, Ciudadanos won over a broad range of voters on the left and right who were opposed to secessionism, while in the Spain-wide political arena, Ciudadanos directed its fire mainly at the PP and attracted mostly younger voters from the center and right.[96] This flexible strategy allowed Ciudadanos to rapidly expand its electorate, winning 3.5 million votes (13.9 percent) in the 2015 general election, and becoming the biggest single party in Catalonia after the 2017 Catalan elections, with 25 percent.

This strategy rested on an increasingly uncompromising Spanish nationalist discourse, which raised the stakes of the territorial conflict. But rather than succeeding in monopolizing the center-right political space, Ciudadanos found itself with a new competitor to the right in the far-right party Vox, which burst onto the scene in the autumn of 2018, winning 11 percent of the vote in Andalusian regional elections. This electoral breakthrough ended the anomaly of Spain lacking a significant far-right party,[97] and in the general election held in Spring 2019, Vox won 10 percent of the vote nationally, making it the first far-right party to enter the Spanish Congress since 1982. But unlike the experience of the anti-system Right in northern Europe, Vox's success was not built on a sudden shift in Spanish attitudes toward migrants, nor did it appeal to "left behind" voters. Instead, it mobilized especially around the territorial issue and the threat of "separatism" in Catalonia and elsewhere.[98]

The leader of Vox, Santiago Abascal, was a former activist in the PP, and most of its voters were conservatives disillusioned with the PP, a party hemorrhaging votes after a succession of corruption scandals. Vox combined a traditional social authoritarian message with an aggressive Spanish nationalism and an intense hostility to Catalan and Basque nationalism and Spain's decentralized political arrangements more broadly.[99] Vox came to prominence by ably exploiting a quirk of Spanish law whereby a private individual or organization can file a charge of criminal offense in the courts and take part in the court proceedings alongside the public prosecutor (the so-called *acusación popular*).[100] When the Catalan crisis hit the courts, with the main Catalan independence activists being charged with sedition and rebellion, Vox filed as a plaintiff and won the right to take part in the high-profile trial, allowing its leaders to promote the party's ideas to a wide audience.

Vox is unusual among parties of the anti-system Right in having relatively little to say about immigration, although references to the Reconquest—the historical battle against the Muslim presence in Spain in Medieval times—permeated its discourse. Instead, the unity of Spain and the purging of corruption from the political institutions were its main themes. Its launch document emphasized four principles: opposition to abortion, family, the unity of Spain, and opposition to ETA (the Basque terrorist organization).[101] The party's three-thousand-word Founding Manifesto did not mention immigration once, but instead made repeated references to the need to resolve Spain's territorial issues, as well as combating corruption and promoting "moral values" and "national cohesion."[102] Specific party commitments ranged from the promotion of the Spanish language in education to easing restrictions on hunting licenses and protecting bullfighting from the challenge of animal rights activists. Unlike many parties of the anti-system Right, Vox appeared to perform better in high-income areas in cities, and its strength correlated with that of the PP and Ciudadanos in past elections. In other words, Vox reflected a splintering of Spanish conservatism, attracting a hardline section of the most socially and culturally conservative voters.[103]

With the emergence of Vox to the right of the PP, the stretching out of the political space in Spain after the crisis took a further step. The main establishment parties of the center-left and center-right saw their space curtailed by anti-system forces attacking them from more radical positions. Cutting across the left-right divide, the center-periphery dimension of Spanish politics has also stretched out, with more voters advocating either secession on the one side or recentralization on the other. Not only do we observe a challenge to the established party system, but we can also see how the anti-system challenges feed off each other, with the rise of Podemos and Catalan secessionism provoking the emergence of a new anti-system Right.

Immigration was a lesser concern for Spanish voters than in most other European countries, but the resurgence of nationalism and the mobilization around cultural identities was very strong. Unlike elsewhere, however, identity politics in Spain was directed more toward internal rivalries and disputes about the unity of the state than toward migrants or the European Union. The high salience of national and regional identities is a persistent feature of Spanish history, and predictably distributional tensions in a period of economic crisis ran along an identitarian axis as well as the more conventional economic one. The Spanish case shows that a powerful economic crisis hitting a political system suffering from elite collusion and public mistrust inevitably produces major anti-system challenges. However, it also shows that anti-system reactions are shaped by existing institutions, particularly the economic and social arrangements that determine how economic losses are distributed among different groups.

Conclusion

Spain provides an eloquent illustration of the direct impact of economic distress on anti-system politics. The country suffered one of the deepest financial crises, with some of the most severe effects on wealth and incomes , of all the Western democracies. This was followed by a surge of political instability, voter volatility, and electoral shifts away from the establishment parties to anti-system forces. The political discourses of the anti-system parties, and the kinds of voters they appealed to, confirm that economic factors were the driving force behind this transformation. As in Greece and Portugal, anti-austerity movements reflected the ways in which patterns of social spending and labor market policies shifted the costs of the crisis onto younger voters, leading to mainly socially liberal forms of anti-system politics prevailing. In contrast, migration was mostly a marginal issue in political debates following the financial crisis.

But Spain also reveals the complexity of anti-system politics, with anti-austerity politics contributing to the intensification of the conflict between Catalan nationalism and its opponents, both within Catalonia and across the rest of Spain. The crisis forced moderate Catalan nationalists to radicalize their position in response to the growth of more left-leaning anti-system forces that threatened their hegemony within Catalonia. This lurch toward an anti-system position accelerated the polarization of Catalan politics between nationalists and nonnationalists, but also exacerbated long-standing tensions between different territories of Spain. The fragmentation of the Spanish center-right into three parties—Ciudadanos, the PP, and Vox—each attempting to outbid the others over the territorial issue, diverted cultural or identitarian conflict toward constitutional issues, and away from migration.

The lower salience of migration in southern Europe had one notable exception: Italy. The refugee crisis in the Mediterranean provided an opportunity in 2018 for Spain's Socialist prime minister, Pedro Sánchez, to burnish his left-wing credentials by offering a haven to the *Aquarius*, a ship carrying migrants rescued off the Libyan coast. The ship had been denied entry to Italy, whose interior minister, Matteo Salvini, had made opposition to migration the main focus of his successful election campaign in March 2018. The next chapter explains how Italy's anti-system parties won power, and why migration politics was more salient there than in neighboring countries.

CHAPTER 7 | Basta!: Anti-System Politics
in Italy

I N SEPTEMBER 2007, just as the first tremors of the Global Financial
Crisis were felt across Europe, Italian comedian Beppe Grillo organized
a bizarre rally in Piazza Maggiore, Bologna, as part of the quirkily titled V-
Day (*Vaffanculo-day*: "**** you day"). The aim was to gather signatures for
a referendum banning anyone with a criminal record from standing for election to the Italian parliament. The initiative achieved a spectacular 336,000
signatures, far more than the 50,000 necessary to hold a vote. The campaign
was the parting shot of what became the Five Stars Movement (Movimento
Cinque Stelle, M5S), perhaps the most innovative and unpredictable exemplar of contemporary anti-system politics, and the big winner of the 2018
Italian election.

Italy is an unusual case in our panorama of anti-system politics, having
already experienced a thorough clear out of its political establishment back
in the early 1990s. After a financial crisis and a wave of corruption scandals
swept away the main political parties, the 1994 election ushered in the "business politician" Silvio Berlusconi, allied with anti-system forces on the Far
Right, and promising "a new Italian miracle." Yet despite these upheavals,
Italy embarked on a period of austerity and reform to ensure entry into the
first wave of European Monetary Union in 1999. It did not enjoy the pre-
crisis boom seen in Spain or Greece, but neither did it suffer a similar financial collapse, managing to survive the sovereign debt crisis of early 2010s
without a formal bailout. But in 2016, Italian GDP per capita was lower

than in 1999,[1] and public debt had grown to beyond 130 percent of GDP, despite yet further doses of austerity.

The depth and duration of the economic crisis made Italy fertile ground for anti-system politics, but the nature of the reaction was less predictable. Alongside the M5S, the other main beneficiary was the Northern League, which began life as a regionalist party campaigning for the breakup of Italy, but then smartly reinvented itself as an Italian nationalist party, hostile to Europe, and especially to immigration. In 2018 these two parties came together in an unlikely coalition, making Italy the second country in the European Union to form a government completely dominated by anti-system parties. This chapter explains why anti-system politics was so successful in Italy, and why the anti-system Right was so much stronger than in the rest of southern Europe.

The Dress Rehearsal: The 1992 Financial Crisis and the End of the "First Republic"

For most of the period after World War II, Italy followed a very different path than the rest of southern Europe. After the collapse of Mussolini's fascist regime, Communists, Socialists, and Christian Democrats came together to write a democratic constitution, paving the way for Italy to become a founding member of the European Economic Community, and one of the fastest-growing economies in Europe, with GDP per head quadrupling between 1950 and 1992.[2] Italian democracy gave an appearance of instability and permanent crisis, yet survived grave threats from the mafia and terrorist movements on the right and the left to deliver some of the highest living standards in the world.

Key to this achievement was a complex system of horse-trading between political parties, and patterns of distributional politics that won the consent of disparate social interests to the democratic political order. Governments were coalitions of several parties, dominated by the Christian Democrat party, itself divided into organized factions, all of which used their political power to channel public resources and regulatory favors to their supporters. The postwar economic boom delivered a bonanza of tax revenues, which were used to build a fragmented and complex welfare system that redistributed income, eased social and geographical divisions, and constructed reliable reservoirs of political support for the main political parties. The development of the Italian welfare state in the boom years of what became the "First

Republic" (roughly, 1948-1992) shaped the subsequent politics of economic decline over the next quarter century.

As in the rest of southern Europe, the Italian welfare state was strongly biased toward the elderly, with pensions dominating social spending. By 2013, public spending on pensions amounted to over 16 percent of GDP, the highest in the OECD.[3] Some occupational categories, such as civil servants, the military, teachers, and the self-employed, enjoyed benefits far exceeding contributions and could retire on reduced pensions well before the normal retirement age, the so-called baby pensions.[4] Italy also handed out large numbers of invalidity pensions, especially in areas of high unemployment in Italy's less economically developed South. Needless to say, many supposed invalids were in decent health: one case saw a 58-year-old pensioner who, despite being registered blind, worked on weekends as a football referee.[5]

Over time Italy developed into what Julia Lynch describes as "a welfare state that rewarded older male breadwinners handsomely but crowded out spending on benefits for families and young adults."[6] Pensions accounted for well over half of social spending, the highest in western Europe, and contributed to the Italian public sector spending over half of GDP, almost as much as the more advanced welfare states of northern Europe, but with markedly poorer coverage of social risks and patchy public services. This high level of spending was in part the product of widespread corruption and clientelism (the trading of political favors for votes), which grew alongside a modern welfare state.[7] The central role of political parties in this system became known as *partitocrazia*, and was widely tolerated for a long time, especially since Italy's healthy economic growth provided a steady flow of tax revenues to pay for clientelistic redistribution.

The inefficiencies and inequities of Italy's system of government were well understood, but despite frequent scandals that revealed the sordid hidden workings of the political system, there was little appetite for change. This suddenly ended in spring 1992, after the arrest of a minor Socialist politician in Milan, Mario Chiesa, who was caught taking a bribe of 7 million lire (around 3,500 euros). Chiesa agreed to tell magistrates everything he knew after his estranged wife revealed he kept billions of lire in Swiss bank accounts. He testified to delivering envelopes of cash to the Socialist leader Bettino Craxi's offices in Piazza Duomo, Milan, and subsequent investigations in the so-called *Mani pulite* ("clean hands") inquiry revealed a vast network of corrupt dealings involving bribes worth the equivalent of millions of dollars, popularly known as *"tangentopoli"* ("bribesville").[8]

The *tangentopoli* system was in any case on its last legs, because the Italian economy was no longer able to sustain the costs of a corrupt political system.[9] Public spending was growing faster than tax revenues, in part because of corruption, but also in part because of political pressure from the left to increase welfare provision. At the same time, governments tolerated widespread tax evasion by Italy's large and politically powerful small business sector.[10] These conflicting pressures meant that budget deficits grew steadily, peaking at 11 percent of GDP in the early 1990s, while total government debt hit 100 percent of GDP. Politicians' inability to balance the books was initially absorbed by monetary policy, as the Bank of Italy was subordinate to the Treasury and forced to buy any government bonds not picked up by the market. But the central bank lobbied successfully for greater independence in the hope that politicians would be forced to face the fiscal consequences of deficit spending without the monetary safety valve.[11]

Attempts to raise more revenue ran up against a tax revolt in the wealthy North of the country, spearheaded by a new anti-system political movement: the Northern League (Lega Nord). [12] The League was an alliance of regionalist movements across the North, chiefly in Veneto and Lombardy, and expressed, in truculent and earthy language, the anger of the small business class at the iniquities of the tax system, the demands for bribes from politicians and bureaucrats, and the wasteful spending of *Roma ladrona* ("thieving Rome"). Its electoral breakthrough in spring 1992 coincided with the opening of the *Mani pulite* investigations, and with the acceleration of Italy's financial difficulties, as currency speculators attacked the lira, ultimately forcing it out of the European Monetary System, alongside the pound sterling, in September 1992.

This combination of political, judicial, and financial pressures blew apart the political establishment, which no longer had the votes or the money to sustain the *tangentopoli* system. A third of the members of the Italian parliament, including former prime ministers Bettino Craxi and Giulio Andreotti, found themselves arraigned on charges of corruption, embezzlement, illegal financing of political parties, tax evasion, and complicity with organized crime.[13] This led to a redrawing of the political map and the emergence of a completely new party system, but it also brought about a fundamental change to Italy's economic governance, which progressively marginalized these parties from the conduct of economic policy.

Italy's "Second Republic": Vote Berlusconi, Get the Bank of Italy

Italy's financial and political crisis produced the most transformative election in western Europe since World War II. By spring 1994, when parliament was dissolved, the Italian political map had become unrecognizable. The main governing parties fell apart, their leaders discredited or in some cases under arrest. Bettino Craxi escaped to Tunisia on a vacation that turned into permanent exile, while others gave up on politics to focus on their legal battles. The disintegration of the "First Republic" parties not only left many voters orphaned, it also threatened a variety of political and business interests that had benefited from their political protection.

Silvio Berlusconi, an entrepreneur in the construction and media sectors, was particularly exposed, both economically and legally. Berlusconi had built an effective monopoly of the private television market and the related advertising market, thanks to the Craxi government's acquiescence in his bending broadcasting law. In return, Berlusconi's channels offered Craxi political support. The political demise of Berlusconi's political backers at a time when his Fininvest corporation faced financial pressures was bad enough, but there were also judicial threats: Berlusconi's lawyer, Cesare Previti, had bribed Roman magistrates to deliver a sentence he himself had written, which allowed Berlusconi to take control of Mondadori, a major Italian publisher.[14] The *Mani pulite* investigations risked bringing down Berlusconi's business empire and miring him in charges of corruption.

So Berlusconi entered politics—or "took the field" as he put it—creating a new political party called Forza Italia to contest the 1994 elections, at the head of a broad-ranging electoral alliance with the Northern League and Alleanza Nazionale (National Alliance, or AN), a new formation with roots in the postwar Italian fascist movement (the Italian Social Movement – MSI). These parties were united by their hostility to the Left, but had little else in common: the Northern League wanted the secession of northern Italy into an independent Republic, while National Alliance was strongest in Rome and the South. Berlusconi's party bound these disparate groups of voters together with a catch-all message of optimism, anti-communism, and vague promises of economic reforms to unleash a "new Italian miracle." This unlikely coalition won a majority of seats, defeating a broad left-wing alliance led by the Democratic Party of the Left (PDS), composed of former members of the Italian Communist Party. Berlusconi, despite never having held elective office, was appointed prime minister.

The Berlusconi government, deeply divided from the start, lasted little more than six months before the Northern League brought it down. The motive was a pensions reform that would raise the retirement age, a measure that particularly affected the League's electorate of older northern Italians. But throughout the convulsions unleashed by *Mani pulite*, apparent political chaos masked an underlying policy stability as technocrats took over the key offices. In 1993 a caretaker government was formed under Carlo Azeglio

Ciampi, the governor of the Bank of Italy, imposing harsh austerity to confront Italy's precarious financial and economic situation. Automatic wage indexation (the so-called *scala mobile*) was abolished, public spending and public sector salaries were frozen, some pension benefits were deferred, and a raft of privatizations and tax increases came in to boost revenues.[15]

This stabilized the public finances and initiated a long period of fiscal rectitude, in which the government consistently ran a primary budget surplus (net of interest payments). After the brief interlude of the Berlusconi government in 1994, the president of the Republic called on Lamberto Dini, a former Bank of Italy director general, to form a nonpartisan administration composed entirely of "experts": mostly bankers, economists, and lawyers without party affiliations. The all-important Treasury portfolio went to Carlo Azeglio Ciampi, while Foreign Affairs was handed to Susanna Agnelli, from the family that owned FIAT, Italy's largest private company. The government, sustained by the parties of the left, the remaining Christian Democrats, and the Northern League, set about making further fiscal adjustments, including a politically sensitive pension reform. In twelve months, budgetary measures were passed to cut the deficit by over 50 trillion lire, around 3 percent of GDP.[16]

Even after further elections, in 1996, delivered a majority for the center-left Olive Tree (Ulivo) coalition led by Romano Prodi, policy followed a similar path, with Ciampi not only remaining in his post at the Treasury but also adding the Budget and Economic Planning to his portfolio. The fiscal squeeze continued, with ad hoc measures such as the "Eurotax," a supplementary income tax of up to 3.5 percent, sold as a temporary measure to meet the criteria for entry into the euro. The sell-off of state-owned entreprises and other assets worth more than 164 trillion lire (85,000 million euros) between 1993 and 2001[17] was the most extensive and rapid process of privatization of any Western country.[18] The Prodi government also introduced significant structural reforms, such as the "Treu package" of labor reform measures, which eased the requirements for temporary work contracts and legalized private employment agencies, with the aim of lowering unemployment by facilitating the creation of low-paid short-term jobs.

This program of fiscal stabilization and reform reflected faithfully the recommendations of orthodox liberal economists, and was justified by the demands of European Monetary Union, a key objective of Italy's policymaking and business elite in this period. These measures had long been demanded by the most influential economists in Italian universities and institutions, such as the Bank of Italy. An eloquent expression of this view is the report of a team of economists from the National Research Council (CNR) published in

1993, which was "unanimous . . . that the time has now come in Italy for a shift in the weight assigned to the long hand of the state by comparison with the invisible hand of the market, with the former receding and improving."[19] The same report confessed some puzzlement over the failure of Italy's "strong tendency towards egalitarianism" to produce the "expected outcome . . . of a homogeneous, non-selective, non-competitive country," but still expressed confidence that "the Italian economy would grow even more strongly and rapidly if it were not hampered by the present policy-induced rigidities."[20]

The CNR team was building on a long-standing tradition of pro-market and anti-state thinking in the Italian economics profession. Italy's history of an often oppressive and inefficient state had engendered a deep-rooted skepticism of government interventionism, promoted by Luigi Einaudi in the postwar era, and still influential through the "Bocconi school" of the present day.[21] Driven to despair by the venality of the "First Republic" cartel of parties, neoliberal economists saw Europe as a useful pretext to limit corrupt politicians' ability to manipulate economic policy and interfere with market forces for electoral advantage. By sharing a currency with the more rigorous countries of northern Europe, Italy would be "tying its hands,"[22] insulating policy from short-term political pressures. The apparently virtuous circle of liberal reforms, fiscal adjustment, and monetary stability that allowed Italy to qualify for euro entry in 1998 led many observers to conclude that Italy had been "rescued by Europe."[23] But this was achieved by cutting off government policy from the demands of voters, a strategy with obvious risks should the promised economic pay-off of euro membership not materialize.

Italy in the Euro: Slouching toward Crisis

As in other southern Eurozone countries, the introduction of the euro marked a pause in the drive for reform and fiscal stabilization in Italy. Berlusconi won power once again in 2001, on a promise of "less tax for everyone." The long period of austerity—tax revenues had increased from just over 36 percent of GDP in 1990 to over 42 percent in 1997[24]—made this a politically appealing message, but Berlusconi's government was not the fiscal free-for-all some expected. The promised income tax cuts were watered down and largely offset by increases in a variety of other levies,[25] and Italy continued running primary surpluses. Figure 7.1 shows that the budget deficit, which had been cut dramatically as a share of GDP in the 1990s, increased slightly, but Italy continued to run a budget surplus before debt interest payments through the Berlusconi years. With the exception of the crisis year of 2007, the Italian

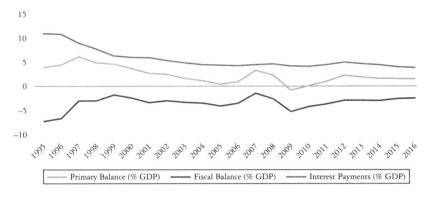

FIGURE 7.1 Italy, Fiscal Position, 1988–2017
Source: FRED database, Federal Reserve Bank of St. Louis, Economic Research Division (https://fred.stlouisfed.org).

government raised more money in taxes than it spent every year after 1993. This steadily reduced the public debt, which dipped briefly below 100 percent of GDP just before the financial crisis.

Not only did Italy run a tight ship fiscally, it also avoided the private sector credit boom seen in Greece, Spain, and Portugal. Italy was running a trade surplus before euro entry, and although it slipped into trade deficit in the 2000s, it had far less exposure to external creditors than the other southern European countries.[26] The flipside of this was a low growth rate: lacking the credit-fueled boom enjoyed by Greece and Spain, the Italian economy failed to take off once the objective of euro entry had been achieved. As Figure 7.2 shows, Italy's growth performance in the euro era managed to achieve the worst of both worlds: it had the same sluggish growth as Germany before the crisis, and a contraction just as deep, but instead of recovering strongly its post-crisis growth was the weakest of any Eurozone economy except Greece. Almost two decades of austerity failed to protect Italy from the contractionary effects of the crisis.

Fearful of spooking the markets, the Berlusconi government refrained from significant fiscal stimulus, depressing demand without achieving any compensatory boost to investment. Government borrowing bottomed out at just over 5 percent in 2009, less than half of the post-crisis deficits in financially distressed countries such as the United Kingdom, Greece, Ireland, or Spain. Moreover, Italy's banking sector was far less affected by the global financial meltdown than the other southern countries. Italian banks had maintained highly conservative lending practices throughout the early years of the euro while other southern countries engaged in a borrowing binge.

FIGURE 7.2 Cumulative GDP Per Capita Growth, Eurozone, 1999–2016
Source: OECD (2019), "Gross Domestic Product (GDP) (indicator)," doi: 10.1787/
dc2f7aec-en (accessed January 4, 2019).

House prices increased, but there was only moderate growth in mortgage credit and household borrowing for consumption.[27] Italian banks did not suffer any short-term panic in the immediate aftermath of the global credit crunch.

Notwithstanding this cautious approach, Italy soon found itself dragged into the eurozone's sovereign debt crisis. As GDP shrank, the ratio of debt to GDP deteriorated, and nervousness in bond markets pushed up interest rates, leading to higher debt-servicing costs. The Berlusconi government responded to these pressures by raising taxes and cutting spending. With such a high stock of debt, interest rates higher than GDP growth rates spelled high default risk in the future, leading to the risk premium on Italian debt spiking through 2010–2011.[28] An austerity budget of tax increases and spending cuts, supported by all the major parties, not only failed to stave off the market pressure, but also depressed demand further, in a familiar self-defeating spiral. To avert a bailout, Berlusconi was forced out and replaced by a technocratic administration under former European commissioner Mario Monti.

The Monti government did manage to avert the impending financial collapse of the Italian state, but at the price of illustrating with great clarity the near irrelevance of the Italian electorate to policymaking in crisis conditions.

The European institutions, in particular the European Central Bank (ECB), effectively forced a change in the Italian government, thanks to their ability to manage access to liquidity for Italian banks and protect Italy from bond market pressure.[29] Like Spain, Italy was on the receiving end of a missive from ECB presidents Trichet and Draghi, stipulating the need for more austerity and outlining specific policy measures such as labor market and public administration reforms, and even constitutional amendments to enshrine balanced budgets in Italy's basic law.[30] As in Spain, it was widely interpreted that ECB support for Italian government debt (under the Securities Market Program) could be withdrawn in the event of noncompliance.[31] According to some accounts, the German chancellor, Angela Merkel, was directly involved in forcing Berlusconi out when he failed to follow through quickly enough on his commitments to the ECB.[32]

The Monti government took office just a few days after the Papademos technocratic government in Greece, reflecting a concerted Europe-wide strategy to deal with the sovereign debt crisis by intervening actively in member state politics at the highest levels. As Stefano Sacchi describes, "the government led by Monti quickly adopted the ECB letter—and the structural reforms it prescribed—as its roadmap."[33] This extraordinary suspension of normal democratic politics was deemed necessary in order to implement the kinds of drastic austerity measures that elected politicians would have balked at, in the hope of calming the bond markets. The Monti government went ahead and imposed a brutal fiscal adjustment worth 3 percent of GDP,[34] through measures such as a VAT increase, cuts in local and regional government funding, and pension changes. It also brought in a labor market reform, known as the Fornero Law after the minister responsible, which proved extremely controversial for its changes to rules on dismissals (the iconic "Article 18" of the Italian labor statute) and its replacement of some existing unemployment compensation schemes. The Fornero reform was signed into law on June 27, 2012, and just a month later the ECB president, Mario Draghi, made his speech at the Global Investment Conference in London, in which he assured his audience that "within our mandate, the ECB is ready to do whatever it takes to preserve the euro. And believe me, it will be enough."[35]

Whether or not the Monti government's labor reform was a condition for the ECB to make such an open-ended commitment, market pressure on periphery debt certainly did abate from summer 2012.[36] More generally, the Monti government's fiscal squeeze pushed Italy once again into deep recession, with GDP shrinking by 2.8 percent in 2012, and a further 1.7 percent the following year. Ironically, one result of this drop in GDP was that the public debt to GDP ratio, the headline measure that investors paid most attention to, rose significantly, hitting 129 percent in 2013 and more than eroding all the debt reduction achieved since the early 1990s.[37] By 2013, Italy had been running primary budget surpluses for twenty straight years, meaning that Italians were paying out more in tax than the government was spending on pensions, welfare, and other public services. Yet not only was the national debt higher than ever, by the middle of the 2010s, household incomes in Italy had fallen back to the levels of the late 1980s, a stagnation of living standards unique among the major advanced economies.[38] The efforts to join the euro had resulted in stagnant living standards, higher debt, and a system of governments increasingly in thrall to the demands of the European institutions and other external creditors.

Who Pays? The Distributional Consequences of Crisis

This context of decline provides the broad backdrop to the political upheavals Italy experienced, but the distributional consequences of decline are also a key factor in determining which forms of anti-system politics have prevailed. Italy is a high inequality country by the standards of the advanced democracies, and it has also seen one of the biggest increases in inequality since the 1980s: the Gini coefficient for household disposable income stood at 0.29 in 1985, but had risen to 0.33 by 2013, among the highest levels in western Europe, surpassed only by Spain, Portugal, Greece, and the United Kingdom.[39] This meant that for the middle and lower income groups in Italy, life got harder from the early 1990s, with the bottom 60 percent worse off in real terms in 2010 than in 1991 (see Figure 7.3), with the bottom tenth of Italians suffering particularly large losses.

The income distribution itself reflects other sociodemographic divides that are relevant in shaping the political response to economic distress. As across the rest of southern Europe, age is an important social dividing line, with older citizens generally enjoying much better protection from the welfare system, and often holding significant capital assets. The pension system is a key source of inequality, since the very generous arrangements of the late twentieth century have been reformed for future generations, but the principle of protecting acquired rights means that current retirees continue to enjoy incomes far in excess of past contributions, funded on a pay-as-you-go basis through the contributions of a shrinking working-age

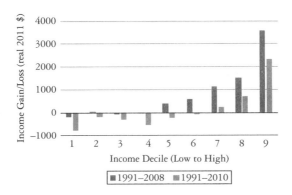

FIGURE 7.3 Real Income Changes for Decile Groups, Italy, 1991–2010
Source: Stefan Thewissen, Brian Nolan, and Max Roser (2016),
"Incomes across the Distribution Database" (https://ourworldindata.org/
incomes-across-the-distribution).

population.[40] Older households enjoyed a degree of social protection shared
by no other category in Italy: in the 2007–2012 period, poverty rates
increased in every category of households except those headed by someone
over sixty-five.[41]

Older households were also better off because of their disproportionate
access to financial assets. In a context of low or negligible real wage growth,
household incomes in Italy were held up by returns on capital or running
down savings, resources available only to those who held some kind of
wealth.[42] This meant mainly older households, particularly in North and
Central Italy, where wealth holdings averaged two or three times those of the
typical household in the South.[43] Due to the tenacity of familial ties, pension and financial wealth was redistributed across the generations, but very
unevenly across social classes and regions, with lower-income households,
especially in the South and the islands of Sardinia and Sicily, benefiting
least.[44]

But even the middle classes of the comparatively wealthy North were
exposed to significant economic threats in this period. Large northern industrial firms such as the FIAT auto manufacturer shifted much of their production overseas, while small and medium-sized manufacturing firms in areas
such as textiles were particularly exposed to Chinese competition. Lacking
the resources to invest in innovation[45] and locked into wage bargaining
structures that raised unit labor costs,[46] many of these firms responded by
hiring more workers on low-paid temporary contracts, or by outsourcing to
eastern Europe. Large numbers of northern Italian workers were exposed to

greater economic insecurity, losing their jobs or having to accept a deterioration of working conditions to hold onto them. Italy shed a million manufacturing jobs in the first two decades of the twentieth century.[47] On top of this, cuts to welfare provision meant income loss and a greater risk of poverty for many northern Italians.

Pension cuts were also a big issue in the North. Internal migration from the South was especially intense during the postwar years of rapid industrialization, so very large numbers of Italians at or close to retirement age lived in northern Italy. The protection of pension rights became especially salient after Monti's government imposed a hasty increase in retirement ages combined with the abolition of an unemployment benefits system known as the "mobility allowance," leaving thousands of redundant Italian workers stranded without state support, in some cases for several years. The numbers of these so-called *esodati* (the "exiled"), initially estimated at just 65,000, grew to over 300,000, provoking predictable outrage and demands for the reversal of the reform from the trade unions and the opposition parties. The Northern League was especially vocal in protesting these changes.

Overall, labor market conditions worsened significantly in Italy after the reforms of the 1990s, with wages for new entrants to the labor market falling and subsequent earnings growth failing to compensate.[48] Italy has ended up with one of the most flexible labor markets in Europe,[49] with younger workers, women, and migrants, the classic "outsiders," particularly affected. This entrenched an insidious generational divide, as the younger population faced significantly worse labor market conditions and was paradoxically increasingly dependent on its better-protected parents and grandparents.[50] As job losses after the crisis were concentrated among younger workers with insecure employment, this family "shock absorber" played an important role in cushioning them from poverty.[51] Immigrants, usually lacking this safety net, were in consequence the group most affected by the crisis.[52]

Italy's familistic traditions compensated for the gaps in welfare coverage and protected most of the population from the worst effects of economic decline, but also entrenched a lack of opportunity for the younger generations. In turn, the growing political veto power of older Italians made reforms to equalize welfare and labor market protections across age groups more and more difficult, a problem further accentuated by the state's declining public finances. This political economy trap goes a long way to explaining Italy's lurch toward anti-system politics in the 2010s, and indicates which groups were most susceptible to anti-system appeals.

The Political Backlash: From Crisis to Comedy?

It is difficult to imagine a scenario more damaging to the established parties than a grand coalition to vote through painful cuts, designed by EU officials and implemented by unelected technocrats, at the urging of the German government. The elections of spring 2013 provided a stark illustration of this point. As Figure 7.4 shows, the joint vote share of the two main parties fell from a peak of 70.6 percent of the vote in 2008 to just 47 percent five years later, with the center-right Party of Freedoms (PDL) losing over six million votes and the main opposition party, the center-left Democratic Party (PD), losing three and a half million. In 2013 voter loyalty hit its lowest level in the history of Italian democracy: almost 40 percent of voters failed to cast a vote for the same party or coalition as in the previous election.[53] In a further indication of voter malaise, turnout also fell, to 75 percent, again the lowest in postwar history.[54]

This collapse of the established party system—the second in Italy in less than two decades—mostly benefited a completely new party, Beppe Grillo's Five Stars Movement (M5S), which won just over a quarter of the vote in its first general election, the best performance ever for a new party in postwar western Europe. Grillo's transition from comedian to blogger and political agitator, launched with the quirky "V-Day" campaign, had in less than a decade put him in charge of the most voted political party in Italy.

What kind of party was the M5S? First of all, the word "party" was used only pejoratively in the M5S lexicon, and one of its main slogans was "no more parties" (*Basta partiti!*). Born out of Grillo's blog (http://www.

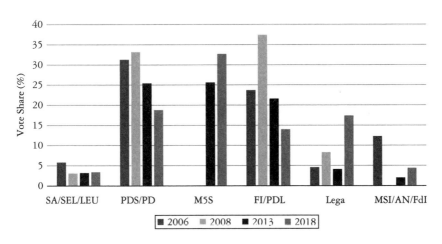

FIGURE 7.4 Patterns of Party Support, Italy, 2006–2018

beppegrillo.it), which he used to promote his ideas about political regenera-
tion and environmental policy, the M5S was a forum that brought together
social movements and ordinary citizens who shared his concerns. The M5S
resisted both the label and the typical structure of a political party, insisting
that the traditional party form was at the root of Italy's political problems.
Instead, the Movement shunned the conventional role of political parties
as intermediaries between the state and civil society, by limiting itself to
coordinating spontaneous citizen participation and advocating Web-based
solutions to the failings of representative democracy. From his blog, Grillo
encouraged his followers to use the Meetup platform (used by Howard Dean
in his ill-fated presidential run of 2004) to build local networks and act on
issues of local concern. These "Friends of Beppe Grillo" groups grew up in all
the major cities and numbered over a hundred in early 2007.[55]

The Movement initially focused on local, particularly environmental, issues, for example opposing large infrastructure projects such as the high-
speed trainline (TAV) from Turin to Lyon and the new motorway bypass in
Genoa (Grillo's home town), and campaigning against the privatization of
the water supply. With the "V-day" demonstrations of 2007, Grillo made
the leap to mobilizing on a national scale, connecting local action to the
sweeping critique of the entire Italian political class he had developed in
his comedy act. Grillo's speech at the V-Day event in Bologna condemned
the corruption, collusion, and mafia connections of the political establishment, and also took aim at the media, attacking the mainstream press and
promoting new social media as an alternative. A key theme was to attack *la
casta*: the corrupt "caste" of politicians, journalists, and well-connected business people whose abuses were documented in a best-selling book published
that same year.[56]

The event gave the Movement a national profile and accelerated the development of the "Friends" network, as well as signaling a shift away from
the local focus of its origins. The next major move was Grillo's bid to stand
as a candidate in the primaries for the leadership of the PD in 2009, which
was predictably rejected, leading to the formal creation of the M5S in 2009.
Although the Movement's formal program revolved mostly around the more
practical, concrete, and often local issues of clean energy, water, Internet
connectivity, garbage collection, and social services (the "five stars" in the
Movement's name representing these five themes), Grillo's discourse was
more ambitious and took aim at the whole political system. The denunciation of a corrupt political class became the leitmotif of the M5S, and specific policy objectives took second place to the aim of cleaning up politics,
overturning the party system, and replacing it with a new form of Web-based

participatory politics. This anti-elitist message was expressed in aggressive tones of a "war against the parties,"[57] with frequent use of earthy language and crude personal insults toward his political adversaries,[58] which has clear parallels with Trump's discourse.

The Movement's critique of existing arrangements was far more developed than its proposed alternative—a system of Web-based political decision-making that would allow ordinary citizens to take direct control, bypassing the corrupt elite. This idea came from the M5S's cofounder, Gianroberto Casaleggio, a tech entrepreneur and publisher who had also dabbled in politics. As well as inchoate ideas about how the Internet could transform democracy,[59] Casaleggio contributed technological expertise and corporate resources to the Movement, most notably by developing a platform for online political participation called *Rousseau*.[60] Rousseau was to provide a structure through which the Movement could mobilize supporters and develop policies through grassroots initiatives and online voting, fulfilling Grillo's ambition to "let the citizens decide."

This almost exclusive focus on the structures of political decision-making made M5S a very unusual political party, in that it lacked any consistent ideological identity, or even discernible positions on many key policy issues. The emphasis on mass participation, and the emergence of the Movement as an electoral force in the early 2010s, points toward a similar strategy of mobilization to the anti-system left parties we have analyzed in Spain, Greece, and the United Kingdom. For example, the M5S had similarities with Podemos: both claimed that the traditional left-right conceptualization of politics was exhausted, condemned the corruption of the existing political class, and advocated participatory democracy through the use of new technologies.[61] Like other parties on the anti-system left in southern Europe, the M5S was also critical of the euro and related austerity measures.[62]

The official program on which the M5S fought the general election of 2013 was heavily skewed toward reforms to the political system, media policy, energy, transport, and health, while the "economy" section was little over a page long and consisted of a mix of extremely vague ambitions such as "favoring local production" and "the abolition of monopolies," alongside very specific commitments such as "the abolition of stock options."[63] The heavy attention to energy and transport issues spoke to the environmental concerns that animated many grassroots campaigners involved in the Movement, and the program included commitments to reducing private car use in urban areas and expanding cycle networks and public transit. But Grillo's blistering critique of the Italian political system was at the heart of the Movement's message. The party program declared that "Parliament no longer represents the citizens" and promised to abolish Italy's provincial tier of government, limit parliamentarians to two terms in office, ban anyone with a criminal conviction from standing for parliament, and drastically reduce parliamentarians' salaries and pensions.

While not falling into any conventional position on the left-right scale, the Movement's approach to the economy did reflect a consistent skepticism toward the motives and behavior of big business and finance, and an aspiration to reduce their power through institutional reforms. Beppe Grillo's shows and blog had consistently attacked the actions of large corporations and banks, and these attacks were especially directed at businesses leveraging political connections to exploit consumers. The M5S program cited several areas of corporate governance legislation to reform, such as cross-ownership of corporations, and specifically those involving banks, multiple board memberships, leveraged buyouts, monopoly positions, shareholder rights, and executive pay. It also argued for a drastic reduction in Italy's public debt through the elimination of "waste" and the use of technology to reduce the costs of citizens' interactions with the state. Together with the Movement's denunciation of the political parties, this constituted a broad assault on both the political and economic elites of Italy, seen as jointly responsible for the country's dire situation.

This generic anti-system stance was not entirely devoid of ideological content. For instance, perhaps with an eye on the most available sectors of the electorate, the M5S was quite specific in its promise to reverse the liberalizing labor market reforms introduced since the early 1990s by both center-left and center-right. Beppe Grillo's Bologna speech in 2007 included a *vaffanculo* personally to Pietro Ichino, a labor law professor and PD leader, blaming his ideas for the precarious conditions and low wages suffered by millions of temporary workers.[64] The Five Stars program also promised support for guaranteed unemployment benefits and commitment to equality of access in education and healthcare, policies that place the Movement clearly to the left of center.

Key features of the Movement's discourse were strangely absent from the program. Immigration was not mentioned at all in the document, although Grillo had on various occasions expressed opposition to migration and naturalization of the Italian-born children of migrants.[65] The M5S program remained vague on issues of market governance, beyond a vague promise to promote domestic food and industrial production and prevent the breakup of Italian industrial groups (a promise that sat awkwardly alongside the promise on the same page to attack large monopolists). However, Grillo's discourse had become increasingly skeptical toward the euro, going as far as to advocate, albeit inconsistently, a referendum on Italy's exit from the European Monetary Union.[66] Here the M5S parted company with Podemos and Syriza, expressing a deep skepticism about European integration as a political project.

The lack of economic policy clarity is unsurprising given the party's origins. Grillo himself and many of his supporters were drawn to conspiracy theories about money and banking that saw the euro as a plot to extract unwarranted interest from citizens through the national debt, views generally associated with outsider groups on the Far Left and Right.[67] However, the Movement did develop specific policies to reverse labor market and welfare reforms, and spend public money to provide a minimum income to the unemployed and the retired. In 2013 the party adopted the policy of a *reddito di cittadinanza* (citizens' income), a universal minimum income guarantee (worth €600 a month) for all Italians, which became its best-known policy commitment.[68]

Although the M5S's ambiguous ideological moorings and unusual organizational form mark it out as distinct from other southern European anti-austerity movements, its pattern of electoral support was rather more similar. The M5S's origins in the mobilization around environmental issues at the local level and the emphasis on networked political participation attracted a younger, more urban, and generally highly educated electorate, mostly former voters for center-left parties. Polling data from early 2012 showed that around 75 percent of M5S voters had some form of further education (as against an average of less than half of the population at large), around 60 percent were between twenty-five and forty-five years old (twice their share in the population), around 40 percent lived in cities of more than 100,000 inhabitants, and their interest in politics was twice the population average.[69] This pattern is similar to other new left-wing anti-system parties, such as Podemos in Spain, although what marks the M5S as distinct is the absence of a sustained anti-austerity mass movement in post-crisis Italy on which the party could build. Instead, it sought to mobilize a more fragmented and inchoate range of activists, on the basis of a more generic discourse focused less on specific austerity measures and more on the structural failings of the political and economic system.

As the M5S expanded beyond its initial activist base, it became more ideologically and sociologically heterogeneous. In 2011 the vast majority (almost two-thirds) of M5S supporters identified with the Left or Center-Left, and less than 10 percent identified with the Right or Center-Right, but as the Movement grew in strength it attracted increasing numbers of voters from the Right.[70] As well as being a natural evolution as it fished in a bigger pool of voters, this was also by design, as under Casaleggio's tutelage the Movement used the data gathered from the Rousseau platform to analyze and hone supporters' responses to different aspects of its message.[71] One example was the Movement's position on immigration: the progressive left origin of many of its activists pushed it toward supporting changing the law to naturalize second-generation migrants born in Italy, but Grillo swiftly shut down any such policy on the grounds that it would cost votes.[72] This catch-all strategy was all the more effective because the M5S had little in the way of formal policy documents or ideological symbols to constrain it, and its largely Web-based form of communication with activists and voters allowed distinct customized messages to be targeted at different groups, maximizing the Movement's reach while hiding from view some of the resulting contradictions.

This approach brought spectacular success with the electoral breakthrough in February 2013. Although the center-left and center-right coalitions received more votes, the M5S became the largest single political party, with more than eight and a half million votes and a share of 25.6 percent in the election for the Chamber of Deputies.[73] The M5S grew by winning votes from both the PD and the PDL in almost equal measure,[74] reflecting the success of Grillo's catch-all strategy of proclaiming that "left and right no longer exist." However this did not mean that the M5S voters resembled Italian society as a whole: over half of them (52 percent) self-identified as left-wing, just under a third (31 percent) as "centrist," and only a small minority (17 percent) placed themselves on the right of the political spectrum.[75] Sociologically, the Movement's support followed a consistent pattern: the younger the voter, the more likely they would vote for the M5S, which was the most popular party in every age group under 55, but failed to clear 12 percent of the vote among the over-65s.[76] The M5S was by far the most successful in attracting new voters and those that had not voted in the previous election,[77] a pattern that fits with its appeal to voters disillusioned with the incumbent political class.

The M5S was unusual, almost unique, in its origins as the spinoff of a comedy show and its vague ideological profile. However, its electoral footprint was similar to that of other similar parties that mobilized the discontents of the "outsider" generation hit hardest by austerity, and the most affected by unemployment and job insecurity. The M5S was the most voted party among those with educational qualifications, but received only 13 percent support among those who had failed to complete high school.[78] In occupational terms, pensioners were the group least likely to vote M5S (11 percent), but it was by some distance the most popular party among the unemployed (34 percent), homemakers (38 percent), students (44 percent), and those in temporary employment (52 percent).[79] As in the rest of southern Europe, the bill for the crisis was passed on disproportionately to the younger generation, many of whom voted for the party most hostile to the political establishment.

Saving the System? Renzi's Reform Project

The M5S's spectacular success in 2013 not only blew open the Italian party system once more, but also undermined the logic of alternation in government between the two main parties. The main party of opposition, the center-left PD, was unable to exploit Berlusconi's crushing defeat, falling well short of a parliamentary majority. The PD's lackluster electoral performance marked the failure of a political project to unite the opposition to Berlusconi under one banner. Why was the Italian Center-Left unable to articulate an alternative to the Center-Right's mishandling of the economic crisis? The answer to this question lies in the PD's detachment from the ideological traditions of the Italian Left.

The PD was founded in 2007, merging the Democratic Left (formerly the PDS), the heir to the Italian Communist tradition, with a collection of centrist factions whose origins were mostly in the now defunct Christian Democratic Party. The PD's political identity was therefore a hybrid, and the logic of the merger was to build a broad coalition capable of monopolizing the political space to the left of Berlusconi. But by maximizing its electoral reach, the PD also dropped the last vestiges of communist and Christian democratic ideological identities, converging around a broadly market liberal position, with a focus on economic reform and commitment to Europe. The PD stressed the need for Italy to undertake a "liberal revolution" of institutional reforms aimed at dismantling opportunities for corruption and rent-seeking, and expanding market competition.[80] Much of the intellectual impetus behind the PD's agenda came from neoliberal economists associated with Bocconi University in Milan, most of them convinced that Italy's difficulties inside the euro were due to institutional weaknesses rather than any demand shortfall caused by austerity measures.[81]

After the 2013 elections, it fell to the PD, as the largest party in the Chamber of Deputies, to attempt to form a governing coalition. Its first move was to approach the M5S, whose leaders insisted that any talks between the parties should be held in public, so the PD's dour veteran leader Pierluigi Bersani was persuaded to meet the Movement's inexperienced parliamentary leaders on live streaming. This meeting, opened by Bersani with a dry thirteen-minute monologue, which served mainly to confirm the staleness of the political establishment, failed to even discuss the basis on which an agreement could be negotiated.[82] The aim of the M5S was to replace the ruling elite rather than compromise with them: Beppe Grillo christened the PD the "*pdmenoelle*"—the PD without the "L"—to drive home the Movement's message that the two main parties were fundamentally the same. The PD was forced into yet another "grand coalition" government (under the PD's Enrico Letta) supported by most of the Center-Right, and with nonpartisan technocrats in key positions, notably Economy Minister Saccomani, a veteran of the Bank of Italy and the IMF.

The Letta government lasted less than a year before an internal shift within the PD brought a new leader and a new prime minister. Matteo Renzi, the young mayor of Florence, saw an opportunity to latch on to the demand for political renewal represented by the M5S, launching a leadership campaign based on the slogan of "scrapping" (*rottamazione*) the political system as one would an old car. Renzi initially enjoyed some electoral success, with the PD winning 41 percent of the vote in the 2014 European elections. His strategy was to make ostentatious gestures of change and novelty, calling for the "destruction" of the old PD and bringing a younger generation into government, including an unprecedented number of women (half of the ministers).[83] The M5S's relatively poor performance in the 2014 election, where it lost around three million votes compared with the year before, mostly to abstention but around 13 percent to the PD,[84] suggests that Renzi enjoyed at least a short-term success in selling his PD as a new political force capable of responding to demands for change.

But Renzi's energetic style embellished what was actually a high degree of continuity in the fundamentals of economic and social policy. He maintained existing commitments to Italy, fulfilling the demands of the European institutions to reduce budget deficits and set about pursuing yet another liberalizing labor reform, this time labeled the Jobs Act (a name borrowed from a law of the Obama administration in the United States). The reform sought to overcome some of the rigidities in Italian employment law by introducing contracts that could transition over time into becoming open-ended, overcoming the sharp dualism between temporary and permanent contracts.[85] As a result, the controversial Article 18 of the Italian labor statute, which gave workers the right to be rehired in the event of a successful claim for unfair dismissal, was finally abolished. To compensate for this loss of job security, the reform incentivized employers to hire on open-ended contracts rather than temporary ones with social security contribution discounts.[86]

The other plank of Renzi's agenda was a plan for constitutional reform to concentrate power around the executive and downgrade the role of the Italian Senate. The proposed reform would have replaced the elected Senate, whose approval is required not only for all legislation, but also for all votes of confidence, with a nonelected body nominated by regional councilors that would no longer have the power to install or overturn the government.[87] The reform would have undermined the broadly consensual policymaking traditions of postwar Italy, ostensibly to facilitate the liberalizing reforms favored by Renzi and his supporters in the business world. Renzi's plan got through parliament but failed to get past the hurdle of winning popular approval in a referendum. Supporters of the League and the M5S voted against Renzi's plan in large numbers: attitudes to the reform correlated strongly with unemployment levels, suggesting that the No vote was interpreted by many voters as a vote against the incumbent government and the economic situation.[88]

Renzi's reformist zeal failed to achieve much in the way of improving living standards, with the economy emerging very slowly from its double-dip recession and the underlying fiscal position of the government remaining contractionary. Although his political style emphasized his youth and energy and sought to deliver reforms at breakneck speed, the policy practice was one of continuity, with Europe's fiscal straitjacket establishing the parameters of taxation and spending, and a further venture down the path of labor market deregulation. Moreover, Renzi's government relied for its survival on a broad coalition of center-left and center-right parties, playing into the hands of anti-system politicians who decried the political establishment. This favored the M5S, which hoped to pick up disenchanted voters from the PD. But it also opened up a space to the right of the established parties.

"Italy First": The Rise of the Right and the End of the Center

The weakness of the PD was mirrored on the right by the decline of Berlusconi, the dominant figure on the center-right since the early 1990s, who was personally discredited by various scandals and increasingly seen as a representative of the old political establishment. The M5S's ideological ambivalence allowed it to fish in this pool of newly available center-right voters, but the main beneficiary was the Northern League, a long-standing ally of Berlusconi, but now under a new leader, Matteo Salvini, who seized the opportunity to expand beyond his party's core base of northern voters. The

League had initially found itself exposed to the anti-system backlash itself, as the clique around party founder Umberto Bossi was implicated in a series of corruption scandals,[89] dropping from over three million votes in 2008 to less than half that number in 2013 (see Figure 7.4). After this defeat, Salvini was able to win control of the party, clear out the old guard, and adopt a new political strategy similar to the xenophobic and Euroskeptic message typical of anti-system right parties across continental western Europe.

Salvini's move represented a dramatic departure from the League's long-standing identity as the defender of the North against the inefficiency and corruption of the Italian central state, and the fiscal burden of the country's economically underdeveloped South in particular. In the early 1990s, the League had a broadly positive view of the European project, seeing it as an opportunity to free the North's vibrant economy from the dead hand of a corrupt and fiscally onerous Italian state.[90] This confident approach to the North's economic prospects informed a broadly neoliberal and anti-statist view of the economy, in which the European Union and the euro would protect free market values from Italy's inefficient institutions. But after euro entry, the northern electorate became much more pessimistic about its economic future and more receptive to a protectionist appeal.[91] This position reflected the increasing economic strain on the industrial system of the League's stronghold regions of Lombardy and Veneto from emerging Chinese and eastern European competition. Growing migration from eastern Europe completed a picture of economic threats associated with the European project.[92]

The League had briefly won support from exasperated northern business leaders in the early 1990s, but as the party institutionalized it focused increasingly on building mass support with an anti-European and anti-globalization message, entrenching itself as the strongest party among working-class voters in the North.[93] Concerns that the euro favored the core European countries over the periphery, and large firms over small ones, resonated particularly among the League's core electorate of workers, artisans, and small businesspeople in the smaller northern cities and towns. The League therefore began to make (largely symbolic) demands for tariff barriers to protect northern production from foreign competition. The party message was less appreciated in the more dynamic and prosperous metropolitan area around Milan, where a more service-based economy enjoyed strong growth.[94] In other words, the League began to occupy a similar kind of political space to radical right-wing nativist parties in the wealthy countries of continental and northern Europe.

The journey to becoming a party of the radical nationalist Right was complicated by tensions between the League's anti-system roots and the opportunities to exercise political power presented by its electoral successes. After radicalizing its territorial claims to the extent of advocating secession from Italy in the late 1990s, Bossi's pact with Berlusconi to join a broad center-right coalition government from 2001 on brought access to political power and a shift toward working within the system rather than simply railing against it, especially as it also won control over regional governments in Lombardy and Veneto.[95] The party's response was to seize the trappings of power but maintain a fiery anti-system rhetoric that was increasingly directed toward "external" threats such as migrants and the European Union, rather than the internal adversaries with which the League was now allied.[96] Xenophobic outbursts against migrants, Islamophobia, and hostility toward the euro featured heavily in this new discourse, although the party maintained its distinctive northern identity.[97]

Salvini built on this tradition but saw an opportunity to expand beyond northern Italy by abandoning regionalist claims and seeking support in parts of the country the League had previously ignored. Salvini's discourse was a potent mix of anti-migrant, anti-euro, and anti-establishment rhetoric. He deployed the imagery of the excavator (*ruspa*), to evoke not only sweeping away the rotten political elite, but also the idea of forcibly clearing out Roma camps.[98] Xenophobia was not a new theme for the party—its founder, Umberto Bossi, had once advocated firing cannon shots at refugee boats in the Mediterranean[99]—but under Salvini hostility to migration no longer coexisted with the League's message of preservation of regional identity, but instead supplanted it. Where Bossi had sought out other regionalist and secessionist parties as European partners, Salvini courted Marine Le Pen's National Front and other right-wing nativists, consciously adopting a similar discourse and advertising their support for his cause.[100]

Instead of invoking the specific interests of "Padania" (a vague neologism for northern Italy), Salvini's League took aim at alleged threats to the Italian nation as a whole, going so far as to organize an anti-immigration rally with Casapound, a small but well-known far-right group with a history of violent activism, and allying with the Brothers of Italy (Fratelli d'Italia, FDI), a nationalist party of fascist inspiration.[101] Salvini also echoed the language of Donald Trump, going so far as to adopt the slogan of "Italy First" (*prima gli Italiani*), an extraordinary step for a leader whose party had advocated the outright secession of "Padania" from Italy less than twenty years earlier. This shift from regionalism to nationalism was undertaken without any attempt to rationalize the contradiction between the League's identity as a party of the North and its new push into the poorer regions it had previously wanted to secede from.

To finesse this contradiction, Salvini identified foreigners—migrants and the European Union—as common enemies to unite against.[102] The sharp increase in arrivals of refugees by sea after 2013, which peaked at 180,000 in 2016,[103] provided an opportunity to mobilize opposition to the Renzi government and expand the League's vote beyond its northern core. The party set out to establish an organized presence even in southern Italy, under the label *Noi con Salvini* (Us with Salvini), studiously avoiding the terms "Northern" and even "League." With popular concern about immigration spiking between 2014 and 2016—the numbers citing immigration as one of the main problems facing Italy jumped from 5 to over 40 percent[104]—Salvini's strategy offered huge potential for growth. His discourse revolved not only around stoking resentment against the refugees and migrants in general, but also specifically targeted the European Union and its failure to relieve the pressure on Mediterranean member states by redistributing refugees around the Union. Since the South of Italy was particularly affected by refugee arrivals, anti-migrant rhetoric had the potential to win support there, too.

Salvini's discourse on migration dovetailed with a similarly Euroskeptic position on the economy. Like the M5S, the League had moved toward a very critical position on the euro and the pressures from European institutions to curb Italy's budget deficit and debt levels. Salvini began to campaign under the slogan "basta euro,"[105] promising that if the League won power it would take Italy out of the European Monetary Union.[106] The League also adopted an anti-austerity line, promising to slash taxation by establishing a "flat tax," while also abolishing the Fornero reform and lowering the retirement age. These redistributive promises reflected the preferences of the League's core electorate of older workers and small businesses, and stood to favor the North overall, given its higher average earnings and large share of pensioners.[107] The League's electoral program also revived Bossi's promise of protective tariffs for Italian manufacturing, which appealed mostly to hard-pressed small companies in the North. However, the focus on immigration and the euro proved an effective way of mobilizing voters across the Italian territory, winning substantial support where the party previously had no presence and eliding the interregional tensions the League had historically fed off.

A Third Republic? The Election of March 2018

The election of March 2018 confirmed Italy's turn away from its established parties and delivered the majority of votes and seats to anti-system movements (see Figure 7.4). The M5S made further gains, establishing itself as the biggest party by a large margin, with almost a third of the vote (32.7 percent), more than ten and a half million votes. Salvini's League also enjoyed unprecedented success, winning a record 17.4 percent of the vote, almost quadrupling its 2013 performance. To complete the anti-system picture, the far-right Brothers of Italy won over 4 percent, double its 2013 share. The mainstays of the pre-crisis party system—the PD and Forza Italia—won barely a third of the vote between them (18.8 and 14 percent, respectively). The cartel of established parties that guaranteed Italy's adherence to the rules and ethos of the European Union and the single currency was roundly defeated.

Italy's tale of economic decline, debt, and austerity, combined with technocratic governance that downgraded the role of elections, presents the ideal conditions for the growth of the anti-system vote. We have also seen that the political and electoral beneficiaries of this climate challenged the economic status quo and argued for changes to Italy's macroeconomic framework and enhancements to its system of social protection. This mirrors developments in the other crisis-stricken countries studied in this book, all of which found themselves at the epicenter of the debt crisis and the Great Recession. Italy also reflects the distinctive pattern of the southern European model of anti-system reaction, with the electoral response to establishment failures disproportionately favoring the mobilization of younger, more educated voters around progressive and liberal rather than reactionary and xenophobic options. However the peculiarities of the M5S, and the extraordinary transformation and electoral success of the League under Salvini, do require some further discussion.

Italy was, along with Greece, one of the countries most affected by the refugee crisis of the mid-2010s, and the surge in support for the League took place after the spike in arrivals in 2013–2014, and after Salvini had taken over the party and adopted an aggressive anti-refugee discourse, focusing on domestic security issues ahead of economic concerns. Opinion polling confirms that most of the rise in League support took place during 2014, which was the year in which the arrivals of refugees on the Italian coast dramatically increased (around fourfold).[108] Studies of the League's social media strategy show a marked increase in posts about immigration and security in the same period, at the expense of those about the economic situation or the European Union.[109] However, opinion data also suggests that public concern about migration lagged behind the rate of refugee arrivals. The numbers expressing fear about migration increased by around 10 percent (to just under 40 percent), but this simply returned it to the average level over the pre-crisis period (the peak of negative attitudes was in 2007, at 60 percent).[110] It is therefore unclear whether immigration attitudes were the driver of the League's electoral rise, or were instead a consequence of Salvini's discourse and his growing political profile over this period.

Voting patterns in 2018 also suggest that economic factors were an important part of the League's electoral success. Although the League enjoyed a spectacular rise in vote share across the Italian regions, one marked tendency was its relative weakness in the larger towns and cities: in its heartland region of Lombardy, the League polled 28 percent of the vote, but only 17 percent in the capital, Milan, while it polled 10 percent less in Venice (22 percent) than in the Veneto region (32 percent).[111] This is a typical pattern of support for the anti-immigration Right, which in other countries has also tended to perform better in smaller and more rural communities than in the economically more successful cities. Even within the major cities, the League and the M5S enjoyed much stronger growth in the most economically vulnerable districts, while the mainstream parties, the PD and Forza Italia, instead performed better in the generally more prosperous city centers.[112] The Italian case confirms the trend toward anti-system politics prospering in the more peripheral and declining areas, but Italy's much more profound economic problems meant a larger reservoir of potential support than in most of the other advanced democracies.

The geographical pattern of anti-system support in Italy reflects the differing ways in which economic vulnerability could be mobilized in different areas. In the South and Islands, where average living standards were lowest and unemployment highest, the M5S was by far the strongest party, winning the support of almost half of all voters (47.3 percent). The League, despite making an unprecedented breakthrough in regions where it had never previously stood candidates, polled on average just over 5 percent in the South, where the direct impact of the refugee problem was felt. The anti-system vote in the South was therefore much more oriented to the kinds of redistributive demands represented by the M5S, and in particular its proposal for a minimum income, than toward immigration and law and order issues. Polling showed that M5S voters gave highest priority to employment and the integrity of the political system, and lower priority to migration and security issues than the average across all Italian voters.[113] This is exactly what we would expect if the anti-system vote was driven by mainly economic insecurity and resentment toward the failures of the political system, rather than by the cultural and security concerns associated with migration.

The League, on the other hand, still won the majority of its votes in its northern heartlands (reaching close to 30 percent in the North-East and over

25 percent in the North-West), but expanded significantly in the central regions, notably the "Red Belt" of Tuscany and Emilia-Romagna, traditionally dominated by the Left, where the League won just under 19 percent of the vote. The anti-migrant message was central to this success, with League supporters giving far greater priority to migration and security issues than other voters (see Figure 7.5).[114] But League voters were also the most likely voters to cite unemployment, taxes and living standards, and pensions as their main concern, far more so than M5S voters. The League may have been strongest in Italy's most prosperous regions, but it was also appealing in particular to economically vulnerable parts of the population in those regions. In terms of socioeconomic profile, the League won its highest vote share among workers, artisans, and the self-employed, and its lowest among public sector workers and professionals.[115] League voters, despite mostly hailing from Italy's richest regions, displayed by far the most pessimistic outlook on the economy—close to half of them agreed that the worst of the crisis was yet to come (46 percent, as opposed to 33 percent for the whole electorate). This is exactly the pattern of voting for far-right and nativist parties that the comparative analysis in chapter 2 would lead us to expect.

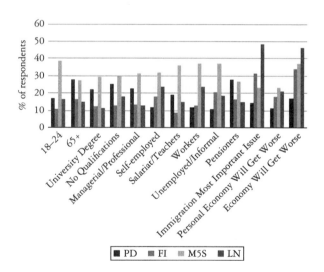

FIGURE 7.5 Sociodemographic and Attitudinal Characteristics of Party Vote, 2018

Source: Ipsos Mori survey, reported in Luca Comodo and Mattia Forni, "Chi vota cosa e perché: Il profilo elettorale dei partiti," in Marco Valbruzzi and Rinaldo Vignati (eds.), *Il vicolo cieco: Le elezioni del 4 marzo 2018* (Bologna: Il Mulino, 2018), pp.213–234, (Table 4, p.226).

Why did poorer and more economically insecure voters opt for anti-system parties like the League and the M5S, instead of voting for parties of the left that stood for redistribution and equality? The clue to this lies in the transformation of the Italian Left since the end of the Cold War. The PD under Renzi presented a liberal, modernizing image, in line with European Union priorities of fiscal austerity and market openness. The PD had become perceived as the party of the "winners" from globalization, and the party of well-protected "insiders." While the League won twice the share of worker votes than the PD, the PD won its largest share among professionals and the managerial class (22 percent), voters with university degrees (22 percent), and the over-65s (28 percent). Of the established parties, the PD was the one whose voters were most economically secure, leaving more vulnerable voters with little option but to support anti-system forces promising protection against economic threats. The M5S was the largest party in every occupational category, but was particularly strong among workers, winning three times the vote share of the PD.

It made perfect sense for these vulnerable voters to opt for anti-system forces if they wished to see policy changes that might improve their economic situation. The M5S promised an unconditional basic citizens' income, the abolition of the Fornero pensions reform, increased health spending, and cuts in taxation.[116] The League was also committed to reversing the Fornero reform and easing retirement rules. Other issues, such as the abolition of public funding for political parties or a pushback against illegal immigration, were also important, but the underlying patterns of voter support for the Italian anti-system parties reflected the country's deep-seated economic problems.

The Yellow-Green Government: When Anti-System Becomes the System

The collapse of the mainstream parties and the surge of the M5S and the League implied a profound change in the Italian party system and a very awkward dilemma for the party leaders. The PD's weak performance made any hope of staying in power contingent on an agreement with other parties, but the equally poor performance of Berlusconi's Forza Italia (what was left of the PDL had returned to its original name), which polled just 14 percent of the vote, losing more than two million votes, made even a grand coalition difficult. On the other hand, the League and the M5S, which did enjoy a majority of parliamentary seats between them, were deeply divided in terms of geographical representation, ideology, and discourse. Moreover, the League had stood in the election as part of a broad center-right alliance with Berlusconi, on a shared program, with the implied aspiration to govern together in coalition. These two parties were also working in coalition in several regional governments in the North of Italy, so breaking the pact at the national level would have broader ramifications.

The impasse produced by this fragmented parliament led to an attempt, yet again, to form a "government of experts" with cross-party support, invoking the urgency of responding to pressure from the bond markets. Carlo Cottarelli, another economist with the Bank of Italy and the IMF on his CV, attempted to form a government with a view to at least passing a budget law before holding new elections. However, only the PD, long resigned to propping up unpopular technocratic governments, could bring itself to back Cottarelli. The parliamentary arithmetic ultimately imposed itself as the M5S and the League, alongside the far-right Brothers of Italy, voted together to back a coalition government, once a compromise candidate for prime minister, Giuseppe Conte, had been agreed to. The long process of government formation was punctuated with controversy, as the president of the Republic vetoed attempts by the League to nominate Paolo Savona, a long-standing advocate of Italy leaving the euro, to the Treasury. These events served to reinforce the impression that the political cartel of mainstream political parties, business interests, and senior government officials were determined to obstruct the implementation of the anti-system mandate.

The first months of the new "yellow-green" administration,[117] the first government in Europe to be backed solely by anti-system parties, offered some clues as to the likely consequences of the rise of anti-system politics. Given the size of Italy's debt burden and its poor growth prospects, the election of a Euroskeptic government, led by parties that had both at various points advocated euro exit, disconcerted markets. The spread of Italy's ten year bond (BTP) to the German Bund stood at 136 basis points prior to the election, leapt to 303 when Cottarelli stepped down, and then hit a new peak of 311 in November 2018 prior to approval of the government budget. Markets were unsettled by the new government's decision to pick a fight with the European Commission over the projected budget deficit, a fight in which the Italians backed down (embarrassingly settling for a deficit target of 2.07 percent, which had the merit of sounding almost identical to their original proposal of 2.7 percent). After first dropping plans for a euro referendum, the anti-system parties' surrender on the fiscal rules suggested a reluctance to go beyond the aggressive rhetoric and formulate a serious challenge to the policy orthodoxy. The removal of a huge *basta euro* ("no more euro") banner from the League's headquarters in Milan the day after the coalition agreement was reached indicated a hasty recognition of the political risks of this policy reversal.[118]

The failed attempt to break with EU fiscal rules was not only a consequence of the League and the M5S's Euroskeptic rhetoric, but also reflected the difficulties of resolving the distributional battles within the government coalition. The two parties agreed on the abolition of the Fornero reform and reduction of the retirement age, but differed over the direction of fiscal policy: the M5S and its mostly southern electorate favored further social spending through a new minimum income scheme, while the League and its more prosperous northern voters preferred tax cuts through an ill-defined flat tax. Implementing all these measures together while remaining within the fiscal rules, at the same time that the ECB was exiting its bond-buying scheme, appeared to be an "impossible trinity." Other divisions within the coalition included migration, where Salvini's unwavering hostility to refugees conflicted with the much more ambivalent line of the left-leaning factions of the Five Stars, and infrastructure, where the League favored continuing the TAV high-speed train project while the M5S minister of transport, Toninelli, insisted it would be halted. Anti-system politics in Italy collided with the harsh realities of constraints that were easier to remove in opposition than in government.

Conclusion

The Italian case has all the familiar ingredients of an anti-system revolt: a severe economic crisis, high levels of inequality, and an unresponsive and discredited political system. It also follows to some extent the pattern typical of the rest of the southern Eurozone: a sovereign debt crisis that forced governments into harsh austerity, the imposition of policies from outside, and an economic crisis that hit "outsider" groups of younger people especially hard. However, the form anti-system politics took differed from the rest of the South in intriguing ways.

The M5S, which was most successful in tapping into the frustration of younger Italians, was less clearly anchored on the left than parties such as Podemos, Syriza, or the Bloco Esquerda. The Left has been markedly absent from post-crisis politics in Italy, with the post-communist left parties almost disappearing from the scene, and the main center-left party, the PD, adopting an increasingly neoliberal stance. Italy differed from Greece, Spain, and Portugal in lacking a strong anti-austerity movement, which could have acted as a focal point for a left alternative. M5S's ideological ambiguity allowed it to expand its support beyond the younger, politically progressive voters that typically support the anti-system Left, but meant it also lacked a clear agenda for government. Its electoral success in 2018 propelled the Movement into government, but without having clarified to its 10 million voters what it stood for, apart from being against the system it now had to govern.

The other exception of the Italian case is the strength of the anti-system Right. Italy experienced a sharp rise in migration, as well as having to manage the refugee crisis in the Mediterranean, though Greece and Spain were equally exposed. But the sharp rise in support for Salvini's League was not solely down to migration. Italy's long economic stagnation left the League's heartlands in the small cities and countryside of northern Italy facing deindustrialization and declining support from the state. League voters look very much like the "left behind" voters of post-industrial Britain, northern France, or eastern Germany, who also supported the anti-system Right. Migration may have mobilized some voters, but the failings of the established parties to address a serious economic crisis offers a powerful explanation of the collapse of Italy's party system, just as it did in the early 1990s.

Conclusions

THIS BOOK HAS presented an explanation of anti-system politics in rich democracies rooted in fundamental changes to the political economy. This group of highly successful societies, which had all, to varying degrees, achieved economic prosperity and social cohesion in the second half of the twentieth century, came under strain as market economies could no longer deliver consistent and equitably shared improvements in living standards. Politicians not only failed to regulate an increasingly unstable global economy, but also withdrew many of the social protections that had cushioned society from market fluctuations. Faced with growing inequality and instability, established political parties farmed out key areas of policymaking to nonpartisan experts, and retreated from articulating competing visions of society. This "neoliberal democracy" could be sustained while economies continued to grow, but it was not strong enough to withstand a policy failure on the scale of the Global Financial Crisis of the late 2000s.

It is tempting to explain anti-system revolts in terms of the short-term events that precede them, the quirks of the individual political leaders involved, and the specificities of each country's institutional and political context. Donald Trump's campaign mobilized long-standing racial divides in the United States and exploited weak leadership within the Republican Party. Brexit leveraged the long-standing Euroskepticism in the United Kingdom, especially inside the Conservative Party, and connected the failings of the European Union to a variety of grievances, many of which had little to do with Europe. In Italy, the Berlusconi experience paved the way for Beppe

Grillo's incursion into politics, while the Catalan conflict had its origins in the early modern period. But if one steps back and places these anti-system movements in a comparative and historical perspective, it is clear that they share many common features, quite apart from having come about at almost exactly the same time.

All these movements appealed to a widely shared sense among citizens that the existing political order had failed. Elections failed to deliver significant changes in the most important policy areas, while political parties retreated from ideological appeals and abandoned their traditional grassroots constituencies. Party politicians seemed far more interested in listening to corporate interests and super-wealthy individuals, who caught their attention by offering money, support in the media, or simply by leveraging the outsized influence enjoyed by the owners of mobile capital in an interconnected world. As the structures of collective action through which citizens had been able to shape policy withered, a growing number of people simply turned away from conventional politics, either focusing on the private sphere or involving themselves in other forms of political action.

This slow deterioration of democratic health was sharply accelerated by the Global Financial Crisis. Suddenly, discontent at a perceived lack of voice escalated into a sense of serious threat to social well-being, as economic losses hit home, and any certainties about the future dissolved. Yet politics in a sense continued as usual. The firefighting of 2007–2009, where politicians and technocrats ripped up the copybook to avoid financial catastrophe, gave way to a doomed attempt to restore the prior political and economic order by curbing the state's capacity to protect the nonwealthy and tightening the constraints on governments' ability to protect the "real economy." Rather than an opportunity to rethink the market liberal orthodoxy, the collapse in government finances following the crisis was exploited as an opportunity to double down on this orthodoxy. In the Eurozone, the process of emptying out the sovereignty of the indebted nations was accelerated, as financial assistance was made conditional on locking in harsh fiscal austerity and pushing through further market liberalizing reforms. Outside the Eurozone, debtor countries enjoyed much greater freedom to relax fiscal and monetary constraints to ease the costs of adjustment, but dominant interests aggressively moved to shift those costs onto the most economically exposed groups.

This attempt to offload the costs of a crisis caused by the unchecked behavior of a wealthy elite onto ordinary voters could hardly have failed to provoke a political reaction—not only because political science tells us that voters punish governments who preside over economic failure, but also because the crisis lasted well beyond the usual electoral cycle. Normal patterns of partisan turnover did not suffice to exorcise public rage: elections threw the "rascals out," only to produce no real relief. The discrediting of governing parties became the discrediting of an entire system. The French presidency transferring from the Gaullist Sarkozy to the Socialist Hollande had no appreciable policy impact. In Britain, the defeat of the Labour Party brought in a Conservative-led government that pushed through a recovery-killing austerity program. In Spain, the Socialist Zapatero was thrown out to be replaced by the conservative Rajoy, who imposed harsh austerity and an "aggressive" labor reform. In Italy, Berlusconi came and went, to be replaced first by a technocrat, then by a series of center-left prime ministers, none of whom was willing to challenge a failed policy of austerity.

What was challenged by the political turbulence of the mid-2010s was not just a ruling elite, or the political parties that underpinned it. The anti-system forces besieging the "establishment" were all, with varying degrees of coherence and clarity, challenging a specific way of doing politics. If the era of market liberalism and centrist politics was an era of political impotence in the face of public demands, the anti-system wave was characterized by demands for action. Anti-system parties on both the left and right challenged the notion that financial markets and nonelected supranational authorities should dictate policy. The guiding logic of the market liberal form of democracy, although rarely openly expressed, was that politics could, and should, do as little as possible to avoid disturbing the smooth functioning of the capitalist system, and should certainly not be involved in distorting the distributional consequences of the market to satisfy political demands.

These arrangements made political parties' ability to respond to voter demands conditional on markets accepting the relevant policies. Faced with this market blackmail power, the resort to delegation of key policy choices to nonelected technocrats sympathetic to financial actors made perfect sense for fragile political parties struggling to win over an increasingly demanding electorate. The similarity between the basic macroeconomic stances adopted by whichever of the mainstream parties was elected to office was difficult to explain away to the large number of voters suffering declining living standards after the financial crisis. If voting for mainstream political options meant continuity, the logical response to a desperate situation was to vote for someone who promised to break the system and replace it with something better.

This book has shown how the upheavals of the second decade of the twenty-first century stem from the failure of neoliberalism to deliver widely shared economic prosperity and democratic accountability. The much discussed "cultural backlash" thesis is superficially plausible, in that many of the anti-system parties that exploited the failures of neoliberalism advocated a return to conservative values and a reversal of the social and cultural changes resulting from migration. Undoubtedly some anti-system votes were motivated primarily by anger at the emerging multicultural society and perceived cultural and economic threats from outside. But there is also substantial disconfirming evidence. Voter attitudes toward migration have tended to soften over time, particularly in countries such as the United States and the United Kingdom, where the cultural backlash appears to be most powerful.[1] Yet at the same time, some countries where attitudes to migration were less tolerant had little or no support for right-wing anti-system parties. Within most countries, the areas with the smallest migrant presence had the highest support for right-wing anti-system parties.

Instead, the role of migration in the crisis is best seen as one of many possible focal points for a range of political and economic grievances. In Greece, Portugal, and Spain, right-wing xenophobic nationalism was a marginal political force in the post-crisis years. There, political opposition was mostly inspired by left-wing anti-capitalist ideas, in some cases accompanied by secessionist opposition to the nation-state itself. Even in the United States and the United Kingdom, the noise generated by Trump and the Brexiters distracts from the clear evidence that left-wing anti-system forces were a powerful driver of political change, too. It is also misleading to reduce the anti-system Right to a racist, authoritarian appeal. Most anti-system right-wingers addressed economic grievances head-on, identifying migration as an economic threat as much as a cultural one, and advocating trade protectionism and welfare chauvinism (the preferential treatment of "natives" in social policy). The anti-system forces on the left and right may differ in ideological positioning and philosophy, but they shared a rejection of the primacy of markets over politics inherent in contemporary neoliberal democracy.

In this sense the events of the 2010s bear a striking, and deeply troubling, resemblance to the 1930s. Faced with the socially destabilizing consequences of an inadequately regulated market economy and a spiraling debt crisis, democratic rule and the international order collapsed under the weight of fascist and communist pressures. Once again, Western countries are faced with existential choices between fascism, socialism, and liberalism as guiding principles of the political economy. The failure of democracies to adequately protect citizens from the potential of markets to overturn the social and economic order unleashed opposition to neoliberalism on both the left and the right. In their different ways they advocate what Sheri Berman called "the primacy of politics"[2]—the empowering of society to control the economy, rather than the other way around. Whether by closing borders or regulating capitalists, the anti-system impulse is always to "take back control" (one of the key slogans of the Brexit campaign), while neoliberalism implies letting the market take its course.[3]

The neoliberal utopia of the "self-regulating market" failed in the 1930s and in the 2000s. In both cases, recognition of the failure preceded a correct diagnosis and the design of solutions by some years. Karl Polanyi explained the catastrophic descent into Nazism, world war, and genocide in the 1930s as the result of the impasse resulting from the inability of politics to liberate societies from the strictures of the Gold Standard. Politics in the 2010s presented a similar scenario. The neoliberal regime lost all legitimacy and the politicians representing its values and policies were unable to keep their grip on power. Yet this time the anti-system forces struggled to do much more than remove the neoliberal elites, lacking credible programs of reform or strategies for fundamental institutional change.

Perhaps the most obvious example of this was Brexit. The extraordinary and unexpected victory of the Leave campaign in 2016 gave way to exactly the kind of impasse that Polanyi described for the 1930s. The British economic model rested on a very open economy in which the United Kingdom's most competitive sectors—finance and business services, pharmaceuticals, the auto industry, research and universities—had full access to overseas markets, labor forces, and supply chains. This model generated huge imbalances, with high levels of inequality between regions and social classes and weak redistributive policies, with only a minority of voters unambiguously benefiting. But the EU referendum was only won by cobbling together a coalition of quite incompatible interests and ideologies: the Leave vote combined wealthy rural and suburban Conservative-leaning voters together with the Labour-voting urban poor. These groups may have agreed on the need for Britain to recover political independence and reduce migration, but there was no Leave consensus on the economic model that the United Kingdom should pursue outside the European Union. Not surprisingly, attempting to actually deliver Brexit proved extraordinarily complex and costly.

The Trump presidency displayed many of the same symptoms. Trump acted in a decisive and aggressive way on some issues, exploiting the unique global power the United States enjoys. The trade war with China and aggressive harassment of migrants reflected the right-wing authoritarian and protectionist values Trump promoted in the 2016 election campaign. Such moves made good headlines and kept his base riled up, but the underlying challenge to the neoliberal order in the United States Trump appeared to articulate, thanks to his initial reliance on Steve Bannon, made far less progress.

The US trade deficit with China and Europe remained stubbornly high despite tariffs levied on some politically symbolic products, and nothing was done by the Trump administration to alleviate the adverse distributional consequences of the "China shock" that were evoked so powerfully in the 2016 election campaign.

Instead, the signal economic policy of the Trump administration was the 2017 Tax Cuts and Jobs Act, worth $1.5 trillion, which one observer described as "largely focused on reducing taxes for rich business owners."[4] Not only did this measure benefit Wall Street far more than the "white working-class Americans" that Trump mobilized so successfully, but also, by increasing the federal budget deficit, it likely increased the trade deficit that Trump saw as America's main economic problem. By introducing debt-financed redistribution to the wealthy, while cutting social provision and undermining the Obamacare health reforms and other progressive measures, Trump followed a well-trodden path of Republican administrations since Reagan. The rhetoric and international alliances may have changed in fundamental ways, but in terms of domestic politics and the conflict between the wealthy and the struggling middle class, Trump failed to genuinely challenge what he consistently described as a "rigged system."

Similar tales can be told about Europe. The European episode of the Global Financial Crisis, which crippled the most indebted countries inside the euro area, brought much political instability, but far less in the way of substantial reform to the workings of the political and financial system of the European Union. The first major challenge to the EU response to the crisis was the election of the Syriza government in Greece, a left coalition that began by sending a maverick economics professor, Yanis Varoufakis, to Brussels to renegotiate the terms of Greece's financial bailout. This attempt failed spectacularly, with Greece's creditors refusing to relax the austerity and reform conditions for financial aid, which Syriza correctly identified as having provoked an economic and even a humanitarian disaster in Greece. The Syriza government even held a referendum in which Greek voters decisively rejected the financial bailout package it had been offered, only for the European Union to respond by putting an even harsher offer on the table, which Greek Prime Minister Alexis Tsipras felt compelled to accept. The Syriza government's diplomatic ineptitude may have played an important role in this failure, but it also suggested that in a collision between the democratic demands of an electorate and the financial rules of the European Monetary Union, there could only be one winner.

Greece was in many respects the European member state least likely to be able to disturb the financial, economic, and political order established after the Maastricht Treaty of 1991. Not only were Greece's economy and its public finances in a parlous state, which made a "Grexit" an extraordinarily risky and painful step to take, but Greece was also diplomatically isolated and too small to be able to threaten to unleash financial catastrophe on its neighbors. Greece was not "too big to fail," especially once the initial market panic had been stemmed by the first Troika bailout, which stabilized the position of the northern European banks that were on the hook for hundreds of billions of euros of Greek debt.

The other "sick man" of the Eurozone, Italy, was quite a different story. With the fourth-largest national debt (by volume, after the United States, Japan, and Germany) in the world, Italy was too big to bail, but also too big to fail. Were Italy to exit the euro, over €2 trillion of Tier One assets held by financial institutions over the European Union would be in default, a financial shock of a magnitude comparable to the crisis of 2008. Worse, Italy, in decline since joining the euro, had one of the most Euroskeptic electorates in the Eurozone.

Italy elected an anti-system coalition to government in an environment quite different from Greece, with the Eurozone enjoying some economic growth and international financial conditions being relatively stable. Unlike Greece, though, the left-wing anti-system impulse was weak in Italy, and the largest parties in the 2018 elections had little to say about reforming capitalism. The government coalition between the Five Stars Movement and the revamped League under Salvini brought together two movements representing very different economic and social interests: the Five Stars entrenched especially in the South and among younger voters, while the League represented the wealthy North and an older and less-educated electorate. Addressing Italy's economic decline from such different standpoints, and with very underdeveloped policy proposals, was unlikely to bring radical change, yet the "yellow-green" government did have sufficient Euroskeptic credentials to spook financial markets and irritate European policymakers.

The Italian, Greek, and British cases illustrate the difficulties of breaking with a model of neoliberal politics that provokes demands for government intervention while closing off many of the channels through which such intervention has traditionally taken place. Anti-system parties can take over the machinery of government, but during the period since the 1980s, Western democracies reformed their institutions in such a way as to give prominence to market over nonmarket relations, and to constrain governments from recalibrating the balance in favor of collective over individual decision-making. The neoliberal project not only involved privatizing government-run industries and agencies, cutting taxes and welfare spending and removing some kinds of regulation, but also more fundamentally altered the capacity of the government and civil society to intervene in economic life. This placed severe obstacles in the way of anti-system forces seeking to win power and use it to change the way the political economy works.

This is most obvious in the case of money and finance. After the breakdown of the postwar Bretton Woods arrangements in the 1970s, capital controls were removed by Western governments, and open capital accounts became the standard for the developed economies. The high level of mobility of capital, with few legal and progressively fewer practical constraints, significantly diminished the room for maneuver among democratic governments, which were exposed to volatile movements of large amounts of money into and out of their economies. In response to this volatility, democratic governments all converged around similar institutions: independent central banks that could provide credibility against the risk of inflation, fiscal rules to commit governments to limited borrowing, and regulatory authorities to oversee markets at arm's length from elected politicians. In the case of the European Monetary Union, this went much further, with national governments renouncing any control over monetary policy whatsoever.

Some of these policies were potentially reversible, but others, especially euro membership, were extremely costly to exit. This was by design, since the underlying thinking behind these institutions was to "tie the hands" of democratic authorities to prevent them from undermining market competition, threatening property rights, and exploiting the opportunity to use fiscal or monetary policy for partisan benefit. Public choice theory, a key theoretical inspiration for redesigning economic institutions from the 1970s on, was quite explicit about its goal to strip elected politicians of the power to regulate, control, or suppress markets, often seeing government as an unfortunate necessity that needed to be constrained at all costs. But by denying elected politicians the tools to undermine markets through rent-seeking, fiscal profligacy, or inflation, these institutions robbed government of the ability to intervene in the public interest when markets failed, which is precisely the scenario that unfolded after 2007. As a result, the burden for fixing the market meltdown fell on central bankers not directly accountable to voters, with the consequence that policy prioritized stabilizing the banking system rather than addressing the broader social and economic damage caused by the crisis.[5]

Governments' ability to manage the economy was also limited by another, perhaps less obvious, consequence of neoliberal reforms. One of the main sources of anxiety among free market thinkers and their allies in the business community was organized labor, and in some countries the failure of collective bargaining to curb inflationary pressures in the 1970s turned neoliberal reformers against trade unions. The decline of unions was almost universal in the rich democracies, although they hung onto some of their functions in continental Europe, and this decline was facilitated by the strong pressure from the policy community and international organizations to dismantle collective bargaining and deregulate labor markets. The loss of political influence and organizational capacity of trade unions undermined progressive politics by isolating workers from each other and limiting the ability of broad social interests to mobilize and pressure business and government. Strikes became a rarity, and governments in many countries abandoned systematic consultation with unions over social and economic policy, while business interests maintained a direct line to decision-makers.

As a result of these deep structural changes to the political economy, deviating from the neoliberal playbook became increasingly difficult for elected politicians, lacking as they do the political and economic clout to resist market pressure and business lobbying. The experiences of anti-system politicians reaching government demonstrated in a short time just how difficult it is to implement serious change, when so many of the policy instruments that would be needed are lacking. The situation was not helped by the incoherent, oversimplified, and amateurish approach of anti-system politicians to policy development and implementation. The opportunistic nature of many anti-system movements, their lack of experience, their limited organization and grassroots presence, and the lack of any serious intellectual grounding for their rhetoric made successful policymaking unlikely. But even in cases where anti-system politicians could draw on deeper thinking and more plausible policy ideas, the impediments to realizing them were severe.

The social and economic forces underpinning anti-system politics will remain powerful as long as the rich democracies continue to be trapped in a low growth equilibrium with unbalanced demographics, high levels of debt, and weak government institutions. The collapse of the neoliberal economic model and the political actors that sustained it make continued mass opposition to the status quo the most likely scenario, especially in the countries worst hit by the financial crisis. Anti-system politics will not go away while the "system" is perceived by a growing share of the population to have failed. The job of politicians is to develop a diagnosis of this failure, and a set of proposals for fundamental change, that make sense and resonate with voters.

The idea that markets can resolve most social problems, and that government should simply provide the basic institutions to allow this to happen, has run out of political capital. Whatever new paradigm emerges must facilitate meaningful mass participation in political decision-making over whatever matters society thinks are important. In other words, what most people understand by the word "democracy."

NOTES

Introduction

1. Giovanni Sartori, *Parties and Party Systems: A Framework for Analysis* (New York: Cambridge University Press, 1976), p.117.
2. Richard Katz and Peter Mair (1995), "Changing Models of Party Organization and Party Democracy: The Emergence of the Cartel Party," *Party Politics* 1(1): 5–28.
3. Colin Leys, *Market-Driven Politics: Neoliberal Democracy and the Public Interest* (London: Verso, 2003).
4. See the work of Roberto Foa and Yascha Mounk, who argue that current trends in electoral behavior and public opinion point to a process of "democratic deconsolidation": Roberto Foa and Yascha Mounk (2017), "The Signs of Deconsolidation," *Journal of Democracy* 28(1): 5–15. For a critique, see Paul Howe (2017), "Eroding Norms and Democratic Deconsolidation," *Journal of Democracy* 28(4): 15–29.
5. Amy Alexander and Christian Welzel (2017), "The Myth of Deconsolidation: Rising Liberalism and the Populist Reaction," ILE Working Paper No. 10 (Hamburg: University of Hamburg, Institute of Law and Economics [ILE]).
6. See, for example, Cas Mudde (2004), "The Populist Zeitgeist," *Government and Opposition* 39(4): 541–563, and *Populist Radical Right Parties in Europe* (New York: Cambridge University Press, 2007); Cristóbal Rovira Kaltwasser, Paul Taggart, Paulina Ochoa Espejo, and Pierre Ostiguy, "Populism: An Overview of the Concept and the State of the Art," in Cristóbal Rovira Kaltwasser, Paul Taggart, Paulina Ochoa Espejo, and Pierre Ostiguy (eds.)

The Oxford Handbook of Populism (Oxford: Oxford University Press, 2017), pp.1-24.

7. Rovira Kaltwasser et al., "Populism: An Overview of the Concept and the State of the Art," p.5.

8. Jan Werner Mueller, *What Is Populism?* (Philadelphia: University of Pennsylvania Press, 2016).

9. Usually by economists suspicious of policies inimical to market liberal orthodoxy: see, for example, Rudiger Dornbusch and Sebastian Edwards (1989), "Macroeconomic Populism in Latin America," NBER Working Paper No. 2986; Luigi Guiso, Helios Herrera, Massimo Morelli, and Tommaso Sonno (2017), "Populism: Demand and Supply," Center for Economic Policy Research Discussion Paper No. 11871.

10. For a classic statement of this distinction, see William Riker, *Liberalism against Populism: A Confrontation between the Theory of Democracy and the Theory of Social Choice* (San Francisco: W. H. Freeman, 1982). For a positive view of populism as a progressive force, see Chantal Mouffe, *For a Left Populism* (London: Verso Books, 2018).

11. Adam Smith, *An Inquiry into the Nature and Causes of the Wealth of Nations* (Edinburgh: T. Nelson and Sons, 1887).

12. Mark Blyth and Richard Katz (2005), "From Catch-All Politics to Cartelisation: The Political Economy of the Cartel Party," *West European Politics* 28(1): 33–60.

13. Data from World Inequality Database, https://wid.world.

14. Richard Wilkinson and Kate Pickett, *The Spirit Level: Why Equality Is Better for Everyone* (London: Penguin UK, 2010).

15. For an optimistic view of the policy response to the crisis, see Daniel Drezner, *The System Worked: How the World Stopped Another Great Depression* (New York: Oxford University Press, 2014).

16. Mark Blyth, *Austerity: The History of a Dangerous Idea* (New York: Oxford University Press, 2013).

17. For example, Roger Eatwell and Matthew Goodwin, *National Populism: The Revolt against Liberal Democracy* (London: Penguin, 2018).

18. Pippa Norris and Ronald Inglehart, *Cultural Backlash: Trump, Brexit, and Authoritarian Populism* (New York: Cambridge University Press, 2019).

19. Eatwell and Goodwin, *National Populism*.

20. Norris and Inglehart, *Cultural Backlash*, ch.4.

21. Philip Manow, *Die Politische Ökonomie des Populismus* (Berlin: Suhrkamp Verlag, 2018).

22. Norris and Inglehart, *Cultural Backlash*, chs. 2, 4.

23. Andrés Rodríguez-Pose (2018), "The Revenge of the Places That Don't Matter (and What to Do about It)," *Cambridge Journal of Regions, Economy and Society* 11(1): 189–209.

24. Mark Blyth (2003), "Structures Do Not Come with an Instruction Sheet: Interests, Ideas, and Progress in Political Science," *Perspectives on Politics* 1(4): 695–706.

25. Perhaps the most important contributions to this debate come from Harvard's Dani Rodrik; see his paper "Populism and the Economics of Globalization," Harvard University, 2018 (copy at http://tinyurl.com/y5djhn5f); and previous books such as *The Globalization Paradox: Democracy and the Future of the World Economy* (New York: W. W. Norton 2011).

26. Christoph Lakner and Branko Milanovic (2016), "Global Income Distribution: From the Fall of the Berlin Wall to the Great Recession," *World Bank Economic Review* 30(2): 203–232.

27. Karl Polanyi, *The Great Transformation* (Boston: Beacon Press, 1944).

28. See, for example, Barry Eichengreen, *Hall of Mirrors: The Great Depression, the Great Recession, and the Uses—and Misuses—of History* (New York: Oxford University Press, 2014).

29. Joseph Stiglitz, *The Roaring Nineties: Paying the Price for the Greediest Decade in History* (New York: Penguin, 2003).

30. Paul Krugman, *The Return of Depression Economics and the Crisis of 2008* (New York: Penguin, 2009); Blyth, *Austerity*.

31. Sheri Berman, *The Primacy of Politics: Social Democracy and the Making of Europe's Twentieth Century* (New York: Cambridge University Press, 2006).

32. To paraphrase political economist Paul Pierson (1998), "Irresistible Forces, Immovable Objects: Post-Industrial Welfare States Confront Permanent Austerity," *Journal of European Public Policy* 5(4): 539–560.

Chapter 1

1. Most notoriously by Francis Fukuyama, *The End of History and the Last Man* (New York: The Free Press, 1992).

2. Karl Polanyi, *The Great Transformation* (Boston: Beacon Press, 1944).

3. Elmer E. Schattschneider, *Party Government* (Westport, CT: Greenwood, 1942), p.1.

4. Maurice Duverger, *Political Parties: Their Organization and Activity in the Modern State* (London: Methuen, 1954).

5. Richard Katz and Peter Mair (1995), "Changing Models of Party Organization and Party Democracy: The Emergence of the Cartel Party," *Party Politics* 1(1): 5–28.

6. Thomas Piketty, *Capital in the Twenty-First Century* (Cambridge, MA: Harvard University Press, 2014).

7. See Charles Beard, *An Economic Interpretation of the Constitution of the United States* (New York: Macmillan, 1913).

8. John Stuart Mill, *Considerations on Representative Government* (London: Parker, Son, and Bourn, 1861), ch.8.

9. Giovanni Sartori, *Parties and Party Systems: A Framework for Analysis* (New York: Cambridge University Press, 1976).

10. Barry Eichengreen, *Golden Fetters: The Gold Standard and the Great Depression 1919–39* (New York: Oxford University Press, 1992).

11. Ruth Berins Collier, *Paths towards Democracy* (New York: Cambridge University Press, 1999).

12. Barry Eichengreen, *Hall of Mirrors: The Great Depression, the Great Recession and the Uses—and Misuses—of History* (New York: Oxford University Press, 2014), ch.1.

13. For compelling accounts of the period, see Gregory Luebbert, *Liberalism, Fascism or Social Democracy: Social Classes and the Political Origins of Regimes in Interwar Europe* (New York: Oxford University Press, 1991); Sheri Berman, *The Primacy of Politics: Social Democracy and the Making of Europe's Twentieth Century* (New York: Cambridge University Press, 2006).

14. Piketty, *Capital*, p.147.

15. On the shifts in the international financial system after Bretton Woods, see Eric Helleiner, *States and the Reemergence of Global Finance: From Bretton Woods to the 1990s* (Ithaca: Cornell University Press, 1996). For an analysis of the challenges for postwar managed capitalism and the labor movement, see Fritz Scharpf, *Crisis and Choice in European Social Democracy* (Ithaca: Cornell University Press, 1991).

16. John Gerard Ruggie (1982), "International Regimes, Transactions, and Change: Embedded Liberalism in the Postwar Economic Order," *International Organization* 36(2): 379–415.

17. Tony Judt, *Postwar: A History of Europe since 1945* (London: Pimlico, 2005); Peter Hall, "The Political Origins of Our Economic Discontents," in Miles Kahler and David Lake (eds.), *Politics in the New Hard Times: The Great Recession in Comparative Perspective* (Ithaca: Cornell University Press, 2013), pp.129–149.

18. This concept, used by Wolfgang Streeck, among others, captures the very general sense in which the postwar order sought to reconcile the market economy with popular demands for social protection and stability. Other terms from the literature ("managed capitalism" or "embedded liberalism," for example) could be used, but have more specific meanings. See Wolfgang Streeck, *Buying Time: The Delayed Crisis of Democratic Capitalism* (London: Verso, 2014).

19. For a classic overview of this postwar system, see Andrew Shonfeld, *Modern Capitalism* (Oxford: Oxford University Press, 1965).

20. Stefano Bartolini, *The Political Mobilization of the European Left, 1860–1980* (Cambridge: Cambridge University Press, 2000).

21. Douglas Hibbs (1977), "Political Parties and Macroeconomic Policy," *American Political Science Review* 71(4): 1467–1487; later research posited that parties on the left achieved systematically better outcomes on both

variables: David Cameron, "Social Democracy, Corporatism, Labour Quiescence, and the Representation of Economic Interest in Advanced Capitalist Society," in John H. Goldthorpe (ed.), *Order and Conflict in Contemporary Capitalism* (Oxford: Oxford University Press, 1984), pp.143–178.

22. Goesta Esping-Andersen, *Politics against Markets: The Social Democratic Road to Power* (Princeton: Princeton University Press, 1985).

23. Vito Tanzi and Ludger Schuknecht, *Public Spending in the Twentieth Century* (Cambridge: Cambridge University Press, 2000).

24. See Peter Mair, "Party Organizations: From Civil Society to the State," in Richard Katz and Peter Mair (eds.), *How Parties Organize: Change and Adaptation in Party Organizations in Western Democracies* (London: Sage, 1994), pp.1–22.

25. Angus Campbell, Philip Converse, Warren Miller, and Donald Stokes, *The American Voter* (Chicago: University of Chicago Press, 1960); Sartori, *Parties and Party Systems*, pp.293–297.

26. Stein Rokkan, *Citizens, Elections, Parties: Approaches to the Comparative Study of the Processes of Development* (Oslo: Universitetsforlaget, 1970).

27. Bartolini, *The Political Mobilization of the European Left*, fig.6.3, p.279.

28. Goesta Esping-Andersen, *The Three Worlds of Welfare Capitalism* (Cambridge: Polity Press, 1990).

29. Julia Lynch, *Age in the Welfare State* (New York: Cambridge University Press, 2006).

30. The model originated in Bismarck's reforms in late nineteenth-century Germany. The term "Bismarckian" refers to welfare arrangements that are tied to employment status and funded by worker and employer contributions; for more, see Giuliano Bonoli (1997), "Classifying Welfare States: A Two-Dimension Approach," *Journal of Social Policy* 26(3): 351–372.

31. Torben Iversen and David Soskice (2006), "Electoral Institutions and the Politics of Coalitions: Why Some Democracies Redistribute More Than Others," *American Political Science Review* 100(2): 165–181.

32. Sven Steinmo, *Taxation and Democracy: Swedish, British and American Approaches to Financing the Modern State* (New Haven: Yale University Press, 1996); Alberto Alesina, Edward Glaeser, and Bruce Sacerdote (2001), "Why Doesn't the United States Have a European-Style Welfare State?," *Brookings Papers on Economic Activity* 2: 187–278.

33. See Peter Lindert, *Growing Public,* vol. 1, *The Story: Social Spending and Economic Growth since the Eighteenth Century* (New York: Cambridge University Press, 2004).

34. Mark Blyth, *Great Transformations: Economic Ideas and Institutional Change in the Twentieth Century* (New York: Cambridge University Press, 2002).

35. Andrew Glyn, *Capitalism Unleashed: Finance, Globalization, and Welfare* (Oxford: Oxford University Press, 2007).

36. Milton Friedman, *Capitalism and Freedom* (Chicago: University of Chicago Press, 1962).

37. Friedman himself went as far as to state: "I don't believe in democracy." See Edward Nik-Khah and Robert Van Horn, "The Ascendancy of Chicago Neoliberalism," in Damien Cahill, Melinda Cooper, Martijn Konings, David Primrose (eds.), *The Handbook of Neoliberalism* (London: Sage, 2016), pp.100–112 (p.105).

38. See, for example, Russell Hardin, *Liberalism, Constitutionalism and Democracy* (New York: Oxford University Press, 2003).

39. See Nancy McLean, *Democracy in Chains: The Deep History of the Radical Right's Stealth Plan for America* (New York: Penguin/Random House, 2017). McLean writes an intellectual history of neoliberalism in the United States, detailing the connection between conservative business leaders and public choice theorists in academia, and their shared hostility to organized labor and collective action more generally.

40. For an academic discussion of this argument, see Richard Rose, *Challenge to Governance: Studies in Overloaded Polities*, vol. 1 (Beverly Hills: Sage, 1980).

41. Michel Crozier, Samuel P. Huntington, and Joji Watanuki, *The Crisis of Democracy* (New York: New York University Press, 1975), p.8.

42. Kathleen McNamara (2002), "Rational Fictions: Central Bank Independence and the Social Logic of Delegation," *West European Politics* 25(1): 47–76.

43. Mark Thatcher and Alec Stone Sweet (2002), "Theory and Practice of Delegation to Non-Majoritarian Institutions," *West European Politics* 25(1): 1–22.

44. Peter Mair, *Ruling the Void: The Hollowing Out of Western Democracies* (London: Verso, 2013).

45. Carles Boix, *Political Parties, Growth and Equality: Conservative and Social Democratic Economic Strategies in the World Economy* (New York: Cambridge University Press, 1998); Geoffrey Garrett, *Partisan Politics in the Global Economy* (New York: Cambridge University Press, 1998).

46. See Goesta Esping Andersen (ed.), *Why Deregulate Labour Markets?* (Oxford: Oxford University Press, 2000); Lucio Baccaro and Chris Howell, *Trajectories of Neoliberal Transformation: European Industrial Relations since the 1970s* (New York: Cambridge University Press, 2017).

47. Recently released documents show that Thatcher and her advisors were quite explicit about this aim: Alan Travis, "National Archives: Margaret Thatcher Wanted to Crush Power of Trade Unions," *Guardian*, August 1, 2013, https://www.theguardian.com/uk-news/2013/aug/01/margaret-thatcher-trade-union-reform-national-archives (retrieved May 18, 2019).

48. Russell Dalton and Martin Wattenberg (eds.), *Parties without Partisans: Political Change in Advanced Industrial Democracies* (New York: Oxford University Press, 2002), fig.2.1, p.27.

49. Otto Kirchheimer, "The Transformation of the Western European Party Systems," in Joseph La Palombara and Myron Weiner (eds.), *Political Parties and Political Development* (Princeton: Princeton University Press, 1966), pp.177–200.

50. This combination of a "catch-all" approach to electoral mobilization and an increasing focus on modern technology and marketing was described by Angelo Panebianco as the "electoral-professional party": Angelo Panebianco, *Political Parties: Organization and Power* (New York: Cambridge University Press, 1988).

51. Katz and Mair, "Changing Models of Party Organization and Party Democracy."

52. Jonathan Hopkin (2004), "The Problem with Party Finance: Theoretical Perspectives on the Funding of Party Politics," *Party Politics* 10(6): 627–651.

53. Donatella della Porta, *Corrupt Exchanges: Actors, Resources, and Mechanisms of Political Corruption* (London: Routledge, 2017).

54. Seymour Martin Lipset and Stein Rokkan, "Cleavage Structures, Party Systems, and Voter Alignments: An Introduction," in Seymour Martin Lipset and Stein Rokkan (eds.), *Party Systems and Voter Alignments: Cross National Perspectives* (New York: Free Press, 1967), pp.1–64 (p.50).

55. Labour in the United Kingdom, the Parti Socialiste in France, the SPD in Germany, and the SAP in Sweden.

56. This measure of volatility is known as the Pedersen index: Mogens Pedersen (1979), "The Dynamics of European Party Systems: Changing Patterns of Electoral Volatility," *European Journal of Political Research* 7(1): 1–26.

57. Mair, *Ruling the Void.*

58. Susan Pharr and Robert Putnam (eds.), *Disaffected Democracies: What's Troubling the Trilateral Countries?* (Princeton: Princeton University Press, 2000); Mariano Torcal and José Ramón Montero (eds.), *Political Disaffection in Contemporary Democracies: Social Capital, Institutions and Politics* (London: Routledge, 2006); Colin Hay, *Why We Hate Politics* (Cambridge: Polity, 2007).

59. Katz and Mair, "Changing Models of Party Organization and Party Democracy."

60. Mark Blyth and Richard Katz (2005), "From Catch-All Politics to Cartelisation: The Political Economy of the Cartel Party," *West European Politics* 28(1): 33–60.

61. See, for example, the British Election Studies of the early twenty-first century, which adopted the "valence" model of electoral competition, arguing that there was fundamental consensus about the values and goals of politics, and that parties simply competed over the best way of fulfilling them: Paul Whiteley, Harold Clarke, David Sanders, and Marianne Stewart, *Affluence, Austerity and Electoral Change in Britain* (Cambridge: Cambridge University

Press, 2013); Jane Green and Will Jennings, *The Politics of Competence: Parties, Public Opinion and Voters* (Cambridge: Cambridge University Press, 2017).

62. For a discussion of the methodology, see Ian Budge and Hans-Dieter Klingemann, *Mapping Policy Preferences: Estimates for Parties, Electors and Governments, 1945–1998*, vol. 1 (New York: Oxford University Press, 2001).

63. Geoffrey Evans and James Tilley, *The New Politics of Class: The Political Exclusion of the British Working Class* (Oxford: Oxford University Press, 2017).

64. Richard Rose and Ian McAllister, *Voters Begin to Choose: From Closed Class to Open Elections in Britain* (London: Sage, 1986).

65. Ibid.

66. Leys, *Market-Driven Politics*. See also Fred Block and Margaret Somers, *The Power of Market Fundamentalism* (Cambridge, MA: Harvard University Press, 2014).

67. Piketty, *Capital*.

68. Piketty, *Capital*, fig.6.5, p.222.

69. Citigroup, "Plutonomy: Buying Luxury, Explaining Global Imbalances," Industry Note, October 16, 2005, https://delong.typepad.com/plutonomy-1.pdf (retrieved February 15, 2019).

70. Quoted in Ben Stein, "In Class Warfare, Guess Which Class Is Winning," *New York Times*, November 26, 2006, https://www.nytimes.com/2006/11/26/business/yourmoney/26every.html (retrieved February 14, 2019).

71. On war and taxation, see Kenneth Scheve and David Stasavage, *Taxing the Rich: A History of Fiscal Fairness in the United States and Europe* (Princeton; Princeton University Press, 2016).

72. For a classic statement of the labor market rigidities thesis, see Horst Siebert (1997), "Labor Market Rigidities: At the Root of Unemployment in Europe," *Journal of Economic Perspectives* 11(3): 37–54.

73. See Ernesto Dal Bó (2006), "Regulatory Capture: A Review," *Oxford Review of Economic Policy* 22(2): 203–225.

74. Even critics of the neoliberal project embraced trade liberalization; see, for example, Paul Krugman, *Pop Internationalism* (Cambridge, MA: MIT Press, 1996).

75. See, among many others, Susan Strange, *Casino Capitalism* (Manchester: Manchester University Press, 1998); Greta Krippner, *Capitalizing on Crisis* (Cambridge, MA: Harvard University Press, 2011).

76. "Profile: EU's Jean-Claude Juncker," *BBC News*, July 15, 2014, https://www.bbc.co.uk/news/world-europe-27679170 (retrieved February 14, 2019).

77. John Quiggin, *Zombie Economics: How Dead Ideas Still Walk among Us* (Princeton: Princeton University Press, 2012).

78. See David Howell, Dean Baker, Andrew Glyn, and John Schmitt (2007), "Are Protective Labor Market Institutions at the Root of Unemployment? A Critical Review of the Evidence," *Capitalism and Society* 2(1): 1–71.

79. Ibid.

80. Paolo Barbieri and Giorgio Cutuli (2015), "Employment Protection Legislation, Labour Market Dualism, and Inequality in Europe," *European Sociological Review* 32(4): 501–516.

81. Baccaro and Howell, *Trajectories of Neoliberal Transformation*.

82. See, for example, Paul Pierson, *Dismantling the Welfare State? Reagan, Thatcher, and the Politics of Retrenchment* (New York: Cambridge University Press, 1994); Monica Prasad, *The Politics of Free Markets: The Rise of Neoliberal Economic Policies in Britain, France, Germany and the United States* (Chicago: University of Chicago Press 2006).

83. This was especially the case in the English-speaking countries, but moves in this direction could also be observed in some of the northern European social democracies. See Klaus Armingeon and Giuliano Bonoli (eds.), *The Politics of Post-Industrial Welfare States: Adapting Post-War Social Policies to New Social Risks* (London: Routledge, 2007).

84. Herman Mark Schwartz and Leonard Seabrooke, "Varieties of Residential Capitalism in the International Political Economy: Old Welfare States and the New Politics of Housing," in Herman Mark Schwartz and Leonard Seabrooke (eds.), *The Politics of Housing Booms and Busts* (Basingstoke: Palgrave Macmillan, 2009), pp.1–27.

85. Paul Pierson (1998), "Irresistible Forces, Immovable Objects: Post-Industrial Welfare States Confront Permanent Austerity," *Journal of European Public Policy* 5(4): 539–560.

86. Perhaps the best account of the crisis and its global ramifications is by Adam Tooze, *Crashed: How a Decade of Financial Crises Changed the World* (London: Allen Lane, 2018).

87. See Naseem Nicholas Taleb, *The Black Swan: The Impact of the Highly Improbable* (New York: Random House, 2001).

88. For a Keynesian interpretation of the crisis, see Robert Skidelsky, *Keynes: The Return of the Master* (London: Penguin, 2010); see also Hyman Minsky, *Stabilizing an Unstable Economy* (New Haven: Yale University Press, 1986); Charles Kindleberger and Robert Aliber, *Manias, Panics and Crashes. A History of Financial Crises* (Basingstoke: Palgrave, 2005, 5th edition).

89. For example, Robert Shiller's work on bubbles in the stock and housing markets (Robert Shiller, *Irrational Exuberance* [Princeton: Princeton University, 2000]), or Susan Strange's analysis of financial deregulation, including a prescient outline of a future crisis of the euro (Susan Strange, *Mad Money: When Markets Outgrew Governments* [Ann Arbor: University of Michigan Press, 1998]).

90. For a critical discussion of theories of financial market efficiency, see Quiggin, *Zombie Economics*, ch.2.

91. "Greenspan 'Shocked' That Free Markets Are Flawed," *New York Times*, October 23, 2008, https://www.nytimes.com/2008/10/23/business/worldbusiness/23iht-gspan.4.17206624.html (retrieved February 15, 2019).

92. Jacob Hacker and Paul Pierson, *Winner-Take-All Politics: How Washington Made the Rich Richer—And Turned Its Back on the Middle Class* (New York: Simon & Schuster, 2010).

93. OECD, "Income Inequality Remains High in the Face of Weak Recovery," *OECD Income Inequality Update*, November 2016, http://www.oecd.org/social/OECD2016-Income-Inequality-Update.pdf(retrieved October 4, 2019.

94. Mark Blyth, *Austerity: A History of a Dangerous Idea* (New York: Oxford University Press, 2013).

95. The chart presents Gini coefficients of disposable household income inequality for selected OECD countries. Unlike the World Inequality Database data for pre-tax incomes shares cited earlier, these data present inequality between households rather than individuals, and of income after taxes have been paid and government transfers have been received. See OECD Income Distribution Database (IDD), http://www.oecd.org/social/income-distribution-database.htm.

96. See, for example, Michael Kumhof, Romain Rancière, and Pablo Winant (2015), "Inequality, Leverage, and Crises," *American Economic Review* 105(3): 1217–1245.

97. Torben Iversen and David Soskice, "Modern Capitalism and the Advanced Nation State: Understanding the Causes of the Crisis," in Nancy Bermeo and Jonas Pontusson (eds.), *Coping with Crisis: Government Reactions to the Great Recession* (New York: Russell Sage Foundation, 2012), pp.35–64.

98. See, for example, Raghuram Rajan, *Fault Lines: How Hidden Fractures Still Threaten the World Economy* (Princeton: Princeton University Press, 2011).

99. See Anat Admati and Martin Hellwig, *The Bankers' New Clothes: What's Wrong with Banking and What to Do about It* (Princeton: Princeton University Press, 2014).

100. Alberto Alesina, "Fiscal Adjustments: Lessons from Recent History," presentation to ECOFIN meeting, Madrid, April 2010. For a recent defense of the austerity doctrine, see Alberto Alesina, Carlo Favero, and Francesco Giavazzi, *Austerity: When It Works and When It Doesn't* (Princeton: Princeton University Press, 2019).

101. Carmen Reinhart and Kenneth Rogoff (2010), "Growth in a Time of Debt," *American Economic Review* 100(2): 573–578.

102. This was particularly the case in the southern Eurozone. See Sotiria Theodoropoulou (ed.), *Labour Market Policies in the Era of Pervasive Austerity: A European Perspective* (Bristol: Policy Press, 2018).

103. Vivien Schmidt and Mark Thatcher (eds.), *Resilient Liberalism in Europe's Political Economy* (New York: Cambridge University Press, 2013).

Chapter 2

1. For a typical example of the genre, see Eric Kaufmann, "Trump and Brexit: Why It's Again NOT the Economy, Stupid," *British Politics and Policy at LSE Blog*, November 9, 2016. Also Larry Bartels (2017), "The 'Wave' of Right-Wing Populist Sentiment Is a Myth," *Monkey Cage*, June 21, https://www.washingtonpost.com/news/monkey-cage/wp/2017/06/21/the-wave-of-right-wing-populist-sentiment-is-a-myth/?utm_term=.03cdb7ee201d.

2. Mattia Zulianello (2017), "Anti-System Parties Revisited: Concept Formation and Guidelines for Empirical Research," *Government and Opposition* 53(4): 653–681.

3. Hanspeter Kriesi (2014), "The Populist Challenge," *West European Politics* 37(2): 361–378.

4. See the discussion of Riker, *Liberalism against Populism*, in the Introduction to this book.

5. See Catherine de Vries and Sara Hobolt, *The Rise of Challenger Parties* (Princeton: Princeton University Press, 2019).

6. This two-dimensional approach was popularized by Ronald Inglehart, *The Silent Revolution: Changing Values and Political Styles among Western Publics* (Princeton: Princeton University Press, 1977).

7. See Pippa Norris and Ronald Inglehart, *Cultural Backlash: Trump, Brexit, and Authoritarian Populism* (New York: Cambridge University Press, 2019), ch.2.

8. Klaus von Beyme, *Political Parties in Western Democracies* (Aldershot: Gower, 1985).

9. The Chapel Hill Expert Survey, https://www.chesdata.eu/our-surveys. See Jonathan Polk, Jan Rovny, Ryan Bakker, Erica Edwards, Liesbet Hooghe, Seth Jolly, Jelle Koedam, Filip Kostelka, Gary Marks, Gijs Schumacher, Marco Steenbergen, Milada Vachudova, and Marko Zilovic (2017), "Explaining the Salience of Anti-Elitism and Reducing Political Corruption for Political Parties in Europe with the 2014 Chapel Hill Expert Survey Data," *Research and Politics* (January–March): 1–9.

10. Andrea Volkens, Werner Krause, Pola Lehmann, Theres Matthieß, Nicolas Merz, Sven Regel, and Bernhard Weßels, *The Manifesto Data Collection: Manifesto Project (MRG / CMP / MARPOR)*, version 2018b (Berlin: Wissenschaftszentrum Berlin für Sozialforschung, 2018), https://doi.org/10.25522/manifesto.mpds.2018b.

11. The Socialist International, the International Democrat Union (for conservative and center-right parties), the Liberal International, and the Christian Democrat International.

12. The European People's Party, the Alliance of Liberals and Democrats for Europe, Progressive Alliance of European Socialists and Democrats, and the European Green Party. Green parties in the European United Left–Nordic Green Left are coded as anti-system.

13. The dataset with parties coded as established or anti-system is available at https://www.jonathanhopkin.com.

14. In Europe these parties are mostly affiliated with the Movement for a Europe of Nations and Freedom party group.

15. The main European party group for the radical Left is the Party of the European Left and the Nordic Green Left.

16. Ronald Inglehart, *Cultural Evolution: People's Motivations Are Changing and Reshaping the World* (New York: Cambridge University Press, 2018).

17. Devin Caughey, Tom O'Grady, and Christopher Warshaw (2019), "Policy Ideology in European Mass Publics, 1981–2016," *American Political Science Review* 113(3): 674–693

18. Norris and Inglehart, *Cultural Backlash*, ch.2.

19. Morris Fiorina, *Culture War? The Myth of a Polarized America* (New York: Pearson/Longman, 2005).

20. Jane Gingrich and Silja Häusermann (2015), "The Decline of the Working-Class Vote, the Reconfiguration of the Welfare Support Coalition and Consequences for the Welfare State," *Journal of European Social Policy* 25(1): 50–75.

21. Mark Blyth, Jonathan Hopkin, and Riccardo Pelizzo, "Liberalization and Cartel Politics in Europe: Why Do Centre-Left Parties Adopt Market Liberal Reforms?," paper presented to 16th Conference of Europeanists, Montreal, 2010.

22. Caughey et al., "Policy Ideology in European Mass Publics." Compare with Hee Min Kim and Richard Fording (1998), "Voter Ideology in Western Democracies, 1946–1989," *European Journal of Political Research* 33 (1): 73–97.

23. Silja Hausermann and Hanspeter Kriesi, "What Do Voters Want? Dimensions and Configurations in Individual-Level Preferences and Party Choice," in Pablo Beramendi, Silja Hausermann, Herbert Kitschelt, and Hanspieter Kriesi (eds.), *The Politics of Advanced Capitalism* (New York: Cambridge University Press, 2015), pp.202–230.

24. Nick Pierce and Eleonor Taylor, "Government Spending and Welfare: Changing Attitudes towards the Role of the State," in Alison Park, Caroline Bryson, Elizabeth Clery, John Curtice, and Miranda Phillips (eds.), *British Social Attitudes: The 30th Report* (London: NatCen Social Research, 2013), pp.33–59.

25. See Larry Bartels (2005), "Homer Gets a Tax Cut: Inequality and Public Policy in the American Mind," *Perspectives on Politics* 3(1): 15–31.

26. Thomas Piketty, "Brahmin Left vs Merchant Right: Rising Inequality and the Changing Structure of Political Conflict (Evidence from France, Britain and the US, 1948–2017)," WID World Working Paper No. 2018/7, March 2018, http://piketty.pse.ens.fr/files/Piketty2018.pdf.

27. Geoffrey Evans and James Tilley, *The New Politics of Class: The Political Exclusion of the British Working Class* (Oxford: Oxford University Press, 2017).

28. Jacob Hacker and Paul Pierson, *Winner-Take-All Politics: How Washington Made the Rich Richer—and Turned Its Back on the Middle Class* (New York: Simon & Schuster, 2010); Martin Gilens, *Affluence and Influence: Economic Inequality and Political Power in America* (Princeton: Princeton University Press, 2012).

29. Riccardo Pelizzo, *Cartel Parties and Cartel Party Systems*, PhD dissertation, Johns Hopkins University, Baltimore, Maryland, November 2003.

30. See Gregory Luebbert, *Liberalism, Fascism, or Social Democracy: Social Classes and the Political Origins of Regimes in Interwar Europe* (New York: Oxford University Press, 1991); Sheri Berman, *The Primacy of Politics: Social Democracy and the Making of Europe's Twentieth Century* (New York: Cambridge University Press, 2006).

31. Adam Smith was well aware of this revolutionary power of liberal markets and their ability to undermine the traditional hierarchies and privileges of the preindustrial social order: see Goesta Esping-Andersen, *Three Worlds of Welfare Capitalism* (Cambridge: Polity, 1990), p.9.

32. See, for example, Herbert Kitschelt and Anthony McGann, *The Radical Right in Western Europe: A Comparative Analysis* (Ann Arbor: University of Michigan Press, 1995).

33. Hans-Georg Betz, *Radical Right-Wing Populism in Western Europe* (Basingstoke: Macmillan, 1994); Piero Ignazi, *Extreme Right Parties in Western Europe* (Oxford: Oxford University Press, 2003).

34. David Autor, David Dorn, and Gordon Hanson (2016), "Importing Political Polarization? The Electoral Consequences of Rising Trade Exposure," NBER Working Paper No. w22637 (Washington, DC: National Bureau of Economic Research); Italo Colantone, and Piero Stanig (2018), "The Trade Origins of Economic Nationalism: Import Competition and Voting Behavior in Western Europe," *American Journal of Political Science* 62(4): 936–953.

35. Alexandre Afonso, "Social Class and the Changing Welfare State Agenda of Radical Right Parties in Europe," in Philip Manow, Bruno Palier, and Hanna Schwander (eds.), *Welfare Democracies and Party Politics: Explaining Electoral Dynamics in Times of Changing Welfare Capitalism* (Oxford: Oxford University Press, 2018), pp.171–194.

36. Hanspeter Kriesi, Edgar Grande, Romain Lachat, Martin Dolezal, Simon Bornschier, and Timotheos Frey (2006), "Globalization and the Transformation of the National Political Space: Six European Countries Compared," *European Journal of Political Research* 45(6): 921–956. On the blurring of party positions, see Jan Rovny (2013), "Where Do Radical Right Parties Stand? Position Blurring in Multidimensional Competition," *European Political Science Review* 5(1): 1–26.

37. Menno Fenger (2018), "The Social Policy Agendas of Populist Radical Right Parties in Comparative Perspective," *Journal of International and Comparative Social Policy* 34(3): 188–209; Laurenz Ennser-Jedenastik (2018), "Welfare Chauvinism in Populist Radical Right Platforms: The Role of Redistributive Justice Principles," *Social Policy and Administration* 52(1): 293–314.

38. Ernesto Dal Bó, Frederico Finan, Olle Folke, Torsten Persson, and Johanna Rickne (2018), "Economic Losers and Political Winners: Sweden's Radical Right," unpublished paper, University of Stockholm, http://perseus.iies. su.se/~tpers/papers/CompleteDraft190301.pdf.

39. Which in practice is the actually existing state of affairs, but Salvini appeals to an underlying resentment that migrants should access any forms of welfare. Marco Valbruzzi (2018), "L'immigrazione in Italia tra realtà, retorica e percezione," *Il Mulino* 5 (September–October): 789–795.

40. See Vanessa Williamson, Theda Skocpol, and John Coggin (2011), "The Tea Party and the Remaking of Republican Conservatism," *Perspectives on Politics* 9(1): 25–43.

41. "Trump Railed against Wall Street. His Victory Is Going to Be Great for Big Banks," *Washington Post*, November 9, 2016, https://www.washingtonpost. com/news/wonk/wp/2016/11/09/trump-railed-against-wall-street-his-victory-is-going-to-be-great-for-big-banks/?utm_term=.a6ab6a14181f (retrieved April 25, 2019).

42. "Pledges Made by Italy's Populist Government Come Up against Economic Reality," *Wall Street Journal*, January 8, 2019, https://www.wsj.com/articles/ italy-offers-bank-bailout-despite-past-pledges-11546954204 (retrieved April 25, 2019).

43. Zsolt Enyedi (2016), "Paternalist Populism and Illiberal Elitism in Central Europe," *Journal of Political Ideologies* 21(1): 9–25 (p.11).

44. Akos Valentinyi, "The Hungarian Crisis," *VOX: CEPR Policy Portal*, March 19, 2012, https://voxeu.org/article/hungarian-crisis.

45. Alen Toplišek (2019), "The Political Economy of Populist Rule in Post-Crisis Europe: Hungary and Poland," *New Political Economy*, online first, March 29.

46. Cas Mudde, *Populist Radical Right Parties in Europe* (Cambridge: Cambridge University Press, 2007).

47. Matthijs Rooduijn, Brian Burgoon, Erika Van Elsas, and Herman Van de Werfhorst (2017), "Radical Distinction: Support for Radical Left and Radical Right Parties in Europe," *European Union Politics* 18(4): 536–559.

48. Takis Pappas and Paris Aslanidis, "Greek Populism: A Political Drama in Five Acts," in Hanspeter Kriesi and Takis Pappas (eds.), *European Populism in the Shadow of the Great Recession* (Colchester: ECPR Press, 2015), pp.181–196 (p.193).

49. Hilde Coffé and Rebecca Plassa (2010), "Party Policy Position of Die Linke: A Continuation of the PDS?" *Party Politics* 16(6): 721–735.

50. See David Hanley (2017), "Left and Centre-Left in France—Endgame or Renewal?" *Parliamentary Affairs* 71(3): 521–537.

51. Herbert Kitschelt (1988), "Left-Libertarian Parties: Explaining Innovation in Competitive Party Systems," *World Politics* 40(2): 194–234 (p.197).

52. Pablo Iglesias (2015), "Understanding Podemos," *New Left Review* 93: 7–22.

53. Christopher Bickerton and Carlo Invernizzi Accetti (2018), "'Techno-Populism' as a New Party Family: The Case of the Five Star Movement and Podemos," *Contemporary Italian Politics* 10(2): 132–150.

54. Kate Hudson, *The New European Left: A Socialism for the Twenty-First Century?* (Basingstoke: Palgrave Macmillan, 2012).

55. On economic voting, see Michael Lewis-Beck and Martin Paldam (2000), "Economic Voting: An Introduction," *Electoral Studies* 19(2–3): 113–121.

56. Benjamin Friedman (2006), "The Moral Consequences of Economic Growth," *Society* 43(2): 15–22.

57. Jeffrey Chwieroth and Andrew Walter, *The Wealth Effect: How the Great Expectations of the Middle Class Have Changed the Politics of Banking Crises* (New York: Cambridge University Press, 2019).

58. Mark Blyth, *Austerity: The History of a Dangerous Idea* (New York: Oxford University Press, 2013).

59. This measure of volatility—which simply sums the gains and losses of all the parties in the system and halves the number to get the total net vote change—is also called the Pedersen index: see Mogens Pedersen (1979), "The Dynamics of European Party Systems: Changing Patterns of Electoral Volatility," *European Journal of Political Research* 7(1): 1–26.

60. Arend Lijphart, *Patterns of Democracy: Government Forms and Performance in Thirty-Six Countries* (New Haven: Yale University Press, 2012); Torben Iversen and David Soskice (2006), "Electoral Institutions and the Politics of Coalitions: Why Some Democracies Redistribute More Than Others," *American Political Science Review* 100(2): 165–181.

61. See, for example, the account of the Greek crisis in Yanis Varoufakis, *Adults in the Room: My Battle with Europe's Deep Establishment* (London: Random House, 2017).

62. See Dani Rodrik, "Populism and the Economics of Globalization," NBER Working Paper No. 23559 (Washington, DC: National Bureau of Economic Research), http://www.nber.org/papers/w23559.

63. Philip Manow, *Die Politische Ökonomie des Populismus* (Berlin: Suhrkamp Verlag, 2018).

64. Hans-Georg Betz and Susi Meret, "Right-Wing Populist Parties and the Working Class Vote: What Have You Done for Us Lately?," in Jens Rydgren (ed.), *Class Politics and the Radical Right* (London: Routledge, 2012), pp.107–121.

65. Noam Gidron and Peter Hall (2017), "The Politics of Social Status: Economic and Cultural Roots of the Populist Right," *British Journal of Sociology* 68: S57–S84.

66. Dominik Hangartner, Elias Dinas, Moritz Marbach, Konstantinos Matakos, and Dimitrios Xefteris (2019), "Does Exposure to the Refugee Crisis Make Natives More Hostile?" *American Political Science Review* 113(2): 442–455.

67. Andrés Rodríguez-Pose (2018), "The Revenge of the Places That Don't Matter (And What to Do about It)," *Cambridge Journal of Regions, Economy and Society* 11(1): 189–209.

68. For evidence on the US case, see Judith Goldstein and Margaret Peters (2014), "Nativism or Economic Threat: Attitudes toward Immigrants during the Great Recession," *International Interactions* 40(3): 376–401.

69. Norris and Inglehart, *Cultural Backlash*, ch.4.

70. Christian Dustmann, Bernd Fitzenberger, Uta Schönberg, and Alexandra Spitz-Oener (2014), "From Sick Man of Europe to Economic Superstar: Germany's Resurgent Economy," *Journal of Economic Perspectives* 28(1): 167–188.

71. Michael Burda (2016), "The German Labor Market Miracle, 2003–2015: An Assessment," SFB 649 Discussion Paper No. 2016-005 (Berlin: Sonderforschungsbereich 649, Humboldt University); Philip Manow and Hanna Schwander link this deterioration directly to the rise of the AfD: "A Labor Market Explanation for Right-Wing Populism—Explaining the Electoral Success of the AfD In Germany," paper presented at the London School of Economics, March 2019.

72. Christian Franz, Marcel Fratzscher, and Alexander Kritikos (2018), "German Right-Wing Party AfD Finds More Support in Rural Areas with Aging Populations," *DIW Weekly Report* 8(7/8): 69–79.

73. Markus Gehrsitz and Martin Ungerer (2017), "Jobs, Crime, and Votes: A Short-Run Evaluation of the Refugee Crisis in Germany," ZEW Discussion Paper No. 16-086 (Mannheim: Zentrum für Europäische Wirtschaftsforschung [ZEW]).

74. Dal Bó et al, "Economic Losers and Political Winners: Sweden's Radical Right,".

75. See David Rueda, *Social Democracy Inside Out: Partisanship and Labor Market Policy in Advanced Industrialized Democracies* (Oxford: Oxford University Press, 2007).

76. Manow and Schwander, "A Labor Market Explanation for Right-Wing Populism."

77. For example, David Goodhart, *The Road to Somewhere: The Populist Revolt and the Future of Politics* (Oxford: Oxford University Press, 2017); Eric Kaufmann (2018), "Go Back to Where You Came From: The Backlash against Immigration and the Fate of Western Democracy," *Foreign Affairs* 97(5): 224–231.

Chapter 3

1. Jacob Hacker and Paul Pierson (2010), "Winner-Take-All Politics: Public Policy, Political Organization, and the Precipitous Rise of Top Incomes in the United States," *Politics and Society* 38(2): 152–204.

2. Goesta Esping-Andersen, *The Three Worlds of Welfare Capitalism* (Cambridge: Polity Press, 1990)., ch.2; Peter A. Hall and David W. Soskice (eds.), *Varieties of Capitalism: The Institutional Foundations of Comparative Advantage* (Oxford: Oxford University Press, 2001), ch.1.

3. Jacob Hacker, *The Great Risk Shift: The New Economic Insecurity and the Decline of the American Dream* (New York: Oxford University Press, 2019).

4. João Paulo Pessoa and John Van Reenen (2013), "Decoupling of Wage Growth and Productivity Growth?: Myth and Reality," CEP Discussion Paper No. 1246 (London: Centre for Economic Performance, London School of Economics and Political Science), p.1, http://cep.lse.ac.uk/pubs/download/dp1246.pdf.

5. Eighty-five percent of Americans had income growth lower than the mean: see Thomas Piketty, Emmanuel Saez, and Gabriel Zucman (2017)http://users.ox.ac.uk/~polf0487/papers/Ansell%20Brexit%20Memo.pdf, "Distributional National Accounts: Methods and Estimates for the United States," *Quarterly Journal of Economics* 133(2): 553–609.

6. Fated Guvenen (2017), "Understanding Income Risk: New Insights from Big Data" (Federal Reserve Bank of Minneapolis, June 26), https://www.minneapolisfed.org/publications/the-region/understanding-income-risk-new-insights-from-big-data.

7. Austin Nichols and Philipp Rehm (2014), "Income Risk in 30 Countries," *Review of Income and Wealth* 60 (Supplement Issue): S98–S116.

8. Jacob Hacker, *The Great Risk Shift*.

9. Kavya Vaghul and Marshall Steinbaum (2015), "An Introduction to the Geography of Student Debt," (Washington, DC: Washington Center for Equitable Growth, December 1), https://equitablegrowth.org/an-introduction-to-the-geography-of-student-debt/.

10. See Richard Wilkinson and Kate Pickett, *The Inner Level: How More Equal Societies Reduce Stress, Restore Sanity and Improve Everyone's Well-Being* (London: Penguin, 2018).

11. Anne Case and Angus Deaton (2015), "Rising Morbidity and Mortality in Midlife among White Non-Hispanic Americans in the 21st Century," *Proceedings of the National Academy of Sciences* 112(49): 15078–15083.

12. Anne Case and Angus Deaton (2017), "Mortality and Morbidity in the 21st Century," *Brookings Papers on Economic Activity* (Spring): 397–476.

13. See, for example, Seymour Martin Lipset and Gary Marks, *It Didn't Happen Here: Why Socialism Failed in the United States* (New York: W. W. Norton, 2000).

14. See, for instance, Alberto Alesina, Edward Glaeser, and Bruce Sacerdote (2001), "Why Doesn't the US Have a European-Style Welfare System?," NBER Working Paper No. 8524, (Washington, DC: National Bureau of Economic Research), http://www.nber.org/papers/w8524.

15. See Martin Gilens, *Why Americans Hate Welfare: Race, Media and the Politics of Antipoverty Policy* (Chicago: University of Chicago Press, 1999).

16. Benjamin Page and Lawrence Jacobs, *Class War? What Americans Really Think about Economic Inequality* (Chicago: University of Chicago Press, 2009), ch.2.

17. Ibid., chs.3–4.

18. See Sven Steinmo, *Taxation and Democracy: Swedish, British and American Approaches to Funding the Welfare State* (New Haven: Yale University Press, 1993).

19. Most famously Charles Beard, *An Economic Interpretation of the Constitution of the United States* (New York: Macmillan, 1913).

20. Larry Bartels, *Unequal Democracy: The Political Economy of the New Gilded Age* (Princeton: Princeton University Press, 2008); Christopher Achen and Larry Bartels, *Democracy for Realists: Why Elections Do Not Produce Responsive Government* (Princeton: Princeton University Press, 2017).

21. Thomas Frank, *What's the Matter with Kansas? How Conservatives Won the Heart of America* (New York: Henry Holt, 2007).

22. Nolan McCarty, Keith Poole, and Howard Rosenthal, *Polarized America: The Dance of Ideology and Unequal Riches* (Cambridge, MA: MIT Press, 2016).

23. Hacker and Pierson, "Winner-Take-All Politics," pp.189–196.

24. David Autor, David Dorn, and Gordon Hanson (2016), "The China Shock: Learning from Labor-Market Adjustment to Large Changes in Trade," *Annual Review of Economics* 8: 205–240.

25. Andrés Villareal, "Explaining the Decline in Mexico-U.S. Migration: The Effect of the Great Recession," *Demography* 51(6): 2203–2228.

26. Larry Bartels (2005), "Homer Gets a Tax Cut: Inequality and Public Policy in the American Mind," *Perspectives on Politics* 3(1): 15–31.

27. Hacker and Pierson, "Winner-Take-All Politics," p.178.

28. Martin Gilens and Benjamin Page found that where the policy preferences of elites and average citizens diverged, Congress tended to adopt the preferences of the elites: Martin Gilens and Benjamin Page (2014), "Testing Theories of American Politics: Elites, Interest Groups, and Average Citizens," *Perspectives on Politics* 12(3): 564–581.

29. For a historical account of the influence of business on party politics, see Thomas Ferguson, *Golden Rule: The Investment Theory of Party Competition and the Logic of Money-Driven Political Systems* (Chicago: University of Chicago Press, 1995).

30. Andrew Gelman, *Red State, Blue State, Rich State, Poor State: Why Americans Vote the Way They Do* (Princeton: Princeton University Press, 2009).

31. Jeff Winters and Benjamin Page (2009), "Oligarchy in the United States?," *Perspectives on Politics* 7(4): 731–751.

32. Roberto Stefan Foa and Yascha Mounk (2016), "The Democratic Disconnect," *Journal of Democracy* 27(3): 5–17.

33. Lydia Saad, "Congress Ranks Last in Confidence in Institutions," *Gallup: Politics*, July 22, 2010, http://www.gallup.com/poll/141512/congress-ranks-last-confidence-institutions.aspx, cited in Lawrence Lessig, *Republic, Lost: How Money Corrupts Congress—and a Plan to Stop It* (Boston: Twelve, 2011), p.2.

34. For example, Joseph Stiglitz, *The Price of Inequality: How Today's Divided Society Endangers Our Future* (New York: W. W. Norton, 2012).

35. British sociologist Colin Crouch described this arrangement as "privatized Keynesianism": Colin Crouch (2009), "Privatised Keynesianism: An Unacknowledged Policy Regime," *British Journal of Politics and International Relations* 11: 382–399.

36. Ahmed Tahoun and Laurence van Lent (2016), "The Personal Wealth Interests of Politicians and the Stabilization of Financial Markets," Working Paper No. 52 (New York: Institute for New Economic Thinking), https://www.ineteconomics.org/uploads/papers/WP_52-Tahoun_final.pdf (retrieved October 14, 2018).

37. Ken Bensinger, "Masses Aren't Buying Bailout: Indignant Americans Stage Protests, Deluge Congressional Offices," *Los Angeles Times,* September 26, 2008, http://articles.latimes.com/2008/sep/26/business/fi-voxpop26 (retrieved August 14, 2017).

38. Ryan Lizza, "The Summers Memo," *New Yorker*, January 23, 2012, http://www.newyorker.com/news/news-desk/the-summers-memo (retrieved August 14, 2017).

39. Michael D. Hurd and Susann Rohwedder (2010), "Effects of the Financial Crisis and Great Recession on American Households," NBER Working Paper No. 16407, (Washington, DC: National Bureau of Economic Research), http://www.nber.org/papers/w16407.

40. Employment Policy Institute (2010), "State of Working America: The Great Recession," http://stateofworkingamerica.org/great-recession/ (retrieved August 16, 2017).

41. Arne L. Kalleberg and Till M. von Wachter (2017), "The U.S. Labor Market during and after the Great Recession: Continuities and Transformations," *RSF: The Russell Sage Foundation Journal of the Social Sciences* 3(3): 1–19.

42. Elise Gould (2015), "2014 Continues a 35-Year Trend of Broad-Based Wage Stagnation," Issue Brief #393 (Washington, DC: Economic Policy Institute), http://www.epi.org/publication/stagnant-wages-in-2014/ (retrieved August 16, 2017).

43. Employment Policy Institute, "State of Working America: The Great Recession."

44. Jesse Bricker, Brian Bucks, Arthur Kennickell, Traci Mach, and Kevin Moore (2011), "Surveying the Aftermath of the Storm: Changes in Family Finances from 2007 to 2009," Finance and Economics Discussion Series (Washington, DC: Division of Research and Statistics and Monetary Affairs, Federal Reserve Board).

45. Olivier Coibion, Yuriy Gorodnichenko, Lorenz Kueng, and John Silvia (2012), "Innocent Bystanders? Monetary Policy and Inequality in the U.S.," NBER Working Paper No. 18170 (Washington, DC: National Bureau of Economic Research).

46. For example, Paul Krugman, "The Stimulus Tragedy," *New York Times*, February 20, 2014, https://www.nytimes.com/2014/02/21/opinion/krugman-the-stimulus-tragedy.html (retrieved May 25, 2019).

47. Robert Prasch (2012), "The Dodd-Frank Act: Financial Reform or Business as Usual?" *Journal of Economic Issues* 46(2): 549–556.

48. Emmanuel Saez (2013), "Striking It Richer: The Evolution of Top Incomes in the United States (Updated with 2012 Preliminary Estimates)," University of California, Berkeley, https://eml.berkeley.edu//~saez/saez-UStopincomes-2012.pdf.

49. Mark Blyth, *Austerity: The History of a Dangerous Idea* (New York: Oxford University Press, 2013), p.5.

50. Eric Etheridge, "Rick Santelli: Tea Party Time," *New York Times*, February 20, 2009, https://opinionator.blogs.nytimes.com/2009/02/20/rick-santelli-tea-party-time/ (retrieved August 17, 2017).

51. Theda Skocpol and Vanessa Williamson, *The Tea Party and the Remaking of Republican Conservatism* (New York: Oxford University Press, 2012).

52. Robert Frank, "Why the Rich Recovered and the Rest Didn't," CNBC.com, June 13, 2012, https://www.cnbc.com/id/47802283 (retrieved September 1, 2017).

53. Jeff Winters, *Oligarchy* (New York: Cambridge University Press, 2011), ch.5.

54. Skocpol and Williamson, *The Tea Party and the Remaking of Republican Conservatism*, p.53.

55. Michael A. Gould-Wartofsky, *The Occupiers: The Making of the 99 Percent Movement* (New York: Oxford University Press, 2015).

56. William Gamson and Micah Sifry (2013), "The #Occupy Movement: An Introduction," *Sociological Quarterly* 54: 159–228.

57. Jonathan Matthew Smucker (2013), "Occupy: A Name Fixed to a Flashpoint" *Sociological Quarterly* 54: 219–225.

58. Emmanuel Saez (2016), "U.S. Top One Percent of Income Earners Hit New High in 2015 amid Strong Economic Growth" (Washington, DC: Washington Center for Equitable Growth, July 1), http://equitablegrowth.org/research-analysis/u-s-top-one-percent-of-income-earners-hit-new-high-in-2015-amid-strong-economic-growth/ (retrieved August 25, 2017).

59. "Donald Trump Heckled by New York Elite at Charity Dinner," *New York Times*, October 20, 2016, https://www.nytimes.com/2016/10/21/us/politics/al-smith-dinner-clinton-trump.html (retrieved May 26, 2019).

60. "$2 Billion Worth of Free Media for Donald Trump," *New York Times*, March 15, 2016, https://www.nytimes.com/2016/03/16/upshot/measuring-donald-trumps-mammoth-advantage-in-free-media.html (retrieved April 3, 2019).

61. Donald Trump, *Crippled America: How to Make American Great Again* (New York: Threshold Editions, 2015).

62. Trump, *Crippled America*, p. x.

63. Robert Costa, "Donald Trump and a GOP Primary Campaign Like No Other," in Larry Sabato, Kyle Kondik, and Geoffrey Skelley (eds.), *Trumped: The 2016 Election That Broke All the Rules* (Boulder, CO: Rowman and Littlefield, 2017), pp.97–111 (p.98).

64. Chris Haynes and Jessica Sattler, "The Twitter Effect: How Trump Used Social Media to Stamp His Brand and Shape the Media Narrative on Immigration," in Jeanine Kraybill (ed.), *Unconventional, Partisan, and Polarizing Rhetoric: How the 2016 Election Shaped the Way Candidates Strategize, Engage, and Communicate* (Lanham, MD: Rowman and Littlefield, 2017), pp. 135–171.

65. Case and Deaton, "Rising Morbidity and Mortality."

66. Rhodes Cook, "Presidential Primaries: A Hit at the Ballot Box," in Larry Sabato et al., *Trumped*, p.90.

67. Matea Gold, Tom Hamburger, and Anu Narayanswamy, "Two Clintons, 41 Years, $3 Billion," *Washington Post*, November 19, 2015, https://www.washingtonpost.com/graphics/politics/clinton-money/.

68. Bernie Sanders, *Our Revolution: A Future to Believe In* (New York: Macmillan, 2016), pt.2, ch.3.

69. Robin Kolodny, "The Presidential Nominating Process, Campaign Money, and Popular Love," *Society* 53(5): 487–492.

70. "WikiLeaks Release Reveals Hillary Clinton's Sympathy for Wall Street," *Wall Street Journal*, October 15, 2016, https://www.wsj.com/articles/wikileaks-release-reveals-hillary-clintons-sympathy-for-wall-street-1476581312 (retrieved May 26, 2019).

71. Center for Responsive Politics, "Sen. Bernie Sanders—Vermont," https://www.opensecrets.org/members-of-congress/summary?cid=N00000528&cycle=CAREER (retrieved April 2, 2019).

72. Greg Sargent, " 'Feel the Bern': Hillary's Agonizing Loss and the Future of the Democratic Party," in Sabato et al., *Trumped*, pp.112–122.

73. Cook, "Presidential Primaries," p.87.

74. See Andrew Gelman, "19 Lessons for Political Scientists from the 2016 Presidential Election," *Slate*, December 8, 2016, http://www.slate.com/articles/news_and_politics/politics/2016/12/_19_lessons_for_political_scientists_from_the_2016_election.html (retrieved September 8, 2017).

75. See Amie Parnes and Jonathan Allen, *Shattered: Inside Hillary Clinton's Doomed Campaign* (New York: Crown Publishing, 2017).

76. See for example, Joan Williams, *White Working Class: Overcoming Class Cluelessness in America* (Cambridge MA: Harvard Business Press, 2017).

77. See Gurminder Bhambra (2017), "Brexit, Trump, and 'Methodological Whiteness': On the Misrecognition of Race and Class," *British Journal of Sociology* 68 (2017): S214–S232.

78. Michael Tesler, "Trump Is the First Modern Republican to Win the Nomination Based on Racial Prejudice," *Monkey Cage*, August 1, 2016, https://www.washingtonpost.com/news/monkey-cage/wp/2016/08/01/trump-is-the-first-republican-in-modern-times-to-win-the-partys-nomination-on-anti-minority-sentiments/?utm_term=.104aa47b7e6d.

79. John Sides, Michael Tesler, and Lynn Vavreck (2017), "The 2016 US Election: How Trump Lost and Won," *Journal of Democracy* 28(2): 34–44 (p.38).

80. For example, Eric Kaufman, "Trump and Brexit: Why It's Again NOT the Economy, Stupid," *LSE British Politics and Policy Blog*, November 9, 2016. https://blogs.lse.ac.uk/politicsandpolicy/trump-and-brexit-why-its-again-not-the-economy-stupid/; Daniel Cox and Rachel Lienesch (2017), "Beyond Economics: Fears of Cultural Displacement Pushed the White Working Class to Trump," PRRI/The Atlantic Report (Washington, DC: Public Religion Research Institute, May 9); German Lopez, "The Past Year of Research Has Made It Very Clear: Trump Won Because of Racial Resentment," *Vox,* December 15, 2017, https://www.vox.com/identities/2017/12/15/16781222/trump-racism-economic-anxiety-study.

81. Judith Goldstein and Margaret Peters (2014), "Nativism or Economic Threat: Attitudes toward Immigrants during the Great Recession," *International Interactions* 40(3): 376–401, p.382, fig.1.

82. Andrew Gelman, *Red State Blue State Rich State Poor State: Why Americans Vote the Way They Do* (Princeton: Princeton University Press, 2008).

83. Diana Mutz (2018), "Status Threat, Not Economic Hardship, Explains the 2016 Presidential Vote," *Proceedings of the National Academy of Sciences* 115(19): E4330–E4339.

84. Daniel Tomlinson and Stephen Clarke, "In the Swing of Things: What does Donald Trump's Victory Tell Us about America?", Resolution Foundation Blog, November 2016. https://www.resolutionfoundation.org/app/uploads/2016/11/In-the-swing-of-things-FINAL.pdf.

85. An ambiguity that appeared to be a deliberate choice. Parnes and Allen, *Shattered*.

86. "Trump Spent Far Less Than Clinton, but Paid His Companies Well," *New York Times*, December 9, 2016, https://www.nytimes.com/2016/12/09/us/politics/campaign-spending-donald-trump-hillary-clinton.html (retrieved April 2, 2019).

87. "Steve Bannon on How 2008 Planted the Seed for the Trump Presidency," *New York Magazine*, August 10, 2008, http://nymag.com/intelligencer/2018/08/steve-bannon-on-how-2008-planted-the-seed-for-the-trump-presidency.html.

Chapter 4

1. Peter Lindert (2017), "The Rise and Future of Progressive Redistribution," Commitment to Equity (CEQ) Working Paper No. 73 (New Orleans: Tulane University, Department of Economics).

2. In the mid-1970s, earnings at the threshold of the top 10 percent of earners (the 90th percentile) were 3 times higher than those at the threshold of the bottom 10 percent (10th percentile), but by the mid-1990s this had grown to 3.5 times higher (OECD Stat Extracts on income distribution and inequality).

3. Martin Rhodes, "Restructuring the British Welfare State: Between Domestic Constraints and Global Imperatives," in Fritz W. Scharpf and Vivien A. Schmidt (eds.), *Welfare and Work in the Open Economy*, Vol. 2, *Diverse Responses to Common Challenges in Twelve Countries* (New York: Oxford University Press, 2000), pp.19–68.

4. Data from World Wealth and Income Database, http://wid.world/country/united-kingdom/ (retrieved August 10, 2017).

5. Colin Hay, *The Failure of Anglo-Liberal Capitalism* (Basingstoke: Palgrave, 2013).

6. Rui Costa and Stephen Machin (2017), "Real Wages and Living Standards in the UK," Paper EA036 (London: Centre for Economic Performance, London School of Economics and Political Science), http://cep.lse.ac.uk/pubs/download/ea036.pdf.

7. David Butler and Donald Stokes, *Political Change in Britain* (New York: St. Martin's Press, 1969).

8. See Anthony Heath, Roger Jowell, and John Curtice, *How Britain Votes* (Oxford: Pergamon Press, 1985).

9. The intellectual inspiration for this shift was the sociologist Anthony Giddens, whose book *The Third Way* (Cambridge: Polity, 1994) articulated the case for a politics "beyond left and right."

10. Colin Hay (1997), "Blaijorism: Towards a One-Vision Polity?" *Political Quarterly* 68(4): 372–378.

11. Jonathan Hopkin and Kate Alexander Shaw (2016), "Organized Combat or Structural Advantage? The Politics of Inequality and the Winner-Take-All Economy in the United Kingdom," *Politics and Society* 44(3): 345–371.

12. Giuliano Bonoli and Martin Powell (2002), "Third Ways in Europe?," *Social Policy and Society* 1(1): 59–66.

13. Robert Joyce and Luke Sibieta (2013), "An Assessment of Labour's Record on Inequality and Poverty," *Oxford Review of Economic Policy* 29(4): 178–202 (fig. 3, p.185).

14. Hopkin and Alexander Shaw, "Organized Combat or Structural Advantage?," p.357.

15. William Keegan, *The Prudence of Mr Gordon Brown* (London: Wiley, 2004), p.139.

16. Philip Gould, *The Unfinished Revolution: How the Modernizers Saved the Labour Party* (London: Little, Brown, 1998), pp.117–130.

17. Geoffrey Evans and James Tilley, *The New Politics of Class: The Political Exclusion of the British Working Class* (Oxford: Oxford University Press, 2016), ch.6; Tom O'Grady (2016), "Careerists versus Coal-Miners: How British MPs' Social Backgrounds Affect Their Support for Welfare Reform," MIT Political Science Department Research Paper No. 2016-17.

18. See, for example, Peter Oborne, *The Triumph of the Political Class* (London: Simon & Schuster, 2007).

19. Alan Grant (2005), "The Reform of Party Funding in Britain," *Political Quarterly* 76(3): 381–392.

20. "How the Ecclestone Affair Unfolded," *BBC News*, September 22, 2000, http://news.bbc.co.uk/1/hi/uk_politics/937232.stm (retrieved May 27, 2019).

21. Colin Hay, *Why We Hate Politics* (Cambridge: Polity, 2007), ch.1.

22. https://www.ft.com/content/6734cdde-550b-11e7-9fed-c19e2700005f.

23. Evans and Tilley, *The New Politics of Class*, ch.8.

24. House of Commons Library (2017), "General Election 2017: Results and Analysis," House of Commons Library: Briefing Paper, CBP 7979 (September 8), p.57.

25. House of Commons Library (2017), "Turnout at Elections," Briefing Paper, CBP 8060 (July), http://researchbriefings.parliament.uk/ResearchBriefing/Summary/CBP-8060#fullreport (retrieved January 10, 2018).

26. Ibid.

27. Matthew Goodwin, *New British Fascism: Rise of the British National Party* (London: Routledge, 2011).

28. Robert Ford and Matthew Goodwin, *Revolt on the Right: Explaining Support for the Radical Right in Britain* (London: Routledge, 2014).

29. Alistair Clark, Karin Bottom, and Colin Copus (2008), "More Similar Than They'd Like to Admit? Ideology, Policy and Populism in the Trajectories of the British National Party and Respect," *British Politics* 3(4): 511–534.

30. Rachel Briggs (2007), "Who's Afraid of the Respect Party?," *Renewal: A Journal of Labour Politics* 15(2/3): 89–97.

31. See, for example, the party's 2005 manifesto: The Green Party of England and Wales, *Green Party Real Progress: The Real Choice for Real Change* (London: Green Party, 2005).

32. Ibid.

33. Andrew S. Crines and Stuart McAnulla (2017), "The Rhetorical Personas of George Galloway and Tommy Sheridan," in Judi Atkins and John Gaffney (eds.), *Voices of the UK Left: Rhetoric, Ideology and the Performance of Politics* (Basingstoke: Palgrave), pp.189–209.

34. Kate Alexander Shaw, *Narrating Boom and Bust: The life-cycle of Ideas and Narrative in New Labour's Political Economy, 1997–2010.* PhD dissertation, London School of Economics, 2018.

35. See Cornelia Woll, *The Power of Inaction: Bank Bailouts in Comparison* (Ithaca: Cornell University Press, 2014); Ray Barrell and Philip Davies (2008), "The Evolution of the Financial Crisis of 2007–8," *National Institute Economic Review* 206(1): 5–14.

36. Pontusson and Reiss estimate the "discretionary" stimulus at 1.45 percent of GDP, smaller than in the United States (at 1.81) but larger than in the large European economies; Jonas Pontusson and Damian Reiss (2012), "How (and Why) Is This Time Different? The Politics of Economic Crisis in Western Europe and the United States," *Annual Review of Political Science* 15:13–33 (p.19, Table 3).

37. Office of National Statistics (2016), "Statistical Bulletin: UK Government Debt and Deficit as Reported to the European Commission: April to June 2016," October 20, https://www.ons.gov.uk/economy/governmentpublicsectorandtaxes/publicspending/bulletins/ukgovernmentde btanddeficitforeurostatmaast/aprtojune2016 (accessed January 8, 2018).

38. Office of National Statistics (2013), "Economic Review May 2013," May 1, http://webarchive.nationalarchives.gov.uk/20160108222452/http://www.ons. gov.uk/ons/dcp171766_308566.pdf (accessed January 8, 2018).

39. "Timeline: Northern Rock Bank Crisis," *BBC News*, August 5, 2008, http:// news.bbc.co.uk/1/hi/business/7007076.stm (retrieved August 14, 2017).

40. Emiliano Grossman and Cornelia Woll (2014), "Saving the Banks: The Political Economy of Bailouts," *Comparative Political Studies* 47(4): 574–600 (p.581).

41. Bank of England (2008), *Financial Stability Report,* No. 24 (October) (London: Bank of England), p.31, cited in Julie Froud, Adriana Nilsson, Michael Moran, and Karel Williams (2012), "Stories and Interests in Finance: Agendas of Governance before and after the Financial Crisis," *Governance* 25(1): 35–59 (p.35).

42. "Gordon Brown Mocked over 'Save the World' Slip-Up in Commons," *The Telegraph*, December 10, 2008, https://www.telegraph.co.uk/news/politics/3701712/Gordon-Brown-mocked-over-save-the-world-slip-up-in-Commons. html (retrieved June 4, 2019). Perhaps Brown had read Paul Krugman's praise in the *New York Times*, "Gordon Does Good," October12, 2008, https://www.nytimes.com/2008/10/13/opinion/13krugman.html (retrieved June 4, 2019).

43. Jonathan Hopkin and Ben Rosamond (2018), "Post-Truth Politics, Bullshit and Bad Ideas: 'Deficit Fetishism' in the UK," *New Political Economy* 23(6): 641–655.

44. Joseph Stiglitz, "The Dangers of Deficit-Cut Fetishism," *Guardian*, March 7, 2010, http://www.theguardian.com/commentisfree/2010/mar/07/deficit-fetishism-government-spending (accessed May 18, 2019).

45. Craig Berry, *Austerity Politics and UK Economic Policy* (Basingstoke: Palgrave, 2016).

46. Valentina Romei, "How Wages Fell in the UK While the Economy Grew: Britain Stands Out among Big Economies with More People in Work but in Lower-Paid Jobs," *Financial Times*, March 2, 2017.

47. Stephen Clarke (2017), "Whose Recovery Is This?," Resolution Foundation, May 11, http://www.resolutionfoundation.org/media/blog/whose-recovery-is-this/.

48. Jonathan Freedland, "Leaders' TV debate: 'I Agree with Nick' Was the Night's Real Catchphrase," *Guardian* April 16, 2010, https://www.theguardian.com/commentisfree/2010/apr/16/leaders-tv-debates-jonathan-freedland (retrieved January 14, 2018).

49. See Gerry Hassan and Eric Shaw, *The Strange Death of Labour Scotland* (Edinburgh: Edinburgh University Press, 2012).

50. "Scottish Independence: Vote 'Will Go to the Wire,'" BBC News, September 7, 2014, http://www.bbc.co.uk/news/uk-scotland-29096458 (retrieved January 20, 2018).

51. John Curtice, "So Who Voted Yes and Who Voted No?," *What Scotland Thinks blog*, September 26, 2014, http://blog.whatscotlandthinks.org/2014/09/voted-yes-voted/.

52. James Mitchell (2015), "Sea Change in Scotland," *Parliamentary Affairs*, 68(Issue suppl. 1): 88–100 (p.90).

53. Ray Collins, *Building a One Nation Labour Party: The Collins Review into Labour Party Reform* (London: Labour Party, 2014).

54. Matt Dathan, "So, Who Are the 'Moronic MPs' Who Nominated Jeremy Corbyn for the Labour Leadership Contest?," *The Independent*, July 22, 2015, http://www.independent.co.uk/news/uk/politics/who-are-the-morons-who-nominated-jeremy-corbyn-for-the-labour-leadership-contest 10406527.html.

55. Koos Couvée, "Corbyn Set to Run for Labour Leadership," *Islington Tribune*, June 4, 2015, http://archive.islingtontribune.com/news/2015/jun/corbyn-set-run-labour-leadership-long-serving-islington-mp-stand-clear-anti-austerity- (retrieved January 24, 2018).

56. Jeremy Corbyn, "The Economy in 2020," Jeremy for Labour Campaign, July 22, 2015, https://web.archive.org/web/20150918143200/https://d3n8a8pro7vhmx.cloudfront.net/jeremyforlabour/pages/70/attachments/original/1437556345/TheEconomyIn2020_JeremyCorbyn-220715.pdf (retrieved January 24, 2018).

57. "Ed Miliband: We'll Tackle Deficit with 'Sensible' Cuts," BBC News, December 11, 2014, http://www.bbc.co.uk/news/uk-politics-30417955.

58. Office of National Statistics (2015), "EU Government Deficit and Debt Return Including Maastricht Supplementary Data Tables: Quarter 3 (July to Sep) 2015," https://www.ons.gov.uk/economy/ governmentpublicsectorandtaxes/publicspending/bulletins/eugovernm entdeficitanddebtreturnincludingmaastrichtsupplementarydatatables/ quarter3julytosep2015.

59. Christina Beatty and Stephen Fothergill, "Hitting the Poorest Places Hardest: The Local and Regional Impact of Welfare Reform," Centre for Regional Economic and Social Research, Sheffield Hallam University, 2013, p.9, https://www4.shu.ac.uk/research/cresr/sites/shu.ac.uk/files/hitting- poorest-places-hardest_0.pdf.

60. Rui Costa and Stephen Machin (2017), "Real Wages and Living Standards in the UK," Paper EA036 (London: Centre for Economic Performance, London School of Economics and Political Science), http://cep.lse.ac.uk/pubs/ download/ea036.pdf.

61. 140 Conservative MPs (out of 330) endorsed the Leave campaign; just 10 Labour MPs (out of 232) did so: *Wikipedia*, "Endorsements in the United Kingdom European Union Membership Referendum, 2016," https:// en.wikipedia.org/wiki/Endorsements_in_the_United_Kingdom_European_ Union_membership_referendum,_2016#Conservative_Party (retrieved January 24, 2018).

62. On the campaign, see Tim Shipman, *All Out War: The Full Story of Brexit* (London: HarperCollins, 2017). On finance, see Robert Wright, "Arron Banks and the Mystery Brexit Campaign Funds," *Financial Times*, November 5, 2018, https://www.ft.com/content/ 4610a4be-dde2-11e8-9f04-38d397e6661c (retrieved June 2, 2019); Adam Ramsey (2018), "Dark Money Investigations: What We've Found Out, and Why We're Looking," *Open Democracy*, December 3, https://www.opendemocracy.net/en/dark-money-investigations/dark- money-investigations-what-we-ve-found-out-and-why-we-re-looking/ (retrieved June 2, 2019).

63. Wen Chen, Bart Los, Philip McCann, Raquel Ortega-Argilés, Mark Thissen, and Frank van Oort (2017), "The Continental Divide? Economic Exposure to Brexit in Regions and Countries on Both Sides of the Channel," *Papers in Regional Science,* December.

64. Marco di Cataldo (2016), "Gaining and Losing EU Objective 1 Funds: Regional Development in Britain and the Prospect of Brexit," LEQS Paper No. 120/2016, (London: London School of Economics and Political Science, November), http://www.lse.ac.uk/europeanInstitute/ LEQS%20Discussion%20Paper%20Series/LEQSPaper120.pdf.

65. Sascha Becker, Thiemo Fetzer, and Dennis Novy (2017), "Who Voted for Brexit? A Comprehensive District-Level Analysis," *Economic Policy* 32(92): 601–650.

66. Christian Dustmann and Tommaso Frattini (2014), "The Fiscal Effects of Immigration to the UK," *Economic Journal* 124(580): F593–F643.

67. Sofia Vasilopoulou (2016), "UK Euroscepticism and the Brexit referendum," *Political Quarterly* 87(2): 219–227.

68. Sara Hobolt (2016), "The Brexit Vote: A Divided Nation, a Divided Continent," *Journal of European Public Policy* 23(9): 1259–1277 (p.1269).

69. Robert Ford and Matthew Goodwin (2017), "Britain after Brexit: A Nation Divided," *Journal of Democracy* 28 (January): 17–30 (p.19).

70. Harold Clarke, Matthew Goodwin, and Paul Whiteley, *Brexit: Why Britain Voted to Leave the European Union* (Cambridge: Cambridge University Press, 2017), p.22.

71. Kirby Swales, *Understanding the Leave Vote* (London: NatCen Social Research, 2016), p.13.

72. Matthew Goodwin and Caitlin Milazzo (2017), "Taking Back Control? Investigating the Role of Immigration in the 2016 Vote for Brexit," *British Journal of Politics and International Relations* 19(3): 450–464.

73. See David Goodhart, *The Road to Somewhere: The Populist Revolt and the Future of Politics* (New York: Oxford University Press, 2017).

74. Danny Dorling (2016), "Brexit: The Decision of a Divided Country," *BMJ: British Medical Journal* 354: i3697.

75. Goodwin and Milazzo, "Taking Back Control?"

76. Swales, *Understanding the Leave Vote*, p.8.

77. Ibid.

78. Data from Lord Ashcroft polls, cited in Noam Gidron and Peter Hall (2017), "The Politics of Social Status: Economic and Cultural Roots of the Populist Right," *British Journal of Sociology* 68: S57–S84 (p.S59).

79. Ben Ansell, "Housing, Credit and Brexit," Oxford University, 2017, http://users.ox.ac.uk/~polf0487/papers/Ansell%20Brexit%20Memo.pdf.

80. Jonathan Portes (2016), "Immigration, Free Movement and the EU Referendum," *National Institute Economic Review* 236(1): 14–22.

81. Marco Alfano, Christian Dustmann, and Tommaso Frattini, "Immigration and the UK: Reflections after Brexit," in Francesco Fasani (ed.), *Refugees and Economic Migrants: Facts, Policies, and Challenges*, VoxEU.org ebook, October 2016, http://giovanniperi.ucdavis.edu/uploads/5/6/8/2/56826033/refugees_and_economic_migrants.pdf#page=65.

82. See, for example, Migration Advisory Committee, "Migration Advisory Committee (MAC) Report on the Impact of EEA Migration in the UK," September 18, 2018, https://www.gov.uk/government/publications/migration-advisory-committee-mac-report-eea-migration.

83. Italo Colantone and Piero Stanig (2018), "Global Competition and Brexit," *American Political Science Review* 112(2): 201–218.

84. Thiemo Fetzer "Did Austerity Cause Brexit?" University of Warwick, 2018.

85. Andrés Rodríguez-Pose (2018), "The Revenge of the Places That Don't Matter (And What to Do about It)," *Cambridge Journal of Regions, Economy and Society* 11(1): 189–209.

86. Thomas Forth (2017), "To Bring Back Trust in Politics, Britain Needs a Local Measure of GDP," City Metric, October 30, https://www.citymetric.com/business/ bring-back-trust-politics-britain-needs-local-measure-gdp-3440.

87. Aditya Chakraborty, "One Blunt Heckler Has Revealed Just How Much the UK Economy Is Failing Us," *Guardian*, January 10, 2017, https://www.theguardian.com/commentisfree/2017/jan/10/ blunt-heckler-economists-failing-us-booming-britain-gdp-london.

88. "Britain Has Had Enough of Experts, Says Gove," *Financial Times*, June 3, 2016, https://www.ft.com/content/3be49734-29cb-11e6-83e4-abc22d5d108c (retrieved June 3, 2019).

89. See Portes, "Immigration, Free Movement and the EU Referendum."

90. "A Pyrrhic Victory? Boris Johnson Wakes Up to the Costs of Brexit," *Guardian*, June 24, 2016, https://www.theguardian.com/politics/2016/jun/ 24/a-pyrrhic-victory-boris-johnson-wakes-up-to-the-costs-of-brexit (retrieved June 4, 2019).

91. "Theresa May's Conference Speech in Full," *The Telegraph*, October 5, 2016, https://www.telegraph.co.uk/news/2016/10/05/theresa-mays-conference-speech-in-full/ (retrieved June 4, 2019).

92. Andrew Gimson, "Profile: Nick Timothy, May's Thinker-in-Chief and co-Chief of Staff," *ConservativeHome*, July 15, 2016, http://www. conservativehome.com/highlights/2016/07/profile-nick-timothy-mays-thinker-in-chief-and-co-chief-of-staff.html (retrieved June 4, 2019).

93. "Brexit: Picking Apart Theresa May's Red Lines on Leaving the European Union: Britain Has Voted to Leave the EU," *Sky News*, January 18, 2017, https://news.sky.com/story/brexit-picking-apart-theresa-mays-red-lines-on-leaving-the-european-union-10732511 (retrieved June 4, 2019).

94. Chris Hanretty (2017), "Areal Interpolation and the UK's Referendum on EU Membership," *Journal of Elections, Public Opinion and Parties* 27(4): 466–483, Table Two, p.477.

95. "Boris Johnson's Brexit Explosion Ruins Tory Business Credentials," *Financial Times*, June 25, 2018, https://www.ft.com/content/8075e68c-7857-11e8-8e67-1e1a0846c475 (retrieved June 4, 2019).

96. See James Sloam and Matt Henn, *Youthquake: Young People and the 2017 General Election* (Basingstoke: Palgrave, 2018).

Chapter 5

1. Ambrose Evans-Pritchard, "Financial Crisis: US will Lose Superpower Status, Claims German Minister," *The Telegraph*, September 25, 2008, https://www.telegraph.co.uk/finance/financialcrisis/3081909/Financial-Crisis-US-will-lose-superpower-status-claims-German-minister.html (retrieved June 5, 2019).

2. "The City of London and Mr Sarkozy: A Clash of Arms," *The Economist*, December 2, 2009, https://www.economist.com/charlemagne/2009/12/02/the-city-of-london-and-mr-sarkozy-a-clash-of-arms (retrieved June 5, 2019).

3. For details of these banking bailouts, see Cornelia Woll, *The Power of Inaction: Bank Bailouts in Comparison* (Ithaca: Cornell University Press, 2014).

4. See Mark Blyth, *Austerity: The History of a Dangerous Idea* (New York: Oxford University Press, 2013), ch.3.

5. Ignacio Sánchez-Cuenca (2000), "The Political Basis of Support for European Integration," *European Union Politics* 1(2): 147–171; Iván Llamazares and Wladimir Gramacho (2007), "Eurosceptics among Euroenthusiasts: An Analysis of Southern European Public Opinions," *Acta Politica* 42(2–3): 211–232.

6. Susannah Verney (2011), "Euroscepticism in Southern Europe: A Diachronic Perspective," *South European Society and Politics* 16(1): 1–29 (p.8).

7. NATO proved more controversial than European integration, with Spanish and Greek Socialists both having to juggle commitments to the Atlantic alliance with a strong current of anti-Americanism in their core electorates.

8. Nauro Campos, Fabrizio Coricelli, and Luigi Moretti (2014), "How Much Do Countries Benefit from Membership in the European Union?," *Vox: CEPR Policy Portal*, April 9, https://voxeu.org/article/how-poorer-nations-benefit-eu-membership.

9. In his study of Greece, Christos Lyrintzis describes this as "bureaucratic clientelism." Christos Lyrintzis (1984), "Political Parties in Post-Junta Greece: A Case of 'Bureaucratic Clientelism'?," *West European Politics* 7(2): 99–118. For cross-national evidence, see Petr Kopecký, Peter Mair, and Maria Spirova (eds.), *Party Patronage and Party Government in European Democracies* (Oxford: Oxford University Press, 2012).

10. Jesús Fernández-Villaverde, Luis Garicano, and Tano Santos (2013), "Political Credit Cycles: The Case of the Eurozone," *Journal of Economic Perspectives* 27(3): 145–166.

11. Thomas Farole, Andrés Rodríguez-Pose, and Michael Storper (2011), "Cohesion Policy in the European Union: Growth, Geography, Institutions," *JCMS: Journal of Common Market Studies* 49(5): 1089–1111.

12. See, for example, Mariano Torcal, Richard Gunther, and José Ramón Montero, "Anti-Party Sentiments in Southern Europe," in Richard Gunther, José Ramón Montero, and Juan Linz (eds.), *Political Parties: Old Concepts and*

New Challenges (New York: Oxford University Press, 2002), pp.257–290. Their data showed increasing hostility to parties through the 1990s, as well as a growing perception among voters that parties were increasingly similar to each other.

13. Luis de Sousa (2001), "Political Parties and Corruption in Portugal," *West European Politics* 24(1): 157–180. Despite the party's misleading label, the Portuguese Social Democrat Party (PSD) is in fact a typical moderate conservative party, affiliated with the European People's Party in the European Parliament.

14. See Kevin Featherstone (2003), "Greece and EMU: Between External Empowerment and Domestic Vulnerability," *JCMS: Journal of Common Market Studies* 41(5): 923–940.

15. Sánchez-Cuenca, "The Political Basis of Support for European Integration."

16. Kenneth Dyson and Kevin Featherstone (1996), "Italy and EMU as a 'Vincolo Esterno': Empowering the Technocrats, Transforming the State," *South European Society and Politics* 1(2): 272–299.

17. Fernández-Villaverde et al., "Political Credit Cycles: The Case of the Eurozone."

18. OECD (2011), "Employment in General Government and Public Corporations as a Percentage of the Labor Force,", OECD, Government at a Glance (Paris: OECD) https://stats.oecd.org/Index.aspx?DataSetCode=GOV_ 2011.

19. Independent Evaluation Office of the IMF (2016), "The IMF and the Crises in Greece, Ireland, and Portugal" (New York: International Monetary Fund), http://www.ieo-imf.org/ieo/files/completedevaluations/EAC%20-%20Full%20Report.pdf (retrieved July 18, 2018).

20. Geithner even revealed in his memoirs that he was told by German Finance Minister Schauble that "there were many in Europe who still thought kicking the Greeks out of the eurozone was a plausible—even desirable—strategy." Timothy Geithner, *Stress Test: Reflections on Financial Crises* (London: Penguin/Random House, 2014), p.483.

21. Yanis Varoufakis, *Adults in the Room: My Battle with Europe's Deep Establishment* (New York: Random House, 2017).

22. C. Randall Henning, *Tangled Governance* (Oxford: Oxford University Press, 2017), p.4.

23. "Dijsselbloem will die Troika auflösen," *Frankfurter Allgemeine*, March 19, 2017, http://www.faz.net/aktuell/wirtschaft/eurokrise/chef-der-eurogruppe-dijsselbloem-will-die-troika-aufloesen-14932856.html.

24. Geithner, *Stress Test*, p.443.

25. See Adam Tooze, "Output Gap Nonsense," *Social Europe*, April 30, 2019. https://www.socialeurope.eu/output-gap-nonsense.

26. See Henning, *Tangled Governance*.

27. Adam Tooze, *Crashed: How a Decade of Financial Crises Changed the World* (London: Allen Lane, 2018), ch.14.

28. Henning, *Tangled Governance*, p.127.

29. Stephen Kinsella (2012), "Is Ireland Really the Role Model for Austerity?," *Cambridge Journal of Economics* 36(1), 223–235 (p.224).

30. For an overview of the recent research on dualism, see Patrick Emmenegger, Silja Hausermann, Bruno Palier, and Martin Seeleib-Kaiser (eds.), *The Age of Dualization: The Changing Face of Inequality in Deindustrializing Societies* (Oxford: Oxford University Press, 2012).

31. Juan Linz defined the southern European dictatorships as "authoritarian" rather than "totalitarian" regimes, emphasizing their lack of clear ideology and the limited pluralism they tolerated: Juan Linz, *Totalitarian and Authoritarian Regimes* (Boulder: Lynne Rienner, 2000).

32. Sara Watson, *The Left Divided: The Development and Transformation of Advanced Welfare States* (Oxford: Oxford University Press, 2015).

33. A "Bismarckian" welfare state is one based on occupational status, where employees and employers pay contributions into a fund that finances pensions and other benefits. The early German welfare system took this form. See Bruno Palier and Claude Martin (eds.), *Reforming the Bismarckian Welfare Systems* (Chichester: John Wiley & Sons, 2009).

34. Cornel Ban, *Ruling Ideas: How Global Neoliberalism Goes Local* (Oxford: Oxford University Press, 2016).

35. Maurizio Ferrera (1996), "The 'Southern Model' of Welfare in Social Europe," *Journal of European Social Policy* 6(1): 17–37.

36. See David Rueda, *Social Democracy Inside Out: Partisanship and Labor Market Policy in Advanced Industrialized Democracies* (Oxford: Oxford University Press, 2007).

37. Julia Lynch, *Age in the Welfare State: The Origins of Social Spending on Pensioners, Workers, and Children* (Cambridge: Cambridge University Press, 2006).

38. Manuela Naldini, *The Family in the Mediterranean Welfare States* (London: Routledge, 2004).

39. Bas ter Weel (2018), "The Rise of Temporary Work in Europe," *De Economist* 166: 397–401.

40. While the average age of leaving the family home in the EU15 western European countries is around twenty-six, for southern Europe it is almost thirty, a number that has increased since the crisis (Eurostat, "Estimated Average Age of Young People Leaving the Parental Household by Sex," April 26, 2018, http://appsso.eurostat.ec.europa.eu/nui/show.do?dataset=yth_demo_030&lang=en).

41. Ferrera, "The 'Southern Model' of Welfare in Social Europe," p.21.

42. Salvatore Morelli, Brian Nolan, and Philippe van Kerm, "Wealth Inequality," in Brian Nolan (ed.), *Generating Prosperity for Working Families in Affluent Countries* (Oxford: Oxford University Press, 2018), pp.312–334.

43. Carlotta Balestra and Richard Tonkin (2018), "Inequalities in Household Wealth across OECD Countries: Evidence from the OECD Wealth Distribution Database," OECD Statistics Working Papers, 2018/01 (Paris: OECD Publishing), Table 2.1, p.15, http://dx.doi.org/10.1787/7e1bf673-en.

44. OECD (2018), "Pension Spending" (indicator), doi: 10.1787/a041f4ef-en (accessed October 30, 2018).

45. Matthias Matthijs (2016), "The Euro's 'Winner-Take-All' Political Economy: Institutional Choices, Policy Drift, and Diverging Patterns of Inequality," *Politics and Society* 44(3): 393–422.

46. Tooze, "Output Gap Nonsense."

47. "As Good as It Gets," *ekathimerini*, December 4, 2009. http://www.ekathimerini.com/66438/article/ekathimerini/comment/as-good-as-it-gets (retrieved November 5, 2018).

48. Georgios Karyotis and Wolfgang Rüdig (2018), "The Three Waves of Anti-Austerity Protest in Greece, 2010–2015," *Political Studies Review* 16(2): 158–169.

49. See Ioannis Andreadis and Yiannis Stavrakakis (2017), "European Populist Parties in Government: How Well Are Voters Represented? Evidence from Greece," *Swiss Political Science Review* 23(4): 485–508.

50. Antonis Ellinas (2013), "The Rise of Golden Dawn: The New Face of the Far Right in Greece," *South European Society and Politics* 18(4): 543–565 (pp.550–552).

51. Ellinas, "The Rise of Golden Dawn," p.555.

52. Kapa Research, "September 2015 Exit Poll Data," https://kaparesearch.com/en/september-2015-exit-poll-data/.

53. Panos Koliastasis (2015), "The Greek Parliamentary Elections of 25 January, 2015," *Representation* 51(3): 359–372 (p.364).

54. Maik Fielitz (2017), "From Indignation to Power: The Genesis of the Independent Greeks," paper presented to ECPR General Conference Universität Hamburg, Hamburg, August 22–25, 2018, https://ecpr.eu/Filestore/PaperProposal/fd58216e-827d-4791-9dc0-291b972f29a0.pdf.

55. Ioannis Andreadis, Monica Poletti, Eftichia Teperoglou, and Cristiano Vezzoni (2014), "Economic Crisis and Attitudes Towards the European Union: Are Italians and Greeks Becoming Eurosceptic Because of the Crisis?," paper presented to Political Studies Association annual conference, Manchester, http://www.gpsg.org.uk/wp-content/uploads/2014/10/Andreadis-Poletti-Teperoglou-and-Vezzoni-2014.pdf.

56. Fielitz, "From Indignation to Power."

57. See Stathis Kalyvas and Niko Marantzidis (2002), "Greek Communism, 1968–2001," *East European Politics and Societies* 16(3): 665–690.

58. Myrto Tsakatika and Costas Eleftheriou (2013), "The Radical Left's Turn towards Civil Society in Greece: One Strategy, Two Paths," *South European Society and Politics* 18(1): 81–99 (p.89).

59. Kostas Gemenis and Elias Dinas (2010), "Confrontation Still? Examining Parties' Policy Positions in Greece," *Comparative European Politics* 8(2): 179–201 (p.189).

60. Tsakatika and Eleftheriou, "The Radical Left's Turn towards Civil Society in Greece," pp.90–93.

61. Syriza (2014), "Salonica programme," https://www.Syriza.gr/article/SYRIZA--THE-THESSALONIKI-PROGRAMME.html.

62. See his account of his brief period in office: Varoufakis, *Adults in the Room*.

63. "How Greece's Left-Wing Election Win Could Reverberate around Europe," *Vice,* January 27, 2015, https://www.vice.com/en_us/article/xd5jm7/what-Syrizas-win-means-for-greece-and-europe-876.

64. Kapa Research, "September 2015 Exit Poll Data."

65. "Ajuda a Portugal só é possível com apoio da Finlândia," *Diário de Notícias,* April 26, 2011, https://www.dn.pt/dossiers/economia/portugal-pede-ajuda-externa/noticias/interior/ajuda-a-portugal-so-e-possivel-com-apoio-da-finlandia-1838131.html.

66. Catherine Moury and Adam Standring (2017), "'Going beyond the Troika': Power and Discourse in Portuguese Austerity Politics," *European Journal of Political Research* 56: 660–679.

67. Marktest (2018), "Todas as sondagems desde 2009," https://www.marktest.com/wap/a/p/id~112.aspx (retrieved November 9, 2018).

68. Pedro Magalhães (2016), "A 'austeridade' nas eleições de 2015," *Pedro Magalhães Political Scientist Blog*, January 18, http://www.pedro-magalhaes.org/a-austeridade-nas-eleicoes-de-2015/?fbclid=IwAR1iT-bi61AfKUECOb9FXfU8WIyfZpx3drnuetwZeEg_UFUS_Z8p4N3aq7I (retrieved November 12, 2018).

69. Partido Comunista Português (2017). "Uma política patriótica e de esquerda," PCP webpage, May 7, http://www.pcp.pt/politica-patriotica-esquerda (retrieved November 12, 2018).

70. Marco Lisi (2013), "Rediscovering Civil Society? Renewal and Continuity in the Portuguese Radical Left," *South European Society and Politics* 18(1): 21–39 (pp.24–25).

71. Guya Accornero and Pedro Ramos Pinto (2015), "'Mild Mannered'? Protest and Mobilisation in Portugal Under Austerity, 2010–2013," *West European Politics* 38(3): 491–515.

72. Lisi, "Rediscovering Civil Society?," pp.35–36.

73. André Freire, Marco Lisi, Ioannis Andreadis, and José Manuel Leite Viegas (2014), "Political Representation in Bailed-Out Southern Europe: Greece and Portugal Compared," *South European Society and Politics* 19(4): 413–433 (p.424).

74. Marina Costa Lobo, José Santana Pereira, and Edalina Sanches (2015), "Relatório Síntese da Bússola Eleitoral, 2 A política económica vista pelos Eleitores" (Lisbon: Instituto de Ciências Sociais da Universidade de Lisboa), http://marinacostalobo.pt/webwp/wp-content/uploads/2014/11/relatório-02-da-Bussola-Eleitoral1.pdf.

75. Elisabetta De Giorgi and José Santana-Pereira (2016), "The 2015 Portuguese Legislative Election: Widening the Coalitional Space and Bringing the Extreme Left in," *South European Society and Politics* 21(4): 451–468 (pp.456–457).

76. Pedro Magalhães (2013), "Os pensionistas nos eleitorados," *Pedro Magalhães Political Scientist Blog*, May 8, http://www.pedro-magalhaes.org/os-pensionistas-nos-eleitorados/ (retrieved November 11, 2018).

77. Rodrigo Quintas da Silva (2018), "A Portuguese Exception to Right-Wing Populism," *Palgrave Communications* 4(1): 1–5.

78. Indeed, Portugal had the second lowest share of non-national citizens in the whole of the European Union in 2016. https://ec.europa.eu/eurostat/statistics-explained/index.php/Migration_and_migrant_population_statistics.

79. Olivier Blanchard and Pedro Portugal (2017), "Boom, Slump, Sudden Stops, Recovery, and Policy Options: Portugal and the Euro," *Portuguese Economic Journal* 16(3): 149–168.

80. Jorge M. Fernandes, Pedro C. Magalhães, and José Santana-Pereira (2018), "Portugal's Leftist Government: From Sick Man to Poster Boy?," *South European Society and Politics* 23(4): 503–524.

81. Joana Almeida (2018), "António Costa: 'Alternativa à política de austeridade resultou no maior crescimento económico do século,'" *Jornal Económico,* March 14, https://jornaleconomico.sapo.pt/noticias/antonio-costa-alternativa-a-politica-de-austeridade-resultou-no-maior-crescimento-economico-do-seculo-280579.

82. See, for example, Liz Alderman (2018), "Portugal Dared to Cast Aside Austerity: It's Having a Major Revival," *New York Times*, July 22, https://www.nytimes.com/2018/07/22/business/portugal-economy-austerity.html.

83. Waltraud Schelkle, *The Political Economy of Monetary Solidarity* (New York: Oxford University Press, 2017).

84. Christian Dustmann, Bernd Fitzenberger, Uta Schönberg, and Alexandra Spitz-Oener (2014), "From Sick Man of Europe to Economic Superstar: Germany's Resurgent Economy," *Journal of Economic Perspectives* 28(1): 167–188.

85. See Varoufakis, *Adults in the Room*, where the former Greek minister claims that northern Eurozone leaders were quite open in admitting that the real bailout was of the French and German banking systems.

86. "Germany, Greece Put Tension in Rearview Mirror during Angela Merkel's Visit," *dw.com*, January 10, 2019, https://www.dw.com/en/

germany-greece-put-tension-in-rearview-mirror-during-angela-merkels-visit/
a-47033131 (retrieved June 6, 2019).

Chapter 6

1. See "Return of the Bond Market Vigilantes," *Wall Street Journal*, May 29, 2008, https://blogs.wsj.com/marketbeat/2008/05/29/return-of-the-bond-market-vigilantes/ (retrieved June 8, 2019).
2. See for example, Josep María Colomer, *Game Theory and the Transition to Democracy: The Spanish Model* (Aldershot: Edward Elgar, 1995), pp.1–2.
3. "Spain: After the Fiesta," *The Economist* November 6, 2008, https://www.economist.com/leaders/2008/11/06/after-the-fiesta.
4. OECD (2018), "Net National Income (Indicator)." doi: 10.1787/af9be38a-en (retrieved November 17, 2018).
5. Guillermo de la Dehesa, "Spain and the Euro Area Sovereign Debt Crisis," paper prepared for conference on Resolving the European Debt Crisis, Chantilly, France, September 13–14, 2011, p.2.
6. Eurostat (2018), "House Price Index," https://ec.europa.eu/eurostat/web/housing-price-statistics/overview (retrieved June 7, 2019).
7. See Eurostat, "Migration and Migrant Population Statistics, 2017," https://ec.europa.eu/eurostat/statistics-explained/index.php/Migration_and_migrant_population_statistics (retrieved June 8, 2019).
8. European Commission (2018), *European Semester Thematic Factsheet: Housing Market Developments* (Brussels: European Commission), https://ec.europa.eu/info/sites/info/files/file_import/european-semester_thematic-factsheet_housing-market-developments_en.pdf (retrieved November 18, 2018).
9. OECD (2018), "Household Debt (Indicator)." doi: 10.1787/f03b6469-en (retrieved November 18, 2018).
10. The airport, ironically named Don Quixote Airport on opening, went into receivership after less than three years. Costing almost half a billion euros, it was eventually sold for just 56 million: "El aeropuerto de Ciudad Real, vendido por 56,2 millones," *El Mundo*, April 15, 2016, https://www.elmundo.es/economia/2016/04/15/5710dc3846163f9f0d8b45c0.html (retrieved November 18, 2018).
11. "La Ciudad de las Artes ha costado cuatro veces lo que se presupuestó," *El País Comunidad Valenciana*, March 16, 2011, https://elpais.com/diario/2011/03/16/cvalenciana/1300306679_850215.html (retrieved November 18, 2018).
12. Jesús Fernández-Villaverde, Luis Garicano, and Tano Santos (2013), "Political Credit Cycles: The Case of the Eurozone," *Journal of Economic Perspectives* 27(3): 145–166.
13. Vicente Cuñat and Luis Garicano (2009), "Did Good Cajas Extend Bad Loans? The Role of Governance and Human Capital in Cajas' Portfolio

Decisions," FEDEA Annual Conference at Bank of Spain, http://www. crisis09.es/mono grafia2009/cajas.html.

14. The Socialist Party's full name was Partido Socialista Obrero Espanol (PSOE).

15. "Nuevos datos en el escándalo de la Asamblea dejan sin aclarar el 'tamayazo,'" *El País,* June 9, 2013, https://elpais.com/ccaa/2013/06/08/ madrid/1370722686_003798.html (retrieved November 10, 2018).

16. Banco de España, *Financial Stability Report*, May 2007 (Madrid: Banco de España), p.12.

17. See Mark Blyth, *Austerity: The History of a Dangerous Idea* (New York: Oxford University Press, 2013), pp.64–68.

18. OECD Data, "Current Account Balance," https://data.oecd.org/trade/current-account-balance.htm (retrieved June 29, 2018).

19. C. Randall Henning, *Tangled Governance* (Oxford: Oxford University Press, 2017), p.133.

20. Letter from https://www.ecb.europa.eu/pub/pdf/other/2011-08-05-letter-from-trichet-and-fernandez-ordonez-to-zapateroen.pdf.

21. European Central Bank (2013), "Press Release: Details on Securities Holdings Acquired under the Securities Markets Programme," February 21, https://www.ecb.europa.eu/press/pr/date/2013/html/pr130221_1.en.html.

22. Henning, *Tangled Governance*, p.137.

23. "De Guindos le dice a Rehn que la reforma laboral será 'extremadamente agresiva,'" https://www.youtube.com/watch?time_continue=3&v=ej8P4jPfsnY.

24. Kenneth Dubin and Jonathan Hopkin (2013), "A Crucial Case for Flexicurity: The Politics of Welfare and Employment in Spain," unpublished paper, London School of Economics, http://personal.lse.ac.uk/hopkin/ DubinHopkinFinal2013.pdf.

25. See Samuel Bentolila, Juan José Dolado, and Juan F. Jimeno (2012), "Reforming an Insider-Outsider Labor Market: The Spanish Experience," *IZA Journal of European Labour Studies* 1: 1–29.

26. "Despite Economic Growth, Spain's Younger Workers See Their Salaries Fall," *El País in English*, June 29, 2017, https://elpais.com/elpais/2017/06/ 29/inenglish/1498725322_738039.html (retrieved November 19, 2018).

27. Henning, *Tangled Governance*, p.140.

28. Statista (2018), "Unemployment Rate in Spain 2005–2018," https://www. statista.com/statistics/453410/unemployment-rate-in-spain/ (retrieved June 30, 2018).

29. See chapter 5, Figure 5.4: OECD Data, "Income Distribution Database," http://www.oecd.org/social/income-distribution-database.htm (retrieved June 29, 2018).>

30. "¿Cuántas familias perdieron su casa por la 'leyenda urbana' de los desahucios?," *Cinco Días: El País Economía*, January 31, 2018, https://

cincodias.elpais.com/cincodias/2018/01/30/midinero/1517339842_922977. html (retrieved November 19, 2018).

31. For an overview, see Ana Guillén and Margarita León (eds.), *The Spanish Welfare State in European Context* (Farnham: Ashgate, 2011).

32. Juan J. Dolado, Carlos García-Serrano, and Juan F. Jimeno (2002), "Drawing Lessons from the Boom of Temporary Jobs in Spain," *Economic Journal* 112(480): F270–F295.

33. Juan García López (2011), "Youth Unemployment in Spain: Causes and Solutions," Working Paper No. 1131 (Madrid: BBVA Bank, Economic Research Department), p.4.

34. Anna Cabré Pla and Juan Antonio Módenes Cabrerizo, "Home Ownership and Social Inequality in Spain," in Karin Kurz and Hans-Peter Blossfeld (eds.), *Home Ownership and Social Inequality in Comparative Perspective* (Stanford: Stanford University Press, 2004), pp.233–254 (p.236).

35. Compared with an OECD average of just under 60 percent. OECD (2016), "Most Youth Live with Their Parents and Patterns Have Changed since the Recession," in *General Context Indicators* (Paris: OECD Publishing), https:// doi.org/10.1787/soc_glance-2016-graph41-en.

36. In contrast, seniors' incomes in the United Kingdom were only 82 percent of the average. OECD, "Pensions at a Glance 2017" (Paris: OECD, 2017), p.20, https://www.oecd-ilibrary.org/docserver/pension_glance-2017-en.pdf?expires =1542377539&id=id&accname=guest&checksum=1D876AE69A81FFB71 0EC39B53CF62717.

37. See Davide Vampa, *The Regional Politics of Welfare in Italy, Spain and Great Britain* (Basingstoke: Palgrave, 2016), ch.7.

38. Jonathan Hopkin (2001), "A 'Southern Model' of Electoral Mobilisation? Clientelism and Electoral Politics in Spain," *West European Politics* 24(1): 115–136.

39. Fernández-Villaverde et al., "Political Credit Cycles: The Case of the Eurozone."

40. ¡Democracia Real Ya!, "Manfiesto," http://www.democraciarealya.es/ manifiesto-comun/ (retrieved November 19, 2018).

41. See Cristina Flesher Fominaya (2015), "Debunking Spontaneity: Spain's 15-M/Indignados as Autonomous Movement," *Social Movement Studies* 14(2): 142–163.

42. For example, one group was called *No les votes* ("Don't Vote for Them," http:// www.nolesvotes.com/ (retrieved November 19, 2018).

43. Eduardo Romanos (2014), "Evictions, Petitions and *Escraches*: Contentious Housing in Austerity Spain," *Social Movement Studies* 13(2): 296–302.

44. Irene Martín and Ignacio Urquizu-Sancho (2012), "The 2011 General Election in Spain: The Collapse of the Socialist Party," *South European Society and Politics* 17(2): 347–363 (p.347).

45. Data from the Centro de Investigaciones Sociológicas, analyzed in Araceli Mateos and Alberto Penadés, "España: Crisis y Recortes," *Revista de Ciencia Política (Santiago)* 33(1): 161–183 (p.174).

46. "Ex-IMF Chief Sentenced over Bankia Card Scandal," *Financial Times*, February 23, 2017, https://www.ft.com/content/7f93082e-f9ed-11e6-bd4e-68d53499ed71 (retrieved November 20, 2018).

47. "Governing Popular Party and Its Ex-Treasurer, Sentenced in Massive Corruption Case," *El País in English*, May 24, 2018, https://elpais.com/elpais/2018/05/24/inenglish/1527154734_539755.html (retrieved November 21, 2018).

48. Pablo Fernández-Vázquez, Pablo Barberá, and Gonzalo Rivero (2016), "Rooting out Corruption or Rooting for Corruption? The Heterogeneous Electoral Consequences of Scandals," *Political Science Research and Methods* 4(2): 379–397 (p.384).

49. The Spanish Congress of Deputies consists of 350 seats. A government can be formed with only an absolute majority of votes in the first round of the investiture motion, or a simple majority after the first vote.

50. Guillem Vidal (2018), "Challenging Business as Usual? The Rise of New Parties in Spain in Times of Crisis," *West European Politics* 41(2): 261–286 (p.278).

51. "Retired Spaniards Earn More than the National Average," *El País in English*, 29 January 2018. https://elpais.com/elpais/2018/01/29/inenglish/1517221833_150575.html.

52. See Irene Martín (2015), "Podemos y otros modelos de partido-movimiento," *Revista Española de Sociología* 24: 107–114; Juan Rodríguez-Teruel, Astrid Barrio, and Oscar Barberà (2016), "Fast and Furious: Podemos' Quest for Power in Multi-Level Spain," *South European Society and Politics* 21(4): 561–585.

53. Daniel Montero, *La casta: El increíble chollo de ser político en España* (Madrid: La esfera de los libros, 2009). Montero was in turn inspired by the Italian book on political corruption, *La casta*. Sergio Rizzo and Gian Antonio Stella, *La casta: Così i politici italiani sono diventati intoccabili* (Milan: Rizzoli, 2007).

54. Samuele Mazzolini and Arthur Borriello, " Southern European Populisms as Counter-Hegemonic Discourses: A Comparative Perspective of Podemos and M5S," in Óscar García Agustín and Marco Briziarelli (eds.), *Podemos and the New Political Cycle: Left-Wing Populism and Anti-Establishment Politics* (Basingstoke: Palgrave, 2016), pp.227–254 (pp.237–238).

55. "Entrevista A Pablo Iglesias, Líder De Podemos: 'Defendemos lo bueno del sistema,'" *El País*, June 17, 2014, https://elpais.com/politica/2014/06/16/actualidad/1402946493_140110.html?fbclid=IwAR07SqUm3RmHlN-mNg4nmxaaxIoFDju-do7PYAf3prELmdYDyi0h_dyuc6Q (retrieved November 12, 2018).

56. Podemos (2014), "Documento final del programa colaborativo," p.2, https://www.eldiario.es/campaña/Programa-electoral-Podemos-Europeas_6_258334180.html (retrieved November 24, 2018).

57. Pablo Cabrera Álvarez (2014), "¿Qué supone la irrupción de Podemos en la izquierda?," *Politikon*, June 30, https://politikon.es/2014/06/30/que-supone-la-irrupcion-de-podemos-en-la-izquierda/ (retrieved November 24, 2018).

58. Karen Sanders, María Jesús Molina Hurtado, and Jessica Zoragastua (2017), "Populism and Exclusionary Narratives: The 'Other' in Podemos' 2014 European Union Election Campaign," *European Journal of Communication* 32(6): 552–567 (p.559).

59. "(Podemos) pretende ser la palanca del cambio político en este país, [. . .] para que los ciudadanos y las ciudadanas recuperemos de modo efectivo el control democrático sobre nuestras instituciones y nuestros destinos" (Podemos, "Documento final," p.6).

60. "Entrevista a Pablo Iglesias, líder de Podemos: 'Defendemos lo bueno del sistema.' "

61. Vicenç Navarro and Juan Torres López, "Un proyecto económico para la gente" (Podemos, November 2014), pp.10–11, http://www.vnavarro.org/wp-content/uploads/2014/12/DocumentoEconomicoNavarroTorres.pdf (retrieved November 20, 2018).

62. José Fernández-Albertos, *Los votantes de Podemos: Del partido de los indignados al partido de los excluidos* (Madrid: Los libros de la Catarata, 2015), pp.45–46; Albert Julià Cano and Pau Marí-Klose (2014), "El socialista enfurecido: No solo jóvenes, aunque sobradamente preparados," *Agenda Pública,* June 26, https://www.eldiario.es/agendapublica/nueva-politica/socialista-enfurecido-jovenes-sobradamente-preparados_0_275072787.html (retrieved November 25, 2018).

63. Oriol Bartomeus (2014), "¿Como es el votante que ha cambiado al PSOE por Podemos?," *Agenda Pública,* June 13, https://www.eldiario.es/agendapublica/nueva-politica/votante-cambiado-PSOE-Podemos_0_270523171.html (retrieved November 17, 2018).

64. Fernández-Albertos, *Los votantes de Podemos*, pp.51–52.

65. Agusti Bosch and Iván M. Durán (2017), "How Does Economic Crisis Impel Emerging Parties on the Road to Elections? The Case of the Spanish Podemos and Ciudadanos," *Party Politics* 25(2): 257–267 (pp.263–264, https://doi.org/10.1177/1354068817710223.

66. Toni Rodon and María José Hierro (2016), "Podemos and Ciudadanos Shake Up the Spanish Party System: The 2015 Local and Regional Elections," *South European Society and Politics* 21(3): 339–357 (p.346).

67. José Fernández-Albertos (2018), "Ideología y voto, septiembre de 2018 edition," *Piedras de papel.Eldiario.es*, September 26, https://www.eldiario.es/piedrasdepapel/Ideologia-voto-Septiembre-edition_6_818278193.html (retrieved November 24, 2018).

68. The 1978 Constitution established seventeen Autonomous Communities within Spain, each of which has its own representative institutions with a range of policy responsibilities and some tax-raising powers. The Basque Country and Navarre have special status, which gives them high degrees of fiscal autonomy. I refer to the Autonomous Communities as regions for ease of understanding in English, although the use of the Spanish term "región" is controversial in Spain. For an overview, see Luis Moreno, *The Federalization of Spain* (London: Routledge, 2013).

69. The Socialists are represented in Catalonia by the Catalan Socialist Party (Partit dels Socialistes de Catalunya, PSC), which is formally an independent party but federated with the PSOE and to all intents and purposes part of the same parliamentary bloc in the Congress of Deputies.

70. See Bonnie Field, *Why Minority Governments Work: Multilevel Territorial Politics in Spain* (Basingstoke: Palgrave, 2016).

71. "Masiva manifestación por la independencia de Catalunya," *LaVanguardia*, September 11, 2012, https://www.lavanguardia.com/politica/20120911/54349943522/diada-manifestacion-independencia-catalunya.html (retrieved November 15, 2018).

72. See for instance, Xavier Cuadras-Morató and Toni Rodon (2019), "The Dog That Didn't Bark: On the Effect of the Great Recession on the Surge of Secessionism," *Ethnic and Racial Studies* 42(12): 2189–2208.

73. "Diez viajes en helicóptero para esquivar el Movimiento 15M en el Parlament," *RTVE Informaciones 24 horas*, June 15, 2011, http://www.rtve.es/noticias/20110615/ocho-helicopteros-trastaladan-presidente-varios-diputados-parlament-para-evitar-movimiento-15m/440256.shtml (retrieved November 25, 2018).

74. "Update 1—Spain Struggles to Meet Regions' 36 Bln-Euro Debts," *Reuters,* May 23, 2012, http://www.reuters.com/article/spain-regions-idUSL5E8GNEXO20120523 (retrieved December 5, 2018).

75. The episode is vividly described in Mas-Colell's memoirs: Andreu Mas-Colell, Albert Carreras, and Ivan Planas, *Turbulències i tribulacions* (Barcelona: Edicions 62, 2018), Ch. 2.

76. Prior to 2016, CDC was in a stable electoral coalition, Convergència i Unió (CiU), with the Christian Democratic Unió Democratica de Catalunya. Unió opposed the turn to independence and left the coalition, after which CDC changed its name to the Catalan European Democratic Party (Partit Demòcrata Europeu Català, PDeCAT).

77. "Mas: 'Con la mitad del déficit fiscal, Cataluña no necesitaría los recortes,'" *El Periódico (Extremadura),* July 25, 2012, http://www.elperiodicoextremadura.com/noticias/espana/mas-con-mitad-deficit-fiscal-cataluna-no-necesitaria-recortes_669765.html (retrieved December 5, 2018).

78. See Astrid Barrio, Oscar Barberà, and Juan Rodríguez-Teruel (2018), "'Spain Steals from Us!' The 'Populist Drift' of Catalan Regionalism," *Comparative European Politics* 16(6): 993–1011.

79. Joan Barceló (2018), "Batons and Ballots: The Effectiveness of State Violence in Fighting against Catalan Separatism," *Research and Politics* 5(2): 1–9.

80. Kiko Llaneras, "El apoyo a la independencia tiene raíces económicas y de origen social," *El País*, September 28, 2017, https://elpais.com/politica/2017/09/28/ratio/1506601198_808440.html (retrieved June 15, 2018).

81. Ibid.

82. Xavier Sala i Martín, "El dividend fiscal de la independència," *Col·lectiu Wilson blog*, November 21, 2012, http://www.wilson.cat/en/mitjans-escrits/articles-dels-membres/item/210-el-dividend-fiscal-de-la-independencia.html (retrieved November 30, 2018).

83. See data in Jordi Argelaguet and Joan Marcet, "Nationalist Parties in Catalonia: Convergencia Democratica de Catalunya and Esquerra Republicana," in Lieven de Winter and Huri Tursan (eds), *Regionalist Parties in Western Europe* (London: Routledge, 2003), pp.88–104.

84. Barrio et al., "The 'Populist Drift' of Catalan Regionalism," p.1002.

85. Candidaturas de Unitat Popular (CUP), *CUP—Alternativa d'Esquerres: Candidatura al Parlament de Catalunya a les eleccions del 25 de novembre del 2012*, Electoral Programme for 2012 Catalan Elections, September 5, 2012, https://www.vilaweb.cat/media/continguts/000/052/905/905.pdf (retrieved November 30, 2018).

86. Barrio et al., "The 'Populist Drift' of Catalan Regionalism," p.1003.

87. "La semana en que el Govern de Torra tuvo que contener a la calle," *eldiario.es*, November 29, 2018, https://www.eldiario.es/catalunya/politica/semana-Govern-Torra-contener-calle_0_840966849.html (retrieved December 1, 2018).

88. The difficulty of attributing responsibility for policy outcomes in Spain's complex system of decentralization makes it more difficult for voters to penalize regional incumbents for economic problems, facilitating blame-shifting toward the central government; see Sandra Leon and Lluis Orriols (2016), "Asymmetric Federalism and Economic Voting," *European Journal of Political Research* 55(4): 847–865.

89. Caroline Gray (2015), "A Fiscal Path to Sovereignty? The Basque Economic Agreement and Nationalist Politics," *Nationalism and Ethnic Politics* 21(1): 63–82.

90. OECD (2011), *OECD Reviews of Regional Innovation: Basque Country* (Paris: OECD).

91. "Cataluña y Euskadi, en las antípodas," *El País*, September 5, 2017, https://elpais.com/politica/2017/09/03/actualidad/1504461950_517938.html?id_externo_rsoc=TW_CC (retrieved November 10, 2018).

92. David Reher and Miguel Requena (2009), "The National Immigrant Survey of Spain: A New Data Source for Migration Studies in Europe," *Demographic Research* 20: 253–278 (p.253).

93. Juan Rodríguez Teruel and Astrid Barrio (2016), "Going National: Ciudadanos from Catalonia to Spain," *South European Society and Politics* 21(4): 587–607 (p.590).

94. The party's position on economic issues is strongly influenced by the pro-market thinking of its economy spokesman, Luis Garicano, a Chicago-trained academic. See his book *El dilema de España* (Madrid: Península, 2014).

95. Ignacio Escolar, "¿Puede ser Ciudadanos el Podemos de la derecha?," *eldiario.es*, January 15, 2015, https://www.eldiario.es/escolar/Puede-Ciudadanos-Podemos-derecha_6_346175409.html (retrieved December 5, 2018).

96. Rodríguez Teruel and Barrio, "Going National," pp.599–600.

97. Sonia Alonso and Cristóbal Rovira Kaltwasser (2015), "Spain: No Country for the Populist Radical Right?," *South European Society and Politics* 20(1): 21–45.

98. Belén Barreiro, "Vox y la identidad vulnerable," *El País*, December 9, 2018, https://elpais.com/elpais/2018/12/08/opinion/1544286928_310121.html (retrieved June 9, 2019).

99. Beatriz Gallardo Paúls, "Vox: El Discurso Enmascarado," *Agenda Pública*, April 12, 2019, http://agendapublica.elpais.com/vox-el-discurso-enmascarado/ (retrieved June 9, 2019).

100. "Cómo ha llegado Vox a ser acusación en el juicio del 'procés,'" *Diario Sur*, February 13, 2019, https://www.diariosur.es/nacional/acusacion-popular-proces-vox-20190213114150-ntrc.html.

101. "Los cuatro pilares de Vox: No al aborto, la familia, la unidad de España y no a ETA," *El Confidencial*, January 16, 2014, https://www.elconfidencial.com/espana/2014-01-16/los-cuatro-pilares-de-vox-no-al-aborto-la-familia-la-unidad-de-espana-y-no-a-eta_76858/ (retrieved June 10, 2019).

102. Vox, *Manifiesto Fundacional*, https://www.voxespana.es/espana/manifiesto-fundacional-vox (retrieved June 10, 2019).

103. Héctor Meleiro, "Vox: Nueva derecha populista o escisión radical del PP," *Piedras de Papel*, December 26, 2018, https://www.eldiario.es/piedrasdepapel/Vox-derecha-populista-escision-PP_6_850474947.html (retrieved June 9, 2019); Juan Rodríguez Teruel, "El difuso malestar de las derechas españolas," *Agenda Pública*, January 31, 2019, http://agendapublica.elpais.com/el-malestar-difuso-de-las-derechas-espanolas/ (retrieved June 9, 2019).

Chapter 7

1. FRED (Federal Reserve of St Louis Economic Data) (2018), "Constant GDP Per Capita of Italy." https://fred.stlouisfed.org/graph/?g=mk5k. (retrieved December 10, 2018).

2. See Nick Crafts (1994), "The Golden Age of Economic Growth in Europe," Warwick Economics Research Paper No. 427 (Coventry: University of Warwick Department of Economics, August), https://warwick.ac.uk/fac/soc/economics/research/workingpapers/1989-1994/twerp_427.pdf.

3. OECD (2018), "Pension Spending (Indicator)," https://data.oecd.org/socialexp/pension-spending.htm (retrieved December 9, 2018).

4. See Julia Lynch, *Age in the Welfare State: The Origins of Social Spending on Pensioners, Workers, and Children* (New York: Cambridge University Press, 2006).

5. "Falsi invalidi, cieco per l'Inps ma faceva il guardalinee," *RaiNews*, May 26, 2017, http://www.rainews.it/dl/rainews/articoli/falsi-invalidi-cieco-inps-faceva-guardalinee-11e0180a-a8f0-419a-915d-e75eab50f6e0.html (retrieved December 18, 2018).

6. Julia Lynch, "Italy: A Christian Democratic or Clientelist Welfare State?," in Kees van Kersbergen and Philip Manow (eds.), *Religion, Class Coalitions, and Welfare States* (Cambridge: Cambridge University Press, 2009), pp.91–118 (p.93).

7. For a classic account of these practices, see Sidney Tarrow, *Between Center and Periphery: Grassroots Politicians in Italy and France* (New Haven: Yale University Press, 1977).

8. See, for example, Donatella della Porta and Alberto Vannucci, *Corrupt Exchanges: Actors, Resources, and Mechanisms of Political Corruption* (London: Routledge, 2017).

9. See Stefano Guzzini (1995), "The 'Long Night of the First Republic': Years of Clientelistic Implosion in Italy," *Review of International Political Economy* 2(1): 27–61.

10. Marcello de Cecco (1996), "Italy and the International Economy," *The International Spectator* 31(2): 37–50.

11. See John Goodman, *Monetary Sovereignty: The Politics of Central Banking in Europe* (Ithaca: Cornell University Press, 1992), pp.169–179.

12. On the origins and early development of the Northern League, see (in English) Anna Cento Bull and Mark Gilbert, *The Lega Nord and the Northern Question in Italian Politics* (Basingstoke: Palgrave, 2001), and (in Italian) Roberto Biorcio, *La Padania promessa* (Milan: il Saggiatore, 1997).

13. Eric Chang, Miriam Golden, and Seth Hill (2010), "Legislative Malfeasance and Political Accountability," *World Politics* 62(2): 177–220 (p.178).

14. Marco Travaglio, "Lodo Mondadori: La storia vera," *L'Espresso*, July 15, 2011, http://espresso.repubblica.it/palazzo/2011/07/15/news/lodo-mondadori-la-storia-vera-1.33970 (retrieved December 8, 2018)

15. For a summary of fiscal measures, see OECD, *OECD Economic Surveys: Italy 1997* (Paris: OECD, 1997), p.77.

16. OECD, *OECD Economic Surveys: Italy 1996* (Paris: OECD, 1996), pp.54–57.

17. Ugo Pagano and Sandro Trento (2002), "Continuity and Change in Italian Corporate Governance: The Institutional Stability of One Variety of Capitalism," Università degli Studi di Siena Dipartimento di Economia Politica Working Paper No. 366 (Siena: Dipartimento di Economia Politica).

18. Marcello de Cecco (1998), "The Euro and the Italian Economy," *The International Spectator* 33(2): 33–42 (p.40).

19. Fiorella Padoa Schioppa Kostoris, *Italy: The Sheltered Economy: Structural Problems in the Italian Economy* (Oxford: Clarendon Press, 1993), p.4.

20. Ibid., pp.229–230.

21. See Mark Blyth, *Austerity: The History of a Dangerous Idea* (New York: Oxford University Press, 2013), pp.166–167.

22. Francesco Giavazzi and Marco Pagano (1988), "The Advantage of Tying One's Hands: EMS Discipline and Central Bank Credibility," *European Economic Review* 32(5): 1055–1075. See also Kenneth Dyson and Kevin Featherstone (1996), "Italy and EMU as 'Vincolo Esterno': Empowering the Technocrats, Transforming the State," *South European Society and Politics* 1(2): 272–299.

23. See Maurizio Ferrera and Elisabetta Gualmini, *Rescued by Europe? Social and Labour Market Reforms in Italy from Maastricht to Berlusconi* (Amsterdam: Amsterdam University Press, 2004).

24. OECD (2018), "Tax Revenue (indicator)," doi: 10.1787/d98b8cf5-en (retrieved December 31, 2018).

25. Roberto Petrini, *L'imbroglio fiscale* (Rome: Laterza, 2005), pp.111–116.

26. Erik Jones (2012), "The Berlusconi Government and the Sovereign Debt Crisis," *Italian Politics* 27(1): 172–190.

27. Andrea Brandolini, Romina Gambacorta, and Alfonso Rosolia, "Inequality amid Stagnation: Italy over the Last Quarter of a Century," in Brian Nolan (ed.), *Inequality and Inclusive Growth in Rich Countries: Shared Challenges and Contrasting Fortunes* (Oxford: Oxford University Press, 2018), pp.190–220 (p.190).

28. Klaus Armingeon and Lucio Baccaro, "The Sorrows of Young Euro: The Sovereign Debt Crises of Ireland and Southern Europe," in Nancy Bermeo and Jonas Pontusson (eds.), *Coping with Crisis: Government Reactions to the Great Recession* (New York: Russell Sage Foundation, 2012), pp.162–197 (p.188).

29. See Andrea Benvenuti (2017), "Between Myth and Reality: The Euro Crisis and the Downfall of Silvio Berlusconi," *Journal of Modern Italian Studies* 22(4): 512–529 (p.511).

30. The letter was published in Italian in "C'è l'esigenza di misure significative per accrescere il potenziale di crescita," *Corriere della Sera*, September 29, 2011, https://www.corriere.it/economia/11_settembre_29/trichet_draghi_italiano_405e2be2-ea59-11e0-ae06-4da866778017.shtml (retrieved January 7, 2019). For a summary in English, see "Trichet's Letter to Rome

Published, Urged Cuts," *Reuters*, September 29, 2011, https://www.reuters.com/article/us-italy-ecb/trichets-letter-to-rome-published-urged-cuts-idUSTRE78S4MK20110929 (retrieved January 7, 2019).

31. C. Randall Henning, *Tangled Governance* (Oxford: Oxford University Press, 2017), pp.133–134.

32. Timothy Geithner, *Stress Test: Reflections on Financial Crises* (London: Penguin/Random House, 2014), p.476.

33. Stefano Sacchi (2015), "Conditionality by Other Means: EU Involvement in Italy's Structural Reforms in the Sovereign Debt Crisis," *Comparative European Politics* 13(1): 77–92 (p.85).

34. For details on fiscal and other measures taken, see Daniela Giannetti (2013), "Mario Monti's Technocratic Government," *Italian Politics* 28(1): 133–152.

35. "Verbatim of the remarks made by Mario Draghi. Speech by Mario Draghi, President of the European Central Bank at the Global Investment Conference in London, 26 July 2012" (Frankfurt: European Central Bank), https://www.ecb.europa.eu/press/key/date/2012/html/sp120726.en.html (retrieved January 7, 2019).

36. Paolo Manasse, Giulio Trigilia, and Luca Zavalloni (2013), "Professor Monti and the Bubble," *Vox: CEPR Policy Portal*, March 19, https://voxeu.org/article/professor-monti-and-bubble.

37. OECD (2018), "General Government Debt (indicator)," doi: 10.1787/a0528cc2-en (retrieved December 31, 2018).

38. Brandolini et al, "Inequality amid Stagnation," p.191.

39. OECD, *In It Together: Why Less Inequality Benefits All* (Paris: OECD, 2015), p.24.

40. See, for example, David Natali, *Vincitori e perdenti: Come cambiano le pensioni in Italia e in Europa* (Bologna: Il Mulino, 2007), ch.6.

41. Andrea Brandolini (2014), "The Big Chill: Italian Family Budgets after the Great Recession," *Italian Politics* 29(1): 233–256 (fig.6, p.245).

42. See Brandolini et al., "Inequality amid Stagnation," p.190.

43. Luigi Cannari and Giovanni d'Alessio, *La richezza degli italiani* (Bologna: Il Mulino, 2006), pp.62–63.

44. Gabriele Ballarino, Michela Braga, Massimiliano Bratti, Daniele Checchi, Antonio Filippin, Carlo Fiorio, Marco Leonardi, Elena Meschi, and Francesco Scervini, "Italy: How Labour Market Policies Can Foster Earnings Inequality," in Brian Nolan, Wiemer Salverda, Daniele Checchi, Ive Marx, Abigail McKnight, István György Tóth, and Herman van de Werfhorst (eds.), *Changing Inequalities and Societal Impacts in Rich Countries: Thirty Countries' Experiences* (Oxford: Oxford University Press, 2014), pp.369–391 (p.372).

45. Marco Simoni, *Senza alibi: Perché il capitalismo italiano non cresce più* (Venice: Marsilio, 2012); Bruno Pellegrino and Luigi Zingales (2017),

"Diagnosing the Italian Disease," NBER Working Paper No. w23964 (Washington, DC: National Bureau of Economic Research).

46. See Alison Johnston and Bob Hancké (2009), "Wage Inflation and Labour Unions in EMU," *Journal of European Public Policy* 16(4): 601–622.

47. OECD, "Employment by Activity," https://data.oecd.org/emp/employment-by-activity.htm (retrieved June 10, 2019).

48. Alfonso Rosolia and Roberto Torrini (2016), "The Generation Gap: A Cohort Analysis of Earnings Levels, Dispersion and Initial Labor Market Conditions in Italy, 1974–2014," Questioni di Economia e Finanza (Occasional Papers), No. 366 (Rome: Banca d'Italia, November).

49. Piergiorgio Corbetta and Pasquale Colloca (2013), "Job Precariousness and Political Orientations: The Case of Italy," *South European Society and Politics* 18(3): 333–354 (p.335).

50. Brandolini et al., "Inequality amid Stagnation," p.206.

51. Sauro Mocetti, Elisabetta Olivieri, and Eliana Viviano (2011), "Italian Households and Labour Market: Structural Characteristics and Effects of the Crisis," *Stato e mercato* 31(2): 223–243.

52. Brandolini et al., "Inequality amid Stagnation," p.215.

53. Lorenzo di Sio and Hans Schadee, "I flussi del voto e lo spazio politico," in ITANES, *Voto amaro: Disincanto e crisi economica nelle elezioni del 2013* (Bologna: Il Mulino, 2013), pp.45–55 (p.47).

54. Gianluca Passarelli and Dario Tuorto (2014), "Not with My Vote: Turnout and the Economic Crisis in Italy," *Contemporary Italian Politics* 6(2): 147–158.

55. Roberto Biorcio, *Il populismo nella politica italiana: Da Bossi a Berlusconi, da Grillo a Renzi* (Milan: Mimesis, 2015), pp.98–99.

56. Sergio Rizzo and Gian Antonio Stella, *La casta: Così i politici italiani sono diventati intoccabili* (Milan: Rizzoli, 2007).

57. Giancarlo Casaleggio and Beppe Grillo, *Siamo in guerra per una nuova politica: La rete contro i partiti* (Milan: Chiarelettere, 2011).

58. See Giovanna Cosenza (2014), "Grillo's Communication Style: From Swear Words to Body Language," *Contemporary Italian Politics* 6(1): 89–101.

59. See the discussion in Antonio Floridia and Rinaldo Vignati (2014), "Deliberativa, diretta o partecipativa? Le sfide del Movimento 5 stelle alla democrazia rappresentativa," *Quaderni di Sociologia* 65: 51–74.

60. See Marco Deseriis (2017), "Direct Parliamentarianism: An Analysis of the Political Values Embedded in Rousseau, the 'Operating System' of the Five Star Movement," *JeDEM-eJournal of eDemocracy and Open Government* 9(2): 47–67.

61. Some scholars have claimed this makes them exemplars of a new party type, the "techno-populist party": see Christopher Bickerton and Carlo Invernizzi Accetti (2018), " 'Techno-Populism' as a New Party Family: The Case of the Five Star Movement and Podemos," *Contemporary Italian Politics* 10(2): 132–150.

62. Piergiorgio Corbetta and Rinaldo Vignati (2014), "Direct Democracy and Scapegoats: The Five Star Movement and Europe," *The International Spectator* 49(1): 53–64 (pp.57–58).

63. "Programma a 5 Stelle," *Il blog di Beppe Grillo*, April 22, 2012, http://www.beppegrillo.it/programma-a-5-stelle/ (retrieved January 18, 2019).

64. A transcript in Italian can be found on Grillo's blog: "Piazza Maggiore, Bologna, otto settembre 2007," September 9, 2007, http://www.beppegrillo.it/piazza-maggiore-bologna-otto-settembre-2007/ (retrieved January 11, 2019).

65. Fabio Bordignon and Luigi Ceccarini (2013), "Five Stars and a Cricket: Beppe Grillo Shakes Italian Politics," *South European Society and Politics* 18(4): 427–449 (p.433).

66. Corbetta and Vignati, "Direct Democracy and Scapegoats," pp.57–58.

67. Salvatore Merlo, "Bilancio degli economisti di Grillo," *Il Foglio*, October 1, 2016, https://www.ilfoglio.it/politica/2016/10/01/news/bilancio-degli-economisti-di-grillo-104778/ (retrieved June 11, 2019).

68. Movimento Cinque Stelle (2014), "#Reddito di cittadinanza—Movimento 5 Stelle," https://www.movimento5stelle.it/parlamento/REDDITOCITTADINANZA.pdf (retrieved January 11, 2019).

69. Roberto Biorcio and Paolo Natale, *Politica a 5 stelle: Idee, storia e strategie del movimento di Grillo* (Milan: Feltrinelli Editore, 2013), pp.55–56.

70. Paolo Natale (2014), "The Birth, Early History and Explosive Growth of the Five Star Movement," *Contemporary Italian Politics* 6(1): 16–36, pp.20–21.

71. Giuliano da Empoli, *La rabbia e l'algoritmo: Il grillismo preso sul serio* (Venice: Marsilio, 2017), pp.18–19.

72. Ilvo Diamanti (2014), "The 5 Star Movement: A Political Laboratory," *Contemporary Italian Politics* 6(1): 4–15, p.13.

73. In the vote for the Senate, which is limited to voters aged twenty-five or above, the M5S polled slightly less: 23.6 percent.

74. See the data in di Sio and Schadee, "I flussi del voto e lo spazio politico," Table 3.2, p.49.

75. Delia Baldassarri, "Sinistra e destra: Un'italia di moderati e conservatori," in ITANES, *Voto amaro: Disincanto e crisi economica nelle elezioni del 2013* (Bologna: Il Mulino, 2013), pp.133–146 (p.137).

76. See data in Marco Maraffi, Andrea Pedrazzani, and Luca Pinto, "Le basi sociali del voto," in ITANES, *Voto amaro: Disincanto e crisi economica nelle elezioni del 2013* (Bologna: Il Mulino, 2013), pp.57–70 (Table.4.1, pp.58–59).

77. Di Sio and Schadee, "I flussi del voto e lo spazio politico," Table 3.2, p.49.

78. Maraffi, Pedrazzani, and Pinto, "Le basi sociali del voto," Table.4.1, pp.58–59.

79. Ibid.

80. See the manifesto published by one of the party's founders, political economist Michele Salvati: *Il partito democratico: Per la rivoluzione liberale* (Milan: Feltrinelli, 2007).

81. Bocconi economists close to the PD have published a number of books advocating liberalizing reforms on progressive grounds: see, for example, Alberto Alesina and Francesco Giavazzi, *Il liberismo è di sinistra* (Rome: Il Saggiatore, 2007); Tito Boeri and Pietro Garibaldi, *Le riforme a costo zero: Dieci proposte per tornare a crescere* (Milan: Chiare Lettere, 2011).

82. The video of this meeting can be viewed at https://www.youtube.com/watch?v=kTaPo4l8Alw (retrieved January 24, 2019).

83. Paolo Segatti, Monica Poletti, and Cristiano Vezzoni (2014), "Renzi's Honeymoon Effect: The 2014 European Election in Italy," *South European Society and Politics* 20(3): 311–331 (p.313).

84. Ibid., Table 2, p.321.

85. Patrik Vesan (2016), "Young Workers and the Labor Market Policies of Renzi's Government," *Italian Politics* 31(1): 191–208 (p.193).

86. Valeria Cirillo, Marta Fana, and Dario Guarascio (2017), "Labour Market Reforms in Italy: Evaluating the Effects of the Jobs Act," *Economia Politica* 34(2): 211–232.

87. See the analysis by Gianfranco Pasquino and Marco Valbruzzi (2017), "Italy Says No: The 2016 Constitutional Referendum and Its Consequences," *Journal of Modern Italian Studies* 22(2): 145–162.

88. Ibid., pp.154–156.

89. Anna Cento Bull (2013), "When the Magic Wears Off: Bossi Loses His Grip and the League Its Appeal," *Italian Politics* 28(1): 95–111.

90. Dwayne Woods (1995), "The Crisis of Center-Periphery Integration in Italy and the Rise of Regional Populism: The Lombard League," *Comparative Politics* 27(2): 187–203 (p.188).

91. Anna Cento Bull (2009), "Lega Nord: A Case of Simulative Politics?," *South European Society and Politics*, 14(2): 129–146 (pp.136–139).

92. See Michel Huysseune (2010), "Defending National Identity and Interests: The Lega Nord's Asymmetric Model of Globalisation," *Studies in Ethnicity and Nationalism* 10(2): 221–233.

93. Heidi Beirich and Dwayne Woods (2000), "Globalisation, Workers and the Northern League," *West European Politics* 23(1): 130–143 (pp.131–132).

94. John Agnew, Michael Shin, and Giuseppe Bettoni (2002), "City versus Metropolis: The Northern League in the Milan Metropolitan Area," *International Journal of Urban and Regional Research* 26(2): 266–283.

95. See John Agnew (1995), "The Rhetoric of Regionalism: The Northern League in Italian Politics, 1983–94," *Transactions of the Institute of British Geographers* 20(2): 156–172.

96. Raj Chari, Suvi Iltanen, and Sylvia Kritzinger (2004), "Examining and Explaining the Northern League's 'U-Turn' from Europe," *Government and Opposition* 39(3): 423–450.

97. Benito Giordano (2004), "The Politics of the Northern League and Italy's Changing Attitude towards Europe," *Perspectives on European Politics and Society* 5(1): 61–79 (especially pp.70–73).

98. See Valerio Renzi, *La politica della ruspa: La Lega di Salvini e le nuove destre europee* (Rome: Edizioni Alegre, 2015), esp. pp.9–10.

99. "Bossi: Abbordaggio alle navi dei clandestine," *Corriere della Sera*, June 16, 2003, https://www.corriere.it/Primo_Piano/Politica/2003/06_Giugno/16/bossi.shtml (retrieved January 27, 2019).

100. Biorcio, *Il populismo nella politica italiana*, pp.63–67.

101. Davide Vampa (2017), "Matteo Salvini's Northern League in 2016: Between Stasis and New Opportunities," *Italian Politics* 32: 32–50 (p.35).

102. Daniele Albertazzi, Arianna Giovannini, and Antonella Seddone (2018), " 'No Regionalism Please, We Are Leghisti!': The Transformation of the Italian Lega Nord under the Leadership of Matteo Salvini," *Regional and Federal Studies* 28(5): 645–671.

103. Pietro Castelli Gattinara (2017), "The 'Refugee Crisis' in Italy as a Crisis of Legitimacy," *Contemporary Italian Politics* 9(3): 318–331 (p.324).

104. Ibid., p.323.

105. See Lega Nord, "Basta euro tour," https://www.leganord.org/basta-euro-tourm (retrieved January 31, 2019).

106. Even in interviews to the international financial press, "Brexit Inspires Salvini Dream of Italy Ditching the Euro," *Financial Times*, October 13, 2016, https://www.ft.com/content/8a24cc84-907d-11e6-a72e-b428cb934b78 (retrieved January 31, 2019).

107. Marco Valbruzzi and Rinaldo Vignati, "Introduzione: Un'elezione storica in tempi staordinari: Tutto cambia?," in Marco Valbruzzi and Rinaldo Vignati (eds.), *Il vicolo cieco: Le elezioni del 4 marzo 2018* (Bologna: Il Mulino, 2018), pp.7–18, (pp.23, 28).

108. See the data in Castelli Gattinara, "The 'Refugee Crisis' in Italy as a Crisis of Legitimacy," fig.2, p.324.

109. Albertazzi et al., " 'No Regionalism Please, We Are Leghisti!,' " pp.653–656.

110. Castelli Gattinara, "The 'Refugee Crisis' in Italy as a Crisis of Legitimacy," fig.2, p.324.

111. Davide Vampa, "Il centrodestra a guida Leghista," in Valbruzzi and Vignati, *Il vicolo cieco*, pp. 57–78 (p.73).

112. Marco Valbruzzi, "Analisi elettorale di un cambiamento 'radicale': Chi ha vinto e chi ha perso," in Valbruzzi and Vignati, *Il vicolo cieco*, pp.147–184 (pp. 175–176).

113. Voters were asked to cite the two most important problems. M5S voters were the most likely to prioritize corruption and the "functioning of the political

system," and the least likely to cite law and order: Luca Comodo and Mattia Forni, "Chi vota cosa e perché: Il profilo elettorale dei partiti," in Valbruzzi and Vignati, *Il vicolo cieco*, pp. 213–234 (Table 4, p.226).

114. 48 percent of League voters cited immigration and 32 percent cited law and order as the most important issues, compared to 28 percent and 23 percent, respectively, on average: Comodo and Forni, "Chi vota cosa e perché." Table 4, p.226.

115. Comodo and Forni, "Chi vota cosa e perché," Table 1, p.215.

116. Cecilia Biancalana and Pasquale Colloca, "Il Movimento 5 stelle alla prova dell'istituzionalizzazione: Una metamorfosi incompiuta?," in Valbruzzi and Vignati, *Il vicolo cieco*, pp. 79–98 (p.86).

117. Yellow being the favored color of the M5S, green that of the Northern League.

118. "Milano, cancellata la scritta 'Basta euro' dal muro della Lega di via Bellerio," *LaRepubblica Milano*, May 31, 2018, https://milano.repubblica.it/cronaca/ 2018/05/31/news/milano_cancellata_la_scritta_basta_euro_dal_muro_della_ lega_di_via_bellerio-197806594/. (retrieved January 17, 2019).

Conclusions

1. Pippa Norris and Ronald Inglehart, *Cultural Backlash: Trump, Brexit, and Authoritarian Populism* (New York: Cambridge University Press, 2019).

2. Sheri Berman, *The Primacy of Politics: Social Democracy and the Making of Europe's Twentieth Century* (New York: Cambridge University Press, 2006).

3. Of course, neoliberalism also implies action, not only to "free" markets but also to shape them for political ends. See Quinn Slobodian, *Globalists: The End of Empire and the Birth of Neoliberalism* (Cambridge, MA: Harvard University Press, 2018).

4. Matthew Yglesias, "Why Millions of People Are Getting Hit with a Surprise Tax Bill This Year," *Vox*, February 6, 2019, https://www.vox.com/policy-and-politics/2019/2/6/18214039/irs-tax-refund-withholding-trump.

5. David Woodruff (2016), "Governing by Panic: The Politics of the Eurozone Crisis," *Politics and Society* 44(1): 81–116.

INDEX

For the benefit of digital users, indexed terms that span two pages (e.g., 52–53) may, on occasion, appear on only one of those pages.

Notes: Figures are indicated by *f* and tables by *t*, respectively, following the page number.

economic (financial) crises. *See also*
   specific countries and topics
   1970s, 29–30
   2000s, 44–45 (*See also* Global
      Financial Crisis; Great Recession)
   political backlash, 50–51
   upheaval from, 50
economics. *See also* neoliberalism; *specific*
   countries and topics
   American model, 89
   economic interventionism, post
      World War II, 25–26
   fissures, neoliberal democracy, 8
   liberalism, 51–52
   policy positions, political parties
      (1945-2017), 37–38, 38*f*
economy. *See also specific countries*
   and topics
   anti-system parties' rise, 73, 75*f*
   Brexit vote, 73
   market-oriented, uncertainty and
      insecurity, 121
   political parties and, US, 94*f*,
      94–95
education, publicly funded,
   Britain, 119
education level
   on Brexit vote, 141, 142–44, 143*f*
   on voting behavior, 11
   on xenophobia, 12
Einaudi, Luigi, 222
EK (Union of Centrists), Greece, 176
electoral competition, valence model,
   265–66n61
electoral market gap, anti-system
   parties and, 57*t*, 58
electoral mobilization, catch-all
   approach, 29–34, 265n50
electoral-professional party, 265n50
electoral volatility, 35–36, 265n56
elites
   Congress favoring policy preferences
      of, 96, 271n28

families, Presidents, 97
financialization and, US, 97
political, 97
ruling, democracy on, 23
embedded liberalism, 262n18
Emergency Economic Stabilization
   Act, 99. *See also* bailouts, Global
   Financial Crisis
employment. *See* labor markets
employment protection
   legislation, reduced, 41, 43
   US, limited, 91–92
enfranchisement
   party cartel model, 35–37, 36*f*
   of poor, Federalists and John Stuart
      Mill on, 23
En Marche (Macron's party),
   53, 55–56
Esquerra Republicana de Catalunya
   (ERC, Catalan Republican Left),
   198*f*, 199*f*, 199–200, 207–8, 209
establishment. *See also specific topics*
   anti-system parties and
      politicians on, 8
   parties opposing, 51, 53
   politicians (*See specific politicians*)
ETA (Basque terrorists), 213–14
Europe. *See also specific countries and topics*
   new North-South divide, 153–86
      (*see also* North-South divide, new
      European)
   southern (*See* southern Europe)
European Central Bank (ECB)
   Italy, 225–26, 246
   Spain, 191–92, 197, 201–2
European Green Party, 55–56, 65–66
European Monetary Union (EMU), on
   southern Europe 156 on southern
   Europe, welfare state expansion
   ideological divides, 155
   reforms required, 156
European Stability Mechanism (ESM),
   162, 192

exogenous shock
  black swan, 44–45
  crises, absence, 44
  crises, after 1970s liberalization, 44

Fail, Fianna, 70
Farage, Nigel, 149
Far Right. *See also specific countries and parties*
  anti-system, 61, 77
  xenophobic, 5–6
Federalists, American, on enfranchisement of poor, 23
Fidesz, 63
financial crises. *See* economic (financial) crises; *specific crises*
financialization, US
  from deregulation, 92
  elites, 97
  shocks, 98
Fine Gael, 70
Finns, The, 55–56, 185
fiscal rules, 31–32
Five Stars Movement (M5S), 82t, 227f
  2018 election, 229f, 240
  as anti-system party, 56
  campaign issues mobilized, 248–49
  as economic crisis reaction, 217
  on globalization, 66
  growth, after economic crisis, 2–3
  origins, 216
  origins through 2013 election, 229
  progressive democratic values, 5–6
  Renzi's reform project, 235
  success, 76–77
  as techno-populist party, 66
  yellow-green government, 244
"flaw in the model," 44
Foa, Roberto, 259n4
Fornero reform, 225, 240, 244, 246
Forza Italia, 1–2, 219–21, 229f, 240–41, 242, 244–45

France
  Communist parties, 1960s, 4–5
  En Marche, 53, 55–56
  Socialist Hollande, 68–70, 73, 249–50
  Socialist Left, 65
France Insoumise, 65
Friedman, Milton
  Capitalism and Freedom, 30–31
  on democracy, 264n37

Galloway, George, 129–30
GDP per capita
  European Economic Community (1950-1992), 217
  Eurozone countries growth (1999-2016), 223, 224f
  Italy, 216–17
General Theory (Keynes), 15
Germany
  Alternative for Germany (AfD), 77, 80–81, 82t, 185
  current account balance (2002-2017), 159f, 159–60
  Die Linke, 65
  government borrowing (1990-2008), 158f, 158
  Great Recession, double-dip, 160–61, 161f
  Green parties, 65–66
  labor movement, early 1900s, 23–24
  refugee crisis, 2010s, 80–81
  social spending (1989-2015), 128f
Gini coefficient
  anti-system vote, post-tax income on (2010), 75f, 75–76
  inequality, disposable household income, 46f, 46, 268n95
  inequality, UK *vs.* Germany and France (1970s), 119
  Italy, 1985 *vs.* 2013, 98–99
Global Financial Crisis, 2, 5, 9–10, 41. *See also specific countries*
  anti-system politics, 67, 69f, 71f, 72f